Claiming
the
Stones

Acknowledgments

This book would have been impossible without the generous efforts of more people than can be named here. The project began as a conference held in 1998 at Saint John's College, Oxford, England. The conference was jointly sponsored by the Getty Research Institute and the Drue Heinz Trust of Oxford University.

We are most grateful to the Getty Research Institute for providing indispensable support. Michael S. Roth, then an Associate Director, encouraged our original proposal; Claire Lyons, Collections Curator, and Charles G. Salas, now Head of Research and Education, brainstormed with us and generously participated in the conference; and Julia Bloomfield, Publications Manager, expertly guided the book through publication. Our thanks also to Michelle Ghaffari, freelance editor, for refining the texts.

At Oxford, the staff of Saint John's College made the conference smoother and more pleasant than either of us imagined possible. Numerous people, in and around Oxford, also made contributions to the conference. The academic staff of the Pitt Rivers Museum (notably Hélène La Rue, Jeremy Coote, Elizabeth Edwards, and Christopher Gosden) contributed substantively to the discussions and hosted receptions at the museum and a concert at the Bate Collection of Musical Instruments. Ruvani Ranasinha of Oxford University and Peter Gathercole of Cambridge University offered thoughtful and stimulating responses to the papers; Graham Dutfield of the Pitt Rivers Museum delivered the paper on which he collaborated with Darrell Posey; and Michael Spence presented a substantial essay at the last minute. Our thanks as well to Linda Waimarie Nakora of the University of Waikato, New Zealand, for her conference paper that could not be included in this collection and to Linda Topp-Sargion of the British Library for her collaboration with Hélène La Rue.

Finally, special thanks goes to Marilyn Bush and Pamela Smith, whose patience and encouragement sustained us.

— Elazar Barkan and Ronald Bush

Introduction

Elazar Barkan and Ronald Bush

Africa needs not only apology and forgiveness, but that these priceless African cultural treasures—artworks, icons, relics—be returned to their rightful owners.... [T]he African art that has found its way into the galleries of former European colonial powers and the homes of the rich in North America, Europe, and elsewhere has deep cultural significance. These works form an integral part of defining our identity and personality as family, as African family. We talk to them. They talk to us. We touch them at certain moments of our lives, from birth through life to death. It is through them that the living spirits of our people, of our history, of our culture interact and interface with us. They are not there, hence the void in our minds and in our hearts. We continue to cry for them to come back home, to complete that cultural, spiritual space.

—Theo-Ben Gurirab[1]

Some calm spectator, as he takes his view
In silent indignation mix'd with grief,
Admires the plunder, but abhors the thief.

—Lord Byron[2]

In the last two decades claims to cultural property have not only roiled legal and art heritage waters but have also reconfigured national and ethnic identities all over the world. Nor are the reasons hard to fathom. As Claire Lyons observes in her essay for this volume, through inexplicable chemistry artworks, religious icons, monuments, literary manuscripts, traditional myths, and rituals "hold the power to create a profound sense of belonging." Moved by this power, communities—including indigenous peoples, ethnic groups, nations that produce the artifacts and nations that will later claim them—come to "locate their historical identity in [these] material expressions." Cultural property consolidates groups, and then reconsolidates them, sometimes differently from the way they had been consolidated before.

As a working example, Lyons intriguingly offers the so-called Steinhardt *phiale*, a shallow gold bowl produced (perhaps in Sicily) in the early third century B.C. and eventually acquired by a prominent New York collector. The *phiale* was the subject of a bitter dispute not only between Italy and the collector but also between the spokesmen of two intellectual disciplines, each brandishing a high-minded intellectual rationale. The American museum

1

world and a group of American archaeologists filed contesting amicus curiae briefs. The museums argued that the return of the *phiale* would lead to obstructing the free circulation of international culture, while the archaeologists insisted on Italy's right to consolidate its culture through the stewardship of its native patrimony, even if that patrimony includes the expression of its extinct antique ancestors. The most striking thing about these arguments was that, for all their elevation, they are incommensurate. In fact, the *real* contest, as Lyons notes, seems to be over which side has the right "to frame and interpret the past of others."

How do courts or diplomats cope with such issues? Sadly, legal attempts to adjudicate cultural property claims often expand rather than diminish their intractability. Legal measures are especially troublesome since they necessarily replicate the universalist and neocolonial assumptions questioned by the non-Western plaintiffs in some of the disputes—assumptions that lie at the very heart of Western law. Thus, arguments about the Steinhardt *phiale* or, more famously, the Parthenon Marbles now threaten to overwhelm the international legal system. Disputes about less straightforward kinds of cultural property, including folk and ethnic traditions, prove even worse.

The difficulties do not stop there. Just as museums in the United States have challenged Italy's right to the Steinhardt *phiale* because the culture that produced it predeceased the advent of modern Italy, many ridicule other claims to alienated property, refusing to recognize the validity of the alienation involved. As the end of this introduction suggests, the difficulty of certifying "true alienation" helps create the riddles of cultural identity and cultural property. Just as no statement of alienation is without conflict, so no claim to cultural property is unproblematic. How, though, does one authorize (or negotiate) the right to have one's alienation acknowledged?

Alas, nothing brings out the conflicting intellectual premises of modern society more powerfully than controversies over *cultural property*—a term that viewed from either the front or the back seems to be an impossible paradox. On the one hand, "property" anchors the West's enlightenment system of universal rights and individual (as opposed to group) liberties. Thanks to the legal fiction that grants corporations the status and privileges of individuals, however, "property" has also become a fundamental building block of Western *social* organization, even more so because corporate ownership constitutes an important model for transforming traditional commonwealths into modern states. The ideological power of modern Western property rights in large part drove the juggernaut that engorged and dismembered traditional societies the world over, perhaps most dramatically in America, where stories of Native Americans giving up their land as a part of agreements whose force they could not comprehend became the stuff of tragedy and farce. (One of the first instances of a modern corporation involved the buying and selling of slaves. And was Manhattan Island really sold for twenty-four dollars of trinkets, or has that story simply become the perfect emblem for the appropriative momentum of European ownership?)

On the one hand, the term *cultural property* reminds us that the steamroller of Enlightenment modernity has not been entirely successful. Almost from its inception, the universalist mandate of "property" rights fomented a reaction in which minority cultures asserted a group-centered symbolic authority that resists property-based definition. Just as "cultures" in the post-Burkean tradition refuse to be characterized entirely in terms of the rights of man, so cultural artifacts, which continued to shape national, regional, and ethnic solidarities, resist the definitions of Western law. From the beginnings of modernity, cultural "patrimony" held out the promise of something that money could not buy.

Cultural property, therefore, discloses a particularly revealing set of contradictions. Consider the arguments over the Parthenon Marbles now housed in the British Museum, London. In the early nineteenth century, in a rush of Enlightenment fervor, Thomas Bruce, seventh earl of Elgin, "rescued" these manifestations of the universal genius of humankind by means of a not unproblematic legal sanction from the Ottoman government. In 1816 he arranged for their sale to the British nation for thirty-five thousand pounds. Even before the sale, however, cries (the most stinging from English poet Lord Byron) held that the purchase was reprehensible because the marbles also represented the mythical spirit of the ancient and modern Greek people and, as such, constituted part of their inalienable cultural patrimony. At the same time, the marbles, once in England, began to shape the cultural identity of Britain. As Timothy Webb suggests in his essay, the symbolic power of the marbles allowed Britain to think of itself as a "natural" successor to the "culture of democracy" that flourished in ancient Athens. This was a very useful kind of ideological strategy at a time when, on the basis of cultural property appropriated from Italy, Napoléon Bonaparte's Paris was vaunting itself the successor to ancient Rome and the natural spearhead of Western civilization. The marbles, in other words, although purchased as simple property, in fact functioned both in the Greek and the British worlds to anchor fluid identities whose shadow extended well beyond the definitions of the marketplace or the courts.

What increasingly were referred to as the Elgin Marbles from early in the nineteenth century became a powerful instance of property that was somehow more than property. The international friction they provoked could not be easily resolved because it engaged two contradictory cultural systems. As well as being universal expressions of human genius and objects of huge financial value, the marbles constituted priceless symbolic vessels of group ethos and carried the seeds of renewal for both Greece and Britain.

Seen from another angle, the marbles—along with antiquities of lesser notoriety—highlight the historical processes by which cultural and group identities are reconstructed over thousands of years. As Clemency Coggins's narrative of the handling of antiquities in Central and South America reveals, such objects, whose origins are shrouded in the mists of prehistory, are subject to appropriation by succeeding regional and national cultures. They acquire so much symbolic value that quarrels over which groups "own" that property are as ferocious as they are difficult to mediate. Coggins questions whether Maya relief sculptures found in the Yucatán currently belong to a local Maya indigenous culture or to the Mexican national culture. Should they be housed in the Yucatán or in the Museo National de Antropología in Mexico City, that "remote capital of the national government, for so long distrusted by the Maya"? Whoever "wins" the sculptures enjoys an enormous increase in group legitimacy, but how is the meaning of "ownership" determined when the objects have been "owned" and ransacked and "owned again" by emerging societies over thousands of years?

This is a difficulty that concerns more than national versus ethnic issues (in Central America, the elements of the "Indian Problem"). It also involves disciplinary arguments. Coggins points out, "Anthropologists who work with the indigenous cultures of America like to emphasize that history is continuous," while "historians and the guardians of the ancient heritage tend to compartmentalize history for the sake of explanation, and … seldom make a convincing connection with the present." Thus, in a way that the topical immediacy of the Elgin Marbles obscures, the long and contested history of South and Central American antiquities suggests that cultural property probably should not be considered simply a locus of national authenticity but rather a contested site of group identity. A great deal depends on whether continuity or discontinuity is emphasized. Claire Lyons would insist on stressing continuity, arguing that the alternative represents "an untenable notion of ethnic essentialism, compartmentalizing cultural and historical developments into a series of discontinuous and bounded phases," and betraying "a serious misunderstanding of the ways that communities evolve, ignoring the role that shifts in the ethnic or religious composition of populations play in directing the long-term course of nation formation." Coggins, however, reminds one that indigenous populations, such as Central American "Indians," often understand alienation differently and insist on a contrary interpretation.

A similar argument lies at the core of the next section of essays in the volume. These consider the ever more heated contest over the so-called Kennewick Man, a skeleton whose provenance and significance are the objects of a classic debate between Douglas Owsley and Richard Jantz, two powerful spokespersons for the objectives of Western science, and Patty Gerstenblith, an internationally known legal scholar who discusses the case of the Native Americans. Their disagreement concerns our difficulty with defining the "indigenous" and displays the complexity of a situation in which the American legal system must deal with two competing value systems. One of these value systems, according to Owsley and Jantz, understands the case as a matter of science versus the politics of religious fundamentalism. The other, in Gerstenblith's view, insists on the value of the skeleton in sustaining the political rights of the Native American in the face of a "national history of conquest, subjugation, and official policies of eradication."

At the heart of the controversy stand the following facts. On 28 July 1996 a well-preserved human skeleton exposed by erosion on the shoreline of the

Columbia River in Washington State was inadvertently discovered and subsequently designated "Kennewick Man." Anthropologists briefly examined the remains, estimated that the skeleton was approximately nine thousand three hundred years old, and linked the characteristics of the skull with European physical types, perhaps due to a migration about twelve thousand years ago (or even earlier). But once a first examination by anthropologists was completed, the United States Army Corps of Engineers appropriated the skeleton and, in line with the Native American Graves Protection and Repatriation Act (NAGPRA), announced they would repatriate the skeleton to a collective of five Columbia River basin tribes, including the Umatilla in Oregon.

This decision was challenged by Owsley and Jantz's group of physical anthropologists, who, acting on their own and putting their careers in jeopardy, argued that to turn the skeleton over without further examination was to lose information about the origins of humanity in the Americas. As part of their argument they questioned whether remains of this type could be labeled Native American or associated with any modern Native American peoples. The "indigenous" in this case might be only a dangerous myth (called into question by the historical reorientation the skeleton demanded) — one that interfered with the scientific understanding of "humanity." In their essay in this volume, Owsley and Jantz affirm that the fundamental context of resolving such a dispute has to be human demographic knowledge and especially its leading edge — "potential biomedical applications." To lose the evidence of Kennewick Man is to forego crucial epidemiological data that could further the understanding and control of genetic and transmissible diseases. In addition, the scientists' allies in Congress added that, if the weight of history and culture were to be allowed, the primary focus should not be on indigenous populations of any kind but on "significant new information concerning the history or prehistory of the United States."

According to Gerstenblith, however, scientific or national-historical objectives are red herrings in a dispute where real import has to do with the distribution of symbolic or cultural capital between unequal parties. In her account, the political significance of NAGPRA is that, for the first time, the government had agreed to treat "Native American cultures as living cultures, worthy of respect for both their past contribution to North American society and their continuing vitality." The psychological and cultural effects of NAGPRA, Gerstenblith argues, are even more significant than its requirements for treatment of human remains and cultural objects. The true purpose of NAGPRA should be seen as the returning to Native American groups the ability to control their own identity, their history, and their heritage (religious, spiritual, and mythic), which is so crucial to the formation of that identity. Deprived of such control, the Umatilla Indians cannot sustain the kind of legitimate cultural authority on which future assertions of autonomy will have to be based, since the establishment of cultural identity is made "particularly difficult when a group of people has been forcibly displaced from its ancestral lands, subjected to intentional policies of cultural eradication, and denied access to both the tangible and intangible remains of its cultural past." Nor should apparent discontinuities in the anthropological record be decisive. According to Gerstenblith, as historian of anthropology James Clifford has shown, "the criteria of cultural and tribal identity over long periods of time are more intricate than the [scientists' and] the court's approach to the question." She goes on to argue that, in Clifford's terms, a culture is less a "static" entity than it is a "fluid" construct based on "a process involving intergroup exchange and continual re-creation."

How is such a dispute resolved? For Owsley, Jantz, and their fellow scientists, the implementation of NAGPRA in this case endangered the scientific basis of a secular society. For Gerstenblith, the debate is not about research but about social justice. Any judicial solution would be offensive to one or the other.

Yet even as cultural property disputes have thrown up such stark oppositions, they have also provided a spur to developing extralegal avenues of resolution, ultimately affecting apparently insoluble disagreements in a host of other situations. As Elazar Barkan shows in his essay, since the 1980s cultural property disputes have blazed a trail for international conflict resolution among divergent legal traditions, and a pattern of consensus has developed about certain kinds of property disputes whose paradigmatic instance is cultural patrimony. The premises in such disagreements have shifted, so that cultural matters sometimes weigh in with more traditional legal categories. Mediators now routinely assume that outcomes should take into consideration identity affiliations between claimant and property, in addition to the property's legal status — allowing sacred land to revert to an indigenous group even though the land had been legally leased to a mining company, for example, or restoring museum objects to a tribe even though museums had legally acquired the objects. The legal frame applied to such property disputes has subtly shifted, so that today an increasing burden of proof is placed on the possessor of alienated property, rather than on a claimant whose identity can be shown to be invested in the object.

As a direct result of this developing consensus, the formal ideal of legal resolution is in such cases more often set aside in favor of a looser diplomacy among equals and legitimacy reconceptualized not as a right but as the product of a "negotiation" concerning what one culture is willing to accept about its neighbor. In the case of the Kennewick Man dispute, where the negotiations occur within a nation-state rather than between separate nations, NAGPRA was legislated by Congress only after extensive negotiation with representatives of the Indian nations. One can argue that those negotiations arrived not at what is "really" Native American culture property, not what was "right" but rather at a solution that was formulated according to what was acceptable to both cultures. Each side was forced to rethink what justice, culture, and property meant in America. From the Native American perspective, as shocking as it is to the scientists even scientific rationality can be viewed as a type of Western cultural property. The process of negotiating

NAGPRA, which has continued through the battles described by Owsley and Jantz and by Gerstenblith, has been slow, but like analogous developments on the international scene, it has narrowed long-lasting cultural misunderstandings and has created a shared space for the parties.

Nevertheless, Western law, even in its most flexible international forays, seems to help only to an extent. In his essay "Selling Grandma: Commodification of the Sacred through Intellectual Property Rights," Darrell Posey portrays the horrors and absurdities of extending Western intellectual property law into places where its categories do not apply. Posey describes indigenous peoples faced with the commodification of their environment by multinational corporations, who would transform traditional ways of life in order to appropriate products newly fashionable in the first world. As Posey points out (concerning one of the prime agents of this appropriation), Intellectual Property Rights (IPR)

> were established to protect individual inventions and inventors—not the ancient folklore and TEK [Traditional Ecological Knowledge] of indigenous and local communities. Even if intellectual property rights were secured for communities, differential access to patents, copyright, know-how, and trade secret laws and lawyers would generally price them out of any effective registry, monitoring, or litigation using such instruments.... [I]ntellectual property rights are considered inadequate and inappropriate for protecting traditional ecological knowledge and collective resources of indigenous and traditional peoples because they
>
> - recognize individual, not collective rights
> - require a specific act of "invention"
> - simplify ownership regimes
> - stimulate commercialization
> - recognize only market values
> - are subject to economic powers and manipulation
> - are difficult to monitor and enforce
> - are expensive, complicated, and time consuming

As Posey also demonstrates, however, even when everything can be swept away in an instant—battles for survival where the stakes are enormous and the odds are terrible—the power of negotiation presents an unexpected if not always satisfying way forward. Negotiations and political discussions can and have taken place to establish the rights of indigenous peoples to control their own lives to some degree, even if it is only to share in the benefits of the exploitation of their knowledge by the commercial world. This may not be comforting—it is an uphill struggle in the best of times—but an increasing number of international organizations have come to recognize some indigenous rights and to subscribe to a code of conduct that will facilitate further recognition. The outcome of these negotiations may be to hasten the assimilation of the indigenous into the technological sphere of global society. Only time will tell.

At present, many indigenous peoples seem to want and need both to limit their exposure to the modern world *and* to benefit from its rewards. Given such contradiction, it may be better (although this is certainly a controversial position) to choose limited co-option as the only result that international organizations can work with. In this case the sustained effort of negotiation involved in defining cultural property—a form at once of preservation and assimilation alike—may be the best outcome these peoples and their sponsors can hope for.

In the meantime, while considering the commodification of traditional ecological knowledge, one is forced to widen the definition of cultural property beyond cases like the Parthenon Marbles, where the stuff in dispute constitutes one-of-a-kind objects that can be locked in a room or spirited off in the middle of the night, and to consider instances that are less concrete. In fact, one might divide cultural property into three "ideal types" according to the "tangibility" of what is involved. One type is material and tangible property, which is unique and indivisible. In cases of disputes over such property, where the condition of sole possession obtains, there is always a potential demand for repatriation and restitution. Another type is intangible property, such as folktales, music, and folk remedies, where the primary issues concern not restitution but license and control, particularly in those cases where the group regards outside appropriation as either "unfair" or "sacrilegious." The third type is still more intangible: trade in "representations," especially those involved in the advancement of an insurgent identity whose embodiment has to do with new forms or discourses.

Nontangible types of cultural property, such as Posey's Traditional Ecological Knowledge, can critically affect group identity and legitimacy, but they increase legal complication in that they are open to reproduction and representation. This category includes practices such as the ritual or communal music discussed in Hélène La Rue's essay, body marking of the kind that Ngahuia Te Awekotuku considers, patterns of architectural ornament, medicinal or nutritive agents or recipes, and so on. All of these can be reproduced or represented in other cultures where an altered context may change the material's symbolic resonance. Such representations can also generate both money and power in which (in the worst scenarios) the producer culture takes no benefit and in which the value of the property at its source may be diminished (or may be seen to be diminished) by the corruption of its "authenticity."

The general issues here are analogues to copyright, licensing, and representational control, and all are inflected by group identity formation. Hélène La Rue's account of the transmission of traditional music takes us into the arena of something similar to intellectual property, only it involves what is traditionally produced by a community rather than by individual artists. Who benefits and who loses as African music is recorded, transmitted, and perhaps transfigured in Western musical traditions? The first set of questions, La Rue points out, has analogues with other kinds of museum disputes, for "it is not only the material being recorded today but also historic recordings in archives that also present . . . problems of ownership and commitments of care. How are they to be managed and how should the resource be used? To whom do these recordings truly belong? Should they be made public?" To these difficulties La Rue adds the problematic impact of the field ethnomusicologists who enter traditional cultures to make and transmit these recordings.

Still these complications pale next to the larger problem of how to handle the artistic and commercial expropriation of traditional music by the global market. Here, well-meaning interventions like the United States Protection for the Products of Indian Arts and Craftsmanship in the Indian Arts and Crafts Act of 1990 quail before the difficulties of licensing "the work of musicians, actors, and writers." Nor is such nervousness unjustified. La Rue raises the issue of whether the original performers have any right to any revenue produced and points by implication to the intractability of choosing between the rights of the group and the rights of individuals within the group when those rights come into conflict.

In Ngahuia Te Awekotuku's account of Maori tattoo, the identity issues involved in the complicated business of reproducible cultural property become more pointed and the intensity level rises. Certainly, images of bodies indelibly marked by patterns of group expression insist that one take the matter of inalienable cultural identity seriously, with all of its power to inspire and disturb. Raised in an extended family of weavers, carvers, genealogists, and storytellers, in 1996 Te Awekotuku encountered Alex Binney, a London-based tattoo artist who asserted his artistic right to take over Maori forms wherever he chooses, "for art surrounds us and is universal." Te Awekotuku's response is that "for many indigenous peoples in the Fourth World, however, this is just another form of pillaging, of extracting the spirit of a tribal people to sate the culturally malnourished appetites of the decadent and industrial West." She allows that some Maori artists disagree with her and that in practice the images cannot be suppressed. They "are there to be seen, interpreted, and consumed by everyone," and even within Maori culture they have been appropriated in nontraditional usages—as emblems of gang membership, for example, or as "an expression of urbanized, or criminal, Maori identity." In these new Maori practices the point is to be, literally, in your face, and Te Awekotuku endorses that aggressiveness as a legitimate modern "assertion of tribal heritage, political activism, and kinship networks . . . [and] commitment to our warrior culture." Te Awekotuku insists, however, that the practice is not simply an art form. "It is an ancestral legacy," she states, "it is a statement of resilience and survival." As such, its reproduction as a work of art or commerce, unlicensed by Maori solidarity—like the alienation of more tangible properties like the Parthenon Marbles under the guise of art—represents a dilution of the Maori legacy and a drain on Maori resilience and survival.

Closely related to the problem of the diffusion and dilution of group solidarity raised by the global reproduction of Maori tattoo, there is a third type of cultural property that is even harder to conceptualize and regulate. This type of ownership involves materials associated with literature: folk stories; dialects; and group images, designations, and experiences. Here difficulty lies not only in controlling an outsider's reproduction or representation of these forms of indigenous symbolic property but also in mediating the conflicting claims to jointly held symbolic property by segments of a large group (sometimes indigenous, sometimes ethnic, sometimes minority), each with different ideas about the nature of the group's identity and significance. The cry here is, "Do not reveal sacred practices to the uninitiated, and keep folktales for traditional use!" This means, however, attempting to control representation and images by censoring offensive depictions that are produced not only by outsiders but by insiders as well. Cultural representation and censorship are Janus faces of each other.

Among the most interesting varieties of this third type of cultural property are representations of an insurgent identity whose embodiment has to do with new forms or discourses. This may be a recurrent feature of the cultural property world. Resisting group censorship multiplies cultural creativity, yet, since a group cannot control images of itself but cannot stop itself from trying to control them, dissent is inevitable (hence the artistic efflorescence of the twentieth-century African American, Jewish, and Irish communities). Prophets attempt to transform their national or minority culture by calling into being new artistic and literary representations, and these new national or ethnic representations take life in revolutionary forms. Born as objects of strife and internal dissent, these are sometimes then appropriated by the culture at large, which makes them over time into icons. Their subsequent "success" (a new cultural understanding) in its turn creates a new fashion, a new style, frequently tied to the way a minority group transforms negative stereotypes of itself into self-validating images that are then embraced by a majority culture.

These phenomena form the basis of Robert Young's essay on identity politics in contemporary Britain, Roy Foster's essay on identity politics in Ireland at the turn of the twentieth century, Marlon Ross's account of how elements of the African American community appropriated different parts of their heritage to define themselves in the furnace of black-white cultural politics, Jonathan Arac's meditation on the way in which a national culture appropriated ethnic representations to help form an American literary identity using Mark Twain's *The Adventures of Huckleberry Finn,* and Ronald Bush's account of censorship and identity in the work of Philip Roth. Young, Ross, Arac, Foster, and Bush specifically highlight the way such issues penetrate the practices of high literature.

Young stresses the complicated situation that arose after minority representations became so prominent in British society that "everyone like the Scots in Britain—and abroad in places like Australia" began to find it harder to define "their identity against" the British. There was, as it were, "no same for the Other." This despite the fact that it became increasingly difficult for minority representations transmitted in the English language to retain their definition. (For example, are Irish authors who write in English manifestations of English literature or Irish culture? It is notoriously difficult to convince libraries or academies of the latter. Since the English language has taken over much of the world's literary commerce, this problem bedevils writers almost everywhere.)

A potential antidote to the frustration of being co-opted by English language expectations, Young suggests, is to seek out nonliterary forms of self-representation, such as popular music and street style. In contemporary Britain, the latter (which resemble each other in that they both make fun of old-fashioned British identity) have become so powerful that they now constitute a kind of common currency that seems to outshine the economic or political property that minority groups in Britain are still denied. With the simultaneous diminishment of old-fashioned British identity, we are left with the paradoxical situation that "marginal identity" has become "the property everyone wants to have." Unbelievably, even at "higher" levels of contemporary culture, the same seems to hold true, so that "Britain's ethnic minorities [seem to] have captured the cultural center ground."

Seeming is not reality, however, and if the center lacks "the cultural properties of what's cool and fashionable," they "can always be bought." Like other kinds of property, cultural property is commodifiable. Hence, Young warns, we should be suspicious in a multicultural society of a claim on behalf of cultural representations to true authenticity or real power. Creative minorities may no longer be "culturally marginalized, but economic disadvantage . . . is as great as ever." The true situation behind the facade of increasing cultural cool is that "there has been a slippage between the representation and the real, between the image and the realities of poverty and social deprivation."

Marlon Ross also focuses on the intricate relationship between cultural property and other forms of power but emphasizes the arena of legal power at play in the African American milieu at the turn of the twentieth century. Ross's point of departure is the curious logic of the landmark United States Supreme Court *Plessy v. Ferguson* decision of 1896, which upheld Jim Crow separate-but-equal statutes in Louisiana. In the process whiteness (or blackness) as a race property was established insofar as it constitutes a real measure of positive (or negative) reputation. The result in the African American community was a concerted effort "to prove the true property value of the [black] race to whites," largely through launching "a massive media campaign to reshape the public image of the race by insisting on the development of what leading African Americans called the 'New Negro.'" That is to say, to "gain the racial authority to invent and market the public image of the New Negro, black uplifters had to claim a sort of racial copyright . . . they persistently had to wrestle away from whites their customary liberty of determining how the black race should be imaged and valued." Here self-representation as cultural property was not merely a refined metaphor but was set in the concrete of American statutes for over fifty years.

The consequence was that "African Americans and their allies began a systematic campaign to police the public image of the race." Their reputation being enshrined in the law of the land as regulated property, African Americans reasoned that they had the collective right to raise the value of that property by means of promotion, as well as the right to authorize or censure representations of blacks, either in the white or in the black community. The positive aspect of this consolidated notion of cultural property, starting with William Pickens's book of 1916, *The New Negro*, was a theorized and ongoing advertising campaign on behalf of a mass body conceived as part of the advance guard of modernity. Its negative aspects included massive protests against the film *The Birth of a Nation*. "Renewing the Negro is an ongoing process of mediating [self-representation] through the voice of African Americans while preventing, policing, and protesting any infringement on that voice made by whites in their customary license to defame the race."

As Ross concludes, however, the literalizing of race identity in the form of legally sanctioned cultural property led to a relentless cycle of quarrel and redefinition about exactly what constituted the identity (the property) of the New Negro. The final product turned out to be a cultivated sophistication about identity difference that would provoke and enlighten the debate over multiculturalism in the America of recent years. It is only by following this debate through the decades, Ross observes, "that we come to recognize the impossibility of answering [a] persistent question." The fallacy, Alain Locke writes in *The New Negro*, "is that there is a type Negro who, either qualitatively or quantitatively, is the type symbol of the entire group." "There are no adequate substitutes for the whole truth of race," Ross concludes, "but as the cultural history of racial copyright [and the idea of racial cultural property] reveals, in the end all we have are inadequate substitutes, for race itself constructs the myth that there can be a whole truth, possessible and reproducible by the voice of one group or another."

As in Young's essay, Ross shows that at the very moment that self-representation seems to solidify into tangible form, we see that its solidity is an illusion. This does not diminish representation's enormous promise to consolidate group legitimacy or its enormous potential to wreck havoc if consolidation is not licensed, policed, and controlled. Both of its faces are viewed in Jonathan Arac's essay, which takes up from Ross the story of how minority and national representations interact and considers the controversial "banning" of *Huckleberry Finn*. Arac argues that *Huckleberry Finn* acquired its enormous status in the American literary canon by appropriating African American materials to make a representation later characterized as "most expressive of who we really are" as Americans. "Some Americans gain a desired identity by this process," he points out, "but at a cost to other Americans." The cost, paid principally by African Americans, is the continuing inequality fostered by a vividly stylized picture of "radically unequal relations of power" and saturated with "the single most symbolically offensive term in the American vocabulary — *nigger*." The gain reaped by whites is the comforting reassurance, reintroduced by a sentimentalized post–Civil War American identity, about the unity and tolerance of American society. Arac offers no guess as to when the angry quarrel over the disposition of this property will cease but concludes by adducing the counsel of the African American novelist Ralph Ellison about some similarly troublesome films. Ellison urged "as an antidote to the sentimentality of these films" that they be seen "in predominantly Negro audiences, for here, when the action goes phony, one will hear derisive laughter."

Ellison's formulation reminds us of classic disputes over tangible property and restitution, where cultural property presented itself as a site for negotiation between perspectives—something that seemed to demand legal arbitration, but whose provocations could only be addressed through dialogue. This time, however, the dialogue takes place between minority and majority groups within a national culture. This is also the narrative presented by Roy Foster as he recounts the way the Anglo-Irish poet William Butler Yeats and his Catholic contemporaries came to navigate their differences over the symbolic property of "Irishry." *Irishry,* Foster reminds us, was a term Yeats deployed to define Irishness in a way "that excluded bourgeois Ireland (the culture of successful Catholic nationalist Ireland) and reinserted the eighteenth-century 'planter' ascendancy, the Protestant elite whence Yeats himself derived." The force of the word, Foster suggests, shows why it is not enough to see Yeats either as a nationalist—"the voice of 'the Irish race' lifted against [British] imperial domination"—or as a Protestant outsider in an essentially Catholic Ireland. Irishness was a property contested, negotiated, and defined by a discourse among cultural parties, and Yeats took part in that process by shaping an interpretation of the legends and the traditions of Ireland.

Foster offers a historically detailed and nuanced picture of the way in which Catholics and Protestants reciprocally fashioned the representation of Ireland from the 1880s to the 1940s. His emphasis on negotiated identity does not, however, have the last word in the volume. Foster's perspective, although wise, is arguably too cool and dispassionate for the kind of hatred kindled when claims to symbolic property are fought out within the little room of a minority culture whose survival is constantly at risk. The minority artist, within the bosom of what to outsiders seems a homogenous ethnicity, inevitably begins to ask, "Why do my contemporaries deserve the right to speak for my group?" and "Why cannot I also draw on my group's symbolic resources to fashion a new identity?" Almost as inevitably, the same artist, as he or she resists group pressures to conform and to "represent" the group accurately in art, will begin to question the group's prevailing understanding of its authenticity and identity.

Thus here it is not the force of appropriation but the claims of free speech that tend to dominate the controversy. Does any individual within a culture have the right to transfer or sell work that draws on traditional group property, even when he or she has produced it? Do groups of African Americans, Muslims, Irish, or Jews have the right to censor a Ralph Ellison, Salman Rushdie, James Joyce, or Philip Roth when they produce representations that "harm" the group's reputation? Or, as it has seemed apparent to each of the writers just named, might it rather be more reasonable to regard matters such as "culture," "race," "identity," "authenticity," and "inalienable property" as part of the problem rather than part of the solution?

Moreover, in cases like Roth's, the symbolic dialectics of group authenticity converge with the more mystified business of personal identity. Perhaps this is why quarrels within minority groups not only have become the focus of a number of celebrated literary works but also have shaped some of the key concerns and procedures of twentieth-century literary practice. In the novels of Ellison, Rushdie, Joyce, and Roth the urgent and difficult project of defining group and personal authenticity has molded the procedures of modernist and postmodernist literary technique and has driven plots in which authenticity is revealed as a kind of dangerous piety that can only obscure discontinuous, constructed, and historical truths.

In the last essay of this volume, this territory is explored by Ronald Bush, who examines Philip Roth's lifetime battle against censure within the American Jewish community. After a number of Jewish elders had charged that Roth's stories had helped "to make people believe that all Jews are cheats, liars, and connivers," Roth found himself in the position of a traitor in a cultural war. He was accused of betraying the tribe's secret shame, and he was threatened with a traitor's deserts. As part of his defense, he crafted a series of stories and novels in which claims to stable group identity are repeatedly unmasked as disguises that majority groups construct to naturalize the contingency of their social values and to gain advantage in the game of cultural politics. Although Roth allows that he cannot *not* write about Jews, in his fiction and his critical prose he constructs a skeptical and antiessentialist account of what a Jew is and is not, and defends his own techniques of "irony, pathos, ridicule, [and] humor" as tools he can use to demythologize the world of conventional identity. Without the "doubleness" that Roth advances as the marker of genuinely contingent identity, there can be, he asserts, only pretence and sorrow. "Doubleness" is a necessity created by the tensions inherent in all matters of identity, and, as Bush suggests, its formulation should remind us of the skepticism of African American self-reflection, and especially of W. E. B. Du Bois's description of American Negro life as a "double-consciousness," a "history of strife" in which "one ever feels his twoness—an American, a Negro."

By now it may be argued that both cultural property and the notion of cultural identity have come to seem categories so loose and inclusive as to lose even their pragmatic usefulness. If cultural property can encompass all of these types and examples, and if cultural identity is as problematic as Roth suggests, what good does it do us to retain the terms?

Let us reconsider Roth's anxiety about whether he is to be regarded as a Jewish writer, a dilemma that may stand in for parallel worries about whether the Parthenon Marbles are Greek, or why Native Americans have a claim over the rituals of a medicine man that New Agers lack. Here Roth's insistence on "doubleness" may point a way forward. If, as Young argues, ethnicity "amounts to a form of differential identity," then it is a composite business of which one aspect is always resistant to majority definition. Further, if self-representation is driven by resistance, the representations of various minority groups within a majority community will resemble one another because of their solidarity in resistance. This does not mean that different minority groups do not have their own identities, only that all of their identities were formed in a dialectical relationship to the same "Other."

Similarly, although the idea of cultural property proves problematic and nearly impossible to constrain within a legal framework, by that very quality it demonstrates the usefulness of extralegal, dialectical frameworks. Roth argues that his "Jewishness" (or, in *American Pastoral*, his "Americanness") should be regarded as an inauthentic and pernicious convention, and yet there seems to be no alternative to defining himself against that convention. So it may be that culture crystallizes as property because it is something that we cannot help but desire to "own" even though, logically, we never can (just as we can never "own" that part of our consciousness that is "Jewish" or "American").

The experience of necessary *alienation* from part of our patrimony thus stands at the core of our dilemmas over group identity and cultural property. However paradoxically, it is always the case that being alienated from the identity or cultural property of one's group helps precipitate our sense of belonging or ownership.

These observations, admittedly provisional, may suggest why claims on cultural property are only made in hindsight, after loss. This phenomenon is not, as skeptics sometimes insinuate, simply proof of the fraudulence of such claims. Only after being appropriated by outsiders or by establishment (or even dissenting) insiders does cultural property disclose its field of force. Its positive existence has a dialectical relation to deprivation, and its significance cannot be clear except in the experience of alienation. This alienation takes the form of a communal subjective experience and at times succeeds in calling on the sympathies of outsiders. In sum, as we come to recognize more levels of group organization between the sovereign state and the individual, it may be that the most important cultural property issue of all will be: Who else besides the state gets to apportion the validity of alienation?

Notes

1. Theo-Ben Gurirab, Foreign Minister of Namibia, quoted in Barbara Crossette, "A Bully Pulpit to Restore Lost African Icons," *New York Times*, 19 September 1999, sec. 1, p. 21.

2. Lord Byron, *The Curse of Minerva* (1811); see idem, *The Complete Poetical Works*, ed. Jerome J. McGann (Oxford: Clarendon, 1980–), 1:326 (no. 151, ll. 196–98).

Amending Historical Injustices: The Restitution of Cultural Property — An Overview

Elazar Barkan

The demand that nations act morally and amend their own gross historical injustices is a relatively new phenomenon. Traditionally, international diplomacy was based on the dictum Might is right. Beginning at the
end of World War II, however, and quickening since the end of the Cold War,
morality and justice have received growing attention as international political
questions. It is in the context of these new moral demands, which are placed
on the rich and powerful in the international arena, that the fate of the cultural property of past victims has come to the fore. This growing attention to
cultural property as part of restitution to past victims also provides a new
framework through which to view the relationship between individual and
group rights.

Cultural identity and, by extension, cultural property, have enhanced the
recognition that victims have rights as members of groups and has called for
a reformulation of our understanding of justice. Our conventional notion of
justice is founded on Enlightenment principles, which see inalienable human
rights as accruing to individuals. Today we have begun to recognize that while
preserving individual rights remains a necessary component of human rights,
this in itself is no longer satisfactory because individuals cannot enjoy full
human rights if their identity as members of a group is violated. This recognition arose from the dilemma presented by the attempt to extend Enlightenment principles of individual rights and justice to minorities, and to the traditional cultures of indigenous peoples, and coincided with the increased
recognition that the representation of history has a role in forming the identity
of the nation. What has emerged may be called neo-Enlightenment morality —
a political sense that groups have rights similar to those that have traditionally
been reserved for individuals.[1] Group rights have come to dominate the political agenda in negotiations over the rights of indigenous peoples and are also
pertinent to any nonsovereign national group.[2]

Negotiation of identities often takes place through the medium of cultural
property, such as art, religious and other artifacts, sacred sites, and even
human remains. Possession of one's cultural property seemingly creates a
level playing field among powerful nations and weaker nations or minorities
within nations. The rationale is that if all cultures are of equal worth, all
cultural property is worth preserving. Control of one's patrimony is seen as

a mark of equality and has become a privileged right in today's world. Restitution of cultural property, therefore, occupies a middle ground that can provide the necessary space in which to negotiate identities and a mechanism to mediate between the histories of perpetrators and victims. The discourse of such restitution revolves around nationalism: whose story and what version of the national narrative will be legitimated by both, as well as by the "impartial" outsider. Heritage is appreciated and cherished because it enriches life in ways that market economy and monetary compensation cannot. Tangible cultural property manifests the cultural identity of a nation or a group disproportionate to other economic resources. The significance of the objects is often enhanced by aesthetic or utilitarian considerations. Thus, the heritage of every nation is projected on its own priceless objects and sites. The identity of these objects, even when separated from ownership, manifests the group's history and tradition.

The Benin bronzes, although neither bronze nor in Edo possession, are significant because of their Edo identity. Their presence in major museums in Europe and the United States does not put their identity into question, only the right to own them. Even more famous is the British Museum's possession of the Parthenon Marbles (also known as the Elgin Marbles; see Timothy Webb's essay in this volume), which the Greeks have been contesting for over 180 years. In a manner that was legally disputed even at the time of the "theft," Lord Elgin took the marbles from the Parthenon in Athens and sold them to the British Museum. On gaining their independence in 1830, the Greeks sought to establish their direct link to the Hellenistic tradition, legislated this aspiration into a protection of heritage through control of antiquities, and demanded the return of the marbles. "Elginized" marbles have a different meaning than Parthenon Marbles.[3]

The presence and the absence of these objects, which cannot be replicated or renewed, add a further layer to the complexity of the object as signifying the national identity. Often the longing itself for these unavailable objects or sites constitutes an essential component of the group's identity. The restitution of cultural property, therefore, plays a central role in attempts to redress historical injustices. Ownership of cultural property has become a prime moral issue in the international community. This includes discussions about inalienable patrimony, about a possible statute of limitations on amending historical injustices, and on the relationship between the individual and the community vis-à-vis ownership of tangible identity.

These discussions began with particular conflicts and have reached the stage in which the United Nations Educational, Scientific and Cultural Organization (UNESCO) now leads efforts to codify these sentiments into moral standards and to translate the resolutions of specific conflicts into a series of international agreements about cultural property. These attempts are excruciatingly slow, and UNESCO and other international organizations are subjected to a continuous barrage of criticism. In the best of cases critics see the international agreements as ineffective rhetoric. Nonetheless, international efforts continue presumably because participants agree that weak policies are better than none.[4]

Historical hindsight of these standards suggests that international agreements do provide a moral agenda and that restitution can play a role in mediating economic interests, culture, religion, and politics among rival societies. In particular, historical examination of cultural property disputes provides a relatively long view of the relationship between ownership and identity. It appears that even when political circumstances change, the identity of patrimony seems to be frozen in time. As an abstract principle, this presumed stability of essence and identity could provide a clear moral principle. This postulated historical edifice of stable identity is, however, built on sand dunes; identity and ownership are never neatly organized. Over time a great deal of cultural patrimony was removed from its original owners through sales, wars, looting, or by other means. At the time of acquisition some of these methods were considered not only legal but also honorable. Today they are considered a violation. To this category belong colonial exploits, exchanges of cultural treasures for trinkets, or purchases of stolen art objects. Consequently, institutions or individuals who have property claims on objects of cultural patrimonies but no affinity to the original owners whose identity determines their significance have a diminished moral claim on their possession. Historical circumstances have also led to the shift in the national identity of the dispossessed, which often find themselves belonging to new nations.

Provenance of Cultural Patrimony

The very notions of cultural property and public patrimony evolved concurrent with nationalism in Europe at the end of the eighteenth century. These notions have played a role in the debate over the control and use of sites, artifacts, and identities ever since. One can trace international concern with the national identity of culture and its property to the French Revolution and the Napoleonic wars. As Napoléon Bonaparte plundered European courts, he left a trail of budding national identities. It is, therefore, not surprising, given the tremble caused by the call of democracy, the novelty of nationalism, the undermining of hereditary sovereigns, and the unprecedented role of "the people" in wars and national politics, that cultural property, too, was "rediscovered" as national, and not merely court, heritage. As national movements in Europe invented their own glorious traditions they relied, in part, on the physicality of cultural property to substantiate their new past. In 1815 when faced with a wish to return to the old order and restitute the art treasures looted by the French army and taken to Paris, the anti-French coalition of European monarchs sought to both reclaim the old regime's lost property and exclude cultural property from being considered legitimate spoils of war in the future. The national character of cultural property was being invented in front of Parisian eyes, as they watched the removal of acquired cultural objects from Paris, this time not as the spoils of war but under the claim of legal ownership based on the previous geographical location of the objects.

Although there had been specific treaties concerning cultural property along these lines since the seventeenth century, and despite the delegitimation of plunder during the eighteenth century by international law, the Napoleonic wars recast the old European order. The new policy regarding war spoils was characterized by internal contradictions as well as by the self-serving principles of the anti-French coalition. The participants who fought the French in the name of the ancien régime did not object in principle to cultural spoils, nor did they care particularly about national sentiments. The new ideology was, however, a practical way of dividing the old war spoils held in Paris. Perhaps the most glaring characteristic of the new "system" was its haphazard implementation. In the post-Napoleonic agreements the monarchs attempted to arrest the legitimacy of national identities and agreed on a geographical principle that called for works of art to be placed in their original locations. The arrangements created precedents that were later used in a very different way than the European monarchs intended in 1815. The immediate purpose of the "geographical priority" was to legitimize the massive redistribution of art objects that had already taken place. Major works were being taken back to Prussia, the Vatican, Venice, and the Netherlands—all to the displeasure of the watching Parisians who viewed themselves as being robbed.[5]

As a result of the new order and in the absence of large-scale European wars in the next century, a near stability was established in which plundering national art within Europe became immoral and illegal. This commitment against the plunder of art and cultural treasures was, however, very narrowly applied. While it respected the center (western Europe), the periphery (the East and the rest of the world) remained fair game.

An early, notable exception to the practices of the nineteenth century—one that specifically privileged cultural property due to the identity of the objects rather than their legal ownership—was the Austrian-Italian agreement of 1871 when Venice was joined to the new state of Italy. The agreement included the restitution of objects of art and science, which were "specifically allocated to the ceded territory." The agreement excluded the return of objects acquired in bona fide individual transactions, which underscored the necessary vagueness involved in defining the "organic" nature (that is, their Venetian identity) of the collection.[6]

Imperial Plunder

While Europeans inconsistently experimented with juggling the priorities of geography, peoples, and private ownership in adjudicating cultural patrimony within Europe, they were uninhibited in exploiting the rest of the world. International morality remained subject to power and expediency. The competition for world domination by European states was manifested in imperial collecting that was equated with a new national glory. As European empires conquered new territories, they looted cultural objects from around the world. Thus, British, French, and German travelers competed for national glory by hauling away Greek, Egyptian, Chinese, African, and other antiquities. The

Vatican's veneration was supposedly enhanced through its extensive and growing collections pouring in from all over the globe. While in the 1990s such policies were viewed as immoral, imperial plunder was the norm in the past. The competition revolved around who could dominate the vast "empty spaces" (at times, literally known as *terra nullius*) of the world, namely those regions that were not under the sovereignty of a recognized power. Looting from these regions was not contested. The growing European domination of other countries was seen as imperial progress. As the symbol of this imperial progress, Cecil Rhodes (1853–1902; British imperialist, business magnate, and prime minister of the Cape Colony in South Africa), was envied for being more successful than other politicians. Communist leader Vladimir Lenin (1870–1924), too, viewed imperialism as a necessary step on the way to the socialist society. Back in the metropolis, looted cultural objects expansively displayed in museums and world fairs were the most concrete demonstration of imperial glories and wealth. Eventually, with the delegitimation of imperialism, even after the European powers withdrew from their empires, they held on to the cultural imperial spoils. It is these possessions that have become subject to criticism.

The vast majority of currently disputed cultural property was displaced under colonial and imperial rule. Much of it was straightforward plunder with little or no legal constraints or local involvement. Taking at will, the military provided a rich supply of cultural objects for museums and individuals. Imperialism at its height was "the heart of darkness." Indeed, plunder was not outlawed before 1907.[7] Joseph Conrad's Marlow evoked for his contemporaries not only the Congo but also the "punitive expedition" to Benin as the "city of blood." While Conrad imagined a new literary aesthetics, the plunder of Benin's extensive art contributed to the revolution of European aesthetics.[8] European imperialism had numerous adventurers—real Marlows, some more violent than others—who saw themselves as bringing civilization to the native while rescuing and restoring to civilization the art and culture of ancient civilizations.

Even in the midst of this imperial plunder, however, there evolved a modus vivendi, a semblance of imperial order that placed constraints on outright plunder. This order included anomalies that recognized some local groups as having agency and, therefore, the right to control and trade their cultural property, or that recognized some local monuments as treasures to be protected from imperial plunder. At the beginning of the twentieth century, as a representative of the British Museum, Emil Torday traded with the Kuba people of the Kasai region of central Africa. His partner, Melville W. Hilton-Simpson, described one purchase:

> Eventually, owing to Torday's persuasive powers, and to the fact that our interest in their customs had caused the elders to take a liking to us, all the dignitaries concerned agreed to use their influence with the king to induce him to sell us the statues.

> At a solemn gathering of the elders the matter was discussed. The Nyimi [king] told us afterwards that he had let it appear that he was not desirous of parting with the treasures, but when the council had urged him to do so in order that all the world might see and marvel at them in the museum he had agreed to let them go too, and the question of price was then raised. The price demanded for the first statue was a very high one, to be paid mainly in a kind of dark red cloth which we could purchase from the Kasai Company, but we could not let such an opportunity go by of securing such an important object, and were, therefore, obliged to pay what was asked.[9]

Although Torday viewed himself as representing the "whole world," the actual transaction suggests a sense of local, independent decision making by the Kuba. Despite the vastly superior imperial power, this was an exchange in which the local Kuba are represented (by Torday) as having agency; they devised their own facade in order to facilitate a transaction that may have violated their local customs, but, when given the opportunity, it was one they were interested in pursuing. The transaction and the described intentions of both the imperial actors and the local leaders suggest that, at times, the local people may have reached independent decisions. Even so, this was done within the limited constraints of a "purchase from the Kasai Company." Benevolence, after all, played a minimal role in collecting. This is not to suggest that there existed equality under imperialism but rather to point out the precursors of today's emerging rhetoric of reciprocity.

There are those who, in hindsight, justify the removal of cultural artifacts from their place of origin as contributing to their preservation, and hence, to contemporary indigenous culture, although they saw it as preserving a dying and disappearing stage of human evolution.[10] The imperial agents were, however, mostly interested in the kind of personal enrichment and institutional glory that pervaded other facets of imperialism and voyages of discovery. Torday employed a different rhetoric in addressing his employers at the British Museum in London than he used to persuade the Kuba leaders. London was worried that the massive collection of the renowned ethnologist and explorer Leo Frobenius (German, 1873–1938), who boasted of amassing everything in Africa, meant that nothing would be left in Africa for the English; however, Torday was quite a match for Frobenius. Calming his superiors, Torday promised that Frobenius would not undersell "the old curiosity shop of Bloomsbury." The rhetoric of "world heritage" he used in Africa to persuade the Africans to part with the objects — "our interest in their custom," and the desire "that all the world might see and marvel at [Kuba objects] in the museum"[11] — disappeared in London under a facade of narrow national competition.

The modern concept of "cultural property" was coined by the Hague Convention of 1954 and is based on the belief that "damage to cultural property belonging to any people whatsoever means damage to the cultural heritage of all mankind since each people makes its contribution to the culture of the world."[12] The ruling morality of the "unity of man" was a rebuttal to the racist divisions that tore the world apart in World War II. In practice, the Cold War determined political divisiveness, but the moral stand and rhetoric were of a unified humanity. This correspondence between every unique culture and global riches was further enhanced in 1972 by UNESCO's definition of significant universal objects as those that contribute to the "world heritage of mankind as a whole."[13] The global perspective is based on the belief that the "deterioration or disappearance of any item of the cultural or natural heritage constitutes a harmful impoverishment of the heritage of all nations of the world."[14] It aims at conserving the world's outstanding cultural and natural properties: a "cultural internationalism" in which all peoples have a stake.[15] A series of committees, negotiations, and declarations articulated the unity of humankind through a host of policies.

Since the 1980s, as the universal and global give way to the national and particular, there has been a reversal in emphasis that is informed by local uniqueness and perspectives and highlights questions of control over cultural objects. The shift comes as a response to practical dilemmas: How is cultural property defined, and who is entitled to define it? Who and what determines whether culture is national and local or global? As the global becomes, in practice, a compilation of the local, the moral commitments remain international yet the operating framework privileges local. Except in extreme cases, the local currently reigns supreme. Ordinarily that means state control, but the struggle within sovereign nations over who represents the local spills on to the international stage where minorities contest what they view as oppressive governments.

The competition over cultural property is a race to appropriate identity. Declaring cultural artifacts as patrimony transforms a particular object or a site into an essence of the nation. Traditionally cultural commodities are produced and consumed by a small minority of the nation, as was the case, for instance, with court culture. Both materially and spiritually, the artifacts are adopted by the nation and are invested with historical memory to become national symbols. The physical objects evoke national historical imagination and provide a focus for communal emotions. While the objects themselves are often aesthetically pleasing and even universally esteemed, their exquisite quality is surpassed by their national significance.

With thousands of peoples around the globe and less than two hundred countries whose borders have repeatedly shifted and still continue to change, the affinity between a sovereign country and the cultural patrimony in its control is often partial at best, as the competition between "new" nations for control confirms. Beyond the internal contradiction between validating local agency and objecting to local mores that contradict the global perspective, the ambivalent global position toward specific local disputes often results from the lack of a unified local attitude. Instead, the local is represented by a number of conflicting and competing perspectives that change over time. Changing historical circumstances often become a source of disputes over the legitimate heirs of cultural patrimony. This is particularly true when empires and traditional states are fragmented into new national and sovereign states and when a country incorporates (and often represses) its traditional ethnic minorities while claiming to represent them.

Consider the struggle between Australia and its indigenous peoples over the ownership of Aboriginal culture. Is Australia the appropriate "representative" of Aboriginal culture? Aboriginal peoples reject the proposition, yet Australia certainly acts as the owner. Since 1960 it has limited the export of indigenous culture, widely defined, and its protection has become more comprehensive since the UNESCO convention of 1972. Limitations on export of Aboriginal culture were, however, the result neither of the yet-to-form Aboriginal political pressure groups nor of any popular interest. Australian archaeology, which operated a generation ago only within the discourse of European discoveries, assigned control to professionals and not to indigenous peoples or the public. Australia's control over indigenous culture was a question of professional parochialism and not an indigenous identity statement. Aborigines were not even Australian citizens until the 1960s, and the onslaught of public racism in Australia since 1996 underscores for the outsider what continues to be the reality for Aborigines. The struggle between the state and Aboriginal organizations for control over dissemination and consumption of Aboriginal cultural property remains a point of contention; however, the Western Australian Aboriginal Heritage Act of 1972, which includes provisions for Aboriginal input, was an early exception that may have acted as a guide in the transition from a universal appreciation of primordial ancestry to appreciation of, and respect for, Aboriginal culture as a concrete and living culture.

Negotiations between the Metropolitan Museum of Art in New York and Mexico over the Maya temple at Campeche demonstrate the duality of center and periphery. The growing moral pressure to restitute illegally purchased cultural objects caught the Metropolitan Museum unprepared before it took possession of the Campeche temple facade, which was offered to it by a private dealer. As the crates were on their way to New York, the museum came under pressure and refused to finalize the purchase. Instead it became instrumental in arranging for the temple facade to be donated to the Museo Nacional de Antropología in Mexico. The episode was compared to the Parthenon Marbles, and the transfer of the facade to Mexico City represented restitution.[16] For Mexico City to own the Maya temple facade from the Yucatán Peninsula is also an appropriation by a center of a periphery. From the Campeche perspective, restitution only meant privileging a closer center over a more distant one. The question of the cultural affinity of traditional cultures to new sovereign states is especially crucial in cases involving Fourth World nations. At present, however, the morality of restitution of cultural patrimony is confined to sovereign actors. The dilemma is yet to capture international attention.

Resolving vague imperial legacies is further complicated when the claim of national patrimony is projected on to a distant historic or prehistoric past.

The identification of distant histories with the peoples who currently populate the same geographic area, to the exclusion of others, faces serious objections. Syria and Iraq demand global recognition and restitution of patrimonial objects, including everything throughout history that falls within its current borders. This includes the antiquities from the ancient Fertile Crescent. The negative global public image of Syria and Iraq predisposes international bodies to reject their demands. The unpalatable possibility of restituting revered cultural objects into the hands of a dictator who positioned missiles in the vicinity of antiquities alleviates the immediate moral contradiction but not the ethical dilemma.

Similar to the dilemma of the relationship between ancient history and contemporary societies, questions arise about the findings from early hominid sites in Ethiopia and Kenya. Recently even the United States has become embroiled in a comparable dispute. The Kennewick Man—the remains of an ancient "caucasoid" found on the banks of the Columbia River—illuminates the moral and cultural question shared by these disputes: Should contemporary national borders and cultures overshadow regional and transnational cultural heritage and legacies?[17] As complicated as these issues are, in the public arena the competition over affinity to a distant historic or even prehistoric period has, at times, become an authenticity pageant. People view their own culture as patrimony, and other peoples' cultures and treasures as global heritage.

The United Nations has become the most important international moral arbiter. Notwithstanding the general and accurate perception of the short-comings of the United Nations, in the long term its policies and organizations shape global morality. Indeed, United Nations debates and resolutions were the first venue to recognize the need to redress the cultural infliction of imperialism as a basis for a new international morality. The political impotence of the United Nations is deservedly frustrating, but with the hindsight of a generation, the organization may enjoy a more favorable historical judgment. Indeed, even when the tools of the United Nations are rejected and its rhetoric viewed as mere duplicity, in the long run governments accept its international standard. An emblematic case occurred in 1973 when, at the height of the Cold War, Zaire (now the Democratic Republic of the Congo) led the charge to reverse the infliction of colonialism and to restitute cultural artifacts to the nations of origin. President Mobutu Sese Seko (Zaire, 1930–1997), a corrupt despot, spelled out the global enlightened position. No matter how hypocritical he may have sounded, the substantial position can hardly be ignored:

> During the colonial period we suffered not only from colonialism, slavery, economic exploitation, but also and above all from the barbarous systematic pillaging of all our works of art. In this way the rich countries appropriated our best, our unique works of art, and we are therefore poorer not only economically but also culturally.... That is why I would also ask this General Assembly to adopt a resolution requesting rich Powers which possess works of art of the poor countries to

restore some of them so that we can teach our children and our grandchildren the history of our countries.[18]

Since then, international conventions and agreements have increasingly recognized the value of cultural property in defining both national and global identities. A United Nations resolution of 1975 called for the restitution of patrimony in order to "strengthen international understanding and cooperation" and viewed justice as a pragmatic resolution and not just an abstract principle.[19] Since the late 1970s, cultural property has become increasingly national and ethnic. The global is no longer seen as a playground of the homogenous omnipotent viewer—the perspective of the globe-trotter—but as a quilt of local cultures with a richness that depends on its components: a richness that, at times, has internal conflict. As an abstract concept, protection of cultural property is laudable; but protection means control. International critics often willfully ignore the specific circumstances and/or the desires and needs of local peoples either by demanding that countries better preserve certain sites or by demanding greater access. In both cases the dispute is over the sovereignty of a government to control the cultural resources under its jurisdiction. Cultural nationalism versus universalism has become the major divisive issue in the politics of cultural patrimony (see, for example, the case of Papua New Guinea below).

The shift in balance from the global to the local was accentuated in the mid-1990s through efforts to restructure laws regarding the acquisition and trade of art objects. These efforts were the result of viewing all cultures as fundamentally equal and the consequent global decentering of culture. The new ideology, even if it was yet to be defined as such, drastically shifted the balance from a system that privileges the center as the possessor of the world patrimony to one that recognizes the periphery as owners of their own local culture. In the new system the appropriation of cultural property and illegal trade of antiquities are seen as existing on one continuum, and combating the former began by fighting the latter. The shift began by first making certain kinds of previously legal transfers illegal. In 1970 UNESCO adopted the Convention on the Means of Prohibiting and Preventing the Illicit Import, Export, and Transfer of Ownership of Cultural Property. The agreement was informed by global perspectives, working to increase "the knowledge of the civilization of Man," which "enriches the cultural life of all peoples and inspires mutual respect and appreciation among nations."[20] Yet, as the most comprehensive convention to protect cultural property in peacetime, it did establish legal hurdles in an attempt to stop the flow of cultural objects from the poor to the rich. These sentiments were explicated when the seemingly obvious premise that "cultural property is a basic element of people's identity" was adopted as a policy in 1976,[21] and its ramifications had to be thought out. By 1980 UNESCO was paying more attention to the cultural heritage of each nation. Its declaration on the need for the "return of cultural property" to "its true context, namely that of maintaining, reconstituting, developing and serving the cultural identity of all peoples,"[22] points to a watershed in the international community's attitude to the question of universalism and particularism. This did not mean that the global perspective was rejected but, rather, that despite contradictions, the agreements elucidate vague international sentiments in favor of particularism without providing precise guidelines.

Perhaps the only currently undisputed fact about the restitution of cultural property is its growing pace. In the past, weaker nations were never able to protect their cultural property. Over the last generation, however, as the demand for cultural objects grew, so did the demand for specific and effective protection to counter market forces.[23] International conventions and national legislation have come to recognize the need for this protection and to justify constraining market forces because of the communal nature and "ownership" of the artifacts. This trend receives continuous further support, such as in the comprehensive treaty of the International Institute for the Unification of Private Law (UNIDROIT) of 1995, which aims at establishing a similar legal standard among countries.[24] The essence of the agreement is to recognize the rights of nations to their cultural property in cases where the current holder does not have a legal proof of ownership. Beyond the legal difficulties that collectors are going to face in numerous individual cases, the significance of UNIDROIT is that, by shifting the burden of proof to the collector, the agreement underscores a global view of justice that places objects not with the collector but with the originator. The purpose is to supplement market economy with moral economy. The legislation, which has been criticized for being too weak, demonstrates the current international morality. The most immediate impact is to engender a political discourse and a moral reasoning that thwart the perpetuation of past policies that are, today, the subject of restitution disputes.

Preservation and Conservation

The growing trend to validate the local over the global comes to a halt when faced with the risk of the destruction of world treasures or when the risk of isolationism endangers cultural exchange. Destruction can result either from armed conflict, willful destruction, or as a by-product of neglect. In the last case destruction presents a practical dilemma but not a moral or cultural predicament. It becomes a moral predicament in cases where the destruction is part of the culture that is supposedly preserved, or even a revered cultural practice, as, for example, in the case of the Zuni war gods or, more generally, in cases of objects associated with cultural performance such as religious practices. Despite an almost uninhibited eagerness by a relativist world to declare a preference for cultural preservation over consumption and destruction, the conflicts between local and global perspectives remain at the heart of the current cultural patrimony debate.

The international order embraces alternative national styles of preservation, but it is much more reluctant to allow for the outright destruction of cultural property, whether by omission to prevent natural aging and erosion or from overt acts of looting, war, or improper excavation. Critics differ over the relative strength that nationalism and universalism ought to play in determining the preservation of cultural property. One reason is the risk to cultural property in times of war, which increasingly seems to be restricted to specific regions. Given the inadequate facilities to preserve and maintain collections in many countries, especially during times of war, it is not easy to determine where the objects ought to be kept for the long-term benefits of the culture. This is particularly apparent given the fate of antiquities during the Gulf War, the total destruction in regions of the former Yugoslavia, and the disappearance of whole collections from African museums as a result of widespread looting, which has been described as "wiping out the memory of Africa" and as a "cultural genocide."[25] Restitution in the context of vanishing collections may only hasten and aggravate the losses. The obvious dilemma is that the threat of destruction becomes a justification for denying restitution.

Certain international treaties convey in strong language the universal standards of preservation over restitution when these come into conflict. These treaties maintain that cultural property is meaningful to the world and that international laws and treaties ought to prevent destruction by a "host state" and allow intervention by foreign forces. For example, such intervention "would sanction internationally coordinated efforts to stop deterioration of the Sphinx."[26] This potential conflict was most evident in Bamiyan Afghanistan over the destruction of the Buddha statues, which instigated international protest but not protection. Afghanistan proved to be a case where the destruction of cultural treasures became the proverbial canary whose death signaled the collapse of all political order.[27] Efforts to save singular antiquities may, indeed, be well intentioned but can only be viewed locally as paternalistic imperialism and a misplaced renewal of the "white man's burden" to civilize the world. This is particularly true when the use of force, which would violate the sovereignty of a country in the name of universal culture, is contemplated. This theoretical proposal is as grave as the motivation may be noble.

By analogy to human rights, the tendency is to validate the growing local autonomy of mores and practices. Until a fundamental conflict emerges between local and global perspectives, the world community is willing to enforce values that it views as superior to local practices. Despite the general moral anxiety of patronizing local sovereignty by global standards, the support of preservation as a global ideology remains stronger. This moral anxiety is ambivalent. The desire to "preserve" is not merely altruistic, since often "protection means control," and some advocates are motivated more by "controlling" than by "protecting" the objects. This relates back to the issue of restitution as a form of neocolonialism. The ambivalence of such universalism is a manifestation of a vague neo-Enlightenment morality that embraces a great number of local variations and group rights but attempts to maintain a core of universal values. These universal values include, in this case, a shared global cultural heritage.

Despite the validation of national patrimony as part of decolonization and of Third World advocacy at the expense of world heritage, there are reasons to consider whether the pendulum is swinging in the direction of a convergence between the two doctrines or perhaps even toward privileging the global perspective.[28] This may be a result of the growing recognition that Third World identities are as fragmented as those in the West and that the local is frequently an imposed center on an "other" localized community. A return to globalism, if it were to take place, would therefore occur under very different political circumstances from the old-time imperialism. Unlike during the classical imperialist era, the pertinent international bodies that formulate current cultural policies are numerically dominated by Third World countries, the voice of which may carry substantial influence. Consequently, the contemporary civilizing impetus, which in the past was always one-directional—from the center to the periphery—struggles to become more multidirectional. This poses seemingly insurmountable obstacles to the international discussion regarding empowering UNESCO or other international agencies to monitor violations of cultural preservation. In the end, powerful countries remain unlikely to relinquish control in these matters, yet the less powerful are not likely to abandon their sovereignty claims. In the midst of this struggle, the nongovernmental organizations of today are likely to receive a hearing, although not always an outcome that they find satisfactory. (This does not mean that there is equality in the new world order: it is, after all, hard to imagine sanctions against a major industrialized country.)

Pivotal international space for negotiating the universal and local dilemma is created by regional organizations that adopt the universal moral language of the international bodies while maintaining the relative cultural homogeneity of their members states. The regional multinational organizations—Southeast Asia, Latin America, Africa—view the adoption of global standards as self-interest and not an imposition from the center. In the process, the definitions of patrimony expand. The establishment of a desired universal ethical norm, even if unfulfilled, creates a standard, which, over time, more states embrace. While the international community is a long way from enforcement, the economic seduction of international goodwill is getting stronger in weak countries and provides a motivation to invest in unprofitable preservation. A weak international regime can only formulate general policies, which creates much frustration. Within the postcolonial ethos there is little reason to think that the world would benefit from a stricter regime.

Restitution and the Cultural Heritage Industry

Despite the internal contradictions among the different approaches and attitudes to restitution, its legitimacy is on the rise, and numerous countries and institutions have embarked on returning objects of cultural patrimony to peoples who are viewed as the rightful owners. At times these are the previous owners, but often the question of who is the rightful owner is determined according to national or cultural identity and not on legal grounds.

International comprehensive agreements provide a model for a potential hierarchy of vague principles and for future cases of restitution.[29]

The main targets in the debate over center and periphery as the repositories of the cultural heritage industry are the few largest museums in the world. These museums possess objects that have been plundered or otherwise acquired from every part of the world. In Western capitals there are many displays of national patrimonies from around the globe. In their own defense the universal museums claim to provide the global citizen with a spectrum of cultures and see their responsibility as exhibiting cultures that would otherwise be unknown outside of the specific area. Both sides present their perspectives as informed by moral arguments but employ these for self-serving purposes. Thus, the controversy is over whether a particular artifact is better used to serve a global perspective in a museum or restituted as part of a living culture. The "world heritage" ideology, which employs practices that privilege museums in metropolises over those in "remote" places, used to be self-evident. Advocates who want to maintain the current museum structure and resist wholesale restitution emphasize better conservation, curatorship, security, and larger public exposure. They view the large museums within the context of international heritage rather than from a "narrow national" context. The British Museum, indeed, often leaves the visitor with the impression that it displays everything but British artifacts, and its spokespersons are frequent advocates of universal institutions and culture.

While the moral claims and potential global benefits of restitution are both legitimate and compelling, they also risk the very existence of major museums. Curators of these museums are trying to defend against the dismantling of their own institutions, which they see as being of universal benefit. This may explain actions and attitudes of these institutions that otherwise would be inexplicable. David Wilson, director of the British Museum from 1977 to 1992, was criticized perhaps more than any other museologist. He has frequently been frustrated by the rhetoric of "a battle between Third World and developed countries in which loaded terms — 'colonialism,' 'loot,' and 'booty' — are bandied about by claimants and ostrich-like silence is maintained by those against whom claims are made."[30] Indeed, Britain's split personality over the question of cultural property is shamelessly self-serving. Despite Britain's strong support for the universal status of cultural property, it tries to maintain control over its own treasures and cultural artifacts of national interest through export regulation. These regulations give any British public institution the option to match an offer and gain precedence over any foreign buyer. Only if the money is not raised within a given time can the foreigner take possession.[31]

The stubbornness of the British Museum has been exposed perhaps more than that of any other cultural institution. It also becomes apparent in cases where the museum's legal claims are shaky, such as in the case of the skull named *Proconsul africanus*. The museum refused a request from Kenya to return the skull, which was loaned to the museum in 1948 by paleontologist

Mary Leakey (British, 1913–1996), who, with her husband, Louis, made key discoveries in East Africa that shaped our understanding of human origins. When the loan was made, Kenya was under British rule. Years later, Richard Leakey (Mary and Louis's son), as director of the National Museum in Nairobi, Kenya, requested the return of the skull to be displayed in Kenya. In the meantime, the British Museum had "accessioned" the skull in a highly ritualized act. Indeed, for the museum to "deaccession" an object, a full meeting of the trustees would be required to approve what some felt would be a betrayal of the museum's mission and would thus throw it into an identity crisis. In this particular case, "deaccession" meant, at best, admitting a "mistake" but, more likely, giving up on an unsuccessful act of appropriation. The British Museum balked until presented with the "proof" that the skull was indeed a loan and not a gift. The bickering did not add to the museum's moral prestige, which had already been wounded on previous occasions in the continuous restitution debate.[32] While the outcome of *Proconsul africanus* was determined by traditional property rights, the moral cachet was its cultural affinity. It belonged to Kenya on cultural grounds, although the precise cultural (as opposed to geographical) affinity of the skull to Kenya was not explicated.

Restitution as a moral good has become such a powerful value that, within the right context, it even validates theft. One notorious case of a restitution that is reminiscent of the Robin Hood story took place in 1982 when an ancient Aztec codex was stolen from the Bibliothèque Nationale in Paris and given to the Instituto Nacional de Antropología e Historia in Mexico City. Legally, this was a simple case of theft; however, indigenous support for restitution of Mexico's heritage led its government to obstruct the codex's return to France. This was viewed as a confrontation between two rights: legal and moral. After the theft, the French requested the return of the codex, which the Bibliothèque Nationale had held in its possession for 150 years. The Mexican government was, however, all too happy to be pressured by public opinion to retain it. Indeed, such an outright illegal act was possible only because it carried a justification that, at a fundamental level, both parties accepted. While the French could not publicly admit that they condoned restitution through theft, their relatively insignificant diplomatic protest suggested a deeper, moral agreement. The codex remains in Mexico.

An earlier attempt at restitution through theft took place in London. The ancient Coronation Stone, which is believed to be Jacob's biblical pillow, was the site where ancient Scottish kings were consecrated. It was moved to London in 1296 and later became part of the British throne. On Christmas Day in 1950 the stone was liberated (stolen) from Westminster Abbey. At the time, cultural restitution was not yet on the public agenda. The search for the stone, which weighs about four hundred pounds, ended four months later in front of the ruined altar at Arbroath Abbey where Scotland's declaration of independence was signed in 1320. It was taken back (confiscated) to London. To confuse matters, it was suggested that the found stone was only a replica.

In 1984 the stone was again the subject of demands by Scottish nationalists who argued for its placement in Edinburgh Castle; however, UNESCO ruled it an internal British matter. The case was resolved unexpectedly when, as a pre-election pro-Scottish propaganda token, Prime Minister John Major returned the stone to Scotland in 1997. It did not keep the Conservative Party from defeat in Scotland.

Restitution through theft, however, remains a fantasy in most cases. Such was the fate of the wish of the Bini (Edo) of Nigeria to exhibit a fifteenth-century ivory mask in Lagos, West Africa, which was frustrated by the British Museum's refusal to loan it in 1976. A Nigerian film, *The Mask* (1979), transformed their frustration in an adventure movie in which the mask is restored through theft.

Another immoral but time-honored tradition is the acquisition by museums of objects through illegal means. The provenance of numerous museum displays is murky at best, but growing legislation and awareness of the morality of cultural patrimony have led to a dramatic decline in the willingness of certain institutions to engage in such transactions (witness the Maya temple facade mentioned previously). Indeed, any public announcements of a new major acquisition by a museum attract the attention of the country from which the objects were robbed. Current legislation enables a reasonably straightforward restitution of such objects. While these cases of restitution are more about legality than about issues of identity, and are not of direct concern in this context, the legislation is certainly a by-product of the growing awareness of culture as patrimony and of the vigilance—although many would argue not enough—in tracing these violations. The increased pace of restitution is a result of the public's realignment with this shifting moral order, and not of repentance by current possessors. These debates force museums to defend their holdings, liberalize access, and justify their existence as international, rather than national, institutions. Screaming and kicking as they do, museums are obliged to subscribe to this shifting moral order.

Those who support a global perspective often argue that countries in which great amounts of antiquities are still largely unexcavated or unexplored should not be entitled to deny the rest of the world access to them. Global connoisseurs argue that nations should not hoard such objects and forbid exports. The ire is directed against governments that restrict archaeological access and export. By such practices, it is said, countries deny themselves an important trade resource and inhibit the cultural improvement of people in other parts of the world.[33] This ostensibly sound approach becomes more perplexing in view of the fact that major museums hoard, and deny access to, multitudes of objects in their basements. They defend this practice on the grounds that the objects are kept there for protection. The "little secret" of archaeology, as it has become known, is the minuscule percentage of excavations that are studied, processed, and displayed. This does not enhance the museums' efforts to resist restitution.[34]

In the postcolonial world the debate is refocused on the protection and return of cultural patrimony to poorer countries. Stripped of high rhetoric, many demands for restitution from poorer nations, beyond the high-profile cases, are often aimed at "representative" or the "most significant objects," and not at wholesale restitution that would empty the large museums. In many cases the intention of restitution is not to deprive the current holders of all the objects in their possession. Rather, it is to return to poorer countries some portion of their own heritage. The terms of the debate seem to shift once it is explicated that the number of objects from the same culture in museum vaults is so large that only a minuscule fraction is exhibited. An Ecuadorian representative described a future utopian moment of restitution: "It would appear to be obvious, easy, and just, and it would extol their scientific stature, if those museums were to add moral prestige by returning some pieces to the museums of the country of origin."[35] Hard as it is to imagine, such a reasonable position is too radical for the contemporary market of cultural heritage, which is dominated by international rivalry.

Despite the weak moral position of the large museums, one should not deny that numerous objects have been saved by being collected and kept in major Western museums. The dilemma is over research and trade versus religion and local culture, of tourism (even if educationally motivated) versus conservation. The specific determinations are, in a certain sense, less consequential than who is entitled to give the answers, which has become the core issue for cultural patrimony and identity during the last generation.

The Question of Inalienability

This relative imagined stability is the basis for a striking if controversial claim for ownership of cultural property beyond the norms that apply to any other forms of property. It is a claim that heritage, like identity, is inalienable. This type of claim for ownership, and often for restitution, is based on the belief that for cultural reasons cultural property cannot be transferred to the possession of others. The demand for restitution is based on the assumption that, notwithstanding economic and political changes over time, or even demographic and cultural discontinuities, cultural property remains part of the identity of its original owners, determined primarily by geographical (read cultural) affinity. The psychological basis for such an attachment is that the object is part of the group's identity and vice versa; the object is meaningful because it conveys the group's identity. Prime examples are national monuments and, by extension, nonmaterial national treasures such as memory of historical events.

Cultural objects are often declared to be "inalienable." Time may or may not be of the essence. Being deprived of possession may, after a long while, terminate the affinity, or it may not. Restitution depends, in part, on how vital the original affinity remains in comparison to the newly established affinity with the identity of the new owners. An object is most likely to be considered inalienable by the "impartial observer" when its essence and value stem from belonging to the original owners: an essence that is also recognized by the current owners. Museum objects, therefore, are often candidates for being viewed as inalienable. The determination of inalienability, however, is fuzzy and is decided separately in each case.

The inalienability argument is that cultural patrimony belongs to the nation of origin by its nature, notwithstanding how the objects may have been transferred into alien hands. Since the objects belong to the community, whether they have been sold or given away, the transfer ought to be judged immoral and illegal. The rationale is that objects embody the group identity, which belongs to future generations, and hence the ownership does not include the right of sale, which is alienation. National patrimony is, by definition, a nonrenewable resource. As such it often appreciates in value, and its current price reaches beyond the resources of poor or subjugated groups who cannot purchase back their own heritage. To let market mechanisms determine the fate of all cultural property would be to allow the rich nations to hoard all objects of value.

The claim of inalienability is, at present, most often raised by indigenous peoples who are least in control of their patrimony. It is most persuasive when combined with continuous, even if partial, possession, and as a protection against future deprivation. This would include, for example, mining rights in areas inhabited by indigenous peoples. It has been shown over and over in cases where the traditional ownership is more likely to be recognized if possession has remained in indigenous hands, even if there are alternative claims (by an oil company). In certain cases it is indispensable to establishing the right to the property. Lack of possession opens the property to conflicting claims. In cases where the cultural identity of a group is invested in a certain property — an indigenous burial ground used by a mining company — the indigenous cultural and religious moral claim would carry more weight if also advanced on the grounds of traditional economic ownership. At present, rights for fishing or hunting are more persuasive than the right to worship gods on a mountain range. In such a case cultural inalienability is weaker than economic interest. Pragmatic moral and economic issues have to be determined in each individual case, often according to vague principles.[36]

One predicament of indigenous nonsovereign peoples is that they have communal but not sovereign ownership (for example, the tribe that is not sovereign owns the land, the fishing rights, and its own tradition), which compounds the dilemma of restitution of inalienable indigenous art. The legal quandary arises from the recognition of private property by the modern state, while indigenous claims are based on the tradition of communal property. Future negotiations will attempt to create international standards for the restitution of objects from the center to the periphery and of cultural property to minorities within national borders. Attention will also have to be paid to objects that have been alienated from the nation before laws to forestall such transactions were put into place. This trend can be seen in the return of cultural property to indigenous peoples within a country, such as in the United States, under the Native American Graves Protection and Repatriation

Act of 1994, or in Australia where the South Australian Museum in Adelaide, among others, returns objects to Aborigine communities.

Saving Angkor: The Limits of Legitimacy

Suffering through many years of wars and genocide, Cambodia is a place of great poverty and misery. The government, when one existed over the last generation, was less than capable and not very interested in actively conserving the cultural legacy. Still, Angkor, located in Siem Riep, northwestern Cambodia, remains one of the world's cultural wonders; it is composed of several cities in an area of over one hundred square miles, at the center of which is Angkor Wat, the "largest" temple in the world.[37] In lawless Cambodia, antiquities deteriorate and are subject to widespread looting. While the Khmer Rouge did not espouse an ideology of destroying the site, much destruction took place, in part because Khmer leaders themselves looted the site. Since the early 1990s there have been increased efforts by archaeologists from India—as well as Japan, France, and the United States—to save the site, but in this divided country there is little to stop continued plundering. One could easily empathize with the Cambodians who, in their effort to survive, lack interest in conserving the site and participate in looting as a source of income. Today, most conservation efforts are made by outsiders. This raises the question of what constitutes the legitimate interests of outsiders in the site. Should the lack of local involvement be a factor? This outside involvement has certain similarities to archaeological investigations of indigenous cultures, but in this case the conflict is between archaeologists and thieves. The local perspective for many years can be said to have been the looters' perspective, which is not validated in the international arena. Thus, it would be easy to dismiss the local perspective, and perhaps this does not present a grave moral dilemma. Morally, the story would have been more complicated had the Cambodian government tried to harvest the antiquities officially, to plunder and loot their own treasures. Would that have been a more valid local moral position? As it happened, in the late 1990s the Cambodian government chose tourism over harvesting. For a while, preservation won out even in the killing fields.

The issue becomes slightly more complicated once stolen objects reach the market. Today's conventional wisdom finds that the legal and moral position is to refuse to buy the objects. Yet, would this position change if one were faced with a rare object worth saving "at any price"?[38] Which is worse: to let the object disappear or to pay the looters? In the past we celebrated this type of plunder and built huge museums to accommodate the trophies. Today we prefer the scientific—excavations and restoration—and reject looting as a means of acquisition, even when the "looters" are those from the country whose identity is tied to the items and who "loot" their own artifacts in order to survive.

A moral standard based on poverty may be difficult to legitimate. Should poor local populations be subject to a distinct moral standard? Do the *huaqueros* (professional tomb-robbers), for example, present a challenge to the global notion of legitimacy?[39] The *huaqueros* are indigenous people who dig mounds in Ecuador to unearth antiquities and sell them worldwide. In a time when the rejection of looting is taken for granted, few are willing to deal with the *huaqueros*. Given the reality of extensive and continuous excavation and plunder by the *huaqueros,* however, should the looted objects be acquired and studied? The scientific community distinguishes between a properly documented excavation and undocumented objects available in the market. There are those who reject any dealings with the *huaqueros,* emphasizing that the effort and expense should be directed toward funding other excavations. Others are not so sure, because certain objects, even when looted, are still valuable. Archaeologists and museum curators often face this conundrum, but in the cultural property debate, the voice of the *huaqueros* is absent. Similar to those in Cambodia, the thieves are often poor, lack viable economic alternatives, and serve themselves in whatever way they can. Does their position deserve validation as an indigenous perspective even though they lack an organization and a voice, and act against accepted international morals? Could there be a moral position toward cultural heritage informed by poverty that is substantially different from one informed by an affluent position?

The morally privileged status of cultural property is tentative and serves more as a rhetorical device than as a comprehensive international commitment. Destruction is not the privilege of the poor. A brief survey of any week's news will show contradictory instances in which countries either do not pay attention to their own essential and irreplaceable cultural objects or actively pursue a contrary national agenda. Emerging as a global player that dwarfs all others, China, for the moment, relegates cultural preservation to a very low position on its national agenda. It is estimated that in the 1990s tens of thousands of Chinese tombs were looted annually, the result of which are antiquities that are freely traded on the world market,[40] and the largest hydroelectric dam in the world was built on the Yangtze River, which inflicts proportional destruction. China is too strong to be opposed, however, and despite the extensive damage to the cultural heritage of China, little can be done in the near future to impress on China the preservation of cultural heritage. Similarly, Turkey, despite its fierce campaign to restitute ancient objects from the West, is about to flood the extraordinary but barely excavated city of Zeugma, comparable in size and wealth to Pompeii, under a new dam on the Euphrates.[42]

The explanation for the apparent disjunction between the declared global consensus and the widely diverse national practices lies, primarily, in the disparity between wealth and poverty. Heritage is for the rich. The poor may wish for it or dream about it, but often they cannot afford to preserve their own cultural heritage. For the poor, in most instances, cultural property becomes sufficiently significant only when it enhances their prosperity or independence. Indigenous peoples who can gain economic resources through focusing political pressure on the conservation and salvage of their heritage will be eager to do so. Otherwise, if such efforts compete with development or inhibit the standard of living, talk about salvaging heritage may be lip service at best. Papua New Guinea serves as one of the more despondent examples.

Papua New Guinea, with its large indigenous population and numerous ethnic groups and languages, still enjoys a great deal of internal diversity.[41] Not a world leader like China, Papua New Guinea is a relatively new and poor nation struggling to develop its economy with limited resources and attracting little attention from the international public. Initially the country had a formal commitment to pay "homage and respect to the memory of our ancestors," as well as "acknowledge the worthy customs and traditional wisdom of our people," which was written into the constitution. The National Cultural Properties Act (1967) even established state ownership of all archaeological and material culture. National goals include the conservation of sacred and historical sites as well as the maintenance of the historical diversity of the country. The rhetoric of conservation is as persuasive as in the best of museums. G. Mosuwadoga, the director of the Papua New Guinea National Museum and Art Gallery at the time, stated that the museum's goals are "to provide adequate facilities to review the material culture and arts for the village people and scholars; to look upon the museum as a united cultural institution for all the ethnic groups; to establish it as a monument to the past and a source of inspiration for the future culture of Papua New Guinea."[43]

The situation changed, however, once heritage and prosperity collided. Papua New Guinea's heritage is far from the minds of most people and politicians. In the face of unabashed efforts to develop the country, environmental and cultural preservation gives way to market forces. The past became a low priority. Developmental policies, deforestation, mineral exploration, and industrialization, are all privileged over preservation. As well, similar to the case of most indigenous peoples, in the cultural sense, modernization in Papua New Guinea is inextricably involved with missionaries who see it as their holy duty to reject the local tradition and its cultural artifacts of idols, "indecent" and otherwise. An additional motivation for actively forgetting the past was provided by Australia, which itself was shy about both its Aboriginal and European heritage and, consequently, committed Papua New Guinea to progress. Seeking quick economic progress hinders preservation of the past, from the traditions to the environment. Whether the change is welcomed or traumatic—assuming the Papuan's perspective is not rejected as mere expediency or false consciousness—Papuans have to accommodate and attempt to strive under the new market economy, and they do so by elevating development as the most important national goal. In the process they have become indifferent to the past, or at least to certain aspects of the past. Anthropologists and environmentalists who criticize these policies are viewed as enemies and are even attacked on occasion. While the traditional ethnic and geographical divisions (as well as new colonial and postcolonial rivalries) are maintained as part of the political culture of the country, other traditions that contradict the newly validated Western norms—such as bride-price—have lost their attractiveness. Given Papua New Guinea and other instances, privileging cultural heritage

over progress and prosperity is feasible only after a minimum level of affluence has been achieved. This underscores the provisional and vague status of
supremacy that cultural patrimony enjoys over other national priorities, as
well as the innumerable moral impediments on the road to promoting the
inalienability of tradition as an option for global legislation.

The Illusive Postcolonial

Over the last generation, the International Council of Museums (ICOM) elaborated a global standard. ICOM contributed to the creation of a vague moral
international norm by defining an ethical code, illuminating points of crises
through lists of existing and lost cultural objects, commenting on various
bilateral agreements, formulating minimum professional standards for the
maintenance of restituted objects, and advocating restitution from a global
perspective. Perhaps anticipating the future, ICOM asserted in 1975 that restitution had become "an ethical principle recognized and affirmed by the major
international organizations."[44]

A conventional argument against restitution has been that much of the
cultural property now subject to the debate has survived precisely because it
has been collected and kept in institutions that have valued conservation.
From the risks posed to the Parthenon in Athens (neglect in the past, pollution
at present) to Australian artifacts that may have been burned in the fire that
destroyed the Australian National Museum in the nineteenth century, over the
long run certain artifacts may have faired better because they were alienated
and held in geographically distant locations. Although by and large contemporary opinion rejects the "benevolence" of collecting in its broader repudiation of the "white man's burden," indigenous peoples, it is said, may come to
view as "good fortune that European collectors preserved fragments of their
cultural heritage."[45]

The act of preservation was, at best, a by-product of imperialism. Successful conservation is the tip of an iceberg of a dismal record of appropriation
and ruin in previously colonized countries. When the argument for preservation is measured against what colonialism destroyed, rather than what it
preserved, a polarized picture emerges. Collecting is often the residue of the
devastation.

The destruction of cultural property is not, however, the prerogative of
Western imperialism in the Third World. Indeed, perhaps the strongest con-
tenders for the most widespread concentrated desolation of cultural objects
include the Nazi invasion of Europe (especially Russia) and China's internal
destruction during the cultural revolution. One could not begin to compare
the relative ruin in numerous other wars and revolutions.

The rhetoric of preservation by museums often encourages exaggeration
and effaces local subtleties, while self-righteousness colors museums as unrepentant imperialists. Such is the claim that art of previously colonized peoples
was collected through gifts and barter and was due to the "genuine spirit of
scientific inquiry by Europeans eager to know more about the people with

whom they came into contact. They claim that much of what was collected was of no more value to the original owners than were the trinkets which they received in exchange from the collectors."[46] It is hard not to view this as incredible. After all, transforming the motivation of more than five centuries of exploration and colonialism into a curiosity of other peoples surely leaves something unsaid. Notwithstanding Torday's description above, the exchange of the "trinkets" for museum artifacts cannot be embraced in hindsight as moral. Furthermore, the universal rhetoric shared by museums of emphasizing their "superior display" is not only offensive but also untrue. In the best of cases it applies in practice only to a small minority of the objects while most of the collection is routinely stored away. Additionally, the argument of an exposure to a "large public" assumes that the significant public is the international tourist rather than the local population. Justifiably, proponents of restitution are unimpressed by museum rhetoric and see in it a veiled attempt to legitimize imperialism and colonialism. Indeed, if the local people were considered the significant public, placing artifacts far away in European or American cities makes the objects unavailable. Furthermore, notwithstanding the major preservation efforts of world museums, the value of local cultures displaying the objects in "context" and with "integrity" has become a powerful rhetorical tool in discussing patrimony.

A different argument favoring Western collectors of indigenous peoples' artifacts and denouncing restitution is the claim by these same collectors and their supporters that collecting and preserving have largely been Western value. It is only "recently" that peoples around the globe have even cared about preserving the artifacts of their heritage. The exception, the story goes, was preservation through cultural performance (often classified in the West as "religious ceremonies"), but not for the sake of conservation or display. Again, this argument is false. There were numerous other circumstances of indigenous preservation of cultural property, evident by the antiquities collected around the globe that were kept, stored, and abandoned (the terminology is as significant as the act) by local populations. From ancient civilizations to past kingdoms, much evidence is continuously discovered in the Americas, in Asia, and in Africa. Where poverty had fewer exceptions, the evidence is more scarce. In addition, even if the concern for patrimony in certain societies is a recent phenomenon, it is hardly a justification for denying its validity.

The Mephistophelian relationship of imperialism with dominated cultures, however, may have a more constructive future. Contemporary conservation and collecting often work to the mutual benefit of both larger museums and local culture. The Ägyptisches Museum in Berlin, among others, participated in salvaging Egyptian antiquities as part of the Aswan Dam project, which flooded major archaeological sites in Egypt. In return, the Egyptian government granted certain impressive antiquities to the museum, which were prominently displayed there. This is in contrast to the notorious controversy that was widely reported, but apparently never happened, between the museum and the Egyptian government concerning the restitution of Nefertiti.[47] There are numerous other examples of cooperation where major museums and curatorial staffs assist fledgling museum cultures to salvage and exhibit their treasures. These include locations in post-Communist Europe, where substantial preservation efforts are assisted by experts from larger museums. One example of this is how British curators have stepped in to salvage disintegrating late-medieval churches in Moldavia and Albania. The British Museum and others have also been instrumental in returning various stolen goods to their countries of origin. Although the big issues remain contentious, the working morality is somewhat more harmonious.

The growing awareness of a new moral perspective on the part of museums may serve, at present, as the best guarantee that the worst abuses of the past stemming from power disparities are less likely to occur in the future. However well intentioned, rich institutions possess, by definition, controversial power. This is also true regarding many aspects of indigenous peoples' culture, from intellectual property rights to material objects. Defenders of indigenous rights argue that indigenous peoples should "retain the right to 'market' themselves if they want to—no matter how crass it might seem to the upper middle-class liberal elite."[48] Marketing, however, carries risks to the very survival of indigenous culture. The ideological opposition by an "elite" that advocates pristine primordialism is undermined by its eager consumerism, not only of fancy natural medication but also the products sold on Main Street in stores like The Body Shop that built their reputation on indigenous images. The commodification of indigenous culture, at times by indigenous societies themselves, is controversial because the collection, processing, and publishing of any indigenous culture transforms its very uniqueness. Economically, however, the temptation is irresistible. After all, ignoring market forces only weakens the indigenous response, making it neither stronger nor more moral. Some see the challenge facing museologists as winning the acceptance of indigenous peoples and cooperating with them on equal terms. Museums have to persuade indigenous peoples to exhibit their culture without amalgamating it into the Western tradition and to affiliate indigenous individuals in all aspects of the museums' work.[49] This attitude may consolidate, for some, the best possible goals. Even without resorting to questions of discourse and to how the poor understand what their informed consent means, Torday's dealing with the Kuba in central Africa suggests that informed consent in these matters may not be all that it claims to be.

The challenges arising from new communication technologies accumulated by the multinational moguls focus on legislation that serves large companies. The choice indigenous peoples face leaves much to be desired: they can either cooperate with the expanding global system and try to benefit financially by marketing their culture or resist the incursion of capitalism and, perhaps, suffer continued or worsened poverty. Either way, it is unlikely that the pace of the multinationals will slow down.[50] The question remains, What will happen to the cultures in the process? The ability of large corporations to copyright new technologies and traditional knowledge cannot be matched by the best intentioned supporters of the indigenous cultures that are deprived of their uniqueness. The center's consumption of indigenous material culture is often out of context and always with little understanding of the traditional culture from which it comes; in a way it replicates the old "cabinet of curiosities" in its detachment from any living culture. This exploitation is further aggravated by the race to harvest biological knowledge. Do indigenous peoples deserve compensation from the pharmaceutical, agricultural, and mineral industries, among others, for the use of their territories and knowledge? From music to cosmetics, there is a race by various industries to harvest the indigenous knowledge of (mostly) tropical habitat in addition to anthropological investigation of traditional religious knowledge. Furthermore, in the commercialization of their knowledge, indigenous peoples face a direct challenge from loggers and farmers who invade indigenous space; they have an urgent need to create resources to hold back the invaders. Indigenous advocacy groups, primarily environmental and human rights organizations also hold a Western agenda that incorporates the indigenous peoples into a global system, one that may well be more attuned to their needs and is preservationist but is, nonetheless, not the traditional isolated culture. Faced by invading capitalism, indigenous peoples play a growing role in these global movements as they try to enhance their chances of survival. Even here, however, it seems that advocates of indigenous causes, even more than indigenous peoples, lead the way.[51] Occasional successes are evident at the local level and provide a source of optimism for activists, but globally opinions are still polarized.[52]

Indigenous peoples face the criticism that nature belongs to all and is not owned by any indigenous population of the tropics. There is also opposition to the neo-Enlightenment notion that groups have rights separate from individuals.[53] Both claims are presented as principled positions but serve to further anti-indigenous policies. There is nothing exceptional in recognizing the legal rights of groups. After all, corporations are legally treated as individuals, as are states. Establishing the communal legal nature of indigenous groups would not break any new legal ground but would merely extend equality to discriminated groups. Similarly, natural resources are everywhere under the control of specific countries, and recognizing the "ownership" of indigenous peoples over the tropical diversity is not essentially different from the ownership of any country over its mineral reserves or companies over their trademarks. The legal recognition of ownership of indigenous rights over their cultural knowledge is merely a matter of extending well-established rights to a new population. It is the limitation of rights to the rich and powerful that is a cruel manipulation of abstract morality to justify inequality, not their extension to indigenous peoples. (Formally the substantive distinction is that copyright is given to new knowledge but not to traditional knowledge. Given the new situation, however, such an extension of rights would signal the recognition that the traditional knowledge is fundamentally transformed when it is made available to a wide alien public.)

Public opinion has begun to recognize this fundamental unfairness. The growing criticism of pharmaceutical moguls who, in search of profits, destroy or corrupt the local indigenous culture has led some multinationals to offer compensation to indigenous peoples.[54] It seems that the prime motivation for these offers is to receive good press and avoid lawsuits or demonstrations. An essential question is, How symbolic is the compensation? In every case agreements were based on the political judgment by the multinationals that compensating the tribes would ease public pressure. There is still no legal mechanism to enforce compensation and agreement prior to harvesting the indigenous culture or for evaluating fair compensation. Installing such a legal system would be very complex. Furthermore, the economic disparity between companies and indigenous groups presents a fundamental dilemma; a substantial compensation from the perspective of the indigenous group is minuscule in comparison with the company's anticipated profits and most likely would fall under the legal category of "unjust enrichment." Nor is there a system to deal with the fact that the payment to one indigenous group would deprive other groups who possess comparable knowledge. A global fund to distribute and share royalties among indigenous peoples carries its own limitations, not least of which would be the incorporation of all indigenous peoples under one capitalist organization. This is a small indication of how difficult it would be to satisfy the moral demands for fair distribution, and that compensation may be not only possible but also necessary.[55]

Fuzzy Principles and International Agreements

Not surprisingly, global cultural diversity frustrates efforts for homogenous generalizations and international agreements regarding cultural property. In the last generation there have been yearly international resolutions and agreements laying out rules for restitution. Consequently, results are vague and are the target of criticism. Expectations from international conventions far surpass any potential consensus regarding policies of cultural patrimony. It seems futile to attempt a global definition of cultural patrimony that will answer the needs of every group; however, this has never stopped international and legislative bodies from explicating long complex definitions, which, at the end of the day, reiterate the self-designated heritage of each group. Such open-ended definitions strike fear into legal bodies, conjuring up widespread cultural manipulations and anarchy.

How useful are these vague definitions? Being too general, the accords lack the legal specificity needed in cases of conflict to facilitate restitution or compromise. As cultural property and heritage have become all inclusive, they have not only been elevated to constitute a national identity but have also been devalued by the inflationary usage. This hinders legal action against those who damage national patrimony. The permissive, often frustrating, use of the terms has led to suggestions to limit the definitions in order to facilitate legal action. There have also been attempts to distinguish among patrimony, cultural property, and natural objects.

The frustration has led to discussions about an international tribunal and a more specific international code. The disillusionment arises from the discrepancy between the vague accepted moral judgment and political impotency. Despite the generalities, however, the value of international agreements and conventions is precisely in creating the framework and in demonstrating that the vague moral standard is a basis for discussion, while leaving legal demarcations murky and open to negotiation in particular contexts. International awareness becomes a major motivation in initiating dialogues. Acceptance and public opinion create motivation for embracing the new morality and provide for domestic rather than external enforcement. Consequently, new claims are made by peoples who apply the novel moral economy of international justice to their own situation. The publicity surrounding restitution and compensation bestows legitimacy on previously ignored grievances, opening the possibility for compromise and resolution. This will depend on the recognition of an alternate theory of justice, one that relies not so much on abstract principles but on a more general principle of negotiated justice.

Notes

1. I develop these issues in Elazar Barkan, *The Guilt of Nations: Restitution and Negotiating Historical Injustices* (New York: Norton, 2000).

2. See Will Kymlicka, *Multicultural Citizenship: A Liberal Theory of Minority Rights* (Oxford: Clarendon, 1995); and Amy Gutman, ed., *Multiculturalism: Examining the Politics of Recognition* (Princeton: Princeton Univ. Press, 1994).

3. See David Lowenthal, *Possessed by the Past: The Heritage Crusade and the Spoils of History* (Cambridge: Cambridge Univ. Press, 1998), 142, 244–46, for Greek appropriation of the classical legacy. See also Timothy Webb, "Appropriating the Stones: The 'Elgin Marbles' and English National Taste," this volume, for the early controversy over the looting of the marbles.

4. For example, the attempts to conclude a treaty for indigenous human rights have faced a long and tortuous process. See the International Covenant on the Rights of Indigenous Nations, authorized version, initialed 28 July 1994, Geneva, Switzerland; posted at http://www.cwis.org/icrin-94.html (14 February 2002).

5. See Jeanette Greenfield, *The Return of Cultural Treasures,* 2d ed. (Cambridge: Cambridge Univ. Press, 1996), 279–81.

6. See Gael M. Graham, "Protection and Reversion of Cultural Property: Issues of Definition and Justification," *International Lawyer* 21 (1987): 755–93.

7. See the Convention for the Protection of Cultural Property in the Event of Armed Conflict, held at the Hague 14 May 1954, entered in force 7 August 1956; posted at http://www.unesco.org/culture/laws/hague/html_eng/page1.shtml (14 February 2002).

8. See Elazar Barkan, "Aesthetics and Evolution: Benin Art in Europe," *African Arts* 30, no. 3 (1997): 36–41, 92–93. See also Elazar Barkan and Ronald Bush, "Introduction," in idem, eds., *Prehistories of the Future: The Primitivist Project and the Culture of Modernism* (Stanford: Stanford Univ. Press, 1995).

9. M. W. Hilton-Simpson, *Land and Peoples of the Kasai; Being a Narrative of a Two Years' Journey among the Cannibals of the Equatorial Forest and Other Savage Tribes of the South-western Congo* (London: Constable, 1911), 209. Hilton-Simpson describes the political structure of the Kasai society, comparing it to England, and talks about the prime minister and the representative of art and crafts as similar to the London guilds and so forth.

10. The Nationalmuseet (National Museum of Danish History) in Copenhagen collected cultural artifacts from Greenland for one century. Then, in the 1980s, the museum cooperated with the growing population in transferring much of the goods back to Greenland, which had not preserved any significant local culture of its own in the past; see Helge Schultz-Lorentzen, "Return of Cultural Property by Denmark to Greenland: From Dream to Reality," *Museum* (UNESCO) 40, no. 4 (1988): 200–5.

11. John Mack, *Emil Torday and the Art of the Congo, 1900–1909*, exh. cat. (Seattle: Univ. of Washington Press, 1991), 28–29.

12. Convention for the Protection of Cultural Property (note 7), preamble.

13. See the preamble to UNESCO General Conference (17th session, 1972), Convention Concerning the Protection of the World Cultural and Natural Heritage, doc. code WHC.2001/WS/2; posted at http://www.unesco.org/whc/world_he.htm (14 February 2002).

14. Convention Concerning the Protection of the World Cultural and Natural Heritage (note 13), preamble.

15. See John Henry Merryman, "Thinking about the Elgin Marbles," *Michigan Law Review* 83 (1985): 1881–923; and John Henry Merryman, "The Public Interest in Cultural Property," *California Law Review* 77 (1989): 339–64.

16. Other cases are less visible. Compare, for example, the case of a Colombian monstrance, which was offered to the San Antonio Art Museum in 1982 but was discovered to have been exported by illegal means; see Greenfield, *Return of Cultural Treasures* (note 5), 267, 273.

17. Compare the chapters by Patty Gerstenblith and by Douglas Owsley and Richard Jantz, both this volume.

18. United Nations General Assembly (28th session, 1973–74), Speech by Mobutu Sese Seko, plenary meeting, 1973, Agenda: A/9201 & Add.1–4, UN doc. sym. A/PV.2140; quoted in Douglas N. Thomason, "Rolling Back History: The United Nations General Assembly and the Right to Cultural Property," *Case Western Reserve Journal of International Law* 22, no. 1 (1990): 50.

19. United Nations General Assembly (30th session, 1975), Resolution 3391: Restitution of Works of Art to Countries Victims of Expropriation, 19 November 1975, UN doc. sym. A/RES/3391(XXX); quoted in Thomason, "Rolling Back History" (note 18), 56.

20. See the preamble to the Convention on the Means of Prohibiting and Preventing the Illicit Import, Export, and Transfer of Ownership of Cultural Property, adopted by the General Conference of UNESCO on 17 November 1970, entry in force 24 April 1972; posted at http://exchanges.state.gov/education/culprop/unesco01.html (14 February 2002).

21. A 1976 UNESCO panel; quoted in Rosemary J. Coombe, "The Properties of Culture and the Politics of Possessing Identity: Native Claims in the Cultural Appropriation Controversy," *Canadian Journal of Law and Jurisprudence* 6, no. 2 (1993): 249–85, esp. 264.

22. UNESCO General Conference (21st session, 1980), Intergovernmental Committee for Promoting the Return of Cultural Property to Its Countries of Origin or Its Restitution in Case of Illicit Appropriation, doc. code 21 C/83; as quoted in Greenfield, *Return of Cultural Treasures* (note 5), 255.

23. See Jonathan S. Moore, "Enforcing Foreign Ownership Claims in the Antiquities Market," *Yale Law Review* 97 (1988): 466.

24. UNIDROIT Convention on Stolen or Illegally Exported Cultural Objects, 24 June 1995; posted at http://www.unidroit.org/english/conventions/c-cult.htm (14 February 2002).

25. Christina Lamb, "Looted Treasure Floods Europe," *Sunday Times* (London), 18 June 1995, sec. 1, p. 22.

26. Luke Harding, "Debris of the Past," *The Guardian*, 27 March 2001, 12.

27. See M. C. Vernon, "Common Cultural Property: The Search for Rights of Protective Intervention," *Case Western Reserve Journal of International Law* 26, no. 2/3 (1994): 435. Given the recent prolonged restoration of the Sphinx, this may be a particularly inappropriate example.

28. See Thomason, "Rolling Back History" (note 18), 48.

29. For example, the International Council of Museums (ICOM) Code of Professional Ethics was adopted unanimously by the Fifteenth General Assembly of the ICOM meeting in Buenos Aires, Argentina, 4 November 1986; posted at http://www.icom.org/ethics_rev_engl.html (19 February 2002).

30. David Wilson, "Return and Restitution: A Museum Perspective," in Isabel McBryde, ed., *Who Owns the Past? Papers from the Annual Symposium of the Australian Academy of the Humanities* (Melbourne: Oxford Univ. Press, 1985), 99–106.

31. In 1979 the United Kingdom adopted the Ancient Monuments and Archaeological Areas Act, which extended protection of cultural property by the state and provided for a more aggressive policy of state acquisition of antiquities; posted at http://www.cruithni.org/resources/legislation/primary/ancient_monuments_and_archeological_areas_act_1979/index.html (19 February 2002).

32. See Greenfield, *Return of Cultural Treasures* (note 5), 271–72. Two comparable incidents took place involving the British Museum. The first is the case of an object that belonged to King Saud of Saudi Arabia. The second is the case of the skull of Broken Hill Man. Zambia demanded its restitution, but it seems that, since no evidence supporting or disproving the legality of the export of the skull from Zambia (in 1921) existed, the British Museum trustees found it a perfect case to hold on to their "trust." Since Zambia could not prove their ownership, the trustees refused restitution. See A. H. Mulongo, "The Broken Hill Skull: A Zambian Case," *Museum* 44, no. 2 (1992): 103–4. It would not be unfair to assume that other similar cases, which have not come to light, are buried in tombs of correspondence.

33. John Henry Merryman, "Two Ways of Thinking about Cultural Property," *American Journal of International Law* 80 (1986): 831.

34. Brian Fagan, "Archaeology's Dirty Secret," in Karen D. Vitelli, ed., *Archaeological Ethics* (Walnut Creek, Calif.: AltaMira, 1996), 247–51.

35. United Nations General Assembly (40th session, 1985–86), Speech on return of cultural property by M. A. Albornoz (Ecuador), 21 November 1983, Agenda: A/40/251, UN doc. sym. A/40/PV.87; quoted in Thomason, "Rolling Back History" (note 18), 86.

36. See the International Covenant on the Rights of Indigenous Nations (note 4).

37. Russell Ciochon and Jamie James, "The Glory That Was Angkor," in Karen D. Vitelli, ed., *Archaeological Ethics* (Walnut Creek, Calif.: AltaMira, 1996), 117–27.

38. Greenfield, *Return of Cultural Treasures* (note 5), recounts several cases of the refusal of museums and dealers to buy significant objects, which led to the return of those objects; however, these are still the exceptions.

39. Carol L. Howell, "Daring to Deal with the Huaqueros," in Karen D. Vitelli, ed., *Archaeological Ethics* (Walnut Creek, Calif.: AltaMira, 1996), 47–53.

40. Lawrence M. Kaye and Carla T. Main, "Law, Ethics and the Illicit Antiquities Market," *Asian Art and Culture* 9, no. 1 (1996): 22–37.

41. Les Groube, "The Ownership of Diversity: The Problem of Establishing a National History in a Land of Nine-Hundred Ethnic Groups," in Isabel McBryde, ed., *Who Owns the Past? Papers from the Annual Symposium of the Australian Academy of the Humanities* (Melbourne: Oxford Univ. Press, 1985), 49–73.

42. See http://www.zeugma2000.com/zeugma.html (19 February 2002).

43. Robert Edwards and Jenny Stewart, eds., *Preserving Indigenous Cultures: A New Role for Museums* (Canberra: Australian Government Publishing Service, 1980). Quoted in John Mulvaney, "A Question of Values: Museums and Cultural Property," in Isabel McBryde, ed., *Who Owns the Past? Papers from the Annual Symposium of the Australian Academy of the Humanities* (Melbourne: Oxford Univ. Press, 1985), 94.

44. Quoted in Thomason, "Rolling Back History" (note 18), 93.

45. Mulvaney, "A Question of Values" (note 43), 86–98.

46. Wilson, "Return and Restitution" (note 30), 104.

47. The Egyptians were said to demand restitution, but there is no reliable evidence for such a demand. There was a demand by the East Germans to return the bust from West Berlin to the Pergamonmuseum where it was displayed before the war.

48. J. Anthony Paredes, "Preface," in Tom Greaves, ed., *Intellectual Property Rights for Indigenous Peoples* (Oklahoma City: Society for Applied Anthropology, 1994), vii.

49. See Mulvaney, "A Question of Values" (note 43), 95.

50. See Ronald V. Bettig, *Copyrighting Culture: The Political Economy of Intellectual Property* (Boulder: Westview, 1996).

51. Tom Greaves, "IPR, a Current Survey," in idem, ed., *Intellectual Property Rights for Indigenous Peoples* (Oklahoma City: Society for Applied Anthropology, 1994), 10.

52. Greaves, "IPR, a Current Survey" (note 51), 1–16.

53. Barkan, *Guilt of Nations* (note 1), conclusion.

54. Several articles in Tom Greaves, ed., *Intellectual Property Rights for Indigenous Peoples* (Oklahoma City: Society for Applied Anthropology, 1994), illuminate the

cooperation between the pharmaceutical industry and indigenous peoples, including proposals for compensation and establishing standards of reciprocity. The demonstrations around the World Trade Organization and the International Monetary Fund in 1999 and 2000 signaled a political expansion of these sentiments.

55. Greaves, "IPR, a Current Survey" (note 51), 1–17, sees a recent, astonishing rise in indigenous success in retaining their ownership.

Part I

Nationalizing Identity

Appropriating the Stones: The "Elgin Marbles" and English National Taste

Timothy Webb

> It has always appeared to me rather extraordinary to consider Lord Elgin as a destroyer. I venture to think that he is more entitled to be considered as the saviour of the finest part of the building, and deserves the thanks of every man of feeling and taste throughout Europe.
>
> — An English Student[1]

Origins and Naming

The case of the "Elgin Marbles" brings into focus many of the central issues that characterize the discipline of cultural history.[2] The removal of a substantial group of marbles from the Acropolis in Athens, Greece, first to London and then to the British Museum, is the focus of a passionate debate, one that is long and hotly contested and is by no means finally resolved. Recent newspaper reports suggest that the fundamental disagreements involved have now reached a point that reveals very clearly the underlying values and assumptions on both sides of the argument and brings into urgent perspective many of the forces implicated in creating a great international museum. Most of the sculptures originally formed part of the Parthenon, the temple sacred to Pallas Athene, or Minerva, the virgin goddess who presided over Athens and the Athenian state, but the acquisition also included a statue from the Erechtheion (or, in Latin, Erechtheum), which stood close by on the Acropolis. For nearly two hundred years this daring and extensive example of seigneurial acquisition has been associated with Thomas Bruce (1766–1841), seventh earl of Elgin and from 1799 to 1803 ambassador to the Sublime Porte (that is, Constantinople). Elgin conceived the acquisition of the sculptures, carried it out through his representatives and emissaries in Athens, gradually transported the collection to London, and displayed it there to the public first in a large shed behind the house he rented at the corner of Picadilly and Park Lane and then, in less than ideal conditions, at Burlington House. Finally, after long and frustrating negotiations and an almost one-year delay since his petition had first been formally presented to the House of Commons, Elgin testified at the celebrated hearings that culminated in the *Report from the Select Committee of the House of Commons on the Earl of Elgin's Collection of Sculptured Marbles* (1816) and strongly argued debates in the Commons. As a result, in June 1816, Elgin sold the collection to the nation for £35,000.

From that point on, it became a pilgrimage at the British Museum, which was slowly redesigned to acknowledge the new range of its responsibilities both as a source of scholarly materials and as an inspirational center to the growing British Empire and to conceptions of Englishness itself.

Elgin paid for the privilege of removing the marbles from the Acropolis. As the Greeks have consistently reminded those who eventually obtained his collection, however, his agreement (the terms of which have often been disputed) was made not with the Greeks themselves but with the local *disdar* (warden of a castle or fort), who embodied the authority of the Ottoman occupying force. No attempt to consult Greek opinion seems to have been made because it was widely assumed that it did not meaningfully exist (since modern Greeks were a sadly degenerate version of their predecessors) or that, even if it did, it could not be usefully identified. Both Elgin and many of those who supported his actions were animated, at best, by an admiration for classical Athens and what they interpreted as its values and achievements. In preserving the heritage of Western civilization, they do not seem to have envisaged the possibility that they were infringing the rights of contemporary Greeks or of a Greek heritage that might still have national significance. Still less have they seemed to recognize that within the Greek tradition, and despite centuries of desecration, the Parthenon was a sacred temple and a national shrine. A few witnesses registered a more profound local sentiment, which seems to have touched even some of the permissive Turks, and which was sometimes matched, if briefly, by a sense of violation. Yet even these stirrings of reluctance were usually compromised, with very few exceptions, by a lordly rapacity on the part of the observers and a desire to collect, or merely to acquire, on their own account. British association with the War of Greek Independence (1821–32) was not insignificant, both materially and emotionally, but it was already too late to reclaim successfully an essential part of a national heritage whose value and importance were now more fully acknowledged, in keeping with the growth of a new national self-consciousness. This case exemplifies with unusual clarity the kind of assumptions that caused the initial misunderstandings and the ways in which the claims of individual national traditions may be overridden in the presumed interests of something "higher" or more obviously accessible. The issues at stake are urgently relevant to those who are concerned with the proper function of the museum. They are best approached, perhaps, through the medium of an analysis that attempts to be as dispassionate and objective as possible.

Even before the sculptures were acquired by the state on behalf of the British Museum, they were regularly referred to as the Elgin Marbles. Elgin had stamped the marbles with his identity, in a sense, by so memorably collecting such a large group of them on his own initiative. Whatever hesitations or objections were made on the part of individuals and at a cost far below that which Elgin required in order to reimburse himself, the state authenticated this apparently provisional identity by including them so prominently in the national collection. Naming is rarely a neutral activity since it so often involves the imposition of identity or the staking of claims toward wider recognition and even fame by association. The history of these remains from the Acropolis is a frequent reminder that collectors sometimes achieved "immortality" by enclosing their collections within the defining bounds of their own identities. Such assumptions could be supported by the institutions that acquired their collections and perpetuated the original relationship within the framework of a larger whole.

On the one hand, other labels were possible: the Aigina Marbles at the Glyptothek in Munich, the Phigaleian Marbles at the British Museum, and the Pergamon Altar in the Pergamonmuseum in Berlin are known not by the names of those who collected or transplanted them from Greece but by their place of origin. On the other hand, the Towneley Marbles retained their owner's name and identity when they provided the foundation of the antique collection at the British Museum. Some commentators were reluctant to see this principle applied to Elgin's collection; thinking of opportunistic highwaymen, Lord Byron bluntly observed: "I suppose we shall hear of the 'Abershaw' and 'Jack Shephard' collection."[3] Six years later an anonymous writer in the *Gentleman's Magazine* noted, more equably but inaccurately, that the Elgin collection "will henceforward be properly called the Athenian Marbles or Sculptures."[4] Yet, whatever delicacies may have prompted this prediction, the connection between Elgin and the stony fruit of his enterprise had already been institutionalized by the official acceptance of a title that had been granted formal authority by an act of Parliament. The statute recorded the earl's wish that this acquisition should "be called by the Name of 'The Elgin Marbles'"; according to the enacting clause, it was to be "distinguished by the Name or Appellation of 'The Elgin Collection.'"[5] With whatever qualifications, the connection between Thomas Bruce and his collection was to be acknowledged by formal and official recognition.

The growth of nationalism and national self-consciousness has ensured that, for many, such a title is necessarily provocative. While older historians and curators experienced no problems in referring to "the Elgins," recent writers, experts, and visitors have become much more circumspect and more anxiously conscious of difficulty. So the Elgin Marbles can now be encountered as the Athenian Marbles, the Parthenon Marbles, or even the Phidian Marbles. While such titles are understandably directed toward the claims of repossession, however, they are often inaccurate by their very partiality since in none of these cases is the term strictly confined to the pieces brought to London by the efforts of Elgin. The Musée du Louvre, for example, contains some works that also derive from the Parthenon and find themselves in Paris through the agency of Marie-Gabriel-Auguste-Florent, comte de Choiseul-Gouffier, French ambassador at the Sublime Porte from 1784 to 1792 and author of *Voyage pittoresque de la Grèce*, the first volume of which appeared in 1792.[6]

Admittedly, Choiseul-Gouffier was a great deal more modest in his acquisitive urges, and admittedly (unlike Elgin) he was a traveler and a scholarly connoisseur in his own right. Yet Elgin's bravado, the scale of his transportation of Greek antiquities, and the public recognition of its results have caused a notoriety that has allowed the acquisitions and intentions of Choiseul-Gouffier and other strenuously possessive travelers to go largely unnoticed. As an anonymous correspondent to the *Examiner* pointed out in 1811, Aubin-Louis Millin had celebrated Choiseul-Gouffier's acquisition of the Parthenon fragment and specifically attributed its presence to a "noble passion pour les Arts" (a noble passion for the arts) on the part of the collector. The patriotic correspondent claimed, "M. Choiseul *would* have taken down all if *he could,* but fortunately for *us,* was checked by the Revolution; and French artists were actually at Athens waiting the return of their influence to renew their proceedings."[7] In fact, Choiseul-Gouffier had his own agent in Athens and in later years recorded an envious admiration for his more successful rival:

> Lord Elgin gathered, throughout Greece, a rich harvest of precious monuments, which I had coveted long and vainly; it is difficult for me to see them in his possession without some degree of envy, but it should be a satisfaction for all those who cherish the arts to know these masterpieces have been saved from the barbarity of the Turks, and preserved by an enlightened amateur who will make them available for public enjoyment.[8]

The Elgin collection includes a metope that was originally acquired for Choiseul-Gouffier but was captured by Lord Nelson. Through a series of accidents and misunderstandings, this has long formed part of the London holdings so that, ironically, Choiseul-Gouffier is both implicated in Elgin's seizure of Greek materials and, necessarily, subordinate if not entirely invisible. In various ways, however, Elgin and the marbles he acquired have become consociates. There may be patriotic resistance to the museum's self-allocated role as, in William Hazlitt's phrase to describe the Louvre, "a school and discipline of humanity," but for good or ill, the Elgin Marbles have been a part of museum history and a London sight for nearly two hundred years. Despite the great sense of dislocation unmistakably part of the "Elgin experience," the marbles have achieved an alternative identity that has placed them, permanently it seems, not in Athens but in London. An examination of how that identity has been established and contested should provide an instructive example of cultural history and some of its complexities.[9]

Charles Towneley, the Archetypal Collector

It is useful to start by considering the portrait of Charles Towneley titled *Charles Towneley and His Friends in the Towneley Gallery* (fig. 1), originally painted between 1781 and 1783 by Johann Zoffany. The painting was first exhibited in 1783 and revised about ten years later. According to Towneley himself, this representation owed much to Zoffany's record of a gathering at the Tribuna degli Uffizi in Florence. The institution was widely acknowledged as one of the outstanding points of focus for the eighteenth-century admirer of

Fig. 1. Johann Zoffany (German, 1733–1810)
Charles Towneley and His Friends in the Towneley Gallery, 33 Park Street, Westminster
England, 1781–83, oil on canvas, 127 × 99.1 cm (50 × 39 in.)
Burnley, Lancashire, England, Towneley Hall Art Gallery and Museum

art, to whom the achievements of quattrocento Florence were still largely unknown or unrecognized. While the Tribuna is presented as public and crowded, Towneley's library is peacefully private. Zoffany is not only following his own example in the earlier picture but is also paying a debt to the traditions of the Renaissance, according to which the wealth and discrimination of the collector were celebrated by the vision of the artists who recorded them in meaningful company with representative pieces. Towneley's library is organized deliberately for this purpose; the air of apparent calm and domesticity is as carefully staged as the seeming informality. Contemporary pictures both of the library and the dining room record more common arrangements for display, although even these cannot be entirely trusted as historically accurate. The very crowding of the room does not appear as an inconvenience but a sign of unthreatening range and copiousness. This impression is achieved not only by coloring, which is reassuringly muted, but by the subtle intimations of scale as well. Charles Towneley is unlike the figure in Henry Fuseli's *The Artist in Despair over the Magnitude of Antique Fragments* (1778–80; Kunsthaus Zürich), who seems dauntingly confronted by the gigantic scale of the past in the form of an unattached foot and an unattached hand with pointing index finger, which dwarf the despairing observer. He is unlike the poet in John Keats's *The Fall of Hyperion* (written in 1819, first published in 1856), who finds himself distressingly out of scale with the inexplicable remains of a former world. He is even unlike the black-suited gentlemen captured by Archibald Archer among the marbles in the temporary Elgin Room at the British Museum in 1819.[10] Charles Towneley and his friends are entirely—or almost entirely—at home among his collection, which never seems to threaten or to disturb their equanimity and their good-humored poise by the suggestive presence of naked flesh, by troubling disparities or imbalances of scale, or by energies that are inappropriately dynamic or uncontainable.

The diplomatic harmonies of this delightful group portrait should not, however, blind the viewer to a number of facts that may be largely excluded from the frame of the picture but might inform any attentive reading. Even if the strategy of the painter allows Towneley to assume what seems an unquestioning place in a larger unity, this whole was assembled as a direct result of his initiative, his discrimination, his contacts, and his wealth. The portrait might be seen not only as a tribute to his discriminating powers—his capacity to elicit the best and most interesting examples of the art of classical antiquity—but as a celebration of the achieved objectives of the acquisitive tendency (as is the case of many Renaissance portraits). When one inspects these acquisitions—when one observes them gracefully integrated into the context of a library—one might also recall the extent to which the slightly later debate on the value and utility of the Elgin Marbles, and on their significance to society, was founded on the notion of art as a social commodity. The connoisseur and collector Richard Payne Knight was not alone in objecting to the Elgin Marbles because they were perceived as deficient in what was generally known as "furniture value." For example, the celebrated sculptor Richard Westmacott distinguished Towneley's collection since, as he said, "you can make furniture of them" and the "Elgin Marbles," which did not allow for such uses, and were "only fit for a school" (that is, an art school).[11]

It is not surprising, then, that the *Report from the Parliamentary Select Committee* endorsed the special virtues of Elgin's marbles but distinguished them from the kind of finished objects that normally attracted connoisseurs and dilettanti: "the mutilated state of all the larger figures, the want either of heads or features, of limbs or surface, in most of the metopes, and in a great proportion of the compartments, even of the larger Fri[e]ze, render this collection, if divided, but little adapted for the decoration of private houses."[12] Unhistorical recrimination would be entirely out of place, yet we must notice the exemplary value of Towneley and the precise significance of Zoffany's tribute to his powers as a collector. Towneley belonged to a generation that still allowed for the skill and energy of the individual collector and his entrepreneurial abilities even at the cost of archaeological contexts, or the claims of place, or what would later be seen as national rights of possession. Our responses might be quite different if Zoffany's picture were to be read not as a tribute to Towneley's acquisitive virtues but as an almost surrealistic vision of dislocation in which works of art were not to be approached in terms of their original provenance or their significance within a specific culture. Such a reading would be perverse in terms of the cultural assumptions that helped to assemble the collection and commissioned the picture. Still, it draws our attention to the fact that this world of apparent certainties was based on "civilized" philosophies that would soon be challenged and have long since ceased to be regarded as acceptable.

Charles Towneley was one of the last great examples of the individual connoisseur of antiquities; the tradition that he represented was to be continued, in some ways, by collectors of painting. The classical world, however, was no longer a free zone for the escapades of the adventurous and the enterprising. Zoffany's painting was intended not only to record that role but also to dignify and explain the nature of his contribution. The presence of open books indicates that the pleasure in acquiring and possessing works of classical art is refined and informed not so much by acquisitive impulse as by scholarly curiosity. Towneley's interlocutor is Pierre-François Hugues, baron d'Hancarville, the French art historian and expert on ancient art who had been appointed to catalog the collection. His presence reminds the observer that the origins of collecting were sometimes associated with the early stages of archaeology; even if the brutal depredations of individual travelers or collectors frequently destroyed precisely the kind of contextual evidence that would have been essential to later archaeologists, the personal conjunction points toward the intellectual foundations of the modern museum.[13] The status and the destiny of the classical work of art (especially sculpture) were changed forever by the growth of nationalism and the new and highly sharpened consciousness of national identity that was accelerated by the example and challenge of Napoléon Bonaparte. The European tour continued and even widened its scope in the nineteenth century, but the traditional Grand Tour, with all the temptations and cultural opportunities that it had involved for the British aristocracy, was no longer possible. The connoisseur and the free-lance collector of antiquities such as Towneley were replaced by the museum. What had once been a privilege for the special few was now made available to a much wider public.

Elgin's Collection and Cultural Dislocation

Such issues of cultural dislocation can be detected behind a passage in Byron's *English Bards and Scotch Reviewers* (1809):

> Let coxcombs printing as they come from far,
> Snatch his own wreath of Ridicule from Carr;
> Let ABERDEEN and ELGIN still pursue
> The shade of fame through regions of Virtu;
> Waste useless thousands on their Phidian freaks,
> Mis-shapen monuments, and maimed antiques;
> And make their grand saloons a general mart
> For all the mutilated blocks of art.[14]

Byron's public reaction conceals a complicated set of relationships. When he toured Athens with his countryman John Cam Hobhouse, Byron visited numerous sites in the company of Giovanni Battista Lusieri. This Italian draftsman and artist played a significant role in removing what would become known as the Elgin Marbles, and did not hesitate to use violence when the claims of ownership seemed to demand it. Lusieri was still working on behalf of Elgin in 1809 and would continue to do so until his death in 1821.[15] Although a note to *Childe Harold's Pilgrimage* (1812–18) would later identify Lusieri as "the agent of devastation" and "the able instrument of plunder," it was with him that Byron and Hobhouse had visited Sunium (Cape Sounion) and had spent 5 January (Christmas Day, old style) 1810.[16] It can be presumed, then, that Byron had privileged access not only to the Acropolis but also to Lusieri's accounts of what he had acquired on behalf of Elgin. Byron's knowledge of these operations would have brought him into direct contact with the latest consignment of marbles as they awaited passage to England. By a delicious irony, the ship that carried this batch back to England by way of Malta also brought Byron with the uncompleted manuscript of what would become *The Curse of Minerva* (1812), a satire that engaged damagingly with Elgin's activities and the subsequent display of dislocated marbles in London. In *English Bards and Scotch Reviewers*, Byron enjoys the full satirical privilege of demonstrative indignation, and the name of Elgin is included along with those of many others who had left a mark on the English cultural scene. There Elgin is linked with "the travell'd Thane, Athenian Aberdeen" who was a member of the Society of Dilettanti, excavated in Attica and Amyclae, acquired a metope from the Parthenon, may have been one of "the two English gentlemen" who tried to purchase the Parthenon frieze from Lusieri, and, later in life, was a member of the British Museum Committee, which sat in judgment on the Elgin collection.[17] The pairing of Aberdeen—George Hamilton-Gordon, whose name curiously mimicked that of Byron—with Elgin suggests that Byron had not yet formulated an entirely independent estimate of Elgin. Byron may have associated Aberdeen with his fellow Scot as acquisitive noblemen with misplaced classical interests and because both can be associated with the Grecian fashion. In a canceled stanza for *Childe Harold,* Elgin is linked not only with "sullen" Aberdeen but also with the antiquarian and diplomat William Richard Hamilton and with Thomas Hope, author of *Household Furniture and Interior Decoration* (1807) and *Costume of the Ancients* (1809).[18] The sweeping reference to "grand saloons" takes the poem beyond the cramped arrangements of Elgin's display at the Park Lane house to include the conspicuous display of other aristocrats who had opened their houses to the public. Byron was shrewdly, if unkindly, aware that such pursuits were not usually directed toward altruistic ends. In devoting themselves to following "The shade of fame through regions of Virtu," connoisseurs may have been deceiving themselves; however, as the history of collection in general and of the Elgin Marbles in particular surely demonstrates, they were giving expression to an urge that seems to have motivated many, even the most idealistic. Directly or indirectly, the assembling of a collection was closely associated with hopes of immortality in which the collector or the collection, or both, would share in the apparently unlimited future of the work of art.

The history of *The Curse of Minerva* is even more complex; while it includes a pointed and particularly virulent response to Elgin and his activities, the poem was privately printed but not licensed by Byron for publication during his lifetime.[19] At first *The Curse of Minerva* appeared in a few private copies; it was then pirated, with the result that, although Byron had not publicly expressed himself on the subject in print, his views were well known. *The Curse of Minerva* includes an account of the British role in the history of the Elgin Marbles as part of a larger critique of foreign policy. British policy toward Greece, its sense of its own larger responsibilities, could not be addressed without reference to this episode, which, for Byron, represented a flagrant impropriety. The painful paradoxes are set out in a vivid account of the display of the marbles, which in its alliterative force and the balance of its couplets remind readers that for Byron, Alexander Pope was the supreme model, particularly before Byron had discovered a verse form with a flexible nature that would lend itself more easily to the mobility of his own temperament:

> Be all the bruisers cull'd from all St. Giles,
> That art and nature may compare their styles;
> While brawny brutes in stupid wonder stare,
> And marvel at his Lordship's "stone shop" there.
> Round the throng'd gate shall sauntering coxcombs creep,

To lounge and lucubrate, to prate and peep;

While many a languid maid, with longing sigh,

On giant statues casts the curious eye:

The room with transient glance appears to skim,

Yet marks the mighty back and length of limb;

Mourns o'er the difference of *now* and *then,*

Exclaims, "these Greeks indeed were proper men!"

Draws sly comparisons of *these* with *those,*

And envies Lais all her Attic beaux.

When shall a modern maid have swains like these!

Alas! Sir Harry is no Hercules!

And last of all amidst the gaping crew

Some calm spectator, as he takes his view

In silent indignation mix'd with grief,

Admires the plunder, but abhors the thief.[20]

This description might be addressed not only in terms of the traditions of English verse satire but also of the well-established artistic tradition of observing audiences or gatherings of art admirers, or "connoisseurs." This artistic lineage and its social implications are suggestively examined by John Brewer in *The Pleasures of the Imagination,* where one can discover a number of visual ancestors to Byron's verbal satire. Byron's "gaping crowd" can be related to portrayals of the clientele of the art gallery, with its attention often centered on concerns that were far from aesthetic. Unlike Zoffany's dignified picture of Towneley, Byron's crowd can be directly aligned with satirical presentations in particular. Here the "coxcombs" of *English Bards and Scotch Reviewers* appear again, this time "sauntering," finding occasion to "lounge and lucubrate, to prate and peep"; the alliterating verbs insist on an inappropriateness that might become impropriety.

The hints of voyeurism fit suggestively Thomas Rowlandson's portrayal of three connoisseurs — *The Connoisseurs* (circa 1800) — who examine an unfinished painting of Susanna and the Elders, itself an example of female beauty trapped by the male gaze. Byron's peeping coxcombs have similar social and artistic traditions to what Brewer characterizes as the "ogling gaze" and later the "lubricious gaze of the elders (and connoisseurs) who also desire (private) possession, either of Susanna or of her picture."[21] In fact, Byron's own "gaping crew" was at one time imagined as a "gazing throng."[22] The single-letter switch from "gazing" to "gaping" has the effect of concentrating the reader's attention not on the eyes, "curious" or otherwise, that have provided a central impetus for the previous description but on the mouth, which indicates summarily an incapacity to engage intelligently with the spectacle. Whatever the direct result of this verbal change, however, the erotic potential of these nude sculptures is emphasized but provided with a very different gender orientation by an explicit reference to a distinctly female response, in which "many a languid maid, with longing sigh, / On giant statues casts the curious eye." Although the passage modifies the apparent violence of the encounter with references to "Attic beaux," "swains," and "Sir Harry," seeming perhaps to translate the potentially troubling into a mode that is genially familiar in social and literary terms, there is a strong sense of the more arousingly physical, especially in the references to "mighty back and length of limb." Byron plays over the theme of a tragic lament, which was to feature both in the text of *Childe Harold* and in the confirming notes, as well as in the accounts of other travelers—"the difference of *now* and *then*." Here, however, the mourning is not for the passing of a great civilization that left no direct inheritors but specifically for the physical decline that it may be thought to have involved: "these Greeks indeed were proper men!" In this context, the denotation of *men* is specific and exact: for the languid female observer, the sheer scale of the Elgin Marbles may have been a threat to complacency, especially when the unexpected intensity of perception transformed the nude to the naked.

The poem's concern goes beyond erotic excitements approached under the guise of the antiquarian or the aesthetic because it also suggests not so much the degeneracy of contemporary Greeks as the degeneracy of the contemporary male. The "feeble dotard West" (actually Benjamin West, president of the Royal Academy, who had struggled to appreciate the marbles without unduly upsetting his conservative aesthetics and who, according to Byron, had declared himself a "mere tyro" by comparison), the "brawny brutes" staring in "stupid wonder" (a Popeian locution),[23] the "sauntering coxcombs" (coxcombs also feature in Popeian gatherings), and the other implied male observers in the audience, all present an inadequate, inappropriate, and, in a sense, "effeminate" alternative to the "giant statues" of antiquity who put them, demeaningly, into perspective. Such muscular masculinity (and these statues are unmistakably male) exposes the weakness of those who come to view it. A similar contrast was made by Hazlitt when he welcomed the virtues of the Elgin Marbles by contrasting their energizing possibilities with the emptiness of eighteenth-century English art, which he characterized by a series of disabling ailments that are noticeably "effeminate": "It is to be hoped...that these Marbles...may lift the Fine Arts out of that Limbo of vanity and affectation into which they were conjured in this country about fifty years ago, and in which they have lain sprawling and fluttering, gasping for breath, wasting away, vapid and abortive ever since,—the shadow of a shade."[24]

Artists from Zoffany to Archer have profited meaningfully and sometimes to complex effect from the contrasts between flesh and stone, between the naked and the clothed. In Byron's conjunction, however, the ironies are simply interpreted, and there is a clear suggestion that the statues are superior to those who, with a variety of motives, come to view them. The description places all of those engagements, partial or personal, in a wider perspective by its introduction of a final resolving figure:

> And last of all amidst the gaping crew
> Some calm spectator, as he takes his view
> In silent indignation mix'd with grief,
> Admires the plunder, but abhors the thief.

Unlike the constituents of "the gaping crew," who approach the statues with a naive readiness to be amazed or amused, to be titillated or to wonder, this ideal viewer has the kind of composure that allows for a more reflective response. For some visitors, the experience is essentially superficial ("The room with transient glance appears to skim"); however, this spectator is informed by calmness and inexpressive self-possession (silence), which allows him to transcend the immediate or the merely personal and to experience the powerful but inappropriate presence of the marbles with a reaction that is thoughtfully, if passionately, paradoxical. The calm spectator "Admires the plunder, but abhors the thief": the balanced line, the paired verbs, and the moral discrimination may seem Augustan, or reminiscent of the classical poise of writers such as Pope, but this debt should not conceal the fierceness of the reaction in which the spectator is informed by feelings that may be related to Byron's own. Elgin is characterized as a "thief," and although this indignation is "silent" and combined with "grief," indignation is an emotion proper not only to the offended viewer himself but, more generally, to the satire and to the satirist.

Byron and the Register of Discord

Much of Byron's poem is animated by an indignation that is not concealed by the discipline of the rhyming couplet. The next passage repossesses this privilege for the poem and directs it at Elgin himself, who is here associated, once again by alliterative conjunction, with Eratostratus who set fire to the temple at Ephesus:

> Oh, loath'd in life, nor pardon'd in the dust,
> May Hate pursue his sacrilegious lust!
> Link'd with the fool that fired the Ephesian dome
> Shall vengeance follow far beyond the tomb,
> And Eratostratus and Elgin shine
> In many a branding page and burning line:
> Alike reserv'd for aye to stand accurst,
> Perchance the second blacker than the first.[25]

These lines enact the sacred privilege of the satirist: without reservation they call for hate and vengeance, and the verb *shall* includes both a prophetic indictment and a prediction. It is also suggested, however, that satire is the agent of larger forces and that both Eratostratus and Elgin are, ironically, creators of their own destiny, which is a direct consequence of their actions. The poem therefore proclaims and predicts that Eratostratus and Elgin will "shine / In many a branding page and burning line." Their own activities as plunderers will trigger a sequence of critical and satirical punishments that will avenge their plunders and depredations with a kind of negative immortality ("Alike reserv'd for aye to stand accurst"). Their ultimate blackness is appropriate to those who are connected with firing and plunder (Elgin, of course, metaphorically and by association) just as they will "shine" not through the luster of achievement but through the branding pages and burning lines of satirical denunciation. Even if the punishment of fire is more fitting for Eratostratus ("the fool that fired the Ephesian dome"), the poem is unremittingly severe at the expense of Elgin ("Oh, loath'd in life, nor pardon'd in the dust"), who was not yet dead but whose afterlife was already marked out in terms that were chillingly exact: "So let him stand through ages yet unborn, / Fix'd statue on the pedestal of Scorn."[26] Just as the British burning of Copenhagen in September 1807 (when the city was bombarded and on fire for three days), in some way followed the burning of Ephesus, which was also linked with the actions of Elgin in Athens, so Elgin's ultimate transformation to stone found its parallel in the actions of British foreign policy, which through the alienation of Greece and Greek interests, had the effect of petrifying friends and allies.

The parallels are not, perhaps, entirely exact, but the larger treatment in the passage and in the poem as a whole shows that Elgin could be seen both as a follower of British example and as a powerful local embodiment of the negative effects it could achieve. Within the larger rhetorical structure of *The Curse of Minerva* these connections are central. Although the attack on Elgin might be thought to be incidental or powerful but episodic, it is intimately related to the setting of the poem. Elgin's sacrilege, which involves the desecration of a temple and a site that carried sacred significance for patriotic Greeks, is a painfully vivid example of an insensitivity that might prove destructive to the British empire itself.

Byron's discomfort with the public display of Elgin's acquisitions is driven in part by what appeared to be its obvious commerciality. Some parliamentary speakers would later give voice to similar anxieties concerning Elgin's "dishonesty" and the way he took advantage of his ambassadorial privilege to invoke special help that would ultimately serve to his own financial advantage. Part of the resistance to purchasing the marbles for the nation was motivated by the anxiety that it would be giving official sanction to the use of public office for private gain. Yet Byron's objection was much more than merely pragmatic, or even principled, since it included a strong element of the personally temperamental. Byron's own aristocratic pride kept him at some distance from the self-gratifying concerns of those who only cared about commercial profit. A passage in *English Bards and Scotch Reviewers* had already expressed the case forcefully: "make their grand saloons a general mart / For all the mutilated blocks of art" centers its distaste for this shift of values around a set of images that present unpleasing and uncomfortable paradoxes, confusions, and improprieties. In *The Curse of Minerva* the poem's animus is directed more extensively at Elgin's supposed financial ambitions:

> Long of their Patron's gusto let them tell,
> Whose noblest, *native* gusto is — to sell:
> To sell, and make, may Shame record the day,
> The State receiver of his pilfer'd prey.[27]

"And make,.../ The State receiver" suggests that Elgin is attempting to involve government itself in his crime as an accessory after the fact. Elgin's protracted efforts to sell his collection fit into a continued discourse, which translates such ambitions into criminal activities as indicated by references to Jerry Abershaw, Jack Sheppard, and Jonathan Wild: "larceny," "plunder," and "thieves." Accordingly, Byron's redefinition of "gusto" is designed to dissociate Elgin's activities or interests from a term that was much in vogue to suggest the instinctive discrimination of the connoisseur; and Elgin's materialism is damningly identified as crudely and demeaningly Scottish. Here, the "general mart" has become, if possible, even more debased, because it is now a "stone shop," which attracts the stupid attention of muscular boxers ("brawny brutes" in the poem's uncomplimentary locution).

The appearance of boxers among the marbles on display is no satirist's fancy but an attested historical fact. "Be all the bruisers cull'd from all St. Giles, / That art and nature may compare their styles" points toward a fashion of inviting boxers to pose naked among the marbles or to use such a setting to exhibit their pugilistic virtues. Joseph Farington's diaries record, for example, "much company to see [Bob] Gregson naked amongst the antique figures" on 30 June 1808, while on 29 July 1808 there were sparring exhibitions between John Gully and Jem Belcher, Dutch Sam and Belcher Junior, and finally between John Jackson and Gully. As he notes, the company on such occasions included many of the country's leading experts on Greek antiquities and on art (a significant proportion would later give evidence to the Select Committee).[28] The ostensible pretext was to show that the sculptures were not only idealistic but also satisfyingly realistic; by the same token, surgeons such as Sir Anthony Carlisle used the Greek figures to demonstrate the principles of anatomy.[29] No one crusaded harder or more passionately than Benjamin Robert Haydon, a friend of Keats and the writer Leigh Hunt among others, and himself an ambitious historical painter. Haydon kept a vividly animated private record of his feelings at the time and of his almost obsessive commitment to recording the details of the sculpture and to absorbing its virtues by an intensity of application. Haydon's feelings were no secret: at the appropriate time, he joyfully and very publicly identified in the sculptures an advanced kind of realism that did not eliminate the idealistic but exposed the limitations of the merely realistic endeavors that he associated with Dutch painting.[30] For all the festivity and the celebration of these newly discovered artistic virtues, some observers still could not help but think that conspicuous displays (which were later extended to include a riding master and the actress Sarah Siddons) could be used to enhance the valuation of the Elgin Marbles.

While the discomfort in Byron's descriptions may be largely animated by the sense of inappropriateness—mismatches among the marbles, the spectators, and the location—there is also perhaps a residual element of offended conservative taste. Byron's first account in particular concentrates on the brokenness of the exhibits in a way that both suggests a painful personification and looks forward to the concession of the Select Committee, that for all their artistic virtues, the larger figures were in a "mutilated state." The alliterative point of "Phidian freaks" does not suggest an admiration for the unbroken masterpieces of Phidian sculpture so much as the kind of doubt notoriously expressed by Payne Knight and by William Wordsworth's anxious hostility in *The Prelude* (1805) toward the crowd at Bartholomew Fair, which expresses itself in the form of "freaks of nature."[31] Modern observers have long adjusted to the appearance of the fragmentary, but many initial reactions were motivated by shock rather than admiration. Farington's diaries provide a fascinating insight into this crisis in the history of taste. Ozias Humphry, who had been appointed portrait painter in crayons to King George III in 1792, admitted that while there "certainly was something great & of a high stile of sculpture," he could only see "a mass of ruins" (although his negative view may have been partly influenced by the setting in which Elgin's marbles were originally displayed). Nor did the marbles, at this relatively early stage, find favor with Sir George Beaumont, an amateur painter and draftsman, an important patron (whose clients included Wordsworth), an original member of the Parliamentary Committee for Taste, and a highly influential arbiter whose own collection of paintings established one of the foundations of the National Gallery. Beaumont was decisive in his opinion: "His recommendation [is] that the mutilated fragments brought from Athens by Lord Elgin should be *restored*, as at present, they excite rather disgust than pleasure in the minds of people in general, to see parts of limbs, & bodys, stumps of arms &c."[32] In the eyes of many, such unfinished shapes could only be made acceptable to a larger public if they were submitted to a process of "restoration." This was a standard procedure applied to many of the Towneley Marbles, one that Ludwig I of Bavaria, crown prince and later king, had engaged sculptor Bertel Thorvaldsen to carry out on the Aigina Marbles at the Glyptothek in Munich. Sculptor Antonio Canova was approached by Elgin with a view to carrying out a similar act of reclamation for his own collection; Canova refused, but there is evidence to show that Elgin never entirely abandoned this scheme.[33] Such acts of "restoration" were posited on a concept of an original whole that could be imaginatively reconstructed. Within a short time, their interpretation of artistic responsibility would be challenged by the claims of another kind of restoration, that is, restitution of works of art to their original owners. The early history of the Louvre is marked by the rival demands of both definitions while Byron, whose slightly undeveloped aesthetic sensibility may have first reacted with a kind of dissatisfied shudder, was soon identified as a powerful voice for the transfer of the Elgin collection to its proper home on the Acropolis.[34]

In this resistance to dislocated display, Byron may have been expressing a taste that was, in some ways, neoclassical, which was offended by such fractures of harmony and such discontinuities; he was also expressing a point of view that, for a variety of reasons, was also shared by many of his contemporaries. One example is that of Edward Daniel Clarke, an antiquary and traveler who became a professor of mineralogy at Cambridge University in 1808. Clarke, who had made the Grand Tour from 1800 to 1801, complained that the removal of a horse's head from the east facade proved "the want of taste and utter barbarism" involved in such an operation. Clarke's criticism was perhaps compromised and ambivalent—a writer in the *Quarterly Review* observed that "there is a bitterness always apparent in speaking of Lord Elgin in his pursuits in Greece," while Haydon noticed that Clarke "took away all he *could* take away, and sneers at Lord [Elgin] because he had the power to take & did, thank God, take away more."[35] In spite of this, the force of Clarke's judgment and the accuracy of his observation are unaffected. He had the advantage of knowing the Parthenon before the sculptures were transported, and, like Byron's arguments in poetry and prose, his authority is based on a knowledge of location, although his critique is more aesthetic in its analysis of the effects of "the work of destruction." Certain effects can only be observed on the spot, where they are informed by the function of individual sculpture as part of a larger whole. To remove pieces of sculpture from their original framework was, therefore, not to contribute to the salvation of works that might otherwise be at risk but to collaborate in the very process of damage from which the marbles were to be protected: the removal of the horse's head "from its situation amounted to nothing less than its destruction."[36]

Elgin's depredations were more extensive and more ambitious than those of the majority of travelers, but he seems to have received a share of blame that, historically considered, might be regarded as disproportionate. This may have been in part because he did not fit in to the normal categories. He was never elected to the Society of Dilettanti (he declined a much-delayed offer of membership in 1831), and he seems not to have operated within the recognized circles of collectors. John Brewer aligns his ambitions with those of Napoléon rather than those of the other connoisseurs and collectors, noting that "there is no evidence that he had any special knowledge or interest in the cultures of classical antiquity. He was a collector who was not a connoisseur, an outsider who did not move in the intellectually precious, aesthetically fastidious, predominantly Whig and slightly epicene circles in which the study of classical civilization was more than a gentleman's pastime."[37] According to an unattributed paragraph in the *Examiner* on 19 May 1816, it was mortifying for well-born collectors to be confronted by a nobleman "without pretensions to *virtu*," who deeply wounded their vanity "at the prospect of a new era being effected in Art, by works too dirty for their drawing-rooms, too pure for their propensities, and too elevated for their comprehensions."[38] Elgin's emphases inevitably drew attention to their own inadequacies. Perhaps, too, there was for some of his critics a personal element: one of the published notes to *English Bards and Scotch Reviewers* observes with tart incredulity, "Lord Elgin would fain persuade us that all the figures, with and without noses, in his stone-shop, are the work of Phidias."[39]

Whether Byron's anger at Elgin's activities was fueled by distaste at his appearance or whether his scorn for "the worst, dull spoiler" provided a savage edge to the personal criticism remains uncertain, but there can be no doubt that Byron's reactions both in *Childe Harold* and *The Curse of Minerva* were informed by, and took advantage of, Elgin's Scottish origins. In *Childe Harold* Byron enjoys his satirist's privilege to declare, "Blush, Caledonia! such thy son could be! / England! I joy no child he was of thine." The poem presents an account of nationality that is confused, subtly evasive, or, perhaps, fashionably fluid, since it includes "England," "Albion," "free Britannia," and "British hands," yet clearly distinguishes between such apparently inclusive titles and Elgin's own narrow Scottishness, which personifies the land that it seems to represent: "Cold as the crags upon his native coast, / His mind as barren and his heart as hard." In *The Curse of Minerva,* as the manuscript shows, Byron finally resisted a further insistence on Elgin's nationality since he tried out "the Scotchman's name" and then "the Scot's dull name" before settling on the received version, "The insulted wall sustains his hated name."[40]

The specific introduction of naming is richly ironical. On the surface, Byron is alluding to the fact that Elgin inscribed his name on the Acropolis: such unhappy insistence once again links Elgin with a public infamy, but it also allows Britain the opportunity to issue a disclaimer in its own "injur'd name." The notes give expression to this complex of reactions, stating: "The most unblushing impudence could hardly go farther than to affix the name of its plunderer to the walls of the Acropolis; while the wanton and useless defacement of the whole range of the basso-relievos, in one compartment of the temple, will never permit that name to be pronounced by an observer without execration."[41] Interestingly, the poet was very exact in his own permissions for that name to be pronounced: *The Curse of Minerva* is explicit, but *Childe Harold* takes care not to include the name in the text of the poem but to confine identification to the prose notes. The distinction was obvious to at least one contemporary writer (anonymous but later identified as George Ellis) who notices in the *Quarterly Review* of March 1812 that Lord Elgin was "very plainly designated in the text, and actually named in the notes."[42] The further irony (to be explored below) is that Byron is vituperating Elgin for a practice of which he himself had been famously guilty.

The Importance of Place

Byron's rhetorical strategies are particularly devoted to emphasizing a sense of place. The celebrated rebuke of Elgin in *Childe Harold* involves the invocation of an appropriate Scottish geography that both informs his uncivilized behavior and is an appropriately bleak location for a plunderer so lacking in sensibility or imagination. What gives weight to this judgment is the poet's own presentation of himself as firmly and unarguably part of the disputed scene in Athens itself: "Here let me sit upon this massy stone, / The marble column's yet unshaken base."[43] While this position among the ruins is a traditional setting for melancholy musings, it also offers a firm base for informed observation. This centering of the narrator implies solidity and reliability of observation while it also implies familiarity as a main source of its authority. In *Childe Harold* this is further enforced by the use of annotation that supplements a poetic engagement with Greece and the Greek example by the collaborative evidence of prose, which at times extends to provide alternative essays. Most significantly of all, perhaps, Byron includes in the notes to *Childe Harold* two prose pieces dated 23 January and 17 March 1811, both of which bear the heading "Franciscan Convent, Athens," which, according to A. H. Smith, "stood for Western civilization." Indeed the convent had once been inhabited by John Galt, a writer who published the satirical poem *The Atheniad* in 1820 and a biography of Byron in 1830. Byron himself lived at the convent for most of his stay in Athens. A similar claim is being made when *The Curse of Minerva* is headed "Athens: Capuchin Convent, *March 17, 1811.*" The date and location are precisely the same as that for the second prose piece in the notes to *Childe Harold*, since *Capuchin* is another term for *Franciscan.*[44]

Both canto 2 of *Childe Harold* and *The Curse of Minerva* begin with an evocation of Athens and the Acropolis that includes Athena; the opening passage of *The Curse of Minerva* was later appropriated by Byron himself to introduce *The Corsair* (1814) where its picturesque orientalism gives preliminary expression to a distinctively Byronic sentimental topography. Byron took pains to provide such a sense of authenticity; although the location and date at the head of the text seem to indicate that *The Curse of Minerva* was an Athenian production, the manuscript evidence strongly suggests that although the opening lines were written while he was living in Greece the rest of the poem was added after his return to England.[45] The poem may owe its origins to feelings that can be traced to his time in Athens, but the history of its gradual composition suggests a relation to its raw materials that was more extended and dispersed than the dateline indicates. In both cases the poem's sense of its own sense of place, its deliberate founding in the actualities of Athens itself, provides a base from which the disruptive effects of Elgin may be watched and criticized. Byron's description of "the room" in which the broken marbles are displayed is not only a pointed analysis of a contemporary group of spectators but also an essay in the politics of cultural dislocation. The paradoxes of Byron's account are, on the surface, amusing examples of satirical observation; however, the passage as a whole suggests a mismatch not only between the spectators and the marbles but also between the marbles and their location. The contrast between the brawny brutes and the objects of their stupid wonder, the disparities in scale between the languid maids and the giant statues, contribute to a general sense of alienation. The marbles are out of place because they have been displaced, or misplaced, or because they are, *literally*, out of place. Byron's case is not so much aesthetic as it is focused on the importance of place. As he later wrote in a public letter of March 1821 to John Murray, "I opposed—and will ever oppose—the robbery of ruins—from Athens to instruct the English in Sculpture—(who are as capable of Sculpture as the Egyptians are of skating) but why did I do so?—The *ruins* are as poetical in Piccadilly as they were in the Parthenon—but the Parthenon and it's rock are less so without them.—Such is the Poetry of Art."[46]

An illuminating contemporary French perspective is provided by François-René, vicomte de Chateaubriand, a traveler, diplomat, and an essentially conservative writer who had spent some years in England during his youth and later (briefly) worked in Napoléon's embassy in Rome. Chateaubriand commented on the experience of Athens after Elgin's activities when he visited the Acropolis in the company of the French consul, Louis-François-Sébastien Fauvel, who had given him a room that included casts of the Parthenon Marbles: "The English who have come to Athens since Lord Elgin's visit have themselves deplored these dire consequences of such an unthinking love of the arts."[47] This reaction may have been influenced by French considerations: certainly, "An English Student" controverted Chateaubriand's claims and definitions in a detailed response printed in the *Examiner* on 1 December 1811.[48] According to this interpretation, Chateaubriand's "English" (*Anglais*) and their reported opinions were not representative: "What English? A few young Noblemen, who, after having trotted up Mount Hymettus, would perhaps lament, from mere politeness, to Monsieur Chateaubriand, with all the indifference of colloquial thoughtlessness, that the Parthenon was not perfect for their own immediate gratification."[49] According to the French interpretation, one of the unfortunate consequences of this ill-considered *amour des arts* (love of the arts) was the state of the Acropolis itself; another was to be seen in London where, claims Chateaubriand, the dislocated monuments were disadvantaged by English light: "If the monuments of Athens are torn from the places for which they were made, they will not only lose part of their relative beauty but their actual beauty and will [also] be diminished. It is the light alone that brings out the delicacy of certain lines and certain colors; since this light is missing under English skies, these lines and colors must disappear or remain hidden."[50] Although Chateaubriand may not have personally seen the marbles in London, his account of Athens was based on his own travels, and he knew from experience how the English climate might achieve its own effects, which were quite different from those of the original Greek locations. A work of art was not merely a transportable object or a possession but something whose *very identity* was materially altered by surrounding circumstances and contexts.

This case had already been made with particular exactness and eloquence by another Frenchman, Antoine-Chrysostôme Quatremère de Quincy, a sculptor, archaeologist, and authority on the fine arts who played a significant part in the arguments that accompanied the founding of the Louvre and its translation into the Musée Napoléon and in the later controversies concerning the reception and display of the Elgin collection.[51] *The New Oxford Companion to Literature in French* characterizes Quatremère as "a striking example of the persistence of classical precepts, which, despite tentative modifications, he largely reiterated," but this generalization does not do full justice to the subtlety and force of the arguments with which he defended Rome against the claims of Napoléon, insisting on the fragile but inviolable uniqueness of its identity: "The Antiquities of Rome are a great book, of which time has destroyed or dispersed the pages." The city expresses a complexity that could only be infringed or weakened if parts of it were removed for display in museums; necessarily this would be inferior to Rome itself, which was more complete and authentic than any alleged "museum":

> The true museum of Rome, the museum of which I am speaking, is, it is true, composed of statues, of colossi, of temples, of obelisks, of triumphal columns, of baths, of circuses, of amphitheaters, of triumphal arches, of tombs, of stucco decoration, of frescoes, of bas-reliefs, of inscriptions, of ornamental fragments, of building materials, of furniture, of utensils, etc., etc., but it is also composed fully as much of places, of sites, of mountains, of quarries, of ancient roads, of the placing of ruined towns, of geographical relationships, of the inner connections of all these objects to each other, of memories, of local traditions, of still prevailing customs, of parallels and comparisons which can only be made in the country itself.[52]

This formulation acknowledges the artifacts that might be found in a traditional collection, although it does much to undermine the feasibility of such an enterprise by the copiousness of its range and by the relentless inclusiveness of its cataloging that breaks down after eighteen items into the weary acknowledgment "etc., etc." It should be evident, too, that colossi, temples, baths, and amphitheaters could not be included within the walls of a single building or institution, so any museum would at best be notionally representative, a miniature and highly selective anthology of the unclassifiable diversity of a city such as Rome. In this sense, the only true representative of the city is the city itself. Quatremère's rhetoric has directed his readers to such a conclusion even before he claims that a proper museum would include such uncontainable elements as mountains, quarries, and even places themselves. The sentence goes on to speak not only of objects but of their relations both to one another and to the places in which they have their being—"geographical relationships... the inner connections of all these objects to each other." This redefinition continues by including not only the relations between objects but also the relations between objects and the observer. Finally, it affirms that such acts of connection do not allow for the acquisitive translations without which the collection or the "museum" cannot come into existence: such parallels and comparisons "can only be made in the country itself." Even if the Catholic Quatremère was here defending Rome against the depredations of Napoléon and his agents, the French commissioners,[53] even if his rhetoric was designed for this particular moment of crisis, and even if his taste could not easily admit the new or the radical, his account of a deeper layer of relationship and of the delicate connective tissue between works of art and their originating contexts expresses a discomfort with the concept of a museum that is prophetically critical, and which can now be applied to the status of the Elgin Marbles with an appropriateness that he might never have imagined.

Although he was writing even before Elgin had begun his work, Quatremère's formulation is of particular importance. Whatever its motivations and its own contexts, it expresses with persuasive fullness and exactness the case for leaving certain artworks where they were. Quatremère's later role in the Louvre and Paris (where he became secrétaire-perpétuel of the Académie des beaux-arts), and even in London (where he eventually endorsed the transplanted marbles), is much less significant than the fact that he, together with Chateaubriand, represents the French perspective and influence. The forces that generated the scope of the new British Museum, and of the Elgin collection within it, were partly shaped and at times accelerated by the French example and especially by that of the Louvre, which for a while changed its title to the Musée Napoléon.[54] To some extent, Choiseul-Gouffier and Elgin had contended against each other; French observers such as Chateaubriand were acutely aware of rival British enterprises; and the English measured themselves against the performances of the French, not least through the responses and artistic judgments of experts such as Quatremère, the sculptor Canova who had been invited to "restore" the marbles, and Ennio Quirino Visconti, curator of antiquities at the Musée Napoléon and commissioned author of *Lettre...à un Anglais,* which was published as an appendix to the third edition of Elgin's *Memorandum on the Subject of the Earl of Elgin's Pursuits in Greece* (1815). On the surface, the early development of the British Museum was both opportunistic and, to a point, accidental. According to Ian Jenkins, "The material culture of the great civilisations of antiquity was not gathered out of any sustained motive for national self-aggrandisement, but rather through a series of remarkable accidents."[55] These accidents were centered on and supplemented by the activities of a number of powerful individual personalities. This process of accumulation seems conveniently free from ideological imperatives and characteristically British in its preference for the unplanned and the pragmatic over the programmed and deliberately cultivated acquisition of artifacts. As Jenkins's lucid history also demonstrates, however, the British Museum was, at least partly, assembled as an act of patriotic self-assertion in which British collectors acknowledged the presence and example of the French by way of competition.

Competing with the French

The French are often part of expressed English concerns, especially where the justification of the Elgin collection is at stake. Elgin himself is quite explicit about this on a number of occasions. For example, on 7 May 1802 he warned Lusieri, "I hear that French frigates will soon be coming into the archipelago.

Every moment is therefore very precious in securing our acquisitions." On 9 August he wrote with even more urgency that "the French have it in their minds to occupy themselves immensely with Greece, both in the matter of the arts and in politics." His sense of panic and competitive anxiety is palpable, causing him to note that "artists will be sent into Greece, not without the hope of preventing the completion of my work, and of my collections, and not even without the hope of presenting the same subjects to the public before my works can appear."[56] Again, he is motivated by consciousness of the French in a letter to Lord Keith, who commanded the fleet in the Mediterranean and whom he approached for material help: "Now if you would allow a ship of war of size to convoy the Commissary's ship and stop a couple of days at Athens to get away a most valuable piece of architecture at my disposal there you could confer upon me the greatest obligation I could receive and do a very essential service to the Arts in England. Bonaparte has not got such a thing from all his thefts in Italy."[57] This language is almost embarrassingly free from self-awareness: what might be a "theft" for Bonaparte would be immune from the demeaning implications of such a definition for Keith and for Elgin and would effect "a very essential service to the Arts in England." Perhaps it is unfair to scrutinize Elgin's correspondence with this severity and to point to its self-contradictions and shifts of motive and posture or to its vacillations between private gratification and the more altruistic claims of abstract public responsibilities. Yet its central uncertainties (both here and elsewhere) draw one's attention to a discord at the very heart of the enterprise itself and to the awkward way in which fear of Napoléon and resentment of his achievements exercised a dramatically mobilizing influence on some of the principals.[58] As one writer expressed it, "The fact is, the French are jealous of our good fortune in having secured those inspired productions by Lord Elgin's energy; which puts us above them, notwithstanding all their selections in Italy, Germany, and Spain, as to a School for Art."[59]

There were recurrent rumors that Napoléon actually had intentions of acquiring the Parthenon sculptures for the Louvre, where they were intended to provide further evidence of the centrality of Paris both in taste and acquisitive prowess. As early as 1809 Haydon wrote in his diary that "Buonaparte would have had them the moment he had the power; the French had actually began to take them down before the revolution."[60] Galt, who was in Athens in 1810 when Lusieri was in the process of arranging for a major shipment, reported that Fauvel "was no doubt ambitious to obtain these precious fragments for the Napoleon Museum at Paris; and certainly exerted all his influence to get the removal of them interdicted."[61] Byron's friend Hobhouse recorded a French plan that the entire Theseion should be removed to Paris.[62] Similar considerations influenced others: opening the parliamentary debate on 23 February 1816, Chancellor of the Exchequer Nicholas Vansittart, who had corresponded with Elgin and who had been involved in preliminary negotiations, "saw no prospect but, in the course of a short time, these exquisite works of art must be dispersed, or disposed of to foreign purchasers," while

Henry Bankes, who opened the second debate on 7 June 1816, declared that the "greatest desire . . . had been evinced by the government of France to become possessed of them."[63] There was a time when these potential rivals might have included what Hamilton called "the Sovereigns of Europe," causing Elgin to acknowledge "the importance they attach to the possession of objects of art."[64] One of these was probably Ludwig of Bavaria, who had circumvented Britain's prince regent in buying the Aigina Marbles. He had visited London in 1814 and left a deposit in case the Elgin collection was rejected by Parliament.[65] Perhaps the references to "foreign princes" and "foreign purchasers" by Vansittart and by John William Ward, who had been in Parliament since 1802, were conditioned by knowledge of this fact or by a sense of international competition, but the central and most influential rivalry was with the French.[66] In this way, there was at least an element of the competitive in British interest in the acquisition and purchase of the marbles, even if Elgin himself was inconsistent both in his motivation and his actions. The argument finds classic expression in a letter from Sydney Smith written in December 1816: "I read yesterday the evidence of the Elgin Marble Committee. Lord Elgin has done a very useful thing in taking them away from the Turks. Do not throw pearls to swine; and take them away from swine when they are so thrown. They would have been destroyed there, or the French would have had them. He is underpaid for them."[67] Smith was a man of liberal views and humane sympathies, yet his response to the question of an appropriate location for the Elgin Marbles makes no allowance for national rights or for the claims of Greek, or even Athenian, patriotic sentiment. Such local considerations are eliminated from an equation in which the Turks and the French are, in their different ways, both unsuited to the needs of the sculptures that are better understood by the Select Committee and by Elgin himself, who "has done a very useful thing in taking them away from the Turks."

In 1815 after Napoléon had finally been defeated at Waterloo, Robert Banks Jenkinson, British prime minister and second earl of Liverpool, wrote from London to Robert Stewart Castlereagh, the foreign secretary, who was in Paris:

> Hamilton will go with the messenger from London who carries the despatches of this day. He will explain to you the strong sensation in this country on the subject of the spoliation of statues and pictures. The Prince Regent is desirous of getting some of them for a museum or a gallery here. The men of taste and vertu encourage this idea. The reasonable part of the world are for a general restoration to the original possessors; but they say, with truth, that we have a better title to them than the French, if legitimate war gives a title to such objects: and they blame the policy of leaving the trophies of the French victories at Paris, and making that capital in future the center of the arts.[68]

Hamilton was William Richard Hamilton, once private secretary to Elgin, who was now undersecretary for foreign affairs at the British embassy in

Paris. Liverpool's letter admits elements that were becoming more important to the argument: the fact that the marbles might be included in a public collection ("a museum or a gallery here"), the sponsoring interest of the prince regent (who had earlier bid unsuccessfully for the Aigina Marbles),[69] the opinions of "men of taste and vertu," the debate on "spoliation" and "restoration," and, finally, the contrast between legitimate and illegitimate trophies and the reluctance to allow Paris to be recognized as "the center of the arts." The French, too, were aware that their own example seemed to provide pretexts for British behavior, which they could hardly sanction.

Chateaubriand had already addressed this issue in his account of contemporary Athens: "It is claimed that Lord Elgin excused himself by saying that he had only followed our example. It is true that the French took from Italy her statues and paintings; but they did not mutilate her temples in order to tear out the bas-reliefs, they merely followed the example of the Romans who plundered Greece of her masterpieces of painting and sculpture."[70] The clear distinctions of the contrast formulated here enraged "An English Student," who remarked on the apparent national bias by which "Lord Elgin was censured for what he called *ravaging* the Parthenon" and for committing acts of mutilation, while Choiseul-Gouffier was praised for "a mere detaching" that "shewed a noble passion for the Arts."[71] Whatever its justification, Chateaubriand's argument suggests what is elsewhere evident: that alleged models for Napoléon's artistic appropriations had not been provided by classical Greece so much as by classical Rome. Perhaps one of his exemplars was Sulla, who was responsible for partially sacking Athens in 86 B.C. and whose triumphal return to Rome from Athens had been described by Plutarch (although, alternatively, Byron was reminded of the greed of Verres, who had been governor of Sicily in 73–71 B.C. and whose rapacity and acquisitive taste for Greek art were notorious); this was a particularly noticeable instance of Chateaubriand's "Romans who plundered Greece."[72] Chateaubriand, however, was careful to distinguish between the booty of such expeditions ("masterpieces of painting and sculpture") and Elgin's "monuments of Athens." The difference is clearly formulated in the description of Elgin's booty as "arrachés aux lieux pour lesquels ils étaient faits"[73] (torn from the places for which they were made): the brutality of "arrachés" speaks of acts of violence that cannot be accepted even within the permissive framework of the Sullan precedent. Even Sulla, it seems, confined his appetite to objects that were conveniently portable. After discussing the inappropriateness of London as a setting for the Parthenon Marbles, Chateaubriand concludes by addressing a variety of other considerations, including the claims of patriotism: "Moreover, I will admit that the interest of France, the glory of our native country, and numerous other reasons might demand the transplantation of the monuments conquered by our arms; but the fine arts themselves, as being on the side of the defeated and numbered among the captives, have perhaps the right to be distressed at their lot."[74] Here Chateaubriand allows himself to admit a sentimental qualification: indeed, the sentence devotes its second half to recognizing the alternative rights of the fine arts ("the fine arts themselves"); however, these alternative claims are compromised by the presence of doubt ("perhaps") and, more expansively, by the assertion that the fine arts are, without qualification it seems, at the mercy of conquerors and possessors, perennially "on the side of the defeated and numbered among the captives." The rhetoric of the first half of the sentence has already advanced several significant factors including the interest and the glory of France, which could be supported by "numerous other reasons"; it also makes telling use of the image of war and its conquests, which prevails throughout both parts of the sentence and forms an essential part of the contention between France and England and the debate concerning the destiny of the Elgin collection.

Whatever its qualifications, Chateaubriand's imagery was certainly appropriate to French imperial ambitions. The assembling and construction of the collection of the Louvre, particularly as it was transformed into the Musée Napoléon, had recurrently insisted on its military significance. Art and arms were not opposed; rather, the possession of masterpieces was a proof and an indication of superior military prowess. Even if Chateaubriand had regarded art as ultimately on the side of the defeated, the official policy emphasized the taste and acquisitive powers of the conqueror. The agenda was explicit. On 31 August 1794 it was unblushingly articulated by the abbé Henri-Baptiste Grégoire, constitutional bishop of Blois, an influential deputy, a strong supporter of the French Revolution, and a powerful and regular contributor to its debates: "Certainly, if our victorious armies penetrate into Italy the removal of the Apollo Belvedere and of the Farnese Hercules would be the most brilliant conquest."[75] In 1797 the painter, engraver, and architect Louis-Pierre Baltard wrote, "The National Museum and its precious contents are recompense for the lives and blood of our fellow citizens spilled on the field of honour. French artists are worthy of this prize; they fully recognize its importance."[76] The *tricolore* was displaced by "an ornamental arrangement of captured enemy arms and battle standards": "A trophy of arms and flags taken from the enemy decorate the door of the salon. In the middle, an inscription reads: 'To the Army of Italy.' The sight of this trophy warmed my blood, the words brought tears to my eyes.... One day we will raise monuments of marble and bronze to our warriors. Unnecessary efforts! The true and lasting monuments to their glory will be in our museums."[77]

This emphasis on the power of arms and on the public virtues of conquest was consolidated and demonstrated by a series of triumphal processions that acknowledged the Roman model but asserted its own significance. For example, there was the elaborate festival of 10 August 1793, organized and choreographed by the painter Jacques-Louis David, who at an earlier stage had opposed the idea of a museum and protested against what he regarded as the "plunder" of Italy. Now he was producing what Andrew McClellan has called "his masterpiece of Revolutionary pageantry."[78] On 27 July 1798 another festival was organized to celebrate and publicly note the arrival of the third convoy of artworks from Italy. An inscription on the cart that carried the *Apollo Belvedere* and the *Clio* proclaimed, "Both will reiterate our battles, our victories." The central point was not forgotten: "Meanwhile a song composed for the occasion resounded with talk of prize trophies, vanquished tyrants, and the Republic's eternal right to its plunder."[79] A French history of this period of acquisition published in 1902 is suggestively entitled *Les conquêtes artistiques de la Révolution et de l'Empire*.[80] Cecil Gould's *Trophy of Conquest* records such emphases in detail and charts the growth of a collection with unequivocal reference to its military origins and status. Gould refers to "looting," "the confiscatory organization," and "raiding parties," notes that the confiscations "were a direct result of aggressive warfare," and cites Wellington's judgment that these "specimens of the arts" were "obtained by military concessions, of which they are the trophies." The index provides further examples of how pointedly Gould's history interprets this process of accumulation in terms of "plunder."[81]

It was within such a context that British ministers and supporters of the arts sought to establish a claim that both surpassed those of Napoléon and his museum and, at the same time, undermined those very premises on which the Napoleonic bid for public significance had been based. The prime minister therefore advised his foreign secretary in this way: "It is most desirable...to remove them [the Napoleonic collections] if possible from France, as, whilst in that country, they must necessarily have the effect of keeping up the remembrance of their former conquests, and of cherishing the military spirit and vanity of the nation."[82] The British claim was based on superiority in arms and yet attempted to evade or transcend military implications. One endorsing voice was that of William Wordsworth, who was not yet poet laureate but who increasingly expressed himself as if his opinions were granted such an official validation. In "Ode: The Morning of the Day Appointed for a General Thanksgiving, January 18, 1816," he addressed God from a national perspective and asked "what transcendent monument" might be an appropriate offering in gratitude for the victory over Napoléon at Waterloo:

> —Not work of hands; but trophies that may reach
> To highest Heaven—the labour of the Soul;
> That builds, as thy unerring precepts teach,
> Upon the internal conquests made by each,
> Her hope of lasting glory for the whole.[83]

This formulation celebrates military victory while it aspires toward a situation in which no further external victories would be necessary. The transfer of necessary virtues is made even more explicit in the fourth stanza from Wordsworth's "Ode Composed in January 1816," known, rather misleadingly, as "Ode 1814" since 1845:

> But garlands wither; festal shows depart,
> Like dreams themselves; and sweetest sound—

(Albeit of effect profound)

It was — and it is gone!

Victorious England! bid the silent Art

Reflect, in glowing hues that shall not fade,

Those high achievements; even as she arrayed

With second life the deed of Marathon

Upon Athenian walls;

So may she labour for thy civic halls:

And be the guardian spaces

Of consecrated places,

As nobly graced by Sculpture's patient toil;

And let imperishable Columns rise

Fixed in the depths of this courageous soil;

Expressive signals of a glorious strife,

And competent to shed a spark divine

Into the torpid breast of daily life; —

Records on which, for pleasure of all eyes,

The morning sun may shine

With gratulation thoroughly benign!

The original version of these lines was more immediate in its responses than later, more prudential revisions, and more pointedly adversarial. Wordsworth's choice of "trophies" involved an obvious contrast with the more militaristic trophies exhibited by the Louvre. Much of this precisely targeted antagonism was lost, as "imperishable trophies" became the more indeterminate "imperishable structures" in 1827 and finally "imperishable Columns" in 1845, and the heavily insistent final repetition of "trophies" was avoided by the substitution of "Records" in 1827. The same pattern of tactical retreat can be found in the alteration of the title, which withdraws the poem from the informing context of the aftermath to Waterloo and strategically relocates it at a date when Napoléon posed a threat that was less immediate. In the original, the recent achievement of Waterloo is equated with the Athenian defeat of the Persians at Marathon in 490 B.C.; and here the pattern of the argument equates the French with the Persians and the English with the Athenians themselves. Wordsworth's hope is centered on the inspirational force of the whole range of Greek art, which was integrally related to the political expression of Greek patriotism. His prayer seems to suggest that the Parthenon might provide a model for English administrative architecture ("thy civic halls" were, in fact, much influenced by Greek examples).[84] Although Wordsworth's diction prefers to evade the specific, it is clear that in part at least he is referring to the Acropolis and, in particular, to the Parthenon ("consecrated places"); the stanza is, among other things, a patriotic prayer based on firmly held beliefs about the moral value of the arts. In its preference for a victory that substitutes a nonmilitaristic procedure for the French conflation of military and artistic superiority ("warfare waged with desperate mind / Against the life of virtue in mankind"),[85] Wordsworth's formulation is in keeping with certain expressions of British opinion, although, like them, he seems untroubled by the methods through which the Elgin collection was actually acquired.

In January 1817, the following year, the case was given explicit support in an anonymous essay in the *Gentleman's Magazine*:

> And we are affected at that revolution of empires which has occasioned their transportation from their native city to a country which, in the age of Pericles, was esteemed the most barbarous of all countries, even if its very existence was known. They are, however, a proud trophy, because their display in the British metropolis is the result of public taste; and also a pleasing one, because they are not the price of blood, shed in wanton or ambitious wars.[86]

Not only is the triumph allegedly bloodless but the poem also implies, or even claims, that the English are the descendants of the Greeks and that London has succeeded Athens as the defender of Western freedom. According to Ian Jenkins, "Waterloo became England's Battle of Marathon, and acquisition of the Elgin Marbles by the British Museum was hailed as confirmation of the ancient claim that liberty and the arts rise and fall together."[87]

It is to illustrate that identification that Benedetto Pistrucci designed a set of medals to mark the victory at Waterloo depicting the head of the prince regent placed protectively but possessively above the pillared ruins of the Parthenon; the reverse sides of the medals were devoted to, specifically, a celebration of the Elgin collection, which once formed an integral part of the Parthenon's patriotic display but was now transplanted to London.[88] The identification of Georgian London with Periclean Athens may have been fortuitous in the first instance but its significance did not elude contemporary observers. During the second parliamentary debate on 7 June 1816, for instance, John Wilson Croker argued for the purchase of Elgin's marbles by reference to the effect that the marbles could be thought to have had on the life of the city for which they were designed and to the influence that they might exert on a London that had acquired them. Although Croker was a member of Parliament and secretary to the admiralty, he is now best remembered as one of the most powerful voices of the *Quarterly Review* (which he had helped to found in 1809), where he was often caustic in his defense of conservative positions. A member of the Select Committee, he often credited with having written its influential report. *Hansard* reported part of his speech as follows:

> The bargain was for the benefit of the public, for the honour of the nation, for the promotion of national arts, for the use of the national artists, and even for the advantage of our manufactures, the excellence of which depended on the progress of the arts in the country. It was singular that when 2,500 years ago, Pericles was adorning Athens with those very works, some of which we are now about to acquire, the same cry of economy was raised against him, and the same answer that

he then gave might be repeated now, that it was money spent for the use of the people, for the encouragement of arts, the increase of manufactures, the prosperity of trades, and the encouragement of industry; not merely to please the eye of the man of taste, but to create, to stimulate, to guide the exertions of the artist, the mechanic, and even the labourer, and to spread through all the branches of society a spirit of improvement, and the means of a sober and industrious affluence.[89]

To acquire these masterpieces for the state was not to deprive another nation of its heritage but to make provision for the future not only of English arts but also, it would seem, of "manufactures," "trades," and "industry." As a statement that assumes the energizing influence of good art in general and of high culture in particular, this would be hard to surpass. It is also of special interest because it shows very clearly how the presumed values of Greek art could be translated into terms that were considered appropriate for a developing English economy in the nineteenth century. One encounters here familiar concerns about money well spent even on the "arts"; models of an organic society that would include the artist, the mechanic, and "even the labourer"; and appeals to the ideal of "a spirit of improvement" and "a sober and industrious affluence," which seem much more appropriate to the forces that would soon create a Victorian society than to classical Athens. Perhaps we should remember that much of this debate was affected by the pragmatic and that even the highest ideals are sometimes influenced by the claims of the expedient.

Croker's speech properly addressed itself to financial concerns, since these had been expressed by other speakers, and it was necessary to engage with the arguments raised, for example, in the cartoon by George Cruikshank that bears the legend "The Elgin Marbles or John Bull buying *Stones* at the time his numerous family want *Bread!!*"[90] In the course of the first debate Henry Brougham, who had assiduously represented the Whig position throughout the parliamentary session, had also alluded to the biblical model when he asserted that if "we could not give them bread we ought not to indulge ourselves in the purchase of stones." Viscount Milton, who had established himself as a leading figure of opposition, later drew attention to the financial pressures of the moment "in which the want of subsistence was the cause of riot and disturbances in many parts of the country."[91] Croker had argued, however, that, ultimately, the larger gains and advantages should prevail. Similar arguments were advanced in the final paragraph of the *Report from the Select Committee,* which was widely reprinted at the time (for example, in the *Quarterly Review* and in the *Examiner*), and has often been attributed to Croker himself. The report contends that the cultivation of the fine arts is intimately connected "with the advancement of every thing valuable in science, literature, and philosophy":

In contemplating the importance and splendour to which so small a republic as Athens rose, by the genius and energy of her citizens, exerted in the path of such studies, it is impossible to overlook how transient the memory and fame of extended empires and of mighty conquerors are, in comparison of those who have rendered inconsiderable States eminent, and who have immortalized their own names by these pursuits. But if it be true, as we learn from history and experience, that free governments afford a soil most suitable to the production of native talent, to the maturing of the powers of the human mind, and to the growth of every species of excellence, by opening to merit the prospect of reward and distinction, no country can be better adapted than our own to afford an honourable asylum to these monuments of the school of Phidias, and of the administration of Pericles: where, secure from further injury and degradation, they may receive that admiration and homage to which they are entitled, and serve in return as models and examples to those who, by knowing how to revere and appreciate them, may learn first to imitate, and ultimately to rival them.[92]

Here again, the connection between Athens and London is boldly asserted since, it is claimed, "no country can be better adapted than our own" to providing a home for monuments that were produced under the fostering influence of a free government. Byron, in *The Curse of Minerva* (which had not been published officially at the time), regarded this potential acquisition not as an expression of freedom but as a contradiction of the traditional British role as a supporter of liberty, and a number of other dissenting voices had advanced or imagined the force of Greek claims. The Select Committee, however, like Croker himself and like Wordsworth, expressed no doubts about the rightness of this "inheritance." The title "New Athens" was a trope and often a license for a variety of operations sometimes based on historical interpretation, sometimes on realpolitik presented as history. In spite of the claims of London, hopeful versions of Athens were also located, for example, in Potsdam, Edinburgh, and even parts of Paris (where it jostled, interestingly, with the model of Rome).[93] In all of these identifications, it was assumed that a flourishing of the arts, which might include public architecture, was a sign of civic virtue.

The sonorities of this prose together with its aspirational tone might remind one that it is officially the product of a committee (although it may have been largely or completely composed by an individual member of that group). It emerges as a summary and a recommendation after a consideration of the factors involved in acquisition and other alternative arguments, while it bears a close similarity both to the opinions expressed by Croker and to the views of many contemporaries. Once again, the French example is troublingly apposite. If London could afford "an honourable asylum," Paris could claim that the French would look after the appropriated works better than their original owners and that they were acting in the "cause of Art." Nearly twelve years before, the abbé Grégoire had articulated this view in terms that were clearly political and ideological: "Should the masterpieces of the Greek republics decorate the country of slaves? The French republic should be their final home."[94] Coming from someone who notably contributed to the debate against slavery, a defender of the rights of Jews and of the oppressed in general, a denouncer of despotism, and the coiner of the term *vandalism*, this apparently unquestioning belief in the values of French liberty may seem a little surprising. This attitude, or policy, had been expressed with chilling force by Luc Barbier, the minor painter and military officer who had accompanied a large convoy from Belgium: "The fruits of genius are the patrimony of liberty.... For too long these masterpieces have been soiled by the gaze of servitude. It is in the bosom of a free people that the legacy of great men must come to rest; the tears of slaves are unworthy of their glory."[95] A similar attitude was expressed by Dominique-Vivant Denon, an artist and diplomat who had traveled memorably both in the vicinity of Naples and in Egypt, and who was made director of the Louvre by Napoléon in November 1802, where he proved both efficient and fiercely partisan. Denon was reported as saying, with characteristically uncompromising patriotic pride, that "they have no eyes to see them with, France will always prove by her superiority in the arts that the masterpieces were better here than elsewhere."[96]

"Rescuing" and "Englishing" the Marbles

The case advanced by the Select Committee accepts such assumptions and follows prevailing fashion in pursuing a pattern that is not only Hellenic but specifically Athenian. Even when Towneley's purchases had been Greek, either directly or indirectly they had come from Italy; now the source and the model to be followed was provided by Athens itself. Comparisons with the Renaissance were also offered: "caught by the novelty, attracted by the beauty, and enamoured of the perfection of those newly disclosed treasures, they imbibed the genuine spirit of excellence, and transfused it into their own compositions." The arrival of Elgin's efforts in London would have an effect similar to that of the "abundant harvest" of those who "made gigantic advances" under the impact of the rediscovery of the classical and its values.[97] Hugh Hammersley, who became a member of Parliament in 1812 and was characteristically critical of public spending, questioned some of the assumptions behind this parallel and suggested that the marbles should be held "only in trust till they are demanded by the present, or any future, possessors of the city of Athens." Hammersley's doubts and reservations found some support (the vote after the first debate was eighty-two to thirty), but they were outnumbered by the views of those who, for whatever reason, wanted to acquire Elgin's collection.[98] Many of these members of Parliament linked an admiration for the qualities of Greek art with the fear and disgust so vividly expressed in the previous century by James Stuart and Nicholas Revett, who had published the first volume of their influential *The Antiquities of Athens* in 1762, where they characterized the Turks as "professed enemies to the Arts."[99] Similar arguments were made in 1811 when it was claimed that the "exquisite Remains" in Athens were dangerously neglected: this was a perilous location "where they were considered as mere marble, where their beauties were unfelt, where they were daily suffering destruction, where one half of them had been pounded into lime for mortar, and the other half gradually approaching the same usage." Whatever the damage involved in Elgin's inter-vention, this was a minor consideration when set against the fact that his timely actions had secured "the eternal salvation of some part of the Pedi-ment, the greatest part of the Metopes, and nearly the whole Frieze."[100] Less than five years later, the Select Committee was also in tune with a strong ele-ment in contemporary thinking that argued for London as the safest location for the Parthenon Marbles, a place where they would find (in the words of the report) "an honourable asylum." The need for the marbles to be accepted as refugees from a variety of abuses was one of the contentions of Henry Bankes, chairman of the Select Committee, an original member of the Parliamentary Committee for Taste, and a trustee of the British Museum, whose interests he normally represented in the House of Commons. Bankes, a member of Parliament since 1780, had a reputation both for expressing independent views and for being, in Elgin's words, "a stiff stickler...for public money." Bankes observed, "The climate was no doubt less severe than our northern one; but still they were then making rapid strides towards decay, and the natives displayed such wanton indifference as to fire at them as marks. They had also been continually suffering, from the parts carried off by enlightened travellers."[101]

Similar arguments had frequently been advanced by earlier travelers. Writing in 1768, Stephen Riou, author of *The Grecian Orders of Architec-ture,* had celebrated the achievement of Stuart, whose publications on "the genuine forms of Greek architecture" had rescued them "from that oblivion into which the senseless insults of barbarians would soon have plunged them."[102] Richard Chandler, the antiquary who had led an "Ionian Mission" for the Society of Dilettanti, had already observed the vulnerability of the Parthenon in his *Travels in Greece* (1776): "It is to be regretted that so much admirable sculpture as is still extant about this fabric should be all likely to perish, as it were immaturely, from ignorant contempt and brutal violence. Numerous carved stones have disappeared; and many, lying in the ruinous heaps, moved our indignation at the barbarism daily exercised in defacing them."[103] The perilous condition of Greek remains had also been graphically cataloged by the traveler and archaeologist Edward Dodwell, who lamented "the destructive influence of these tasteless barbarians over the splendid and interesting remains of Greek architecture." Similar cultural contrasts were later made by Haydon, who had not visited Greece himself but who cele-brated the "energetic resolution" and the "vigour of fancy" of Elgin by whose efforts the Greek marbles had been brought to "an enlightened part of the World where their future existence would be safe"; had he acted sooner, "then perhaps the most beautiful productions in the World would not have been pounded into mortar."[104] Elgin himself had told the Select Committee that "there are now in London pieces broken off within our day. And the Turks have been continually defacing the heads; and in some instances they have actually acknowledged to me, that they have pounded down the statues to convert them into mortar."[105]

Essentially, this is a central part of the justification offered by Sydney Smith; a much earlier version can be found in the letters of Lusieri himself where it is expressed in terms of desperate expediency.[106] Byron had combined anxiety for the future of the remains with a sense of their sacred function when he recorded feelingly in the notes to *Childe Harold:* "The Parthenon . . . had been a temple, a church, and a mosque. In each point of view it is an object of regard; it changed its worshippers; but still it was a place of worship thrice sacred to devotion: its violation is a triple sacrilege."[107] A similar argument was expressed by a writer (possibly Robert Southey) in the *Quarterly Review* who was surveying the third and fourth volumes of Clarke's *Travels in Various Countries of Europe, Asia, and Africa* (1810–23). The reviewer both contested Clarke's claim that it was "of itself, worth a journey to Athens" to see the Parthenon frieze and specifically controverted Clarke's criticism of Elgin that "he will not easily convince a candid man that they are more likely to perish when *protected* from the weather and all other violence in *London,* than when *exposed* to weather and depredations of every kind in *Athens.*"[108] Protection from danger was not the only benefit provided by transfer to London. As the reviewer made clear, rescuing the remains of the Parthenon from the effects of weather and Turkish negligence was a service to Western civilization:

> we should hold the revival of Grecian sculpture in the west a satisfactory reason for having deprived the east of treasures which it no longer understood, or any otherwise appreciated than as children value baubles. Nor can we conceive a nobler fate for works, which, however durable, must eventually perish, than to perish in the full gaze of Europe, and in the service of that art of which they are the most brilliant ornaments—leaving behind them the seeds of future works, perhaps not inferior to themselves, and having been the instruments of communicating the arts of Greece to that nation by whom her language and her spirit have been, in every age, most cultivated.[109]

Once again the celebration of Athens expresses a strong cultural preference and a deliberate identification. The suitability of England for this role is based not only on expediency or claims about the nature of the political system but also on a firm belief in the educative virtue of great art. As the *Report from the Select Committee* argued, to possess "these monuments of the school of *Phidias*" was to make it possible to "learn first to imitate, and ultimately to rival them." Throughout the debates there was a widely shared belief that the effect of access to the finest public art was beneficial both to society in general and to the work of individual artists. Such certainties inform the delight of the normally waspish Robert Hunt, a minor artist and art critic, as well as an older brother to his more celebrated sibling, author Leigh Hunt. In 1809 he told readers of the *Examiner,* "The introduction of these grand productions of ancient genius into England is a glorious era in the Fine Arts. They present a new world of beauty and taste to the eye of the young Artist, and awaken a fresh and glowing impulse in the mind of the Professor."[110] Hunt's doubling seems to combine the antiquarian or classical scholar and the practicing artist. A similar faith strongly characterizes the aesthetic responses of Haydon, who was close to the Hunts and whose contentious celebration of the virtues of the Elgin Marbles first appeared in the *Examiner* on 17 March 1816. From the start Haydon had regarded Elgin as a great public benefactor, and in his journal he greeted the eventual acquisition of the marbles in a rapturous manner that fused the personal and the patriotic: "This year [1816] the Elgin Marbles were bought and produced an Aera in public feeling." Publicly, he acknowledged his feelings for "these divine things" in terms that were explicitly religious: "I never enter among them without bowing to the Great Spirit that reigns within them. I thank God daily that I was in existence on their arrival, and will continue to do so to the end of my life." These Greek sculptures will exercise the same attractive powers as holy relics: "Pilgrims from the remotest corners of the earth will visit their shrine, and be purified by their beauty."[111] This imaginary projection attests to a widely shared belief in the influential force of great art, but it also reminds us that the whole controversy was marked from time to time by outbursts of displaced religion: the ritual origins of the original pieces were often translated into terms that carried the aura of the sacred.

In their different ways, these statements draw attention to the importance of ensuring appropriate criteria for the establishing of a taste that was properly informed. As early as 1770 the *Monthly Review* had allowed itself to hope that Stuart and Revett's *Antiquities of Athens* would "contribute much toward improving and fixing our national taste in architecture."[112] The arrival of Elgin's collection focused the attention more on models for art in general and sculpture in particular, and it was also part of a movement that envisaged that taste would no longer be confined to men of virtue or to connoisseurs but could be expressed more widely as museums opened their doors to a range of visitors. Haydon's "public feeling" not only expresses a powerful personal emotion but also welcomes the purchase of the collection as an event of national significance. This is a pluralizing and a broadening of what Hazlitt called a "taste for art."

This view was held very strongly by Haydon, whose own response deserves some attention because he exerted a strong influence on public opinion. Although Haydon's almost religious devotion to a study of Elgin's marbles was primarily motivated by his own artistic needs, his writings both in his journals and in the *Examiner* and the *Annals of the Fine Arts* interpreted their arrival as an occasion when "taste" could be taken away from the connoisseurs and the members of the Society of Dilettanti and made available to a much wider public. The obstinacy of Payne Knight and his failure to recognize the true originality of the Parthenon Marbles embodied for Haydon all the self-protective limitations that he associated with the connoisseur and the amateur of arts. Haydon's enthusiasm reads, at times, like a record of religious conversion: on one occasion, he feels "as if a divine truth had blazed inwardly upon my mind"; while at Burlington House, he records "a depth of mystery and awe."[113] His moments of truth might be compared to those visionary insights recorded by a range of travelers when they first saw with their own eyes a city of antiquity, lost or neglected; however, the diaries show an assiduity of application and an intensity of attention that attempt to prolong these moments of insight. Haydon was concerned that his own special, privileged inspirations should be much more widely available, and he campaigned for a recognition of the virtues of Elgin's collection and for its retention by the state.

At times the force of this aspiration seems almost out of keeping with the facts: "Thank God! The remains of Athens have fled for protection to England; the genius of Greece still hovers near them; may she, with her inspiring touch, give new vigour to British Art, and cause new beauties to spring from British exertions! May their essence mingle with our blood and circulate through our being."[114] Here Haydon is hoping (or praying) for an act of translation that will turn the collection into something that is imagined as almost physically English (or British). Through this process of "Englishing," or perhaps "Britishing," the stones will themselves be assimilated into the body politic and become part of the national bloodstream. This magical process of transformation is presented in ways that emphasize its oddity and difficulty while strongly expressing the wish that such a metamorphosis can be effected for the public good. The heated tone, the rhapsodic tendencies, and the personal intensity are particularly appropriate for a diary but they also appear, with some modifications, in Haydon's more public writings. Knowingly or not, he is here much closer to the German tradition established by Johann Joachim Winckelmann than to the abstractions and formalities of any report; however, Haydon too believed in the possibility of a Renaissance (or renaissance), especially for art. "I knew," he wrote, "that they would at last rouse the art of Europe from its slumber in the darkness" and "their beauty may renovate art." Again, "The Elgin Marbles will as completely overthrow the old antique, as ever one system of philosophy overthrew another more enlightened: were they lost, there would be as great a gap in the knowledge of Art, as there would have been in Philosophy, if Newton had never existed."[115]

The Brutalities of Collecting

What most of this writing, both public and private, ignores, perhaps necessarily, is the brutal and predatory origin of much collecting, a sense of which so vividly informs Byron's satirical visions. Winckelmann, the great discoverer of the values of classical art, may have been indulging both a satirical propensity and a sense of national rivalry when he made a prediction to his German correspondent Heinrich Wilhelm Muzel-Stosch on 26 February 1768. In a passage of Italian that emerges suddenly in the course of a letter otherwise written in German he imagines a future in which Rome will have become a desert because "qualche pazzo Inglese" (some mad Englishman) will have the idea of transporting the ruins to London.[116] Winckelmann's vision records, whatever its distortions, both the presence of English dealers and collectors in Rome and the powerful urge to "domesticate" and reestablish works of art under different credentials. Even the career of Charles Towneley indicates that, by definition, collectors tend to initiate and endorse the process of appropriation. Many of the great museums incorporate materials that were originally acquired in a manner that had little to do with the idealistic, or even moralistic, aspirations of the prose in which they were later celebrated. Jerome Christensen refers to "a kind of cosmetic legality…like that conferred on the Elgin Marbles, cleaned, mounted, and labelled for exhibit in the British Museum."[117] Christensen's reading is harshly critical, but it reminds us that the purity (and even the legality) of such transactions is often only apparent. Chateaubriand acknowledges something of this paradox and its psychological roots when he quickly follows his criticism of Elgin's ill-considered and selfish predilection for Greek remains with an account of his own inability to resist the temptations of stone: "Coming down from the citadel, I took a piece of the Parthenon marble; I had also collected a fragment of stone from the tomb of Agamemnon; and since then I have always taken away something from the monuments I have encountered on my travels."[118] He concedes that these were not as beautiful as those of Elgin or Choiseul-Gouffier, and he is careful to minimize them as "un morceau" (a piece) and "ces bagatelles" (these trifles); but the larger admission both humanizes his critique of Elgin's spoliations and concedes implicitly that there is a primary urge toward possession and toward the personal satisfactions of memory. The presence of stony relics confirms and validates the claims of memory: "When I see these trifles again, I retrace instantly my journeyings and my adventures; I say to myself, 'I was there, such and such happened to me.'"[119] Like Ulysses, but much more modestly and on a smaller scale, he could bring evidence of his traveling when he returned "with a dozen or so stones from Sparta, Athens, Argos, or Corinth."[120]

Others left unmentioned what Chateaubriand openly admits; however, most travelers in Greece at this period were themselves guilty of various acts of appropriation, not least those who passed stern judgment on Elgin. In *Childe Harold,* for example, Byron castigated Elgin for his presumption in associating his name with the remains of the Parthenon, but he carved his own name on a range of monuments at Sunium, Pentelikon, and Delphi, as well as (it is alleged) on the Theseion, the Monument of Lysicrates, and the Erechtheion, all on the Acropolis itself. Such personal indulgences were common to traveling Englishmen who numbered among the passports to "literary distinction" the record provided by having "scratched one's name upon a fragment of the Parthenon" (as the *Quarterly Review* had tartly expressed it).[121] Clarke provided an apparently feeling anecdote about the dismantling of the Parthenon, which Byron included in the second edition of *Childe Harold:* "When the last of the Metopes was taken from the Parthenon, and, in moving of it, great part of the superstructure with one of the triglyphs was thrown down by the workmen whom Lord Elgin employed, the Disdar, who beheld the mischief done to the building, took his pipe from his mouth, dropped a tear, and, in a supplicating tone of voice, said to Lusieri: *Τέλος!*—I was present."[122] It was the same Clarke, however, who had earlier played a major part in removing the image of Demeter from Eleusis in the face of "the superstition of the inhabitants...respecting an idol which they all regarded as the protectress of their fields." Clarke, who presented his Greek statues to Cambridge University and discussed them in a book published in 1809, had taken a fragment from the Acropolis and had bought another inscribed marble "from under the very nose of Elgin's chaplain and his host of Gothic plunderers."[123] Here, as so often, it is hard to distinguish between hypocrisy and strategic blindness. Edward Dodwell, who deplored the influence of the "tasteless" Turks, himself assembled a collection of vases that mostly went to Munich and sold various objects to the crown prince of Bavaria. According to the entry in the *Dictionary of National Biography,* Dodwell "once possessed a marble head from the west pediment of the Parthenon," yet he accused Elgin of a "devastating outrage which will never cease to be deplored."[124] Galt, who would satirize Elgin in *The Atheniad,* made arrangements with his own bankers in case there were financial difficulties for Lusieri and Elgin: "Here was a chance of the most exquisite relics in the world becoming mine, and a speculation by the sale of them in London that would realise a fortune."[125] Had Byron read this recollection, he would certainly have noticed how Galt's cupidity was stimulated not so much by the hope of possessing such "exquisite relics" as by the prospect of making a lucrative speculation.

Another example was that of Robert Smirke, who (like Joseph Mallard William Turner) was at one time considered as a draftsman for Elgin's expedition. Smirke, who later designed a special room for the Elgin collection and designed the new British Museum itself in homage to the models of Greek architecture, recorded with apparent feeling the destruction of the Parthenon: "Each stone as it fell shook the ground with its ponderous weight with a deep hollow noise; it seemed like a convulsive groan of the injured spirit of the Temple."[126] Yet he, too, collected some pieces from the Erechtheion. John Bacon Sawrey Morritt, nicknamed "Troy," a member of Parliament, master of the Yorkshire estate Rokeby, and, later, friend of Walter Scott, was one of the few contemporary observers who seemed at all sensitive to Greek opinion, but he too was explicit and ruthless in his desire for personal accumulation. He regarded Athens as "a perfect gallery of marbles," which was very pleasant for walking the streets: "Over almost every door is an antique statue or basso-rilievo.... Some we steal, some we buy, and our court is much adorned with them." From Athens he wrote home with the news that "our Greek attendant...is, I hope, hammering down the Centaurs and Lapithae." The formula "hammering down" refers to auction procedures but one cannot help noticing the unfortunate presence of other meanings and other practices that show no respect for the architectural integrity of what he calls "the old temple." It seems that Morritt would have purchased a metope and part of the Parthenon frieze for the adornment of Rokeby had he not been thwarted by Fauvel.[127]

Morritt appeared as a witness before the Select Committee, where he had the grace to admit his earlier interests, although his responsiveness to Greek feelings did not prevent him from speaking in favor of paying Elgin and retaining his collection in Britain. Many other antiquarians, antiquity hunters, and collectors acted on a basis that was entirely personal and self-gratifying; usually, there was little or no sense of the alternative rights of the Greeks or the claims of the Greek tradition. Unfortunately, for all their scholarship and targeted sensitivities, this was often equally true of French travelers such as Choiseul-Gouffier. Through the agency of Fauvel, Choiseul-Gouffier did acquire some pieces of the Parthenon. In spite of his partial success, his final collection can hardly have matched the ambitious drive of his instructions: "Do not spare any opportunity to loot anything lootable in Athens and its surrounding area. Spare neither the dead nor the living."[128]

The record is depressing; however, it shows that, even though his depredations were more extensive, Elgin was not as unusual as his reputation might suggest. That the sculptures should bear his name is a sign not of one man's unique vanity but of the origins of a much larger project of appropriation in which many of his contemporaries colluded. This, in turn, suggests significant, troubling, and largely unanswered questions about the nature of great national collections and about the assumptions concerning the national power and virtue they embody.

Notes

1. An English Student, "Grecian Marbles," *Examiner* (London), 1 December 1811, 773.

2. "Elgin Marbles" is the popular name for those marble works at the Parthenon that were removed by Lord Elgin.

3. Lord Byron, *The Curse of Minerva*, in idem, *The Complete Poetical Works*, ed. Jerome J. McGann (Oxford: Clarendon, 1980–93), 1:449 (Byron's note to line 178).

4. "Domestic Occurrences," *Gentleman's Magazine and Historical Chronicle* 87, pt. 1 (January 1817): 80.

5. Cited in A. H. Smith, "Lord Elgin and His Collection," *Journal of Hellenic Studies* 36 (1916): 345. For the growth of the classical collection at the British Museum, see Edward Miller, *That Noble Cabinet: A History of the British Museum* (London: Deutsch, 1973), 102–7; and Ian Jenkins, *Archaeologists and Aesthetes: In the Sculpture Galleries of the British Museum, 1800–1939* (London: British Museum Press, 1992), 13–29.

6. For Choiseul-Gouffier, see David Constantine, *Early Greek Travellers and the Hellenic Ideal* (Cambridge: Cambridge Univ. Press, 1984), 173–82; Richard Stoneman, *Land of Lost Gods: The Search for Classical Greece* (London: Hutchinson, 1987), 136–39; and William St. Clair, *Lord Elgin and the Marbles,* 3d rev. ed. (Oxford: Oxford Univ. Press, 1998), 63–64, 96–97, 122–25.

7. English Student, "Grecian Marbles" (note 1), 773.

8. Jacob Rothenberg, *"Descensus ad Terram": Acquisition and Reception of the*

Elgin Marbles (Ann Arbor: University Microfilms, 1967), 141–42: "Lord Elgin a fait, dans toute la Grèce, une riche moisson de précieux monumens, que j'avais longtemps et inutilement désirés; il m'est difficile de les voir entre ses mains sans un peu d'envie; mais ce doit être une satisfaction pour tous ceux qui cultivent les arts, de savoir ces chefs-d'oeuvre soustraits à la barbarie des Turcs, et conservés par un amateur éclairé qu'en fera jouir le public." See also Smith, "Lord Elgin" (note 5), 355–65.

9. This treatment concentrates on the reception of the marbles as a cultural phenomenon. For detailed analyses of individual reactions, see Grant F. Scott, *The Sculpted Word: Keats, Ekphrasis, and the Visual Arts* (Hanover, N.H.: Univ. Press of New England, 1994), esp. chap. 2; James A. W. Heffernan, *Museum of Words: The Poetics of Ekphrasis from Homer to Ashbery* (Chicago: Univ. of Chicago Press, 1993); David Bromwich, *Hazlitt: The Mind of a Critic* (New York: Oxford Univ. Press, 1983), 205–8, 389–92; Tom Paulin, *The Day-Star of Liberty: William Hazlitt's Radical Style* (London: Faber & Faber, 1998), 98–107; and Noah Heringman, "Stones So Wondrous Cheap," *Studies in Romanticism* 37 (1998): 43–62. Hazlitt's phrase occurs in his account of the Louvre under Napoléon; see William Hazlitt, *The Life of Napoleon Buonaparte, Volume One,* in idem, *The Complete Works of William Hazlitt,* ed. Percival Presland Howe (London: J. M. Dent, 1930–34), 13:213; the formulation itself is adapted from Francis Bacon.

10. For a color reproduction of Archer's painting, *The Temporary Elgin Room* (1819; London, British Museum), see Jenkins, *Archaeologists and Aesthetes* (note 5), pl. 2. For full identification of the figures, which include Haydon and West, see Smith, "Lord Elgin" (note 5), 353–54; and Jenkins, *Archaeologists and Aesthetes* (note 5), fig. 9.

11. For an explanation of "furniture value," see John Brewer, *The Pleasures of the Imagination: English Culture in the Eighteenth Century* (London: HarperCollins, 1997), 285–86; and Rothenberg, *"Descensus ad Terram"* (note 8), 67–73.

12. Cited in Brewer, *Pleasures of the Imagination* (note 11), 286.

13. For the connections between collecting and archaeology, see Ian Jenkins and Kim Sloan, *Vases and Volcanoes: Sir William Hamilton and His Collection* (London: British Museum Press, 1996); see also Suzanne L. Marchand, *Down from Olympus: Archaeology and Philhellenism in Germany, 1750–1970* (Princeton: Princeton Univ. Press, 1996). For the connections between archaeology and empire, see Ronald T. Ridley, *The Eagle and the Spade: Archaeology in Rome during the Napoleonic Era* (Cambridge: Cambridge Univ. Press, 1992); and for the connections between archaeology and creativity, see Carolyn Springer, *The Marble Wilderness: Ruins and Representation in Italian Romanticism, 1775–1850* (Cambridge: Cambridge Univ. Press, 1987).

14. Lord Byron, *English Bards and Scotch Reviewers: A Satire,* in idem, *The Complete Poetical Works,* ed. Jerome J. McGann (Oxford: Clarendon, 1980–93), 1:261, ll. 1025–32.

15. For Lusieri, see Jenkins and Sloan, *Vases and Volcanoes* (note 13), 112–14, 171–74, 251; Christopher Hibbert, *The Grand Tour,* rev. ed. (London: Thames & Methuen, 1987), 167; and Hugh William Williams, *Travels in Italy, Greece, and the Ionian Islands* (Edinburgh: A. Constable, 1820), 2:331–34. For Byron's description of Lusieri, see Lord Byron, *Childe Harold's Pilgrimage, A Romaunt,* in idem, *The*

Complete Poetical Works, ed. Jerome J. McGann (Oxford: Clarendon, 1980–93), 2:190 (Byron's note to canto 2, stanza 12, l. 101).

16. Leslie A. Marchand, *Byron: A Biography* (New York: Knopf, 1957), 1:226; see also 1:221–25, 254, 263, 271.

17. Stoneman, *Land of Lost Gods* (note 6), 180.

18. Byron, *Childe Harold's Pilgrimage* (note 15), 2:48 (canto 2, ll. 18–26n, stanza *a*).

19. For full details, see Byron, *The Curse of Minerva* (note 3), 1:444–47. Critical responses can be found in Robert F. Gleckner, *Byron and the Ruins of Paradise* (Baltimore: Johns Hopkins Univ. Press, 1967), 32–37; and St. Clair, *Lord Elgin and the Marbles* (note 6), 193–200.

20. Byron, *The Curse of Minerva* (note 3), 1:326, ll. 179–98. Compare Anna Jameson's impression of early groups of spectators at picture galleries: "The loiterers and loungers, the vulgar starers, the gaping idlers"; as cited in William T. Whitley, *Art in England* (Cambridge: Cambridge Univ. Press, 1928; reprint, New York: Hacker Art Books, 1973), 1:110.

21. Brewer, *Pleasures of the Imagination* (note 11), 280.

22. Byron, *The Curse of Minerva* (note 3), 1:326, l. 195n.

23. P. Papinius Statius, *The First Book of Statius: His Thebais,* trans. Alexander Pope [1703], in Alexander Pope, *Works* (Dublin: reprinted for G. Grierson, 1718), l. 731: "The Crowd in stupid Wonder fix'd appear."

24. [William Hazlitt], "*Report of the Select Committee of the House of Commons on the Elgin Marbles.—Murray,*" *Examiner* (London), 16 June 1816, 379; reprinted, with slight variations, as "The Elgin Marbles," in William Hazlitt, *The Complete Works of William Hazlitt,* ed. Percival Howe (London: J. M. Dent, 1930–34), 18:100–3.

25. Byron, *The Curse of Minerva* (note 3), 1:327, ll. 199–206.

26. Byron, *The Curse of Minerva* (note 3), 1:327, ll. 207–8.

27. Byron, *The Curse of Minerva* (note 3), 1:326, ll. 171–74.

28. Joseph Farington, *The Diary of Joseph Farington,* vol. 9, *January 1808–June 1809,* ed. Kathryn Cave (New Haven: Yale Univ. Press, 1982), 3306, 3320–21.

29. For Carlisle, see Rothenberg, "*Descensus ad Terram*" (note 8), 252.

30. Benjamin Robert Haydon, "On the Judgment of Connoisseurs Being Preferred to That of Professional Men,—Elgin Marbles, &c.," *Examiner* (London), 17 March 1816, 162–64. For Haydon's responses to the Elgin Marbles, see Benjamin Robert Haydon, *The Diary of Benjamin Robert Haydon,* ed. Willard Bissell Pope (Cambridge: Harvard Univ. Press, 1960), esp. 1:6 (23 July 1808), 54–55 (1 March 1809), 85–91 (September–October 1809), 433–38 (6 May 1815), 439–42 (13 May 1815). On Dutch realism, see his remarks on "all the faculties of men, squeezed into an inside of a tasteless dutch Room, with a woman clouting a child" and "the dutch part, the touching, the knifes, the pewter plates, and tin saucepans"; see 1:4–5 (23 July 1808).

31. William Wordsworth, *The Prelude* (1805 version), 7.688.

32. The opinions of Humphry and Beaumont are recorded in Farington, *Diary* (note 28), 3249, 3290; see also Cecil Gould, *Trophy of Conquest: The Musée Napoléon and the Creation of the Louvre* (London: Faber & Faber, 1965), 116–30.

33. For the "restoration" of the Towneley collection, see B. F. Cook, *The Townley*

Marbles (London: British Museum Publications, 1985), 53. For Thorwaldsen and Canova, see Stoneman, *Land of Lost Gods* (note 6), 199. For Elgin's late intentions, see Rothenberg, *"Descensus ad Terram"* (note 8), 351; for restoration, see Francis Haskell and Nicholas Penny, *Taste and the Antique: The Lure of Classical Sculpture, 1500–1900* (New Haven: Yale Univ. Press, 1981), 103.

34. For a detailed account of these fluctuations of opinion, see Andrew McClellan, *Inventing the Louvre: Art, Politics, and the Origins of the Modern Museum in Eighteenth-Century Paris* (Cambridge: Cambridge Univ. Press, 1994). St. Clair notes that Byron's "*Childe Harold's Pilgrimage* and *The Curse of Minerva* have coloured the world's view of Lord Elgin's activities ever since they first appeared"; see St. Clair, *Lord Elgin and the Marbles* (note 6), 197.

35. See Edward Daniel Clarke, *Travels in Various Countries of Europe, Asia and Africa, Part the Second, Greece, Egypt and the Holy Land, Section the Second* (London: printed for T. Cadell and W. Davies, 1814), 484 n. 1; Haydon, *Diary* (note 30), 1:436 (6 May 1815); and [Robert Southey?], "*Travels in Various Countries of Europe, Asia and Africa*, by Edward Daniel Clarke...," *Quarterly Review* (London) 17 (April 1817): 194.

36. Clarke, *Travels in Various Countries* (note 35), 484 n. 1.

37. Brewer, *Pleasures of the Imagination* (note 11), 283.

38. "Elgin Marbles," *Examiner* (London), 19 May 1816, 317.

39. Byron, *English Bards and Scotch Reviewers* (note 14), 1:418 (Byron's note to line 1027).

40. Byron, *Childe Harold's Pilgrimage* (note 15), 2:47–49, canto 2, stanzas 11–15, esp. ll. 94, 95–96, 110, 113, 131, 102–3; and Byron, *The Curse of Minerva* (note 3), 1:323, l. 106 (and l. 106n).

41. Byron, *Childe Harold's Pilgrimage* (note 15), 2:191 (Byron's note to canto 2, stanza 12, l. 101).

42. [George Ellis], "*Childe Harold's Pilgrimage, a Romaunt,* by Lord Byron," *Quarterly Review* (London) 7 (March 1812): 186.

43. Byron, *Childe Harold's Pilgrimage* (note 15), 2:47, canto 2, stanza 10, ll. 82–83.

44. For the two prose pieces, see Byron, *Childe Harold's Pilgrimage* (note 15), 2:202–9, where it is noted (p. 202) that Byron substituted "Franciscan" for "Capuchin" in the dateline for the first piece. For Smith's comments, see Smith, "Lord Elgin" (note 5), 179. Marchand, *Byron* (note 16), 1:253n, attributes to Byron a difficulty of definition that may have been his own, since Marchand claims that the convent "was Franciscan but then occupied by Capuchins." On Galt and his poem (and its influence on *The Curse of Minerva*), see St. Clair, *Lord Elgin and the Marbles* (note 6), 197–98.

45. Byron, *The Curse of Minerva* (note 3), 1:445–46.

46. Byron, *The Complete Miscellaneous Prose,* ed. Andrew Nicholson (Oxford: Clarendon, 1991), 133.

47. My translation; see François-René Chateaubriand, *Itinéraire de Paris à Jérusalem et de Jérusalem à Paris* (1811), in idem, *Oeuvres romanesques et voyages,* ed. Maurice Regard (Paris: Gallimard, 1969), 2:874: "Les Anglais qui ont visité Athènes

depuis le passage de lord Elgin ont eux-mêmes déploré ces funestes effets d'un amour des arts peu réfléchi." For Fauvel's guestroom, see Chateaubriand, *Itinéraire*, 2:860.

48. English student, "Grecian Marbles" (note 1), 773–74.

49. English Student, "Grecian Marbles" (note 1), 773.

50. My translation; see Chateaubriand, *Itinéraire* (note 47), 2:874: "Les monuments d'Athènes arrachés aux lieux pour lesquels ils étaient faits, perdront non seulement une partie de leur beauté relative, mais ils diminueront matériellement de beauté. Ce n'est que la lumière qui fait ressortir la délicatesse de certaines lignes et de certaines couleurs: or, cette lumière venant à manquer sous le ciel de l'Angleterre, ces lignes et ces couleurs disparaîtront ou resteront cachées."

51. Jenkins, *Archaeologists and Aesthetes* (note 5), 26–28.

52. Brian Rigby, "Quatremère de Quincy," in Peter France, ed., *The New Oxford Companion to Literature in French* (Oxford: Clarendon, 1995), 653. Antoine-Chrysotôme Quatremère de Quincy, *Lettres sur le préjudice qu'occasioneroient aux arts et à la science, le déplacement des monumens de l'art de l'Italie...* [= *Lettres sur le projet d'enlever les monumens de l'Italie*] (Paris: Desenne, 1796); as cited and translated in Stoneman, *Land of Lost Gods* (note 6), 202; and in Haskell and Penny, *Taste and the Antique* (note 33), 110.

53. Haskell and Penny, *Taste and the Antique* (note 33), 110–11.

54. See in particular McClellan, *Inventing the Louvre* (note 34); and Jenkins, *Archaeologists and Aesthetes* (note 5), 26–28.

55. Jenkins, *Archaeologists and Aesthetes* (note 5), 13, 24, 26–27; and St. Clair, *Lord Elgin and the Marbles* (note 6), 149, 217–19.

56. Smith, "Lord Elgin" (note 5), 215, 227.

57. Cited in St. Clair, *Lord Elgin and the Marbles* (note 6), 100.

58. For example, see St. Clair, *Lord Elgin and the Marbles* (Oxford: Oxford Univ. Press, 1967), 133: "He [Napoléon] was the first man to set a proper value on the sculptures of the Parthenon (although his motives were perhaps imperial rather than artistic)." For Elgin's own claims, see Rothenberg, *"Descensus ad Terram"* (note 8), 358n.

59. English Student, "Grecian Marbles" (note 1), 774.

60. Haydon, *Diary* (note 30), 1:87–88 (September 1809).

61. For John Galt, see St. Clair, *Lord Elgin and the Marbles* (note 6), 158. For the general atmosphere of rivalry, see Elgin's correspondence reprinted by Smith, "Lord Elgin" (note 5); Haydon, *Diary* (note 30), 1:86–89 (September 1809); and Stoneman, *Land of Lost Gods* (note 6), 169.

62. Stoneman, *Land of Lost Gods* (note 6), 169.

63. Cited in Christopher Hitchens, *The Elgin Marbles: Should They Be Returned to Greece?* (Athens: nea Synora, 1988), 248, 255, where the parliamentary debates are conveniently reprinted in an appendix.

64. Smith, "Lord Elgin" (note 5), 332.

65. Stoneman, *Land of Lost Gods* (note 6), 193–95.

66. See Hitchens, *Elgin Marbles* (note 63), 127, 131–32.

67. Sydney Smith, *Letters*, ed. Nowell C. Smith (Oxford: Clarendon, 1953), 1:272–73. For these views, see Hitchens, *Elgin Marbles* (note 63), 134–35.

68. Cited in Smith, "Lord Elgin" (note 5), 332.

69. For the interest of the prince regent, see Stoneman, *Land of Lost Gods* (note 6), 191–95; for the Aigina Marbles, see Stoneman, *Land of Lost Gods* (note 6), 185–89.

70. My translation; see Chateaubriand, *Itinéraire* (note 47), 2:874: "On prétend que lord Elgin a dit pour excuse, qu'il n'avait fait que nous imiter. Il est vrai que les Français ont enlevé à l'Italie ses statues et ses tableaux; mais ils n'ont point mutilé les temples pour en arracher les bas-reliefs, ils ont seulement suivi l'exemple des Romains qui dépouillèrent la Grèce des chefs-d'œuvre de la peinture et de la statuaire."

71. English Student, "Grecian Marbles" (note 1), 773.

72. For Sulla, see Gould, *Trophy of Conquest* (note 32), 43. Coleridge was particularly alert to the Roman model: "The finest parts of Europe have been pillaged in order to convert Paris into a new Rome, a metropolis of the civilized world, of this one great European nation; and the books, statues, and pictures of Italy have undergone the same fate from the French conquerors, which those of Greece formerly experienced under the Italian"; see Samuel Taylor Coleridge, *Essays on His Times in the Morning Post and the Courier,* ed. David V. Erdman (London: Routledge & Kegan Paul, 1978), 1:313.

73. My translation; see Chateaubriand, *Itinéraire* (note 47), 2:874.

74. My translation; see Chateaubriand, *Itinéraire* (note 47), 2:874: "Au reste, j'avouerai que l'intérêt de la France, la gloire de notre patrie, et mille autres raisons pouvaient demander la transplantation des monuments conquis par nos armes; mais les beaux-arts eux-mêmes, comme étant du parti des vaincus et au nombre des captifs, ont peut-être le droit de s'en affliger."

75. Cited in Gould, *Trophy of Conquest* (note 32), 41; see also McClellan, *Inventing the Louvre* (note 34), 98.

76. Cited in McClellan, *Inventing the Louvre* (note 34), 121.

77. Quoted (in French) in Jean Chatelain, "Musée Napoléon," in Jean Tulard, ed., *Dictionnaire Napoléon* (Paris: Fayard, 1989), 1209–10; translated in McClellan, *Inventing the Louvre* (note 34), 121.

78. McClellan, *Inventing the Louvre* (note 34), 97.

79. McClellan, *Inventing the Louvre* (note 34), 123.

80. Charles Saunier, *Les conquêtes artistiques de la Révolution et de l'Empire; reprises et abandons des Alliés en 1815, leurs conséquences sur les musées d'Europe* (Paris: H. Laurens, 1902).

81. Gould, *Trophy of Conquest* (note 32), esp. 90, 42, 36, 119, 134.

82. Cited in St. Clair, *Lord Elgin and the Marbles* (note 6), 221.

83. William Wordsworth, "Ode: The Morning of the Day Appointed for a General Thanksgiving, January 18, 1816," in idem, *The Poetical Works of William Wordsworth,* ed. Ernest de Selincourt and Helen Darbishire, 2d ed. (Oxford: Clarendon, 1952–59), 3:161, ll. 169, 171–75.

84. William Wordsworth, "Ode 1814," in idem, *The Poetical Works of William Wordsworth,* ed. Ernest de Selincourt and Helen Darbishire, 2d ed. (Oxford: Clarendon, 1952–59), 3:147, ll. 90–110. For architectural influences, see J. Mordaunt Crook, *The Greek Revival: Neo-Classical Attitudes in British Architecture, 1760–1870,* rev. ed. (London: John Murray, 1995).

85. Wordsworth, "Ode 1814" (note 84), 3:147, l. 101; and Wordsworth, "Ode: The Morning" (note 83), 3:158, ll. 105–6.

86. "Domestic Occurrences" (note 4), 80; partially quoted in Jenkins, *Archaeologists and Aesthetes* (note 5), 19.

87. Jenkins, *Archaeologists and Aesthetes* (note 5), 19.

88. For an illustration of these medals, see Jenkins, *Archaeologists and Aesthetes* (note 5), 17.

89. See Hitchens, *Elgin Marbles* (note 63), 133.

90. Reproduced in St. Clair, *Lord Elgin and the Marbles* (note 6), pl. 10. For a detailed description, including suggestive texts that help to create the political significances of the picture, see Mary Dorothy George, *Catalogue of Political and Personal Satires Presented in the Department of Prints and Drawings in the British Museum*, vol. 9, *1811–1819*, ed. M. D. George (London: British Museum Publications, 1949), 684–85.

91. See Hitchens, *Elgin Marbles* (note 63), 129, 137.

92. Reproduced in, for example, "*Report from the Select Committee on the Earl of Elgin's Sculptured Marbles…*," *Quarterly Review* (London) 14 (January 1816): 547; and "Report of the Committee on the Elgin Marbles," *Examiner* (London), 28 April 1816, 269.

93. For Potsdam, see Constantine, *Early Greek Travellers* (note 6), 105; for Edinburgh, see Crook, *Greek Revival* (note 84), 104.

94. My translation; cited in J. Guillaume, "Grégoire et le Vandalisme," *La Révolution française: Revue d'histoire moderne et comtemporaine* (Paris) 41 (1901): 266–67: "Les chefs-d'oeuvre des républiques grecques doivent-ils décorer le pays des esclaves? La République française devrait être leur dernier domicile." See also Ruth F. Nicheles, *The Abbé Grégoire, 1787–1831: The Odyssey of an Egalitarian* (Westport, Conn.: Greenwood, 1971).

95. Cited in McClellan, *Inventing the Louvre* (note 34), 116; and Gould, *Trophy of Conquest* (note 32), 35–36.

96. Cited in Gould, *Trophy of Conquest* (note 32), 123.

97. Cited in Brewer, *Pleasures of the Imagination* (note 11), 285.

98. See Hitchens, *Elgin Marbles* (note 63), 133–37.

99. See Hitchens, *Elgin Marbles* (note 63), 133–35; and Crook, *Greek Revival* (note 84), 17.

100. English Student, "Grecian Marbles" (note 1), 773.

101. See Hitchens, *Elgin Marbles* (note 63), 130–31.

102. Cited in Crook, *Greek Revival* (note 84), 17.

103. Cited in Terence Spencer, *Fair Greece, Sad Relic: Literary Philhellenism from Shakespeare to Byron* (London: Weidenfeld & Nicolson, 1954), 167.

104. Haydon, *Diary* (note 30), 1:87, 88, 89 (September 1809).

105. Cited in Smith, "Lord Elgin" (note 5), 332.

106. Smith, "Lord Elgin" (note 5), 198: "I am sure that in half a century there will not remain one stone on another. It would be well…to ask for all that is left, or else to do all that is possible to prevent their going on in this fashion."

107. Byron, *Childe Harold's Pilgrimage* (note 15), 2:190 (Byron's note to canto 2, stanza 1, l. 6).

108. [Southey?], *"Travels in Various Countries"* (note 35), 194.

109. [Southey?], *"Travels in Various Countries"* (note 35), 194–95.

110. Robert Hunt, "Lord Elgin's Grecian Sculptures," *Examiner* (London), 8 October 1809, 652.

111. Haydon, *Diary* (note 30), 2:76 (31 December 1816); and Haydon, "On the Judgment of Connoisseurs" (note 30), 164.

112. As quoted in Martin Aske, *Keats and Hellenism: An Essay* (Cambridge: Cambridge Univ. Press, 1985), 14.

113. Benjamin Robert Haydon, *The Autobiography and Memoirs of Benjamin Robert Haydon (1786–1846),* ed. Tom Taylor (London: Davies, 1926), 1:67, 108.

114. Haydon, *Diary* (note 30), 1:87–88 (September 1809).

115. Haydon, *Autobiography and Memoirs* (see note 113), 1:67; and Haydon, "On the Judgment of Connoisseurs" (note 30), 163.

116. Johann Joachim Winckelmann, *Briefe* (Berlin: Walter de Gruyter, 1952–57), 3:372.

117. Jerome Christensen, *Lord Byron's Strength: Romantic Writing and Commercial Society* (Baltimore: Johns Hopkins Univ. Press, 1993), 327.

118. My translation; see Chateaubriand, *Itinéraire* (note 47), 2:876–77: "Je pris, en descendant de la citadelle, un morceau de marbre du Parthénon; j'avais aussi recueilli un fragment de la pierre du tombeau d'Agamemnon; et depuis j'ai toujours dérobé quelque chose aux monuments sur lesquels j'ai passé. Ce ne sont pas d'aussi beaux souvenirs de mes voyages que ceux qu'ont emportés M. de Choiseul et Lord Elgin; mais ils me suffisent."

119. My translation; see Chateaubriand, *Itinéraire* (note 47), 2:877: "Quand je revois ces bagatelles, je me retrace sur-le-champ mes courses et mes aventures; je me dis: «J'étais là, telle chose m'advint.»"

120. My translation; see Chateaubriand, *Itinéraire* (note 47), 2:877: "avec une douzaine de pierres de Sparte, d'Athènes, d'Argos, de Corinthe."

121. St. Clair, *Lord Elgin and the Marbles* (note 6), 193; Catherine P. Bracken, *Antiquities Acquired: The Spoliation of Greece* (Newton Abbot, England: David & Charles, 1975), 55; Spencer, *Fair Greece* (note 103), 229; and *"Researches in Greece, by William Martin Leake," Quarterly Review* (London) 11 (July 1814): 458. By the 1998 edition of *Lord Elgin and the Marbles* (note 6), St. Clair can add that "the names of four bishops of Athens were inscribed on one of the columns" and describe this need to create an association with the marbles as "a new form of cultural appropriation."

122. Byron, *Childe Harold's Pilgrimage* (note 15), 2:191–92 (Byron's note to canto 2, stanza 12, ll. 107–8). This anecdote is also cited by Hazlitt at the end of his two-part anonymous review of the Select Committee's report published in the *Examiner,* where the anecdote acts as a rebuttal to Dr. Philip Hunt's claim to the committee that "no objection was made nor regret expressed by the inhabitants at the removal of the Marbles"; see [William Hazlitt], *"Report of the Select Committee of the House of Commons on the Elgin Marbles.—*(Concluded)," *Examiner* (London), 30 June 1816, 412.

123. For Clarke's role, see Stoneman, *Land of Lost Gods* (note 6), 151–55; and Bracken, *Antiquities Acquired* (note 121), 73–83.

124. The entry for Dodwell in the *Dictionary of National Biography* records: "In

Feb. 1802 he was in Constantinople, whence he wrote home to say that he had seventy-six cases . . . containing antiquities &c. collected during his wanderings."

125. John Galt, *The Autobiography of John Galt* (London: Cochrane & M'Crone, 1833), 1:159.

126. Cited in Crook, *Greek Revival* (note 84), 38.

127. John B. S. Morritt, *The Letters of John B. S. Morritt of Rokeby, Descriptive Journeys in Europe and Asia Minor in the Years 1794–1796*, ed. George E. Marindin (London: J. Murray, 1914; reprint, as *A Grand Tour: Letters and Journeys 1794–96*, London: Century, 1985), 179, 181; and Rothenberg, *"Descensus ad Terram"* (note 8), 140. The evidence of Morritt's observations was invoked both by Hammersley and Croker, who accused Hammersley of misinterpreting the implications. Croker referred to two visits to Athens by Morritt when "he found the greatest dilapidations." Morritt's testimony stated that "Lord Elgin interfered with nothing that was not already in ruins, or that was threatened with immediate destruction"; cited in Hitchens, *Elgin Marbles* (note 63), 134, 135.

128. My translation cited; St. Clair, *Lord Elgin and the Marbles* (note 6), 63: "Ne négligez aucune occasion de piller dans Athènes et dans son territoire tout ce qu'il y a de pillable. N'épargnez ni les morts ni les vivants." For other Parthenon fragments and Greek relics, see Bracken, *Antiquities Acquired* (note 121), 49.

Latin America, Native America, and the Politics of Culture

Clemency Coggins

"Claiming the stones" may conjure the primeval ownership of cultural property, whether living landscape or ancient ruins, whereas "naming the bones" evokes ancestral identity and communal spirit. How and when are cultural property and cultural identity—stones and bones—the same? Once they were the same and simultaneous, but historically and legally they have become estranged by time. On the one hand, ancient property, or stones, may be detached, indeed excised, from a living mother culture that no longer recognizes its maternity. On the other hand, an ancient culture may be reborn in a living people who resurrect, or perhaps create within it, an identity—idealized bones. These are local concerns, but such definitions of culture, and of cultural property, have become international and vulnerable to political, legal, and economic forces remote from community identity, and even ignorant of its existence. In the Americas the high indigenous cultures of Mexico, Guatemala, and Peru that were destroyed by the Spaniards in the sixteenth century are represented today by their living descendants and by innumerable magnificent archaeological monuments, which bear testimony to the brilliance of those civilizations. The relationship between these archaeological remains, "cultural property," and the living peoples has not always been recognized. Only in the twentieth century are the indigenous peoples of these countries slowly acknowledged as the distinctive roots of mestizo Latin America—long after the manifest monumental glories of their pre-Hispanic past had been appropriated.

The tension between claiming the stones and naming the bones is inherent in the twentieth-century Latin American political and intellectual movement known as *indigenismo,* which recognizes and values the aboriginal cultures of the Americas while seeking to redress the irreversible historical injustices of European domination. *Indigenismo* is a key to understanding issues of cultural property and cultural identity in Mexico, Guatemala, and Peru, where the most complex ancient American societies once flourished and where the greatest amount of ancient learning and culture was obliterated. As an educated pursuit, the love of ruins long preceded the scholarly study of exotic peoples in western European culture. Indeed in the New World antiquarianism led first to a science of archaeology toward the end of the nineteenth century and then to ethnology, the study of living (indigenous) cultures; together they formed a new study of "man," or anthropology.[1] In the Americas it is anthropology that subsumes the study and teaching of Native American civilization past and present and, with the intellectual and illustrative support of writers and painters, engendered *indigenismo*.

Ancient Maya civilization and living Maya culture were among the first studied under the rubric of the new science of anthropology. The peninsula of Yucatán and its Maya culture were remote and not easily accessible from the capital city of Tenochtitlán (Mexico City) in central Mexico where, in 1520, the well-documented Aztec emperor had reigned and fallen before the Spanish onslaught. The isolated Maya never entirely capitulated to the power of central Mexico and have continued to rebel intermittently until today, as the oppressor has changed from Aztec to Spanish to Colonial Spanish to the newly independent and then the modern Mexican state. European explorers, fired by neoclassical enthusiasms, had discovered the remains of Maya civilization and, finding the pyramids and relief sculpture, as well as the hieroglyphic writing system so different from the Aztec, concluded that the ancient inhabitants had come from Asia, the Near East, Egypt, or even the sunken Atlantis.

One of these explorers, August Le Plongeon from France, was sponsored by the American Antiquarian Society in Worcester, Massachusetts, which was interested in the study of Maya civilization. He was soon replaced by Edward H. Thompson, a young American engineer who wrote a popular article entitled "Atlantis Not a Myth" (1879).[2] In 1885 Thompson was appointed to the post of United States consul in Mérida, Yucatán, and instructed to report on Maya sites for both the American Antiquarian Society and the Peabody Museum of Archaeology and Ethnology at Harvard University.[3] In the new spirit of a scientific archaeology, Thompson explored and mapped several ancient Maya sites and came to know and admire contemporary Maya culture; in 1895 he bought the large abandoned hacienda of Chichén Itzá, with its well-known archaeological ruins. Today, the Sacred Cenote, or Well of Sacrifice, at Chichén Itzá is a famous tourist destination and a notorious archaeological site, which provided the first cause célèbre for Mexico and its new policies of cultural patrimony after the Mexican Revolution of 1910. The well itself became famous in the latter half of the nineteenth century with the translation into French of a sixteenth-century Spanish document that described Chichén Itzá as an ancient pilgrimage site that would probably have received gold offerings. The translation was made by the French priest and early Americanist scholar Charles-Étienne Brasseur de Bourbourg, whose enthusiasm for pre-Hispanic America inspired several nineteenth-century visitors to Chichén Itzá. Foreign adventurers and romantics were attracted by the possibilities of ancient civilization in the New World.

Although Thompson was not the first to dredge for gold in the Well of Sacrifice, he was the first to find it, together with many other exotic and valuable offerings, during the dry winter seasons from 1904 to 1911. He shipped most of these objects to Boston, where they were received at Harvard's young Peabody Museum of Archaeology and Ethnography as artifacts of scientific value. Thompson began his work during the prerevolutionary phase of Mexican history known as the Porfiriato, when General Porfirio Díaz governed (president, 1877–80, 1884–1911). Díaz represented wealthy landowners, encouraged foreign investment, and took great pride in the modern Mexico he believed he was creating. He had an interest in archaeology, a pursuit seen as both nationalistic and patriotic, and appointed the architect Leopoldo Batres as the national director of archaeology. Hearing of Thompson's excavations at Chichén Itzá, Díaz, Batres, and Justo Sierra, minister of public education, visited the site in February 1906, primarily to check on Thompson's activities, which were being criticized by Mexican nationalists and by envious archaeologists. The genial Thompson entertained them lavishly for three days and showed them the Well of Sacrifice, where there was no archaeological activity. They departed, apparently satisfied. There were no official objections to his work. After Díaz was overthrown in the revolution four years later, however, Thompson ran out of luck. In 1910 he was obliged to apply in Mexico City for a permit to continue his work, and the exportation of artifacts was explicitly forbidden. The Peabody Museum did not renew its sponsorship, and in the wake of national agrarian reform Thompson's hacienda, a large cattle and wood-producing ranch, was settled by squatters, while his title to the land was challenged, although unsuccessfully.

In 1921 his house and museum at the hacienda were burned down and looted. In 1923 the final blow came after Thompson's great friend and sponsor, T. A. Willard, published *The City of the Sacred Well*. In this admiring, uncritical book about Thompson and his work at Chichén Itzá, Willard exaggerated the quantity, quality, and especially the value of the gold found in the Well of Sacrifice. Mexico sued Thompson for one million dollars in compensation. Thompson, who had continually begged his sponsors for money, died a poor man in 1944, nine years before the Mexican supreme court ruled in his favor. The collections from the Well of Sacrifice, procured in the name of science, had not been scientifically excavated, although their dredging was an engineering feat of which Thompson was very proud. Once the court case was settled, however, the Peabody Museum studied and published the collections and presented a representative sample of the metal artifacts to Mexico in 1959. These went to the Museo Nacional de Antropología in Mexico City, the remote capital of the national government, long distrusted by the Maya. An interesting twist in this saga occurred on Christmas Eve 1985, when some of these gold objects on display in the Museo Nacional de Antropología were stolen in a spectacular theft connected with small-time drug dealing; they were recovered some years later after the objects proved too notorious to fence. In 1976 the Peabody Museum had insisted that a selection of newly published jades from the Well of Sacrifice scheduled to be sent to Mexico go to the museum in Mérida, Yucatán, not to the Museo Nacional in the capital.[4]

This story is illustrative of the changing perceptions of the ancient cultural patrimony of Mexico, and indeed of Guatemala and Peru, where there were also highly developed indigenous civilizations and where an analogous sequence of political attitudes may be traced—not always in the same order, although the cast of characters is the same. Historically, pre-Hispanic cultures have been seen variously as comprising degenerate heathen peoples, as utopian societies, as an artifact of classical antiquity, as vanishing and then as enduring culture, as shared ancestry, as the unknowable Other, as dependable economic resources. One constant in Latin America has been the gulf between those who define and those who embody ancient cultural patrimony. This divide everywhere, at every epoch, is at the heart of the "Indian Problem."

Mexico

In 1519 Hernán Cortés, an educated man, and his company of conquistadores were stunned by the magnificence of Mesoamerican civilization; nevertheless, it did not take long to destroy the island capital of the Aztec, claim the land for Charles I of Spain (king, 1516–56, Holy Roman Emperor, 1519–56), and dazzle the Spanish monarch with unimaginable riches of gold and silver. Soon Franciscan friars were sent to this New World to save the souls of the Indians, who the Europeans saw as belonging to a monolithic pagan culture, even though scores of languages were spoken in Mesoamerica by many very different peoples. The friars recognized they could convert the Indians more efficiently if they understood native culture, and one of them, the Franciscan Bernardino de Sahagún, compiled what is described as the first American ethnography—*La Historia general de las cosas de la Nueva España* (1579; General history of the things of New Spain). This was an encyclopedic, illustrated document in which (converted) native informants recorded the beliefs and customs of the Nahuatl-speaking Aztec of the valley of Mexico.[5] Sahagún perceived the underlying religious significance of the universal Mesoamerican calendar and its relation to cyclic time and to the rounds of ritual that structured both daily life and theology. These were of practical interest to the proselytizers, as was the array of deities and the native understanding of the natural world, so that they might be replaced by Christian belief and learning. There was, however, theological speculation about whether the Indians possessed rational souls to be saved, since, if they did not, they might be treated as animals. Were they "noble Indians" or "dirty dogs"?[6] The latter possibility and ensuing enslavement of the native populations led to protests in Mexico and Spain, mostly by friars, and to laws that would to some degree protect the Indians, in a "dawn of conscience" that reflected "the first time in history a people—Spaniards—paid attention to the nature and culture of the peoples they met."[7]

A few members of the native ruling families who survived the conquest kept alive the histories and memories of their past, but these were valued and recorded by only a few criollo historians (criollos were Spaniards born in the Spanish New World). It was not until the eighteenth century that European interest in ancient America led to a search for sixteenth-century written sources about the Aztec. Perhaps the most important single event in the reconstruction of the Mexican cultural patrimony was the discovery, in 1790, of two huge sculptures of extraordinary religious significance for the Aztec. These were found beneath the cathedral in Mexico City, which had been built (as was the Catholic Church's practice) on top of the principal Aztec temple precinct. No surviving examples of Aztec sculpture approached the power and mythic role of these two discoveries, and they were greeted by nationalists and antiquarians alike with an enthusiasm rooted in European neoclassicism. The huge statue of Coatlicue (Serpent Skirt; fig. 1), the beheaded mother of the principal Aztec deity, Huitzlopochtli, was displayed at the national university among the casts of Greek sculpture[8]; it was admired, as it is today, for a terrifying imagery that rivals the most horrible medieval depictions of hell. The authorities found that Coatlicue had not lost her influence on the indigenous people, however, and she was reburied until 1824, when she was exhumed and placed in storage. The other sculpture was the great Calendar Stone, perhaps best known today as the model for a souvenir ashtray. Almost twelve feet in diameter, this fundamental Aztec scriptural stone records the five creations of the Mesoamerican world in terms of the five directions (the four cardinal points and the center) and the count of days since the last creation, which continues unbroken to this day. Appreciated by a scholarly elite, these monuments were condemned by the church when they were found to reactivate a living native heritage, presumed long dead. Ultimately, the two joined the Mexican cultural patrimony in the Museo Nacional de Antropología, where aesthetic and nationalistic meanings have replaced their towering religious significance.

In 1821 Mexico and the rest of Hispanic America achieved its independence from Spain. The reformers in Mexico were liberals who believed in the principles of the Enlightenment that involved the ascendance of reason (and the eclipse of the Catholic Church), freedom and education for every man, land for all, free trade abroad, and progress[9] — although power remained in the hands of the moneyed few who had survived independence by espousing the separatist cause. Many of the founding goals foundered on the rock of agrarian reform that was the most intractable obstacle to solving the Indian Problem for all these countries. The many good intentions behind such reform did not, and still do not, comprehend the radically different native perception of land, and Indian rebellion over this issue has erupted and smoldered from the beginning.[10]

Inspired by the Europeans who were discovering this "new" ancient world, Mexico created a national museum for its own antiquities in 1825.[11] In 1897, under President Díaz, Mexico passed a law that declared all archaeological monuments and objects the property of the nation and prohibited their export without special permit,[12] a law that had little impact on Thompson's activities at Chichén Itzá. President Díaz was overthrown in the Mexican Revolution, which continued episodically from 1910 to 1920, advocating agrarian reform among its many goals. After the revolution, intellectuals and reformers (usually the same people in Latin America) were supremely concerned with establishing a genuinely Mexican identity. *Mestizaje*, a mixing of

Fig. 1. The Aztec earth goddess Coatlicue (Serpent Skirt)
Mexico (Tenochtitlán), 1450s–1520s, stone (andesite?), 3.5 × 1.3 × 1.3 m (11½ × 4¼ × 4¼ ft.)
Mexico City, Museo Nacional de Antropología, Sala Mexica

genes, or descent from the two aristocracies,[13] was promoted as the way to achieve this identity. *Mestizaje* involved the concept of *indigenismo*, which was an ethnopopulism that became the philosophical position of government *indigenistas* who were champions of the Indians and their languages and cultures, as well as advocates of education and land reform. The *indigenistas* resembled the liberals before them—with the important difference that the noble indigenous cultures were newly seen by them as the incarnation of the ancient roots of modern Mexican culture, although at the same time these originating cultures were believed to have no future.[14] This was because the admired ancient civilizations were most purely represented by the modern Indians—Mexico's lowest class—who would be incorporated into modern Mexico through *mestizaje* or intermarriage. This would, inevitably, involve the extinction of remnant indigenous cultures as they were absorbed into a homogeneous Mexican identity and would thus solve the Indian Problem by erasing it.

Indigenismo flowered in the 1930s and the 1940s with the maturing of anthropology and ethnology as disciplines, and the movement was dynamically empowered by the allegiance of Mexican muralist painters such as Diego Rivera and David Alfaro Siqueiros (fig. 2) who combined admiration of Indians and their ancient culture with loathing of the Spanish conquistadors and of United States imperialism to create a rich and evocative pictorial socialist romanticism. In 1934 Mexico created the Instituto Nacional de Antropología e História (INAH). This institution, run by anthropologists and historians, designed and maintained the country's cultural policies until quite recently, when it lost much of its power and influence. The fact that anthropologists were in charge of Mexico's ancient heritage led to a didactic emphasis in schools and museums on the continuity between the original and contemporary peoples, which was very different from such education in most European countries. Whereas Germans in the 1930s were intent on demonstrating the purebred integrity of their "Nordic-Aryan" ancestry,[15] *mestizaje*, which involved assimilation, celebrated the admixture of blood. European national museums were, and are, filled with ancient art from other, unrelated civilizations that was viewed as exemplary and broadly educational, while the national museums of Mexico, Guatemala, and Peru are designed to demonstrate the enduring connection between past and present. In Mexico, it is only Mexican cultural and ethnic continuity that is expressed in the architecture and organization of the Mexican Museo Nacional de Antropología, which opened in 1964. A heroic bronze tree, representing the mythological Maya ceiba that connects the underworld with the heavens, dominates the museum's vast central courtyard, which is surrounded by two-story exhibits of the various Mexican geographic and cultural regions. Each region has its archaeological remains displayed on the first floor, as a substratum, while modern Indian cultures are represented on the floor above. The ancient objects are shown as works of art on the first floor, with minimal labeling (in the traditional European mode), while on the second floor there are ethnographic reconstructions of living cultures, with their music and crafts—a relationship that

Fig. 2. David Alfaro Siqueiros (Mexican, 1896–1974)
Ethnography
Mexico, 1939, enamel on composition board, 122.2 × 82.2 cm (48⅛ × 32⅜ in.)
New York, Museum of Modern Art

might be interpreted as the living Indian emerging from the dead seed beneath.[16] It is interesting that the powerful and gory Aztec culture was so effectively destroyed by the Spaniards that there is no second floor above the Aztec archaeological exhibits; the ethnographic living culture is perhaps best illustrated by modern Mexico City itself. While magnificent as architecture, and admirable in concept, this anthropological museum clearly illustrates the persistent divide between the meaning and uses of archaeology and ethnology and how unconvincingly they have striven to re-create a seamless cultural patrimony.

In Mexico, as elsewhere, the 1960s were a time of intellectual debate and student ferment, which resulted in the complete rejection of *indigenismo* and its corollary *mestizaje* as paternalistic and part of a discredited progressive philosophy that looked to the future and to economic development, concepts viewed as tainted by association with the United States. This period of politicization was strongly ideological, leading also to the rejection of North American scientific methods in the pursuit of Mexican archaeology.[17] From an anthropological point of view, *mestizaje* was then seen as the dilution of Indian identity and culture, as an abomination, and as a perpetuation of the rape of Indian women by Spanish soldiers.[18] This uncompromising position has left only one acceptable possibility—policies of pluriethnicity and multiculturalism.[19] Philosophically these honorable concepts promote freedom of cultural expression and belief, but there are two kinds of problems inherent in the independent coexistence of indigenous groups. One basic problem is that modern Mexico, like much of the rest of the world, lives by the precepts of a Western, linear kind of history, in which the individual is the basic unit of society and property rights are sacred, while indigenous Mexican peoples have always understood time and history as cyclic and the community as the basic unit, with the communal use of land. It is difficult to see how these different (but not separate) cultures can coexist equally when their understanding of time and the meaning and use of land are as irreconcilable as they have always been. The second basic problem derives from the first: in the modern global economy, principles of independent coexistence tend to entail for the indigenous population the bitter freedom to continue as the underclass.

Perhaps because cultural patrimony has always been political in Mexico, and perhaps because the anthropological solution to the Indian Problem has been to withdraw from interference, the INAH has lost much of its influence and its centralized control. The politics of cultural patrimony are heading in two new directions: regionalization and privatization, both involving decentralization. A recent example of regionalization in the state of Oaxaca illustrates the best kind of outcome for this policy, which would cede control of indigenous cultural patrimony, ancient and modern, to the states. Within each state, regional and community museums are being created, ideally by the will of the local inhabitants, who as in Oaxaca, have been involved in design, maintenance, and security, with expertise and some money supplied by the INAH. It is hoped that each such museum can be supported by local artisanal and tourist admission fees. In 1997, there were perhaps a dozen such museums in existence in Mexico; they may be archaeological, historical, and/or ethnographic, with the goal of teaching a community about its own archaeology and history, instead of representing Mexican national patrimony in large regional museums, designed and run by the INAH, as in the past.[20] Such initiatives combine the most constructive use of the ancient and the modern cultural heritage by encouraging local direction and control of the many separate and distinct cultural strands of Mexico's cultural heritage — although it is not clear how such museums can sustain themselves.

In contrast, the INAH, once in command of the cultural patrimony of Mexico, has been subordinated to the Consejo Nacional de Cultura e Arte (CONACULTA), a larger agency that has revived the kind of nationalistic promotion President Díaz pursued, with the added incentive of the proven economic value of archaeological sites as international attractions and generators of touristic revenues. Thus the money that, when the INAH was powerful and independent, might have gone to the mapping, excavation, and publication of Mexico's more than one hundred thousand endangered archaeological sites has recently gone to the renewed excavation, reconstruction, and presentation of the few, well-known tourist sites, in campaigns known as *megaprojectos*, because so much money has been devoted to them. Mexico's understanding of its ancient cultural patrimony has thus evolved from rejection to exploitation through phases of admiration and appropriation.

Guatemala

Many of the same historical processes may be traced in Guatemala, but they seem narrower in scope as well as geographically constricted compared to Mexico, which is eighteen times as large. In the sixteenth century the principal Spanish, and indigenous, settlement was essentially confined to the southernmost mountainous third of what is now Guatemala, and the Spaniards to the southern half of that. Unlike New Spain (Mexico), the southern Captaincy General of Guatemala, where the Indians spoke more than thirty Mayan languages, had no friars dedicated to recording the details of the indigenous culture, although the highland historical account, the Quiche *Popol Vuh*, was written down by the Dominican Francisco Ximenez in the middle of the eighteenth century. The brutal and bloody conquest of Guatemala by Pedro de Alvarado in 1524 set the tone for future subordination and exploitation of the Maya of the highlands. Compared to Mexico and Peru, Central America proved to be of no value to the Spanish Crown as a source of silver and gold, so its agricultural potential was developed through grants by the Crown of free Indian labor, which successively produced indigenous cacao and indigo and cochineal dyes for export until, after 1800, these were replaced by the introduced cultivar, coffee.[21] In return for the grant of free native labor, Spanish and criollo landowners were instructed to convert the Indians, and they were supplied with friars for this purpose. These evangelizing clergy, who had the souls of the Indians in focus, moved them into new towns where they could be converted more efficiently, as their communities were abandoned and cultural roots severed. It is ironic that the pre-Hispanic imperial Inca of Peru had also resettled troublesome populations for purposes of pacification, and that in recent decades the indigenous Maya of highland Guatemala have been forcibly moved again for the same reason—social control.[22]

As in Mexico a mestizo (*ladino* in Guatemala) population emerged, but power and politics were the prerogatives of the conservative criollo landowners who remained loyal to Spain—until independence in 1821, which in Guatemala was more of a family quarrel with Spain than a declaration of new principles of freedom and independence. After independence, Guatemala broke with the rest of Central America and Mexico, to which it lost Chiapas, and went its own way. In search of a national identity, Guatemalans looked to the remains of ancient Maya civilization within the Guatemalan highlands to distinguish themselves from ancient Mexico.[23] Although, as in Mexico, liberal politics were progressive, anticlerical, focused on improving the economy through trade, and concerned with ameliorating the state of the laboring Indians, the Guatemalan ruling class made no connection between their own newly found roots and the downtrodden Indians.

Once the powerful mobilizing and symbolic role played by *mestizos* and Indians in the Mexican Revolution—and the role the revolution continues to play in the Mexican consciousness—is appreciated, it is dramatically illuminating to realize that Guatemala had no revolution. Guatemala was eventually affected by the politics of the Mexican Revolution, but, on the whole, the country ignored it. In the late 1930s, while Mexico, under President Lázaro Cárdenas (1934–40), enacted agrarian and educational reforms and formulated an institutional *indigenismo* in the spirit of the revolution, Guatemala slumbered under the repressive dictatorship of President Jorge Ubico Castañeda (1931–44). After Ubico was overthrown in 1944, a decade of reforms followed that were supported by the interests of newly influential urban and university constituencies, separate from the communities where Maya identity and culture persisted.[24] These initiatives included the founding of an *indigenista* institute as in Mexico; significantly, unlike Mexico, however, Guatemalan intellectuals were not part of the government. Instead, Guatemalan *indigenismo* was most memorably expressed by the writer Miguel Angel Asturias, who won the Nobel Prize for literature in 1967 for novels such as *Hombres de maíz* (1949), which describes the life and worldview of the Maya Indian, who was seen as redemptive in the face of mindless obliteration by a modern world.[25] Consistent with contemporary Mexican *indigenismo*, the Guatemalan version saw *mestizaje*, the racial assimilation of the Maya, as an answer to the Indian Problem. This solution was not, however, the Maya one, and, like Mexico, Guatemala has experienced Indian revolts from the conquest to the present. The Maya, and most indigenous American peoples, simply want their own land.

The second of the two prolabor Guatemalan governments was ousted in 1954 through United States intervention in support of the United Fruit

Company. Since then, military governments, which maintain the power of the small ruling class and support foreign investment, have controlled Guatemala. In response, there arose a highly political, middle-class guerrilla movement located among highland Maya communities that were traditionally originally unpolitical. The successive military governments retaliated by imposing a regime of state terror, generously endowed with United States military expertise and European arms. Finally, a peace treaty was signed between the guerrilla army and the government in December 1996, under Alvaro Arzú Irigoyen, the first nonmilitary president in forty years. In the thirty-six-year civil war, over one hundred thousand Maya were killed, and a similar number fled to Mexico, while tens of thousands more were removed from their homelands, effectively destroying their cultural base. Nevertheless, Maya culture has endured and strengthened, partly in reaction to the years of repression. There is currently a revival in the use of the more than twenty extant Mayan languages, and many refugees are returning from Mexico.[26] The Maya are officially acknowledged as never before; Guatemalans have never described their country in terms of *mestizaje*, or as a *ladino* land, as the Mexicans have tried to do, although the population of Guatemala is 56 percent *ladino;* the rest is "Amerindian."[27] Nevertheless, the more purely Hispanic businessmen and landowners still reign in Guatemala, and they still collect Maya antiquities as a sign of their personal cultivation and national pride. The modern and the ancient Maya are, however, perceived very differently; the former, while colorful, remain an unreliable underclass, whereas the latter have become the second largest source of national revenue, after coffee. Every effort is being made to promote tourism in Guatemala, as it is in Mexico, and the ancient Maya sites and picturesque Indians attract more and more people for whom the government, bypassing the objections of anthropological and historical constituencies, would turn the ancient sites into theme parks and the Maya themselves into ethnic spectacles. In this kind of *indigenismo*, the Maya might be trapped like flies in amber—except that the interface between the Maya and the ruling class is in flux in Guatemala, and the Maya, in a growing Pan-Mayan movement, may choose not to be the designated "living cultural patrimony" (as in the Law for the Protection of the Cultural Patrimony of the Nation of 1997) if this status is primarily for the benefit of Guatemala's role in the international economy. The evocative definition and official benediction on the fractious underclass come from above; fraught with ambivalence and good intentions, the designation overlooks the accelerating obliteration of the remains of the ancient, or nonliving, cultural patrimony of Guatemala.

Peru

The Pizzaro brothers, tough, professional soldiers, more like Alvarado than Cortés, conquered Peru only twelve years after Cortés arrived at the Aztec capital in central Mexico. Their feat was even more incredible than the inconceivable Cortés victories. Cortés had interpreters and powerful Indian allies, and retreat to the coast was always possible for him. The Pizzaro brothers' small company was completely isolated, far from its base on the northern coast, in the hemisphere's highest mountains where the soldiers, equipped with superior weaponry, encountered and demoralized contingents of the equally well-trained Inca imperial army. In the preceding century, the monolithic Inca state had conquered more than three thousand miles of territory, extending from modern Colombia to Chile, and had exerted centralized control by imposing the Quechua language, moving populations, and creating a universal system of governance and tribute. In contrast, in Mexico the Aztec had exercised dominion over a smaller area, also exacting tribute but tending to leave the local cultures alone. In both countries Spanish power supplanted an indigenous state, but in Peru many more native cultures had already been suppressed by Inca subjugation with the effective imposition of Quechua, originally the language of a small band of southern highland people. As elsewhere, the Indians were brutalized and enslaved by the conquistadores, and protests were made by the missionary friars and by morally responsible individuals in Spain. Eventually these protests led to laws that provided some protection and recognition of the humanity of the Indians, although, as in Mexico and Guatemala, there were from the beginning bloody, failed revolts by the Indians. At the end of the sixteenth century, Garcilazo de la Vega, a noble mestizo descendant of the Inca ruling dynasty, nostalgically described Inca society as a utopian, communal, and paternalistic state. In the twentieth century this view led to a romantic, Marxist appreciation of Inca statecraft.

In 1821 Peru was the last American country to declare its independence from Spain, and El Libertador (the liberator), Simon Bolívar, led the battle himself, symbolically visiting the university as part of this historic event.[28] Indeed, his liberal French-inspired goals of intellectual freedom and progress emphasized the ideal of a mestizo Pan-American identity and of political unity throughout the former Spanish colonial empire. The latter goals were never achieved, but in Mexico, Guatemala, and Peru the persistent Indian Problem led to movements of reform that in late-nineteenth-century Peru were expressed in radical didactic novels that championed the Indian cause. Now more often described as *indianista*, these works are seen as transitional, playing on romantic exoticism rather than expressing the more robust social reaffirmation of *indigenismo*.[29] These proto-*indigenista* efforts saw Indian culture as monolithic, separate, and effectively dying. Like Guatemala, Peru had no twentieth-century revolution, but the effect of middle-class intellectuals and writers was greater in Peru, where—unlike in Mexico—liberal thought, influenced by both the Mexican and Russian Revolutions, was alienated from the government. Foreigners attracted by the young discipline of archaeology were eager to unearth the rich and little-known cultures of ancient Peru; some suggesting that the ancient peoples of Peru had come from Asia, but Peruvian archaeologists insisted that they were autochthonous.[30] The historically late Inca state was idealized, and *indianista* writers and painters exalted Indian life (fig. 3). Theoretically, *mestizaje* was still viewed as the only viable solution to the Indian Problem, but Peru's policies of marginalization contrasted with

AMAUTA

DIRECTOR:
JOSE CARLOS MARIATEGUI

SUMARIO:

EDITORIAL.—TEMPESTAD EN LOS ANDES, por Luis E. Valcárcel.—CANCION DE NOCHE, por José M. Eguren.—LA CULTURA FRENTE A LA UNIVERSIDAD, por Carlos Sánchez Viamonte.—EL PERSONAJE Y EL CONFLICTO DRAMATICO EN EL TEATRO, LA NOVELA Y EL CUENTO, por Antenor Orrego.—VIGILIA No. 2, por Armando Bazán.—RESISTENCIAS AL PSICO-ANALISIS, por Sigmund Freud.—UBICACION DE LENIN, por Alberto Hidalgo.—GREGORIO MARAÑON, por Carlos E. Roe.—CARTA A LOS MAESTROS DEL PERU, por Guillermo Mercado.— SPILCA, EL MONJE, por Panait Istrati, traducción de J. Eugenio Garro.—EL INDIO ANTONIO Y CRISTALES DEL ANDE, por Alejandro Peralta.—LA CANCION VIGOROSA, por Alcides Spelucín.—LO QUE HA SIGNIFICADO LA ASOCIACION PRO-INDIGENA, por Dora Mayer de Zulen.—EL ARTE Y LA SOCIEDAD BURGUESA, por George Gros.—LA DICTADURA ESPAÑOLA. MARAÑON, ASUA Y LA MONARQUIA, por César Falcón.—LA IGLESIA CONTRA EL ESTADO EN MEXICO, por Ramiro Pérez Reinoso.—NOCHE DE LA SELVA, por Fabio Camacho.—LAS EXPOSICIONES.—MERCADO DE ARTES Y LETRAS.
DIBUJOS de Sabogal, Pettoruti, Carmen Saco, Grosz, Essquerriloff, Raygada.
LIBROS Y REVISTAS.—INTERVIEWS de "Libros y Revistas".—CON MANUEL BEINGOLEA, por Armando Bazán.—CIRCULOS VIOLETA, por Magda Portal.—EL LIBRO DE LA NAVE DORADA, palabras prologales de Antenor Orrego.—CRONICA DE LIBROS, notas críticas por José Carlos Mariátegui, Alberto Guillén, Ramiro Pérez Reynoso, Armando Bazán y Luciano Castillo.—TOPICOS DE LA NUEVA UNIVERSIDAD.—CRONICA DE REVISTAS.

AÑO I   LIMA, SETIEMBRE DE 1926   NUMERO I

Fig. 3. Front cover of the first issue of the *indianista* publication *Amauta*, September 1926

Mexico's ethic of incorporation.[31] *Indigenismo,* in opposition to an upper-class *hispanicismo,*[32] faded in Peru in the 1950s, before it did in Mexico and Guatemala, perhaps because migration to the cities effectively blurred indigenous identity. From the 1960s, the provincial cities bred middle-class socialist resistance and Maoist-inspired guerrillas, such as Sendero Luminoso (Shining Path), who terrorized both *mestizo* and Hispanic populations while co-opting Indians in the 1980s. Focusing on the radical terrorists, the Peruvian government paid little mind to the Indian, statistically and officially, apparently ignoring their continuing presence.[33]

It is difficult to associate the isolated indigenous Quechua- and Aymara-speaking peoples of the southern mountains with the ancient cultural patrimony of the whole country, so the preservation of that widespread and invisible heritage may be much harder to promote in Peru than in Mexico and Guatemala. Like the Aztec, the Inca had conquered their imperial lands only a century before the Spanish Conquest. They were late on the scene in a country where there is evidence of complex societies well before 2000 B.C. The cultural patrimony of Peru consists of the remains of more than four thousand years of strikingly different cultures, spread throughout the country, while the late Inca were basically a highland people. This diversity was certainly not evident to the Spaniards, who saw only the dominant Inca culture. Most of the ancient cultural property of Peru is actually concentrated close to the long Pacific coast and is not associated with living indigenous cultures or languages, whereas international tourism in Peru is focused on the mountainous Inca capital city at Cuzco and at the Inca site Machu Picchu. These places are not immediately accessible, and Peru has yet to embrace the commercialization of its ancient heritage and living cultures on a scale approaching Mexico, or even Guatemala.

Conclusion

Underlying this exploration of the politics of indigenous culture in Latin America are the questions, What is *indigenismo,* and what has become of it? What are the uses of ancient cultural patrimony in the three countries that harbor the remains of the high civilizations of the Americas?

Indigenismo was inextricably tied to acculturation, assimilation, and *mestizaje;* and now judged paternalistic, it is dead. The word's ideological baggage, however, has apparently invalidated it, as it has the entire *indigenista* enterprise. In the ongoing Zapatista Maya revolt that began in Chiapas in 1994, the Mexican Instituto Nacional de Indigenista has played no significant role.[34] Thus, it seems that in Mexico the *indigenismo* of the 1940s, exemplified by the literary and pictorial glorification of the ancient Aztec deity and cultural hero Quetzalcoatl, has collapsed in the wake of debunking by the social scientists and appropriation by the mythmaking of the tourist enterprise. While such a process has also occurred in Guatemala it has, until very recently, been lost in the horrors of the civil war. In Peru *indigenismo* has yet to recover from the country's internal insurrections and long periods of both glorification and rejection. Unless the term can be infused with new meaning, it is sure to remain dormant.

Anthropologists who work with the indigenous cultures of America like to emphasize that history is continuous. While this is obvious, historians and guardians of the ancient heritage tend to compartmentalize history for the sake of explanation, and they seldom make a convincing connection with the present, which is partly because so many historians in this hemisphere have no real connection with their country's indigenous past or would rather not claim that past. This is a completely different attitude toward cultural patrimony from that found in Germany in the 1930s, for instance, where antiquarianism led to a suspect demonstration of ethnic continuity and thus to the legitimization of racial superiority by association with a primordial and exalted past. Another example of *indigenismo* involves the Greek claim to the classical-period Parthenon Marbles, which are not only emblematic of the country's nineteenth-century political independence but also the very definition of Greek cultural heritage, although a direct link between modern and classical Greeks cannot easily be demonstrated. The British, who now own these Greek classical sculptures, also claim them as central to the nineteenth-century development of their intellectually classicizing, national heritage, but they make no claims of genetic descent. Latin American *indigenismo,* which is a delayed product of the same early-nineteenth-century period of antiquarian enthusiasm and political independence, had an analogous goal of cultural association by appropriation of a glorious past, this was demonstrable in the New World only on grounds of impure blood, although not on grounds of intellectual origins, artistic continuity, or even of historical example.

Current cultural trends in Mexico and around the world seem to be heading in two incompatible directions at every economic and social level. These are, first, toward globalization of the economy and the internationalization of culture to create a global patrimony and, second, toward the reestablishment of separate national languages and cultures—perhaps in reaction to the first impulse. Both these processes, and whichever one prevails, will unavoidably involve cultural heritage.

The question remains, How is it possible to prepare for both globalization and localization? International law may be the only formal global mechanism that presumes to deal with both. In 1970, the United Nations Educational, Scientific and Cultural Organization (UNESCO) adopted the Convention on the Means of Prohibiting and Preventing the Illicit Import, Export, and Transfer of Ownership of Cultural Property.[35] This convention addresses the interests of individual countries that would preserve their cultural heritage, while rejecting the interests of markets and consumer countries, which see cultural property as a global commodity. International law is respected and followed only as far as it is seen as fair and reflective of a truly international ethical consensus. The UNESCO convention is slowly gaining such a consensus and imposing principles of cultural nationalism on the international trade in cultural property. In defiance of global trends, it acknowledges the nascent national identities of poor countries intent, however unsuccessfully, on creating and preserving a distinct cultural heritage. All countries signatory to the convention are equal players in a perpetual international game of cultural property in which one side has the culture and the other has the money. Usually the money wins, and a country loses part of its identity. While apparently remote from questions of *indigenismo*, the UNESCO convention has been used effectively in Latin America, where *indigenismo* still informs cultural policy.[36] Where there is the will, the convention may be used by signatory countries as a weapon against the erosion of their fragile and idiosyncratic cultural heritage in a world war that would expropriate indigenous cultures and flatten them beneath the juggernaut of globalism.

Notes

1. Clemency Coggins, "Professional Responsibility, the Archaeological Institute of America, and the Great Divides," in Susan H. Allen, ed., *Excavating the Past* (Dubuque, Iowa: Kendall/Hunt, forthcoming).

2. Edward H. Thompson, "Atlantis Not a Myth," *Popular Science Monthly* 15, no. 6 (1879): 759–64.

3. Clemency Coggins, "Dredging the Cenote," in idem, ed., *Artifacts from the Cenote of Sacrifice, Chichén Itzá, Yucatán* (Cambridge, Mass.: Peabody Museum of Archaeology and Ethnology, Harvard University, 1992), 9–31.

4. Coggins, "Dredging the Cenote" (note 3), 27–28.

5. Bernardino de Sahagún, *General History of the Things of New Spain: Florentine Codex,* trans. Arthur J. O. Anderson and Charles E. Dibble, 13 vols. (Santa Fe: School of American Research, 1950–82).

6. Lewis Hanke, *The Spanish Struggle for Justice in the Conquest of America* (Boston: Little, Brown, 1965), 11.

7. Lewis Hanke, *History of Latin American Civilization: Sources and Interpretations,* vol. 1, *The Colonial Experience* (Boston: Little, Brown, 1973), 157–59.

8. Octavio Paz, "The Art of Mexico: Material and Meaning," in idem, ed., *Essays on Mexican Art,* trans. Helen Lane (New York: Harcourt Brace, 1993), 30–32.

9. Garmán Arciniegas, *Latin America: A Cultural History,* trans. Joan MacLean (New York: Knopf, 1967), 336.

10. Guillermo Bonfil Batalla, *México Profundo: Reclaiming a Civilization,* trans. Philip A. Dennis (Austin: Univ. of Texas Press, 1996), 54, 100, 112.

11. Enrique Florescano, "La creacion del Museo Nacional de Antropología y sus fines cientificos, educativos y politicos," in idem, ed., *El Patrimonio de Mexico* (Mexico City: Fondo de Cultura Economica, 1997), 2:147–71.

12. Julio César Olivé Negrete, "Reseña histórica del pensamiento legal sobre arqueología," in Jaime Litvak King, Luis González, and María del Refugio González, eds., *Arqueología y derecho en México* (Mexico City: Universidad Nacional Autónoma de México, 1980), 36.

13. William Rex Crawford, *A Century of Latin American Thought,* rev. ed. (Cambridge: Harvard Univ. Press, 1967), 266.

14. Braulio Muñoz, *Sons of the Wind: The Search for Identity in Spanish American Indian Literature* (New Brunswick N.J.: Rutgers Univ. Press, 1982), 219.

15. Karel Sklenár, *Archaeology in Central Europe: The First Five Hundred Years,* trans. Iris Lewitová (New York: St. Martin's, 1983), 159.

16. Bonfil Batalla, *México Profundo* (note 10).

17. Jaime Litvak King, "Archaeological Research and Permits: The Who and the Why," *Mesoamerica: The Journal of Middle America* (winter 1988), 5–8; and Jaime Litvak King, "Mexican Archaeology—Challenges at the End of the Century," *Society for American Archaeology Bulletin* 15, no. 4 (1997): 10, 11, 33.

18. Muñoz, *Sons of the Wind* (note 14), 18.

19. Bonfil Batalla, *México Profundo* (note 10), 166.

20. Teresa Morales Lersch, "El proyecto de museos comunitarios como acción preventativa hacia el tráfico y comercio ilegal de objetos" (paper presented at the conference on the Bi-Lateral Protection of Cultural Heritage along the Borderlands: Mexico and the United States, San Antonio, Texas, October 1997).

21. J. C. Cambranes, *Coffee and Peasants: The Origins of the Modern Plantation Economy in Guatemala, 1853–1897,* English version rev. by Carla Clason-Höök (Stockholm: Institute of Latin American Studies, 1985), 23.

22. Beatriz Manz, "The Transformation of La Esperanza, an Ixcán Village," in Robert M. Carmack, ed., *Harvest of Violence: The Maya Indians and the Guatemalan Crisis* (Norman: Univ. of Oklahoma Press, 1988), 70–89; and Kay B. Warren, *Indigenous Movements and Their Critics: Pan-Maya Activism in Guatemala* (Princeton: Princeton Univ. Press, 1998), 86, 89.

23. Oswaldo Chinchilla Mazariegos, "Archaeology and Nationalism in Guatemala at the Time of Independence," *Antiquity* 72 (1998): 384.

24. Frederick Stirton Weaver, *Inside the Volcano: The History and Political Economy of Central America* (Boulder: Westview, 1994), 135; and Shelton Davis, "The Social Roots of Political Violence in Guatemala," *Cultural Survival Quarterly* 7, no. 1 (1983): 7.

25. Muñoz, *Sons of the Wind* (note 14), 255.

26. Warren, *Indigenous Movements* (note 22).

27. Central Intelligence Agency, *The World Fact Book 2001,* s.v. "Guatemala"; online at http://www.odci.gov/cia/publications/factbook/geos/gt.html (9 January 2002).

28. Arciniegas, *Latin America* (note 9), 294.

29. Tomás G. Escajadillo, *La narrativa indigenista peruana* (Lima: Amaru, 1994), 40, 43.

30. Thomas C. Patterson, "Archaeology, History, *Indigenismo,* and the State in Peru and Mexico," in Peter R. Schmidt and Thomas C. Patterson, eds., *Making Alternative Histories: The Practice of Archaeology and History in Non-Western Settings* (Santa Fe: School of American Research Press, 1995), 73–74.

31. Schmidt and Patterson, *Making Alternative Histories* (note 30), 83.

32. Carlos Ivor Degregori, "The Origins and Logic of Shining Path: Two Views," in David Scott Palmer, ed., *The Shining Path of Peru* (New York: St. Martin's, 1994), 38.

33. Luis Millones, personal communication, February 1999.

34. Jaime Litvak King, personal communication, March 1999.

35. See the preamble to the Convention on the Means of Prohibiting and Preventing the Illicit Import, Export, and Transfer of Ownership of Cultural Property, adopted by the General Conference of UNESCO on 17 November 1970, entry in force 24 April 1972; posted at http://exchanges.state.gov/education/culprop/unesco01.html (14 February 2002).

36. Clemency Coggins, "United States Cultural Property Legislation: Observations of a Combatant," *International Journal of Cultural Property* 7 (1998): 52–68.

Objects and Identities: Claiming and Reclaiming the Past

Claire L. Lyons

Cultural heritage — one's own or a nation's heritage — is central to a sense of purpose and place in the world. Artworks, religious icons, monuments, literary manuscripts, traditional myths, and rituals hold the power to create a profound sense of belonging. As the physical evidence of individual and collective pasts, archaeological heritage is esteemed by communities that locate their historical identity in its material expressions. These communities can include indigenous peoples, ethnic groups, the countries in which the heritage originates, and countries that claim the patrimony of others' pasts to define their political institutions and national character.

As passionately as individuals may embrace the emblems of past achievements, how self and group histories are symbolized is a process that is highly contingent. Different kinds of symbols are precious to different cultures, and symbols — being fluid — can wax or wane in significance depending on any number of circumstances. Among the many forms of cultural production that are considered icons, antiquities are among the most potent and contentious. In its quest to reconstruct the past, archaeology provides the raw material for the study of human origins and the evolution of social structures, languages, and modern nation-states. Based, however loosely, on the remains of the past, political narratives are legitimated by ancestral achievements and are made to appear the result of an inevitable evolutionary process. The physical record may coincide with the way that myths of origin are formulated, or it may be diverted for various political, religious, and psychological ends.

Archaeology frequently finds itself at the center of struggles to establish and maintain identity, a process in which it has not always been an objective bystander. Sustaining identity is not only a matter of valuing heritage but also requires the framing of one's own past against that of others through appropriation and possession. The collecting of antiquities has been essentially a practice of representation as much as ownership. Struggles to come to grips with the question of who owns the past have, consequently, been perennial ones.

Recent developments in the way communities attach value to the past have fomented a rash of acrimonious international disputes. Several shifts stand at center stage. A heightened concern about threats to the preservation of cultural heritage — unlike natural heritage, a *nonrenewable* resource — has revealed the detrimental impact of both development and armed conflict.

Art markets attach spiraling values to an ever wider range of objects, stirring admiration and desire among a broader public. The empowerment of ethnic groups and the emergence of fledgling republics place a premium on symbols of unity. Living communities of indigenous people demand the right to control sacred relics, traditional forms of knowledge, and the mortal remains of their forefathers. Compensation for victims of injustice and exploitation is now sought through the recuperation of property taken from them.

The looting of sites and monuments to supply the illicit traffic in artifacts has grown at an explosive pace over the last four decades. On an issue that impacts nations around the world, few regions have received as much publicity as Italy, with its rich legacy of Etruscan, Greek, and Roman remains. Most of the pillaged objects come from central and southern Italy, where the presence of Greek colonial settlements attracted quantities of imports and stimulated sophisticated local art forms. Densely inhabited in antiquity, many archaeological sites are located in remote rural areas that are difficult to police. Material from these regions is easily recognizable, and archaeologists have been assiduous in tracking objects removed from excavations in this zone. Looting affects nearly 50 percent of recorded sites under the supervision of the archaeological superintencies. During a single sixteen-month period in the early 1990s, Italian law enforcement confiscated over sixty-eight hundred illegally excavated artifacts in the southern Italian province of Taranto alone.[1] Arrests of major traffickers in Italy have exposed an avalanche of evidence that the country's richest archaeological zones are being plundered to supply the pipeline of fresh artifacts to northern markets.[2]

In response, the Republic of Italy petitioned the U.S. State Department to impose import restrictions on a number of categories of prehistoric and classical antiquities, under the 1970 United Nations Educational, Scientific and Cultural Organization's (UNESCO) Convention and the Cultural Property Implementation Act. Hearings on this request highlighted the deep hostilities between heritage and art market proponents.[3] Recent years have seen an escalation in theft and more strident calls for restitution. The crisis of cultural heritage in Italy has crystallized the terms under which ancient patrimony is claimed. Some museums have taken steps to avoid litigation by adopting stricter acquisition policies and undertaking independent investigations of questionable antiquities.[4] In other cases, unofficial requests have been made for the restitution of ancient artworks that have been illegally removed from the Italian peninsula, where protective legislation has been in place for many centuries to restrict the unauthorized export of archaeological heritage.

Two investigations of rare Sicilian antiquities now in New York are being pursued on compelling grounds. A pair of archaic marble heads of female divinities and their associated hands and feet, at present in the collection of New York businessman Maurice Templesman, are thought to come from Morgantina, an ancient city in the central Sicilian province of Enna. According to eyewitness reports, the fragments were removed from a sanctuary within the necropolis and, thus, would have represented key evidence for the practice of Greek religious cults in an indigenous Sikel context. Although the hillsides of Morgantina have been plundered for much of the century, the two heads have aroused sharp local feeling. Schoolchildren in the nearby village of Aidone have organized letter-writing campaigns entreating Templesman to return their goddesses, but, in the absence of incontrovertible proof, the heads remain in New York.[5]

Also alleged to have been taken from the American excavations at Morgantina is a hoard of fifteen gilt-silver vessels acquired by the Metropolitan Museum of Art in 1981 and 1982. Working with a local magistrate and the Soprintendenza Archeologica, excavation director Malcolm Bell III uncovered the precise room and pit that once concealed the silver, reconstructing its history from the Hellenistic period to the moment of its burial circa 212 B.C., and its eventual plunder. Pressure from archaeologists and negative publicity have led the museum, reluctantly, to enter into preliminary negotiations with the cultural ministry in Italy, in hopes of reaching a compromise.[6]

Both the marble heads and the silver treasure are impressive works of art, but they are also vital to understanding the history and cultural identity of one of the most important regions of the ancient Greek world. Despite convincing indications of their origins and dubious routes to American collections, neither of the present owners has indicated a willingness to return these objects in the absence of clear evidence. As is usually the case, the proof of clandestine digging and black-market trading from unassailable sources is difficult to produce. The tools of the archaeologist—stylistic comparisons, forensic investigations like those Bell conducted, local informants—generally do not constitute more than circumstantial evidence, especially when objects pillaged from underground or underwater are undocumented before their appearance on the market. In circumstances where the rewards of the illicit traffic are high and the risks are low, front-page coverage in major news publications and costly litigation have been recognized as the only viable means of changing public perceptions and institutional practice. Despite some notable successes, a consequence of these strategies has been a polarization of the terms in which cultural patrimony is framed.

The Gold Phiale

Concern for ancient objects and modern identities is not merely one of theoretical, anthropological interest. It has immediate implications for the collecting, ownership, and control of artistic heritage—the politics of culture. These issues are at the heart of a recent international dispute involving a claim for restitution of another Sicilian antiquity. Surprising in the extent to which competing interests in the museological, archaeological, and political arenas became involved, the case reached the United States Supreme Court. Its resolution offers a revealing study of the ways in which perennial arguments about control of heritage are now being played out. The case in question is *United States v. An Antique Platter of Gold* and concerns a gold *phiale* (a shallow bowl with a raised central boss of the early third century B.C. (fig. 1).[7]

Fig. 1. *Phiale*
Sicily, ca. 300–250 B.C., gold, H: 3.7 cm (1½ in.), Diam.:
22.75 cm (9 in.)
Palermo, Soprintendenza Archeologica

Fig. 2. Detail of the owner's inscription on the rim of the
phiale
See fig. 1

Because contemporary ideas about the significance of the past for the present are distilled in documents submitted to the court by two groups of learned associations, the case is worth examining in some detail.

Like many archaeological artifacts, the *phiale* has enjoyed several lives. Molded from over two pounds of twenty-four-carat gold, the *phiale* was made in the workshop of a master goldsmith, perhaps in ancient Syracuse, the fabled cultural capital of that area of Sicily and southern Italy settled by colonists from the Greek mainland. It is a fine piece of craftsmanship, decorated with concentric rows of acorns and honeybees in delicate relief. Vessels of this shape were used for making libations in religious observances or for drinking, and the individual who once owned it was clearly a notable figure in the community. Remarkably, his identity is known, for on the rim of the bowl is a neat inscription that reads "From [or "I belong to"] Achyris, the Demarch" (fig. 2). A *demarch* was a form of civil magistracy, a political office instituted in Sicilian cities in the fourth century B.C. The style and dialect of the inscription help pinpoint where he lived and ruled to a region of central west Sicily.[8] One can imagine that Achyris used the bowl in the conduct of sacred and official ceremonies. Whether this prize possession was buried in his tomb, securely hidden in the foundations of his residence, or — as is most likely from the written dedication — offered as a votive gift to the gods in a sanctuary can never be known.[9] The *phiale* remained just as Achyris safely left it for twenty-three hundred years.

The modern history of the *phiale* commences where its ancient existence ended, in northwestern Sicily. In its second life the *phiale* became an art object and investment opportunity. Sometime in the 1970s, laborers carrying out electrical repair work reportedly looted it from Caltavuturo (Sicilian dialect for "Vulture Rock"), a remote interior site not far from Palermo. Excavations sponsored at the site by the University of Palermo uncovered a settlement spanning the period from the fourth to the first century and its cemetery, which has repeatedly been devastated by *tombaroli* (tomb robbers).[10] Shortly thereafter, the *phiale* surfaced in the Pappalardo Collection in Catania, where it was studied by the distinguished scholar and epigrapher Professor Giacomo Manganaro. Manganaro published the *phiale* and confirmed its Sicilian origins and importance.[11]

The *phiale* next came to rest in the hands of another Sicilian collector and antiquities dealer, Vincenzo Cammarata, a notorious figure with reputed ties to the underworld of the illicit antiquities trade. Although this object was in a country with clear, longstanding laws vesting ownership of antiquities in the national government and restricting the unauthorized export of cultural patrimony, a prominent New York antiquities dealer, Robert Haber, examined the *phiale* in Sicily and made arrangements for its sale to his client, Michael Steinhardt, through William Veres, a Swiss intermediary. The *phiale* was removed from Italy via Lugano, a Swiss border town and well-known transit point for antiquities shipped from the southern Mediterranean to northern European markets. In these three transactions, the price of the bowl rose in quick jumps from $20,000, to $90,000, to over $1,000,000. Haber exported the gold bowl by means of customs documents that incorrectly stated the country of origin to be "Switzerland" and declared the value to be less than a quarter of the eventual $1.2 million sales price. A contract between dealer and collector was drawn up, guaranteeing that Manganaro, the scholar who had once studied the piece in Sicily, would testify that it had long been in Switzerland. Anticipating a potential problem with an artwork of its special character, the contract also indemnified Steinhardt against any future claim for restitution by the county of origin, suggesting that both parties were well aware of the status of the *phiale* as nationalized cultural property.

Once it arrived in New York, the *phiale* was tested in the conservation labs of the Metropolitan Museum of Art by an expert on ancient metalwork. The *phiale* is a nearly identical twin of another example in the Metropolitan Museum's collection that was acquired without a documented provenance in the 1960s; this museum's *phiale*, which almost certainly comes from the same workshop as Steinhardt's, shows traces of marine incrustation and a Punic inscription that could link it to the waters off western Sicily. A number of experts have examined and verified Steinhardt *phiale's* authenticity, and subsequent rumors that it may be a forgery appeared to be a final (and unsuccessful) attempt by Cammarata to avoid prosecution in Sicily.

The interest of the Metropolitan Museum in the authenticity of the *phiale* was not purely curatorial and scientific. Michael and Judy Steinhardt are major benefactors of the museum, and other antiquities from their collections are on long-term loan there. Despite Steinhardt's reputation as an experienced collector and successful hedge-fund manager (not to mention Haber's well-established expertise in the classical antiquities market), neither Steinhardt nor Haber made any inquiries to determine provenience or any applicable export restrictions. Both questions could have been readily addressed in a few minute's research, since the *phiale* was published in a major scholarly journal shortly before it was spirited to Switzerland. For several years, the Steinhardts displayed the gold *phiale* in their home, a rare and beautifully wrought work of ancient art, but one whose first life history had been largely erased.

The *phiale*'s existence as a prize artwork was a brief one, because in 1997 it was reborn as the defendant in a forfeiture case, as an illegal alien.[12] Following a request from the Republic of Italy, customs agents seized the piece from its new owner and impounded it in a United States Custom House vault in Manhattan. The seizure was based on false declarations made on the import documents, and proceedings were set in motion for its return to the country of origin. The district court in New York found that the importation of the *phiale* was accomplished by means of materially false statements and, significantly, that it was removed from Italy without permission of its true owner, the Italian government, and therefore could be considered "stolen" under the National Stolen Property Act. The court's recognition of Italy's law of 1939 set a precedent, sparking both approval and outrage among players in cultural properties legislation, art law, and heritage conservation. The decision was appealed, and in July 1999 the United States Court of Appeals for the Second Circuit upheld the lower court's finding that confirmed the grounds for forfeiture based on misstatements on the customs forms and denied Steinhardt an "innocent owner" defense. The court of appeals did not, however, directly address the controversial issue of recognizing Italy's cultural patrimony legislation, which has important consequences for the status of undocumented antiquities held in public and private collections in the United States.[13]

In Sicily, meanwhile, a local court indicted both the Sicilian dealer Cammarata and Manganaro, the scholar who collaborated on the appraisal of the piece, for conspiracy, receipt of stolen goods, and Mafia association. Cammarata was arrested in his villa "bunker" near Enna, which was stocked with thousands of undocumented antiquities.[14] Robert Haber's status, after he invoked his Fifth Amendment rights in the New York proceedings, is currently uncertain. Steinhardt subsequently appealed the circuit court's decision to the Supreme Court, which declined to hear the case.[15] In February 2000 the *phiale* was returned to Italy amid great publicity and fanfare in Rome and Palermo.

On its face, *United States v. An Antique Platter of Gold* should have been a fairly straightforward matter of illegal import of a looted antiquity by individuals who were well aware of the potential consequences of their actions. The case was notable mainly for the prominence of the individuals involved and the availability of extensive documentation, which unusually traces the golden bowl at each step of its journey. By contrast, the vast majority of stolen antiquities on the market are found, smuggled, and bought under cover of silence. The lower court's ruling, nevertheless, became a focus of tremendous concern on the part of the archaeological and museum communities in the United States. It is this aspect of the case that I examine more closely here, leaving aside the legal arguments.[16]

Perhaps the most surprising turn of events was the decision of the American Association of Museums (AAM) and a group of three other associations for museum professionals to enter the case upon its appeal. The AAM submitted an amicus curiae brief in support of Michael Steinhardt and against the return of the gold bowl to Italy. This decision was dismaying to many, because the facts on record appeared to be clear-cut and the grounds for repatriation well founded. The AAM action spurred the Archaeological Institute of America (AIA), in turn, to submit a memorandum of law in support of the Italian claim for restitution.[17] The AAM and the AIA briefs both offer considerable analysis of the legal precedents that informed the court's opinion. It is, however, in the introductions to the opposing briefs that a number of underlying assumptions concerning the connection between ancient artifacts and national heritage claims are made explicit. Striking differences and subtle similarities in perspective, polarized in the context and language of legal disputation, demonstrate the extent to which thinking about antiquities has diverged.

The rationale behind the AAM[18] brief is the concern that, by recognizing

Italian cultural patrimony law, the court has impaired the ability of museums to collect and exhibit works of ancient art. There is little doubt that many acquisitions made over the past several decades have involved pillaged objects supplied with a murky provenance and forged documents. Recognition in the United States of other nations' patrimony laws thus could expose a number of items to calls for restitution. The AAM brief favors fewer restrictions on the free circulation of cultural objects, particularly those on the market and in private collections, both of which constitute the only regular sources of new acquisitions and donations. It opposes the acceptance of foreign laws nationalizing cultural properties on the grounds that they are incompatible with United States laws governing private property and free trade. Museums maintain that their records of conservation, publication, and public education about the material culture of past civilizations offer the best way to preserve heritage for the future.

In the AIA brief, Italy's claims to its Graeco-Roman heritage and the administrative structures it has established in order to manage and preserve that heritage are accepted without question. The chief interests of the archaeological organizations are, first, respect for "original context" in which artifacts and monuments are found and, second, support for legislation that helps to protect archaeological resources. In view of the wholesale demolition that centuries of unregulated trade have caused, archaeologists generally favor export and import restrictions because these are considered to help stem the pillage of sites. The facts surrounding the sale of the *phiale* demonstrate the direct link between the marketing of significant new antiquities and the destruction of sites. Archaeologists hold up the details of the Steinhardt case as a perfect example of how looted objects are laundered through the trade, ending up in prestigious collections. The archaeological perspective stresses the loss of knowledge as selected artifacts are recontextualized as artworks in the setting of a private collection or museum display. At the core of the AIA document is a concern for professional ethics and scientific integrity. Archaeologists do not question the legal regime of the country of origin, which they argue is similar to that of the United States, insofar as it accomplishes these goals.

Both archaeologists and museum professionals care about ancient artifacts and see them as signally important for understanding human history. Both believe they must be preserved for the future. Their perspectives on how to accomplish this, however, diverge widely in three areas: *authenticity* (the connection of past to present), *authority* (who controls the past), and *art and artifacts* (how ancient objects are valued).

Authenticity

On the question of authenticity, the AAM brief observes that "in some cases the countries seeking the return of their 'patrimony' do not have a unique and compelling link to the ancient culture which created the art or cultural objects in question beyond the happenstance of territorial congruence."[19] At many points in the history of collecting, the charge that original owners are not *authentic* descendants of antiquity has been used to justify the appropriation of their cultural heritage. The AAM brief sheds doubt on the role of artifacts as intermediaries between past and present within the national (but not international) spheres. It suggests that the ancient past of modern nations is disconnected, little more than a territorial coincidence having little relevance to the contemporary geopolitical situation. It grants that "some cultural property claims are born of a genuine desire to preserve and exhibit cultural objects that have a unique and powerful link to the culture or history of the claiming country."[20] The questions of how unique and powerful links are to be established, and by whom, however, are not addressed. The gold *phiale*, which bears a historical inscription with the name of its ancient Sicilian owner written in local dialect, would seemingly fulfill the criterion of a "unique link" to the claimant country.

Turkey's claims for objects belonging to its Greek and Roman periods are explicitly rejected in the museum brief on the grounds that the first Turks did not migrate to Asia Minor until the late eleventh century.[21] Here language is taken as a hallmark of ethnicity, and classical heritage is only of tangential significance. Similar arguments have been presented in British parliamentary reports whenever the return of the Elgin Marbles is broached. It is charged that the Greeks are not real "Greeks" because their culture has been transformed by centuries of Byzantine Christianity and Ottoman occupation. Although there is continuity of language, the religious and cultural differences are foregrounded. A frequent response to Native American groups who seek to reclaim their heritage points to their diverse ethnic origins, bringing the racial factor into play. Each of the foregoing ways of defining ethnicity or national identity is beset with pitfalls.

The museum brief does not explicitly disassociate present-day Italy from its Graeco-Roman heritage, a far harder argument to pursue. It does question, however, whether objects made in the Graeco-Roman Empire, which spans numerous modern-day borders, can be claimed as the heritage of any one contemporary nation-state. Because objects were traded across borders in antiquity, museums assert that one country cannot unilaterally declare itself the exclusive owner.[22] This perspective sees artifacts as essentially independent of their context and, curiously, places more weight on an object's place of manufacture two millennia ago than on its current location. It ignores the basic facts that most artifacts came to be located in sites under specific historical circumstances and that the cumulative significance of these sites is nothing less than the history of the region, dynamic and transient as it may be.

Archaeologists find that this line of argument presents serious contradictions, not the least because it invokes an untenable notion of ethnic essentialism, compartmentalizing cultural and historical developments into a series of discontinuous and bounded phases. It betrays a serious misunderstanding of the ways that communities evolve, ignoring the role that shifts in the ethnic or religious composition of populations play in directing the long-term course of nation formation.[23] The meanings that are attached to relics of the past, giving depth and substance to feelings of group identity and patriotic pride, are nullified. By this logic, argues the AIA brief, the United States should not enact legislation to protect its heritage, since most Americans cannot establish a "unique and compelling link" either to the first colonial settlers or to the Native American communities that preceded them.[24]

Identifying historical artifacts with their past place of manufacture rather than the current place of discovery opens the door, ironically, for the sort of parochial demands ("Greek art for Greeks") that museums decry. The multiculturalism that, in the museum view, inspires American interest in the past of other cultures is held against those very cultures, where a history of cultural transformation effected by conquest and migration is used to sever the link between past and present.[25] Although this argument is flawed—and disturbing in its racialist undertones—the way in which the notion of "authenticity" is marshaled by collectors, archaeologists, and by claimant countries owes much to past archaeological theories of cultural identity.

The archaeologist brief avoids the pitfalls of correlating the object too closely with an essentialized view of identity. It argues that the *phiale* is part of the historical patrimony of Italy simply by virtue of its discovery there, important for piecing together a phase of its history. Rather than attempting to establish rightful inheritance or merit, archaeologists concern themselves with understanding the object as part of a network of interrelated clues to the past. The fact that Sicilian history is built of successive layers of invaders— Sikel, Phoenician, Greek, Roman, Arab, Norman—in no way means that a particular phase of the past becomes irrelevant once it is superceded. Just as it is valued today, the Greek contribution to Sicilian history was at the center of cultural discourse in the Renaissance and in the eighteenth century, when the earliest archaeological superintendency in the Mediterranean was formed. The question archaeologists and cultural historians ask is not whether Sicilians are legitimate heirs to antiquities found within their region. This is taken for granted, just as it is taken for granted that certain emblems of American identity—the battlefields of Gettysburg, Mesa Verde, the Liberty Bell—constitute a communal inheritance. Avoiding the impossible issue of "ownership" of an object created by an extinct culture, archaeologists concern themselves instead with the question of stewardship—who will take the main responsibility for caring for heritage. As in the United States, responsibility for natural and cultural heritage rests first with the nation in which it is found.

Current ideas about the fluid nature of identity, which is "performed" through material culture, offer few of the firm and simple correspondences between objects and peoples that museums and nations require in order to present a basic narrative reconstruction of the past. Revealing the identity of the people whose former existence is preserved in found artifacts or visible monuments has always been a primary goal of archaeological research. The nuances of this task are ill suited to the requirements of legal disputes over control and ownership rights, however, especially when these depend on establishing ethnic or racial continuities and one-to-one correspondences between objects and people. By naming anonymous communities as archaeological cultures, ancient peoples are distinguished by sets of recurring assemblages of objects that are understood to mark off one group from others in different locations or periods. Archaeologists establish cultural groupings based on artifacts recovered from "type-sites" where they are first or most fully witnessed, with names like "Beaker Folk" and "Villanovan" culture. Prehistorians rely on the style and function of objects, the type of domestic arrangements, and funerary ritual in order to isolate a series of diagnostic features of a "culture." Historical archaeologists regard characteristic assemblages also in the light of literary texts, mythological accounts, and linguistic evidence. Supporting the process of making sense of all the evidence that centuries of excavation have brought to light is the basic assumption that different people create and use objects in culturally distinctive ways.

The "culture-historical" approach was the dominant paradigm in the archaeology of the 1930s to the 1950s.[26] The predominant view held that artifacts are proxies for past peoples whose cultural traditions are more or less static. Their lifeways were seen to proceed in predictable patterns, changing only in response to ruptures brought about by migration, conquest, environmental factors, and other decisive external events. By isolating diagnostic objects and linking sites where similar types are observed, individual peoples could be named and their movements and contacts with others traced. In traditional archaeological terms, cultural identity is denominated by discarded and abandoned objects, the detritus of everyday life. In museum terms, artworks (or artifacts that have been reconstituted as art) contain the essence of a culture and can stand on their own as aesthetic and spiritual expressions of a people. This approach has many shortcomings—not the least that excavated objects are not dependable markers of who their owners were and how they saw themselves.

Successive thinking about the way artifacts reflect identity has had to confront the problem that, as many came to see, pots are not people. In the wake of racial formulations of ethnic origins and the supposed superiority of certain advanced groups, identity and ethnicity were not on the archaeological agenda in the years following World War II. Marxist, feminist, and postprocessual theory returned to the examination of identity under the categories of gender, age, and class. Theoretical approaches promoted much closer readings of artifacts, their distribution, and the visual imagery they display. The aim was to put the people back into the past by emphasizing the dynamic possibilities of material culture. Interestingly, some current thinking about ethnicity, a subject spurred as much by contemporary global situations as it was in the nineteenth century, has taken a pessimistic view of the role of material culture in signaling identity.[27]

Archaeologies of identity have at their core an interest in the relationship between people and things. By comparison with less tangible although no less significant cultural products, such as ritual, knowledge, and music, artifacts by their very materiality constitute and constrain who we are. They are physical things, a record of social actions and unconscious behaviors that took place at a point in time. *Material culture,* a term in archaeology and anthropology that has come to embrace the totality of objects created in the course of human social life, implies the close interdependence of artifacts and the societal codes of those who create them.

As material manifestations, however, art and artifacts have proved to be just as malleable and subject to ideological redeployment as other elements of traditional and spiritual life. Earlier approaches that viewed people as things — or sums of the things surrounding them — have been reconfigured to see things as agents of social life, not only the passive reflections of it. In order to move beyond the taxonomical arrangement of the museum display case or the manipulations of nationalist discourse, knowing the archaeological context is fundamental.

Authority

On the second point of divergence, *authority,* political motivation is a major flashpoint of the current debate. Those who take the free-trade view make the point that since some claimant countries are not authentic heirs "uniquely linked" to the past, their claims are driven by nationalism and the potential for reaping economic windfalls from recuperated art.[28] The AAM brief asserts that, because of its multicultural heritage, a special "hallmark of American culture is a profound appreciation for and desire to learn about and preserve the culture of other countries and civilizations that span the globe and recorded history."[29] This outlook privileges the tradition of collecting antiquities by museums on the grounds that the ethnic diversity of America encourages a strong desire to understand and experience other cultures through their artistic production. It implies that foreign countries are less keen to engage with others, past and present, whether or not they regularly place cultural objects on public display. By assuming authority over patrimony found within their borders, countries like Italy are termed *parochial* for failing to relocate artifacts to the category of "common cultural heritage" — that is, heritage that can move and be acquired freely.

The idea of common or universal heritage (referred to as the "internationalist" outlook) is used to justify an open market in works of art and craft, one that, in effect, removes pieces from the source country to wealthy and powerful institutions in northern Europe and America. By taking control of important and rare works, museums affirm the right to frame and interpret the past of others and assume to do so in a more broad-minded, objective way than the countries of origin. Archaeological remains of past cultures are recognized in the museum brief as "heritage" so long as they function as internationally available commodities. Insofar as their main identity resides in their symbolic value for local history and national patrimony, their status as heritage is denied. Objects retained or claimed by the country of origin are seen as tools of *nationalistic* regimes, a negative term that is commonly reserved for retentionist policies rather than the acquisitive policies of institutions acting under the "universalist" role.

Drawing such a line between markets and countries of origin, however, does not work well in practicality. On the one hand, it has been observed that northern European and American museums have been "nationalistic" in their quest to own premier examples of world art and point to the obvious imperialist and colonialist roots of museum collecting.[30] On the other hand, a nationalistic or colonialist attitude is not solely the preserve of foreign museums, because similar practices can also characterize the relationship between capital city museums and the provincial regions from which their holdings derive. Such a case has been made for Mexico, where major Maya artifacts were appropriated from the provinces in a display of *indigenismo,* in order to assert the indigenous roots of the newly independent Mexican state (see Coggins, in this volume). Alternatively, the archaeologist brief points to the ninety-odd public galleries displaying antiquities established in Sicily alone, open to hundreds of thousands of tourists, as good examples of the universalist spirit.

Nationalism (like authenticity) is therefore an elusive and loaded term. It is not a singular phenomenon but can assume forms ranging from pride in ancestry and patriotic spirit to more ominous manifestations of chauvinism and ethnic strife. Recalling the achievements of the past in order to formulate national identity is generally associated with nineteenth-century concerns for national character, legitimacy, and ethnic unity. It has a long history, however, that can be traced to ancestor worship in antiquity and operates in the service of many different causes.[31]

In Renaissance Europe, for example, antiquarians were keen to link antiquities to ancestors descended from the classical and biblical past. Speculative scholarship that connected relics with scriptural accounts of the Flood and the scattering of the tribes of Israel aimed to demonstrate the truthfulness of sacred literature. Secular interests in exalting the origins of kingdoms and states likewise saw the present as heir to a glorious "Graeco-Roman-Egyptian" past. In Italy humanist scholars in the papal states celebrated the patrimony of the Roman Empire while the preeminence of Etruscan civilization was promoted in the Medici court of Florence. Naples and southern Italy held up the continuity of the Greek heritage in Magna Graecia, a legacy also constructed by the Venetian Republic for want of a suitably prestigious ancient past.[32]

The simplistic (and often politically motivated) association of selected relics of antiquity with the modern states within whose boundaries they were found gave way, among early-nineteenth-century northern European prehistorians, to a more refined system of chronological and stylistic ordering that provided the foundations for an evolutionary understanding of human development. It also revealed that cultural history is based on a more complex set of material and social circumstances than was hinted at by the literary tradition. Evolution and technological progress were congenial ideologies to the growing middle class, which also began to value local history over universal history. These two trajectories, the twin poles of historical inquiry as Krzyzstof Pomian has defined them,[33] separated the indigenous (for example, Celtic, Anglo-Saxon, Italic, Gallic) past from that of Classical civilization with its reliance on written sources. It created an ideological reservoir of physical evidence (relics), monuments (*lieux de memoir*), and collective memory (myths of origin) on which movements of national unity could draw for symbolic purposes.

The shift in archaeological notions of group identity as a socially constructed performance parallels the understanding that national identities are "invented traditions" used to galvanize the cohesion of groups to a larger political idea. Nationalism, as Eric Hobsbawm has shown,[34] creates nations and is not simply a propagandistic strategy instituted in order to consolidate a nation-state's hold over its constituents. In different contexts during the nineteenth and twentieth centuries nationalist movements have articulated archaeological heritage along very different trajectories, as the well-known cases of Celtic monuments in France, remains of imperial Rome in 1930s Italy, the German uses of "Aryan" prehistory, and Holy Land archaeology have demonstrated.[35] Instances in which archaeologists and political authorities have misused the evidence for ideological purposes are well known.

Some historians of archaeology have drawn a distinction between forms of nationalism by examining the particular social conditions and historical framework in which it emerges. The idea of "symbolic capital" can be used to encompass its many manifestations. Antiquities work as symbolic capital in both the national and international realms—for example, the Parthenon is a symbol that Greece trades on as the birthplace of democracy, but also it is used internationally as a visual proxy for classical Western values. Archaeological heritage is valued as worth preserving insofar as it operates as symbolic capital. It operates in obviously different ways when it is appropriated or exchanged for other types of capital: economic, cultural, and social. In these spheres any difference in the role of antiquities as "capital" between, for example, New York and Athens, is negligible. As an "authoritative resource," the past is involved in relations of power and is used to generate or resist structures of domination.[36] Museums, collectors, nation states, and archaeologists alike are implicated in structures of power by claiming cultural and scientific authority over the object. Symbolic capital, thus, comes much closer to describing how objects can be used and misused than the superficial division between "nationalism" (bad) and "internationalism" (good).

As a locus of knowledge and expertise, the museum configures art and cultural history along aesthetic lines and thus exerts a powerful influence on how other cultures are represented. The artifact's integrity and validity are enhanced by its transfer from the point of origin to the museum display case. Challenges to the authority of source countries to control and interpret their own heritage have been most apparent in the relocation of entire architectural complexes and monumental sculptures to foreign museum galleries. It is this history, so palpably witnessed in Turkey, Greece, Egypt, India, and Indochina, that underlies many of the recent demands for restitution.

Although monuments are generally thought of in heritage circles as "immovables," throughout history they have often proved to be all too movable. Artists and explorers came to understand the technical achievements of ancient architecture and regarded ruins as models of artistic excellence.[37] Travel and archaeological exploration brought to light numerous unknown and exotic structures in their original, non-European contexts. One of the consequences of this thirst for knowledge and inspiration was the dismantling and reconstruction of hundreds of major monuments in national museums. Sometimes the transition was from province to capital city, effecting a marginalization of the periphery, where monuments had local meanings, and empowering capitals as centers of power and nationalist discourses. Notions of progress and superiority supported the rationales given for transferring whole monuments or major fragments of them to distant museums, themselves built in the form of temples. Within the galleries of museums such as the Pergamonmuseum in Berlin, the Louvre, and the British Museum, massive structures and sculptural decorations were exhibited as trophies claimed not only for the enterprise of study and preservation but also as tangible emblems of colonial domination and imperial aspirations.

The patrimony of foreign peoples was not only physically appropriated; it came to be embedded in the very artistic, literary, and intellectual life of its new owners. One need only recall the poetry of Byron, the neoclassical style in architecture and design, or the political ends to which Graeco-Roman antiquity was put in the early years of the French and American republics. Such symbols become deeply rooted in their new contexts. Despite these legacies, a defining aspect of appropriation is the power to know, to name and interpret, and to write history. The authority of knowing is often coupled with the authority to judge. The classic case is, of course, that of the Parthenon sculptures displayed in the British Museum since about 1817. Parliamentary debate produced many arguments both against and in favor of the acquisition of the "Elgin Marbles," in which accusations of Greek inauthenticity and incompetence echoed.[38] British colonial custody of India's archaeological and architectural heritage was likewise staged through the rhetoric of expertise — yet another way that Western powers have mapped their authority onto non-Western national domains.[39]

Through the attitudes and practices of institutionalized art history and collecting, immovable buildings are converted into movable objects, architecture is transformed into sculpture, and monuments of one culture become the prizes of another. In the light of international conventions and legislation enacted to protect immovable heritage, the wholesale dismantling of major architectural monuments is now rare. The principle that buildings and natural formations are part of sovereign territory and cannot be legally alienated except under exceptional circumstances is widely accepted. Citing the Cultural Property Implementation Act of 1983, the AAM brief allows for the restitution of objects stolen from standing monuments or from collections.[40] These narrow parameters, however, exclude unexcavated archaeological features or unrecorded sites from the category of monuments having an architectural and spatial integrity. The implication is that sites are merely random deposits awaiting quarrying to extract what resources may lie buried within. Archaeologists are concerned that such a distinction between "monument" and "site" is untenable, because it leaves the door open for the destructive practices of the past to continue in the future. Although the overt colonialism and imperialism of the nineteenth and early twentieth centuries have been superceded, neocolonialist attitudes are still used to rationalize the commodification of archaeological artifacts.

Art and Artifacts

The third area of fundamental disagreement lies in the interpretation of objects as art or artifact. Both the museum and the archaeologist briefs recognize the inherent value and meaning of objects but diverge on where they locate that value. Like sculptural decorations that are removed from monuments, ancient art and artifacts occupy a middle ground between immovable and movable heritage. Antiquities can be seen both as objets d'art, intrinsically valuable as expressions of individual creativity, and as historical evidence, collectives of data that are most meaningful when considered contextually. The excavation occupies a similarly ambiguous place between immovables and movables. Usually invisible, sites come into being only as they undergo the process of systematic dismantling that is excavation. They exist thereafter as stratigraphic complexes that must be interpreted by a reading of their constituent objects and thus can be viewed both as integral monuments and as assemblages of things. The collector sees sites as generic places where things can be extracted from the ground and given existence as independent artworks. The archaeologist sees things in relation to one another, to structures, and to landscape. Sites, then, are essentially monuments — monuments that go down into the earth rather than rise up from it.

An interesting contradiction in the museum position is apparent in the terminology used to establish the value of objects. In the setting of national collections in "source" countries, objects are seen as "countless." Words such as "surplus" and "repetitive" characterize the holdings of museums in Turkey, Mexico, and Peru. Egypt, ironically, is taken to task for refusing to sell "minor and duplicate" antiquities[41] — that is, for not allowing such material to enter the arena of the marketplace, where economic forces can affect the transformation from surplus to scarcity and thus increase value. Contexts such as domestic structures or tombs are also characterized by proponents of the trade as "all the same," significant only insofar as they produce quality objects. These portable and mass-produced objects, however, become rare and unique exemplars once they are situated in auction catalogs or the display cases of international collections. Here they can be either isolated as masterpieces or ordered within a repertoire of similar objects. In either case, they exist as individualized works of art—clothespins and cooking pots together with statues and paintings—whose meanings have changed entirely from what they were originally.[42]

Archaeological artifacts can share a number of qualities with artworks. There are significant differences, however, and so archaeologists differentiate between a gold *phiale* and a painting by Matisse or a Persian carpet. Unlike ordinary products of commerce, governed by the regulations of international trade, ancient art is not successfully valued in a free market. This is because antiquities from underground or underwater are not simply *older* examples of visual arts. They are the unique physical evidence for entire chronological periods, geographical regions, and peoples, from remote prehistory up to the recent past, for whom no complete or even partial written history may exist. Unexcavated artifacts are like pages from a book or an archive—an interrelated series of documents that elucidate the connections, continuities, shared experiences, and cultural experiments of humankind. Quoting the historian and anthropologist Bruce Trigger, the AIA brief notes that artifacts of the past have "strong implications concerning human nature and why modern societies have come to be as they are." Historical consciousness "helps to guide public action and is a human substitute for instinct."[43] This is very close to the museum notion of the "universality" of art but emphasizes holistic scientific knowledge over the perceived aesthetic qualities of the single object.

Conclusion

The AIA and the AAM briefs share a common appreciation for the importance of understanding our origins and for the study of art and material culture as gateways to the past. While art historians and curators tend to prize individual works as unique expressions of art that manifest the creative spirit of bygone peoples, archaeologists are more inclined to regard artifacts as elements in an assemblage of data that can be used to reconstruct past social life in all its aspects. Despite the ancient Sicilian inscription, rarity, and craftsmanship that imbue it with special historical and artistic significance, the gold *phiale* can only be fully appreciated in context. While the basic assumptions of the briefs are similar, a fundamental dilemma remains. An archaeological approach does not preclude aesthetics and connoisseurship—in fact, some might argue that the field still relies too heavily on the methodology of art history. Collectors and museums that take part (wittingly or unwittingly) in the acquisition of undocumented antiquities, however, place insurmountable obstacles before those whose interest is in reconstructing the larger picture of cultural history, by destroying the evidence.

The case of the Steinhardt *phiale,* however, is not solely one of competing academic practices. Alternative ideologies are invoked to bolster the main point of contention—ownership: who will control increasingly valuable and increasingly scarce artifacts, now that more nations are claiming the right to represent themselves and their past history? Legal considerations of ownership traditionally depend on questions of good title. When applied to cultural "properties," this inevitably leads to accusations that the possessors or heirs do not hold valid title because they are neither authentic nor competent. Two hundred years of disputation over the Elgin Marbles offers an excellent example of the shortcomings and futility of this line of argument. Antiquities are notoriously slippery and poorly adapted to the process of assigning or claiming ethnic, national, and social identities, as theoretical archaeologists have shown. Attempts to utilize antiquities in this way can readily be turned against the parties on all sides. Given the slippages in meanings and the values attributed to archaeological objects and the fragility of the vital evidence that they furnish, shared stewardship (rather than ownership) of artifacts as markers of our *future* identity is likely to be the only viable way to approach the past.

Notes

1. Daniel Graepler and Marina Mazzei, *Provenienza, sconosciuta! Tombaroli, mercanti e collezionisti: L'Italia archeologica allo sbaraglio* (Bari: Edipuglia, 1996), 47. Comprehensive information on the international antiquities trade is assembled in the newsletter *Culture without Context*, published by the Near Eastern Project of the Illicit Antiquities Research Centre, McDonald Institute for Archaeological Research, Cambridge University. See also Kathryn Walker Tubb, ed., *Antiquities: Trade or Betrayed: Legal, Ethical and Conservation Issues* (London: Archetype, 1995).

2. In Italy, arrests of middlemen in the illicit trade of antiquities have recuperated tens of thousands of artifacts; see Peter Watson, *Sotheby's: The Inside Story* (New York: Random House, 1997), 290–93; and Sarah Delaney, "Italian Police Recovering Things That Were Caesar's," *Washington Post*, 24 April 2000, A21.

3. The hearings of the Cultural Property Advisory Committee, held in October 1999, are summarized in David Briscoe, "Clashes over Italy Antiquity Plea" (Associated Press, 13 October 1999), http://www.prosea.org/articles-news/unesco/Clashes_Over_Italy_Antiquity_Plea.html (11 February 2002); "Stemming the Antiquities Flow," *Washington Post*, 18 October 1999, A18; R. Donadio, "Italy Presses U.S. for Help against Art Thieves," *Italy Daily—Corriere della Sera*, 13 October 1999, 2; and Peter K. Tompa, "Cultural Property Advisory Committee Reviews Italian Request for Import Restrictions," *Celator* 13, no. 12 (1999): 32–37.

4. The J. Paul Getty Museum returned three objects that it discovered had been stolen from Italian collections and excavation storerooms; see Suzanne Muchnic, "Getty to Return Three Acquisitions to Italy," *Los Angeles Times*, 4 February 1999, A1. The J. Paul Getty Museum's acquisition policy was revised in 1995 to prohibit the acquisition of artifacts without a documented provenience, which brought the policy into line with the policies of major international museums such as the Berlin Antikensammlung and the British Museum; see *Art Newspaper*, no. 54 (1995): 1.

5. A pair of sixth-century B.C. acrolithic heads of female divinities in the collection of businessman Maurice Templesman are discussed by Alexander Stille in "Head Found on Fifth Avenue," *New Yorker*, 24 May 1999, 58–69.

6. On the hoard of precious silver vessels in the Metropolitan Museum of Art in New York, see Walter V. Robinson, "Italy Calls N.Y. Museum's Prized Collection Stolen," *Boston Globe,* 17 April 1998, A1; and Malcolm Bell III, "La provenienza ritrovata: Cercando il contesto di antichità trafugate," in Paola Pelagatti and Pier Giovanni Guzzo, eds., *Antichità senza provenienza II: Atti del colloquio internazionale, 17–18 ottobre 1997,* Supplement to *Bollettino d'Arte,* nos. 101–2 (1997) (Rome: Istituto Poligrafico e Zecca dello Stato, 2000), 31–41, which offers a full reconstruction of events.

7. The author of the present article served as vice president for professional responsibilities of the Archaeological Institute of America (AIA) from 1994 to 1998, and contributed to the AIA et al.'s brief in the *phiale* case (see below, note 9).

8. Giacomo Manganaro, "Darici in Sicilia e le emissioni auree delle poleis siceliote e di Cartagine nel V–III sec. a.c.," *Revue des Études Anciennes* 91, nos. 1–2 (1989): 302–4, figs. 1–3. An alternative reading of the inscription translates the word *damarchou* as a patronymic: "From [or "I belong to"] Achyrios, son of Demarchos."

9. The history of the *phiale* is described in the brief submitted by amici curiae Archaeological Institute of America (AIA) et al. The texts of the AIA et al. and the American Association of Museums (AAM) et al. briefs are published in Carla J. Shapreau, "Second Circuit Holds that False Statements Contained in Customs Forms Warrants Forfeiture of Ancient Gold Phiale — Hotly Contested Foreign Patrimony Issue Not Reached by the Court: *United States v. An Antique Platter of Gold,*" *International Journal of Cultural Property* 9 (2000): 49–137 (AAM et al. brief, 76–105; AIA et al. brief, 105–30). The *phiale* was reportedly discovered together with a silver cup (now lost), which suggests that it may have been part of a votive deposit or domestic hoard like the Morgantina silver; see AIA et al. brief, in Shapreau, "Second Circuit," 126 n. 21.

10. Nicola Bonacasa, "Scavi e ricerche dell'Istituto di archeologia dell'Università di Palermo a Himera e Caltavuturo (1972–1975)," *Kokalos* 22–23 (1976–77): 710–12; and Carmela Angela Di Stefano, "Ricognizioni archeologiche nel territorio di Caltavuturo," *Sicilia Archeologica* 5, nos. 18–20 (1972): 85.

11. Manganaro, "Darici in Sicilia" (note 8).

12. For a general account, see A. L. Slayman, "Case of the Golden Phiale," *Archaeology* 51, no. 3 (1998): 36–41. The details of this case are drawn from court documents, including the decision issued by District Court Judge Barbara Jones and the briefs submitted to the United States Court of Appeals for the Second Circuit by Michael Steinhardt, the Republic of Italy, the United States of America, and *amici curiae* AIA et al. and AAM et al.

13. The court did address this issue indirectly in holding that the misstatement concerning the country of origin was material because Italy is known to be a country with strong cultural patrimony laws. A declaration that the *phiale* came from Italy would have alerted customs officials at the time of its import.

14. Cristina Ruiz, "Revealed: The Mafia's Interest in Archaeology," *Art Newspaper,* no. 89 (1999): 53.

15. Martha Lufkin, "The Steinhardt Phiale Returns to Italy," *Art Newspaper,* no. 101 (2000): 59.

16. For a legal analysis, see Peter D. C. Mason, "United States Court Issues

Important Ruling on Antiquities," *Art, Antiquity and Law* 3, no. 1 (1998): 61–72; and Shapreau, "Second Circuit" (note 9), 49–76.

17. The AAM was joined by the Association of Art Museum Directors, the Association of Science Museum Directors, and the American Association for State and Local History. On the other side, the AIA was joined by the American Anthropological Association, the United States National Committee of the International Council on Monuments and Sites, the Society for American Archaeology, the Society for Historical Archaeology, and the American Philological Association.

18. I refer to the briefs of the AAM et al. and the AIA et al. as the "AAM brief" and the "AIA brief," but this does not imply that there was unanimity of opinion among the members of those professional associations—the issues are far too complicated! Some archaeologists are more concerned about obstacles to research presented by agricultural development, lack of conservation and research access, and decreasing funding for publication. It should be noted that the AAM brief was a source of discord within the profession. It was apparently drafted by a group of attorneys and museum officials with close ties to the New York collecting and antiquities trade community. The United States committee of ICOM was critical of the confrontational tone of the document and its dismissive attitude toward the right of nations to assume primary responsibility for the protection of their heritage. After the details of the Steinhardt case and the arguments put forth in the AAM brief became more widely known, a number of museum professionals reportedly distanced themselves from its perspectives. Although a small number of institutions still collect aggressively in this field, many museum professionals are increasingly sensitive to ethical considerations that have a bearing on cultural objects of past as well as living communities.

19. AAM et al. brief; see Shapreau, "Second Circuit" (note 9), 76–105.

20. AAM et al. brief; see Shapreau, "Second Circuit" (note 9), 80.

21. AAM et al. brief; see Shapreau, "Second Circuit" (note 9), 100 n. 7.

22. AAM et al. brief; see Shapreau, "Second Circuit" (note 9), 81. The example given is that of the "Sevso hoard," a treasure of Roman silver vessels claimed by three governments, Yugoslavia, Lebanon, and Hungary. Although these competing claims are frequently cited as the example par excellence of nationalistic greed, investigations have since revealed the provenience of the hoard to be Hungary. False rumors that the Sevso hoard was found in Croatia or Lebanon were circulated by the dealers attempting to peddle the hoard in order to deflect attention from the original theft (and associated homicides) in Hungary. See Peter Landesman, "The Curse of the Sevso Silver," *The Atlantic Monthly* 288, no. 4 (November 2001): 63–89.

23. AIA et al. brief; see Shapreau, "Second Circuit" (note 9), 123.

24. AIA et al. brief; see Shapreau, "Second Circuit" (note 9), 123.

25. AAM et al. brief, quoting A. Emmerich, "Importing Antiquities: A Moral Issue?" *Washington Post,* 6 February 1978, A23: "A curious point is that the present-day population of many historically endowed regions consists of the descendants of the invaders who destroyed the very cultures whose remnants their modern governments now so jealously claim is exclusively theirs"; see Shapreau, "Second Circuit" (note 9), 81, 100 n. 11. The AIA et al. brief responds that the majority culture of the United States is no less a product of conquest and yet the United States government protects Native

American and Native Hawaiian cultural patrimony through the Antiquities Act of 1906 as well as an extensive series of federal and state laws; see Shapreau, "Second Circuit" (note 9), 130 n. 45.

26. Bruce G. Trigger, *Gordon Childe, Revolutions in Archaeology* (New York: Columbia Univ. Press, 1980); and Bruce Trigger, *A History of Archaeological Thought* (Cambridge: Cambridge Univ. Press, 1989), 167–74.

27. Jonathan Hall has suggested that who people say they are is more indicative than material markers and that, in the absence of texts, archaeology may reveal only scant and peripheral details about the identity of the people it studies; see Jonathan M. Hall, *Ethnic Identity in Greek Antiquity* (Cambridge: Cambridge Univ. Press, 1997); see also the "Review Feature" discussing Hall's work in *Cambridge Archaeological Journal* 8 (1998): 265–83, with contributions by Ian Morris, Sian Jones, Sarah Morris, Colin Renfrew, and Roger Just, and a response by Hall.

28. AAM et al. brief; see Shapreau, "Second Circuit" (note 9), 81. The AAM brief connects claims for restitution to the rising art market value of objects, which foreign nations are "quick to label" as patrimony (Shapreau, p. 79). The AIA brief counters that there is no evidence that claimant countries have sold or converted repatriated objects for financial gain, but rather they "profit" by regaining patrimony for display, thus stimulating cultural tourism; see Shapreau, "Second Circuit" (note 9), 123–24.

29. AAM et al. brief; see Shapreau, "Second Circuit" (note 9), 79.

30. Tim Barringer and Tom Flynn, eds., *Colonialism and the Object: Empire, Material Culture, and the Museum* (London: Routledge, 1998).

31. Several recent publications have explored the role of archaeology and national identity, including Lynn Meskell, ed., *Archaeology under Fire: Nationalism, Politics and Heritage in the Eastern Mediterranean and Middle East* (London: Routledge, 1998); Margarita Díaz-Andreu and Timothy Champion, eds., *Nationalism and Archaeology in Europe* (Boulder: Westview, 1996); and Philip L. Kohl and Clare Fawcett, eds., *Nationalism, Politics, and the Practice of Archaeology* (Cambridge: Cambridge Univ. Press, 1996).

32. Giuseppe Pucci, *Il passato prossimo: La scienza dell'antichità alle origini della cultura moderna* (Rome: Nuova Italia Scientifica, 1993).

33. Krzysztof Pomian, "Les deux pôles de la curiosité antiquaire," in Annie-France Laurens and Krzysztof Pomian, eds., *L'Anticomanie: La collection d'antiquités aux 18e et 19e siècles* (Paris: École des Hautes Études en Sciences Sociales, 1992), 59–68.

34. Eric J. Hobsbawm and Terence Ranger, eds., *The Invention of Tradition* (Cambridge: Cambridge Univ. Press, 1983); Eric. J. Hobsbawm, *Nations and Nationalism since 1780: Programme, Myth, Reality* (Cambridge: Cambridge Univ. Press, 1990); and Benedict Anderson, *Imagined Communities: Reflections on the Origin and Spread of Nationalism,* 2d ed. (London: Verso, 1991).

35. Michael Dietler, "A Tale of Three Sites: The Monumentalization of Celtic Oppida and the Politics of Collective Memory and Identity," *World Archaeology* 30 (1998): 72–89; Daniele Manacorda and Renato Tamassia, *Il piccone del regime* (Rome: Armando Curcio, 1985); Neil Asher Silberman and David Small, eds., *The Archaeology of Israel: Constructing the Past, Interpreting the Present* (Sheffield: Sheffield Academic Press, 1997); and Suzanne L. Marchand, *Down from Olympus:*

Archaeology and Philhellenism in Germany, 1750–1970 (Princeton: Princeton Univ. Press, 1996).

36. Yannis Hamilakis and Eleana Yalouri, "Antiquities as Symbolic Capital in Modern Greek Society," *Antiquity* 70 (1996): 117–29. D. Byrne applies Bourdieu's concept of symbolic capital to the treatment of antiquities by the Thai state in "The Nation, the Elite and the Southeast Asian Antiquities Trade," *Conservation and Management of Archaeological Sites* 3, no. 3 (1999): 145–53.

37. Claire Lyons, "Archives in Ruins: The Collections of the Getty Research Institute," in Michael S. Roth, ed., *Irresistible Decay: Ruins Reclaimed* (Los Angeles: Getty Research Institute for the History of Art and the Humanities, 1997), 79–99.

38. The debate continued along much the same terms at the 1999 British Museum Classical Colloquium, "Cleaning the Parthenon Sculptures." See the conference report by Claire Lyons in *International Journal of Cultural Property* 9 (2000): 180–84. The comments on this conference by John Boardman, "The Elgin Marbles: Matters of Fact and Opinion," *International Journal of Cultural Property* 9 (2000): 233–62, offer very convincing reasons for the retention of the Parthenon sculptures by the British Museum.

39. Tapati Guha-Thakurta, "Monuments and Lost Histories: The Archaeological Imagination in Colonial India," in Suzanne Marchand and Elizabeth Lunbeck, eds., *Proof and Persuasion: Essays on Authority, Objectivity, and Evidence* (Turnout: Brepols, 1996), 144–70.

40. AAM et al. brief; see Shapreau, "Second Circuit" (note 9), 83.

41. AAM et al. brief; see Shapreau, "Second Circuit" (note 9), 82, 100 n. 12.

42. See Philip Fisher, "Local Meanings and Portable Objects: National Collections, Literatures, Music, and Architecture," in Gwendolyn Wright, ed., *The Formation of National Collections of Art and Archaeology* (Washington, D.C.: National Gallery of Art, 1996), 15–27.

43. AIA et al. brief, quoting Bruce G. Trigger, *A History of Archaeological Thought* (Cambridge: Cambridge Univ. Press, 1989), 3, 14; see Shapreau, "Second Circuit" (note 9), 110.

Part II

Codifying Birthrights

Kennewick Man –
A Kin? Too Distant

Douglas W. Owsley and Richard L. Jantz

The discovery on 28 July 1996 of a well-preserved human skeleton exposed by erosion of the shoreline of the Columbia River led to a lawsuit filed in a United States federal court by eight scientists contesting a federal agency's action. The case of the Kennewick Man is a complicated lawsuit that can be interpreted as a clash between two systems of conceptualizing and tracing human history.[1] The systems arise from differing cultural perspectives: the culture of present-day Native Americans and the culture of science.

In an attempt to explain the perspective and motivations of two of the scientists involved in this case, we want to provide here a foundation for contemplating and evaluating the various views of this dispute by presenting facts from their perspective and expressing our concerns. This legal challenge is not against Native Americans per se, although others frequently characterize it as such. The dispute is based on the action of a federal agency. In developing the scientists' position, the approach must be clear: comprehensive understanding of ancient human history in the Americas requires the study of skeletal remains. It is in the interest of all people that a clear and accurate understanding of the past be available to everyone.

Background

The Kennewick Man was discovered in Kennewick, Washington, by two college students. Erosion had exposed the skeleton on land managed by and under the jurisdiction of the United States Army Corps of Engineers. The discovery was investigated locally as a forensic case by the Benton County coroner with assistance provided by James Chatters, an archaeologist who lives in nearby Richland, Washington. In Chatters's initial opinion the nearly complete, exceptionally well-preserved skeleton seemed European-like and showed craniofacial features unlike those characteristic of Native Americans; therefore, the skeleton was thought to be a nineteenth-century explorer or pioneer. This theory became questionable, however, when a broken projectile point that was embedded in the right pelvic bone was determined to be of an ancient style. Its presence made establishing the skeleton's date essential.

At the coroner's request, a single accelerator test was run using a fragment of a metacarpal. The test indicated that the remains were approximately nine thousand years old,[2] which classifies the skeleton as one of the oldest and best preserved of its kind found in the Americas. According to Chatters,[3] the cranial vault was narrow and relatively long with facial features that included small malars, a narrow facial width, a prominent nose, and a projecting chin. These features are not like those typically found in Native Americans, who commonly have wide faces, large flat malars, a rounded mental symphysis, and a more globular cranial vault. Two physical anthropologists, Catherine J. MacMillan, retired from Central Washington University, and Grover S. Krantz of Washington State University, conducted brief examinations of the skeleton. MacMillan and Krantz assessed that the cranial features could not be biologically linked to existing tribal groups. Krantz added: "The racial affiliation of the skeleton continues to be a problem that should be studied, not ignored, if we are to fully understand the early prehistory of America."[4]

After being notified of the skeleton's age, the Army Corps of Engineers took possession from the coroner, citing requirements of the Native American Graves Protection and Repatriation Act (NAGPRA), which establishes a process for returning remains and associated cultural items found on federal land to Native Americans who can be tribally affiliated. As a starting point, NAGPRA requires federal agencies to contact tribes that are potentially affiliated with found remains. Tribes may claim remains by presenting various kinds of evidence of affiliation such as geography, biology, archaeology, anthropology, language, kinship, folklore, oral tradition, history, or expert opinion. The rationale behind the concept of affiliation is to provide a means for returning remains to a definably linked descendant group.

Five tribes responded to the corps: the Umatilla tribe of northeastern Oregon; the Yakamas, the Wanapum Band of Yakamas, and the Colvilles of Washington; and the Nez Percé of Idaho. They collectively argued for return and reburial under the guidelines of NAGPRA. The coalition demanded immediate reburial of the skeleton in a secret location with no further examination.

The corps ordered termination of the coroner's investigation, including the partially completed DNA tests being run at the University of California, Davis. Then the corps placed the remains, still in their temporary packaging, in a cabinet at the Pacific Northwest National Laboratory in Richland, Washington. It did not create an inventory or conduct a condition assessment of the bones when it took custody. It immediately began consultations with the local tribes to finalize disposition of the remains.

The corps published its intent to transfer the remains within thirty days to the Umatilla, based on the location of the skeleton's recovery. Under NAGPRA, human remains discovered on federal land judicially recognized as having been occupied by an aboriginal tribe can be claimed by that group unless another tribe can show that it is "culturally affiliated" with the remains.[5] In the case of the Kennewick skeleton the Umatilla tribe claimed the skeleton on this basis, asserting that cultural affiliation between the skeleton and any modern tribe cannot be demonstrated because of its great age, and that the discovery occurred on land that was judicially determined to have been aboriginally occupied by the Umatilla tribe.[6] This assertion was later shown to be in error, as there had been no such ruling.

Throughout this process, interested scientists made numerous requests to the Army Corps of Engineers for permission to study the skeleton. Douglas Owsley also contacted the Umatilla tribe through intermediaries and directly in writing to request permission, on behalf of the Smithsonian Institution, to examine the skeleton. He emphasized the importance of the discovery and what could be learned, and offered to release the findings jointly under the auspices of the tribal government and the Smithsonian. Owsley received no response from the tribe.

The corps also failed to respond to repeated requests to study the skeleton. As a result, eight scientists, including the authors of this essay, filed suit in October 1996 to halt the transfer and to enforce what they contend is a legal right to study the skeleton. *Bonnichsen et al. v. United States* is the first major legal challenge to a federal agency's implementation of NAGPRA.

Tribal Views

The Umatilla, a tribe with 2,087 members, refer to Kennewick Man as the "Ancient One." According to Donald Sampson, chairman of the Board of Trustees for the Confederated Tribes of the Umatilla Reservation, religious and cultural beliefs mandate burial of the skeleton as soon as possible. The Umatilla have made it clear that scientific arguments for examining the remains are "shaky to nonexistent."[7] From their viewpoint, religious rights and beliefs should take precedence over study.

A key legal issue of the dispute is whether the skeleton is Native American as defined by NAGPRA. The broken projectile point and the geographical location of the recovery were cited as evidence of Kennewick Man's Native American ancestry, thus implying affiliation as manifested by cultural descent. As the tribe's religious leader, Armand Minthorn, stated: "If this individual is truly over 9,000 years old, that only substantiates our belief that he is Native American. From our oral histories, we know that our people have been part of this land since the beginning of time. We do not believe that our people migrated here from another continent, as the scientists do."[8]

Hundreds of Native American creation and origin stories solidify group identity through symbolic meaning. Many Native Americans are candid regarding their nonbelief in the value of archaeological research as pertinent to questions of origin.[9] This sentiment is intensified when dealing with human remains. Thus, the Umatilla believe they already know their history. According to Minthorn, "It is passed on to us through our elders and through our religious practices."[10] Accordingly, the Umatilla reject the notion that anything relevant can be learned from analysis of a skeleton.

These assertions also dispose some Native Americans against appeals for scientific investigation of the kind now at issue. For example, the following comment was made by Sebastian Le Beau, repatriation officer for the Cheyenne River Sioux: "We never asked science to make a determination as to our origins. We know where we came from. We are the descendants of the Buffalo people. They came from inside the earth after supernatural spirits prepared the world for humankind to live here. If non-Indians choose to believe they evolved from an ape, so be it. I have yet to come across five Lakotas who believe in science and evolution."[11]

These beliefs are not, however, universal among Native Americans. Some tribal groups have permitted study because of local community interest and benefit to the larger majority. For example, scientists are currently investigating human remains from a cave on Prince of Wales Island in Alaska dated to 9,800 B.P. with authorization of the local tribal councils.[12]

Scientific Concerns

From the scientific perspective, repatriation is appropriate in those cases dating to the late prehistoric and early historic periods where affiliation is demonstrable. In response to NAGPRA, museums and scientists now comply positively and willingly with the intent of the legislation by returning museum collections. As of May 1999, the Smithsonian Institution's National Museum of Natural History has deaccessioned and transferred more than 3,225 sets of human remains and 87,000 archaeological and ethnographic objects to forty-five native groups.[13] An additional 3,000 skeletons from the northcentral United States have been repatriated from universities and museums.[14] Nearly all skeletal collections have been returned in some states, as is the case in Iowa, North Dakota, and Minnesota. For example, the number of individual remains reburied in Minnesota between 1978 and June 1998 is 1,608.[15] According to the "NAGPRA Update" of April 1999, collection inventories have been received from 733 American institutions and agencies, as required by this legislation. Many of these inventories have been followed by *Federal Register* notices issued by the United States government, indicating intent to repatriate thousands of remains, funerary artifacts, sacred items, and objects of cultural patrimony to affiliated groups.

In contrast, the Kennewick Man case is the first legal challenge to the repatriation of human remains. From the perspective of the scientist-plaintiffs, NAGPRA becomes problematic when it is applied to remains of greater antiquity where affiliation cannot be easily determined.

In reality, declarations of relationship and continuity become debatable and arguably unrealistic with remains, like Kennewick Man, which are thousands of years old. Human genealogical histories involve various complex combinations of branching and merging, migration and extinction. A genealogical connection extending back nine thousand years, some four hundred and fifty generations, is hard to demonstrate, especially without comprehensive study. Furthermore, many individuals, and even groups, left no descendants. To assume that Kennewick Man is the direct ancestor of a tribe inhabiting the region today assumes no migration in or out of the area for more than nine thousand years. With human mobility as we know it, if there is a relationship at all, Kennewick Man is more likely at the base of a number of scattered populations, rather than the direct kin of a localized group such as the Umatilla. (For an historic example of dispersal, one need only review the geographical distribution of the descendants of those who arrived in America on the *Mayflower*.) Evidence supporting the position of affinity based on geographical location is difficult to establish.

Furthermore, it should be pointed out that NAGPRA was not intended to stop scientific research. The Umatilla contend that this case is an effort by scientists "to lay claim to materials which Congress did not intend them to have."[16] In fact, from its inception, NAGPRA was a compromise that assumed that studies of the kind requested in the Kennewick Man case would be allowed. For example, the report from the Senate Select Committee on Indian Affairs referenced this issue when it recommended the passage of NAGPRA:

> The Committee received testimony from professionals in the scientific community who say that there is an overriding interest in the acquisition and retention of human remains for the purpose of scientific inquiry. Scientists have indicated that recent technological advances allow them to analyze bones and learn new facts and pursue important research on diet, disease, genetics and related matters. Native American witnesses have indicated that they do not object to the study of human remains when there is a specific purpose to the study and a definitive time period for the study.[17]

In a report to the 1994–95 Congress, Secretary of the Interior Bruce Babbitt restates the contention that science is integral to the process:

> Now more than ever, the protection, preservation, and interpretation of America's archeological resources are important activities of federal agencies. Archeological remains, whether related to the ancient inhabitants of our country or from more recent historical times, should be reserved for public uses rather than private gain. We should strive to provide all Americans the opportunity to appreciate the past craftsmanship, understand past ways of life, and better comprehend people's adaptations to changing natural, physical, and social environments during prehistoric and historic times. Information derived from archeological resources should be provided through scientifically based, accessible public interpretation. Archeological collections and associated records should be cared for and used to further public education.[18]

To date, only seven well-preserved and securely dated Paleo-American skeletons have been discovered in the United States. Most are from the western half of the continent, especially Nevada and Texas, where drier conditions facilitate preservation. About twenty more of these skeletons are known, but their condition is fragmentary as a result of poor preservation or, in some cases, because of the mortuary practice of cremation. The sample is so small that each new discovery has the potential of adding significant information to the existing corpus of knowledge.

In recent years, however, research on ancient remains has been blocked or limited by unclear government regulations combined with tribal claims that are not always closely examined. As a result, prehistoric remains have been reburied without adequate study. Examples include the skeleton of a female found near Buhl, Idaho, that is approximately 10,675 years old, which had been claimed under state law for reburial by the Shoshone-Bannock tribe. Little is known about this skeleton because it was reburied without thorough study. In another case, an eight-thousand-year-old skeleton found in Hourglass Cave in the Colorado Rockies was reburied by the Southern Ute tribe. The United States Forest Service has declared the cave sacred and closed to the public.[19] Under NAGPRA, disposition of remains depends on tracing cultural affiliation. These recent transfers are disputable, although no lawsuits were initiated. Based on archaeological evidence, Numic-speaking populations such as the Shoshone, Paiute, and Ute migrated into the Great Basin and Colorado during the late prehistoric period, thousands of years after these ancient individuals died.[20]

Other ancient skeletons have or will be reburied soon, including well-preserved specimens from Minnesota, Nebraska, and Nevada. The Northern Paiute, for example, have claimed the Spirit Cave Mummy from Nevada, compelling the Bureau of Land Management to defer requests to conduct DNA research on this individual and other ancient remains under its control.

The Biological Context of Kennewick Man

The Kennewick Man appears to date to a period similar to four other well-dated skeletons that have provided information about ancestry and biological relationships through morphometric study. As will be demonstrated, morphometric analysis shows how different these four specimens are from modern groups, indicating that it cannot be assumed a priori that the Kennewick fossil is related to modern Native American peoples. Study is absolutely necessary to determine whether Kennewick Man is similar to anyone living today.

Study is also required to test new theories against traditional assumptions about the peopling of the Americas. The traditional model purports that the first Americans crossed the Bering Strait land bridge connecting Siberia to North America during the terminal Wisconsinian Ice Age some 11,500 years ago. Their technology has been referred to as Clovis culture, and their designation as Paleo-Indian was linked to the belief that biologically they were related to northeast Asians, with skeletal, dental, and soft tissue features characteristic of Mongoloid peoples. Scientists assumed that contemporary Native Americans were the descendants of these people.

Bioanthropological studies initiated during the 1990s and accurate dating of early sites have challenged this model, suggesting that Paleo-American may be a better designation than Paleo-Indian for this population. Tantalizing evidence indicates that pre-Clovis arrival with multiple migrations involving diverse populations may be a more accurate assessment of the events involved in peopling the New World. Some of the oldest humans identified on the continent have skeletal features that are distinctly different from modern-day Native Americans. Whether the earliest groups were directly related to later peoples is unknown. Early migrants may have been replaced through competition or changed through gene flow with later arrivals. According to Marta Lahr, "the morphological data are disclosing the complexity of the colonization of the Americas between 15,000 and 5,000 years ago, suggesting that it is likely to have involved higher levels of diversity than were present later, and consequently, high levels of extinction of some of the earlier groups."[21] Studies by Gentry Steele and Joseph Powell, as well as the present authors, indicate that the Paleo-Americans are morphologically distinct from later New World populations, and that they differ in the direction of Europeans and southern Asians.[22] The importance of the Kennewick fossil lies in knowing whether it shares these differences and, if so, to what degree. This can only be determined by thorough study of the skeleton.

One way of examining this question is through morphometric analysis. This approach uses statistical methods to compare the metric data of a fossil to samples representing recent Native American groups and other world populations. It addresses the question of whether the fossil falls within the range of variation of recent populations and, if so, to which group it is most similar. The extensive reference database on this question consists of cranial measurements compiled by William Howells and Richard Jantz for thirty-three world populations, including nine Native American groups from western North America.[23]

To illustrate the power of morphometric analysis, four well-dated fossil crania were incorporated into an analysis—two from Nevada (Spirit Cave, 9,415 years B.P.; Wizards Beach, 9,200 B.P.) and two from Minnesota (Brown's Valley, 8,700 B.P.; Pelican Rapids [Minnesota Woman], 7,900 B.P.)—were incorporated into the reference database. The data were then subjected to canonical analysis with the fossils treated in the same way as the other samples and given equal weight. Canonical analysis is a multivariate statistical procedure that displays Mahalanobis distances in low-dimensional space.[24] Twenty-five measurements were used in this comparison, with the measurements selected to express the size and shape of the cranial vault in the sagittal plane (in effect, heights, vault and face breadths, and facial forwardness and prognathism).

In figure 1, the results are displayed along two orthogonal axes. The first axis, which represents 23 percent of the total group variation, separates the Minnesota crania, and even the Spirit Cave fossil cranium to some extent, from the crania of recent Africa and Southwest Pacific populations. It also highlights the uniqueness of the fossil crania from Brown's Valley and Pelican Rapids relative to all modern populations. This axis reflects variation in vault base width, nose width, frontal flatness, and upper facial forwardness at nasion. The fossil crania from Brown's Valley, Pelican Rapids, and, to a lesser degree, Spirit Cave differ from the crania of other world populations, especially those of Africa and the Southwest Pacific, by having wider vault bases, narrower noses, flatter frontal bones, and upper facial forwardness.

The Minnesota fossils are also extreme on the second axis. This axis

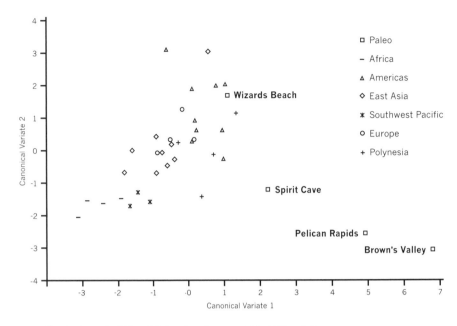

Fig. 1. Canonical Plot of Paleo-Americans and World Populations

represents 15 percent of the total sample variation and separates the crania of most modern Native Americans and Siberians from the Minnesota fossil crania. This axis reflects variation in face height including the nasal and orbital heights, vault breadth, and parietal length. The Brown's Valley and Pelican Rapids fossil crania differ from the crania of modern populations, and especially Native Americans, in having low faces, narrow vaults, and long parietal bones.

The Minnesota fossil crania are extreme on the first two axes of variation and are so differentiated from modern populations that their inclusion tends to compress heterogeneity within the modern series. In fact, it does not make much sense to ask to which groups they are most similar. Spirit Cave fossil cranium falls a bit closer to the modern crania and is nearest the Polynesian-Eskimo part of the two-dimensional space. The Spirit Cave fossil cranium's uniqueness is not fully represented on these two axes, but it appears on subsequent axes. As we have demonstrated elsewhere, the Spirit Cave skull falls outside the range of variation of modern samples, and, in particular, it shows no affinity to Native American samples.[25] The closest biological sample is the Ainu of Japan. In contrast, the Wizards Beach cranium classifies as similar to modern Native Americans.

Overall, the Paleo-American sample exhibits a great deal of heterogeneity, as reflected by the wide spread of the fossil crania within the multivariate distribution. Because the fossils were treated in the same way as the modern samples and given equal weight, it could be argued that the procedure has emphasized unique features of these individual crania. When considering typicality probabilities of group membership, however, only the Wizards Beach skull falls within the range of variation of modern groups. Typicality probabilities are Mahalanobis distances converted to probabilities, and there are no assumptions with regard to group membership. In this regard, the craniofacial morphology of the Spirit Cave, Brown's Valley, and Pelican Rapids fossil skulls falls outside the range of variation of all modern groups. These specimens have a very low probability of belonging to any of the groups represented here.

Motions in Federal Court

Given the importance of the knowledge that could be gained from studying Kennewick Man, one wonders why the corps has been so dogged in its opposition. According to corps spokesman Duane Meier, "We're in court for obeying the law."[26] The *Bonnichsen* scientists dispute that characterization of the corps' behavior. In fact, their lawsuit claims that the corps' administrative process did not follow the law and that the decision for immediate transfer was biased and inattentive to all information pertinent to this discovery.

The main issues in the *Bonnichsen* case are what kind of process federal agencies must follow when they make repatriation decisions; what is required to meet the statute's definition of Native American; and whether it is lawful under the statute to refuse study solely because some contemporary Native Americans do not want the remains studied. What will ultimately matter, then, is the court's interpretation of the law as applied to the facts of this specific situation. As can be imagined with a case of this magnitude where there is little precedence, the process has involved considerable strategy, diversion, and legal maneuvering over a period that has spanned more than five years.

After requesting and receiving a court order to block the transfer of Kennewick Man to the Umatilla tribe, the plaintiff-scientists filed a motion to allow them to study the remains. The scientists proposed an examination protocol using multiple lines of evidence to determine the skeleton's biological and cultural affinities. This motion to study defines how and what would be done, who would do it, how long each test would take, and what potentially could be learned from each part of the analysis.

A human skeleton, depending on its completeness and state of preservation, can tell much about an individual and the conditions he or she experienced. Among other things, skeletal remains can provide information for discerning patterns and trends in ancient population demography, health, origin, migration, gene flow, microevolutionary change, sociocultural interaction, activity, and lifestyle. Examination of the Kennewick Man skeleton would involve observing, recording, and analyzing detailed dental and bone characteristics, conducting mitochondrial DNA research, and obtaining at least two more dates via accelerator. Accurate dating of the skeleton is critical.

Verification of the initial date is necessary, a point emphasized by the scientists who originally dated one of Kennewick Man's bones.[27]

Included in the proposal by the plaintiffs are morphometric comparisons and evaluation of genetic traits in dentition to assess biological affinities to contemporary and prehistoric peoples. Computerized databases allow comparison of Kennewick Man to groups representing different time periods and geographic areas. Comparisons can be large scale (that is, with Africans, Asians, Native Americans, Europeans, and Polynesians) or regionally focused (that is, with regional subgroups or specific North American tribal populations). Comparisons can be evaluated to determine which group (or groups) Kennewick Man resembles most and least — information that will provide insight as to whether there is a definable biological relationship. Also included in the proposal are analyses of dental microwear, nutritional assessments using stable isotopes, and the evaluation of opal phytoliths (crystals found in plants that have unique structures depending on the type of plant) recovered from dental calculus (tartar). These studies can provide information about the availability of high-quality protein and specific plant species in the diet, as well as environmental data (that is, which ecological zones were exploited).

Most plants are highly sensitive to prevailing temperature and moisture conditions. As a result, certain plants are generally found in appreciable numbers only within certain geographically restricted habitats. By reconstructing the Kennewick Man's overall diet (through a combination of phytolith and nutritional analyses) it may be possible to draw inferences about Kennewick Man's geographic range and the prevailing climatic conditions he encountered.[28]

The protocol also calls for the development of a complete image record that includes high-definition photography in black-and-white, color, and digital formats; conventional radiography; computed tomography; and stereolithographic casting.

The Government's Response

The government's first response to the *Bonnichsen* lawsuit was to file a motion to dismiss the case. In this motion the government (represented by the Department of Justice) argued that the scientists did not have a valid cause of action and, therefore, would not be entitled to any relief or protection from the court. The court denied this motion, meaning that, if the scientists can prove what they have alleged in their complaint, they may receive protection.

Next, the government filed a motion for summary judgment (another attempt to have the case dismissed without a trial); the corps asserted that the scientists could not win regardless of the facts. Oral arguments followed on 2 June 1997, and the judge issued several rulings on 27 June 1997.

The Court's Response

The defendants' motion for summary judgment was denied, with the court reaffirming that the scientists had "legal standing" to challenge the government's decisions concerning treatment and disposition of the skeleton. The court noted that the record was clear: if the scientists had not filed the suit, the skeleton would have been reburied. The court also stated that it was left with the distinct impression that early in this case the defendants made a hasty decision before they had all of the facts, or even knew what facts were needed. In addition, some of the facts relied on by the corps were shown to be erroneous.

One such error was the corps' acceptance of the Umatilla's claim that the skeleton was found on land that was determined by the Indian Claims Commission to have been aboriginally occupied by the Umatilla. On further review, however, the corps was forced to admit that this conclusion was in error. The skeleton would have been repatriated to a tribe that does not have the legal status they claimed.

The court vacated all decisions previously made by the corps, and the matter was remanded to the corps for additional deliberations that are consistent with the law and facts. The corps was ordered to follow a logical, reasoned process and to articulate clearly the reasons for whatever new decisions it reaches. Further action in the lawsuit was stayed pending completion of the new administrative proceedings. Since that decision, the corps has transferred responsibility for a portion of the new administrative proceedings to the Department of the Interior.

The judge offered guidance to the corps by suggesting questions that should be considered during the administrative process in order to resolve this controversy "in a timely and orderly manner."[29] Central issues include

- What is meant by terms such as *indigenous* and *Native American* in the context of NAGPRA and the facts of this case;
- Are scientific studies needed to determine whether Kennewick Man is subject to NAGPRA;
- Does NAGPRA apply to remains from a population that is not directly related to modern Native Americans;
- Is there evidence of a link, biologically or culturally, between the remains and a modern Native American tribe or any group, including those of Europe, Asia, and the Pacific islands;
- What level of certainty is required to establish biological or cultural affiliation; and
- Are scientific study and repatriation of the remains mutually exclusive.

Definitions and a reasoned process are critical. For example, from a legal perspective, key observations such as the age of the remains and the presence of an embedded projectile point can be interpreted in various ways, as illustrated by the following two passages:

Even assuming the ancestors of present day Native Americans have always been here as the amici contend, that in itself does not preclude the possibility that non-Indians could also have been present in the Americas at some earlier date [see

Umatilla position paper]. For that reason, the age of the remains is not, by itself, conclusive proof that these remains are related to contemporary Native Americans. On the other hand, conventional scientific theory is that modern Native Americans are descended from immigrants who came to the Americas from other continents. If that is true, then were these original immigrants (who were born elsewhere) "indigenous"? Were their children (born here of immigrant parents) "indigenous"? The analysis is further complicated if there was more than one wave of ancient immigration to the Americas, or off-shoots from the primary group(s). If there were subpopulations whose members survived for a time in North America—perhaps hundreds or even thousands of years—but eventually became evolutionary "dead ends," i.e., all descendants of the group eventually died, leaving no one who today is directly descended from them, would a member of such an extinct subpopulation be considered "indigenous"? Would they be considered "Native American"? It is essential to define what is meant by "indigenous" and "Native American" for purposes of NAGPRA.[30]

A projectile point was found embedded in the remains, which may have led to the man's death. Defendants have suggested that the point was of a type formerly used by Native Americans, and cite this as proof that the man was an ancestor of today's Native Americans. They may be right. However, this also could be seen as proof that the man was not of Native American ancestry, but was part of a competing group—which might tend to explain how he ended up dead with a spear embedded in his side. His group might have lost the competition, while the projectile makers survived and gave birth to succeeding generations. I express no opinion as to which historical view, if either, is correct. My point is simply that it is not enough to take one fact out of context and use it to support a predetermined hypothesis. On remand, the corps must critically examine all of the evidence in the record as a whole, and make specific findings that are supported by reliable evidence.[31]

Plaintiff's Right to Study

While the judge ruled that the scientists have "standing," meaning an arguable claim, he has not yet ruled on whether the scientists have a right to study the skeleton. This question deals with the First Amendment to the United States Constitution and federal statutes as they relate to science. The court stated that the scientists' claims in this regard are not frivolous:

The First Amendment is not limited to "speech" per se. It protects both the right to send and also to receive information. Defendants acknowledge that the First Amendment limits the government's power to suppress knowledge by removing books from a library, but argue that the government has no affirmative obligation to facilitate the dissemination of knowledge by writing and publishing books. That misconstrues plaintiffs' argument. Plaintiffs' contention is that to the trained eye the skeletal remains are analogous to a book that they can read, a history written in bone instead of on paper, just as the history of a region may be "read" by observing layers of rock or ice, or the rings of a tree. Plaintiffs are not asking the government to conduct the tests and publish the results. Plaintiffs simply want the government to step aside and permit them to "read that book" by conducting their own tests. A closer analogy would be a lawsuit brought by scholars seeking access to the Nixon tapes or presidential papers, or the Pentagon Papers, so that scholars may conduct research and publish their own findings.[32]

This concern is not a personal right but instead refers to the ultimate social purpose of such a study, which is to develop knowledge for others to use. The social purpose of science is to obtain information to disseminate to the public. There is no doubt that this is an important concept in this lawsuit. The Army Corps of Engineers, at the request of a small portion of the Native American community, is blocking knowledge that the broader community, as well as future generations, may want and have a right to have. Such information has historical, social, and cultural value, as well as potential biomedical applications. This view acknowledges the rich heritage of the Americas and seeks to avoid denying parts of this history. This is a universalist position projecting the relationship to all and not to one group. The universalist position, one that is entirely responsible but not universally held, is crucial to science and is the basis of our argument.

In contrast, critics see science as an instrument of power as well as knowledge. Within this domain, the perspective is group ownership, for example, of each type of great art or distinctive cultural element. As such, the Kennewick skeleton does not represent the remains of a North American man but rather is the sole proprietary of a specific group.

Case Update

In October 1998 at the court's direction, Owsley conducted an independent inventory of the collection. He concluded that the nearly three hundred and fifty bone fragments recovered from the Columbia River site represent one individual.[33] He also confirmed that significant portions of both femurs had been removed from the collection and were missing. The Department of Justice reports that an investigation is under way. During the inventory process prior to the move, Chatters conducted a condition assessment to document changes in the bones that occurred after he relinquished control in 1996. The skeleton was transferred to the Burke Museum at the University of Washington, Seattle, on 27 October 1998.

In spring 1999 the bones were permanently housed in a secure room at the Burke Museum after acclimating to the new environment. The portion of the metacarpal that had been sent to the University of California, Riverside, for carbon dating and then sent on to the University of California, Davis, for DNA analysis in 1996 was retrieved by federal officials in February 1999 and is now stored with the rest of the collection.[34] Molecular biologists at Davis were not given authorization to finish their study of the DNA.

Given the success of the plaintiffs in their pursuit of the case and faced with the fact that NAGPRA does not prohibit scientific study, the government implemented a two-phase plan of study directed by Francis McManamon, a departmental consulting archaeologist at the National Park Service, on 1 July 1998.[35] The government conducted the first phase of limited studies from 25 February to 1 March 1999. In the government's opinion, the absolute date obtained from the sample sent to Riverside is suspect, so two of their studies focused on establishing a new relative date. These limited studies were conducted by five scientists hired by the government to address questions of whether the remains are Native American as defined by NAGPRA; and whether, if the government determines that the remains are Native American, a modern tribe can be identified to whom the remains can be transferred, if they desire it. Phase one focused on the first question. If a determination is not possible, the government would consider proceeding to phase two, which would involve more invasive tests such as carbon dating and possibly DNA analysis. Phase one includes the following analyses:

Sediment. The objective was to collect sediments from the bones (for example, from inside the skull and the medullary cavities) and then to try to correlate these samples with sediments taken from the discovery site. The intended outcome was to determine a relative date for the skeleton based on geological evidence.

Lithic. The assignment was to note and compare traits of the projectile point lodged in the innominate to lithic types with known dates. The purpose was to determine a date for the skeleton based on lithic criteria.

Skeletal. The procedure was to evaluate the skeleton through osteological measurements, nonmetric traits, and other observations. The objective was to determine whether the skeleton could be identified as a Native American. A second objective was to use these data to determine cultural affiliation.

The government's report of the results of these studies was released on 14 October 1999.[36] The government's studies involved recording some (but not all) of the data (for example, skeletal metrics and pathology information) originally defined in the plaintiffs' motion to study. The government has refused to allow other interested scientists, including the plaintiffs, to study the skeleton and has not invited scientific peer review of the results of their studies. By not allowing other scientists to independently confirm the accuracy and completeness of the data, it is unclear how scientists will be able to resolve questions of interpretation. The plaintiffs' right to study the skeleton is a key question being challenged by the lawsuit.

Case Assessment

The significance of the Kennewick Man lawsuit can be viewed from various perspectives: legal, scientific, tribal, and political. The legal perspective focuses on defining the appropriate processes and standards that must be followed when making repatriation decisions. The scientific perspective is one of ascertaining the origin and cultural affiliation through scientific methods, without prior assumptions about identity or relationship. The tribal view begins with an assumption of Native American relationship. Their religion is a guiding source of cultural integrity, and these "sacred remains" consolidate their culture. While the temptation is to view this case as a clash between science and religion, the suit was brought against a federal agency for lack of compliance with existing laws. With the involvement of the Army Corps of Engineers, the Department of Interior, and the Department of Justice, complex political interrelationships are affecting the defense actions in the lawsuit. These legal, political, scientific, and tribal views have come together in ways not foreseen in 1996.

In the beginning, Kennewick Man was an inadvertent discovery—no one went out looking for him. Similarly, the *Bonnichsen* case is an inadvertent challenge to current NAGPRA processes—no one involved was looking for a way to test its boundaries. Most likely, the Army Corps of Engineers was surprised by the suit and has some right to feel overwhelmed by its consequences. In past decades this agency has demonstrated a commitment to archaeological mitigation and bioarchaeological research.[37] It seems likely that the corps did not expect an opposition involving scientists employed by several major universities and a national museum (itself a government agency) who privately engaged a legal team. The case has extended over five years with no resolution in sight. The legal team and plaintiffs have carried the expense of keeping this case alive.

In defending its actions, the Army Corps of Engineers was placed in the position of using public tax dollars to argue against scientific progress and the acquisition of information for eventual dissemination to the public. By early 1999 the government had spent some $1.2 million to block scientific access to the skeleton and to avoid resolution of the case. A document acquired through the Freedom of Information Act shows that the government's phase one studies cost approximately $30,000, including consulting fees and travel costs for the five scientists. Comprehensive studies proposed by the plaintiffs have been offered free of charge since October 1996.

Clearly the corps did not see the risk of a lawsuit when Colonel Bohn of the Portland Regional Office wrote an internal memorandum stating: "All risk to us seems to be associated with not repatriating the remains." Then what risk did it see? Since the corps regularly deals with various American Indian tribes on a variety of issues, keeping ongoing relationships positive may have influenced its decision to transfer Kennewick Man's remains immediately. In any case, the corps' memo revealed a strong motivation to ignore its own procedures and to comply with the Native Americans' NAGPRA claim. Under normal circumstances, the corps' policy concerning archaeological collections is defined by Regulation ER-1130-2-433:

The Corps has under its guardianship a significant portion of the Nation's cultural materials, which are recognized by public law as important aspects of our cultural heritage. Preservation of this cultural heritage for scientific purposes and for the benefit and appreciation of present and future generations requires that these recovered cultural materials and their associated documentation be properly housed and curated.[38]

The tribes might also have been surprised by the lawsuit and the determination of the plaintiffs to challenge current policies for implementing NAGPRA. Since the passage of NAGPRA, Native American tribes have received thousands of skeletons and cultural items from museums and federal land and have been awarded more than $6.5 million in grants to create their own cultural centers.[39] The Umatilla may have expected the Kennewick skeleton to be turned over to them without protest for reburial, like the Buhl and Hourglass skeletons.

The Umatilla have defended their position regarding Kennewick Man partially on the basis of a traditional belief system, the Washat religion. This system is not the issue; the suit concerns the implications of the corps' apparent policy of favoring a religion over science. This approach is unconstitutional given the First Amendment requirement of separation of church and state. If an agency favors one religion, will it favor all of them? How will an agency choose between religions when their creation doctrines disagree? Furthermore, if these religions restrict scientific study, what about the rights of the public to have access to information about the past? In our view, religion should have no place in developing federal policy, and in this regard we are resisting the claim that one group can force its religious beliefs on the state.

In addition to religious significance, skeletons contain political implications relating to the relationship between Native Americans and the United States government. Political reality for Native American groups has been based on the geographical configuration of different tribal groups at the time of contact with Euro-Americans. These land relationships and distributions became a static model, and now all parties behave as if those patterns had been that way even before contact. There are benefits to this model for both Native Americans and the government: the model ties each tribe to a place and makes that place its homeland, and it forms a basis for decisions about land. In the absence of legal titles and deeds of ownership, claims to the land are based on arguments that a specific group "has always been there."

This current structure of land ownership is simplistic because it is based on a snapshot of time in what anthropologists know is a dynamic process of human mobility. If Native Americans acknowledge mobile populations, however, then they cannot claim to have "always been there." Some suggest that their hold on their land under the current system would be weakened, but there is no basis for this.

Lacking a written record, connections to the land are memory, tradition, and bones—tangible links for reacquiring a right to tribal heritage. If the Kennewick skeleton is put back in the ground without study, we will never know whether this individual represents a much older, different population, one not ancestral to contemporary Native Americans. Some feel that scientific truth could be detrimental to their lives.

As scientists, we believe that knowledge is central to truth and that the role of government does not include suppressing knowledge. We fear that if we cannot study the Kennewick skeleton, a precedent will be set, and scientists will not be allowed to study other ancient skeletons or even the places used by ancient peoples. At stake is the opportunity to explore and ask questions of the past, to reaffirm or challenge conventional views, and to evaluate what we learn against what we have been led to believe. The ancient remains at Kennewick, Spirit Cave, and other sites challenge the established scientific view for the peopling of the Americas. The range of ancient craniofacial morphology suggests the possibility of multiple migrations from Asia, and even Europe, by dissimilar populations. Continued access to ancient remains for examination and analysis is critical to discovering what actually happened long ago.

The Kennewick Man case demonstrates the need for Congress to reexamine how NAGPRA is interpreted and applied. We advocate a more balanced approach to the way the current law is being interpreted, one closer to the original spirit and intent of the law. As noted by Congressman Doc Hastings (R-Washington), "Current law governing the treatment of historic human remains is so vague and confusing that it's no surprise authorities have had difficulty reconciling the need for scientific study with respect for customs and traditions of Indian tribes."[40]

The problem extends beyond the remains themselves. Not only have scientists been prohibited from examining the Kennewick remains but the corps has even refused to release Chatters's photographs of the skeleton because of tribal objections. Further, geoarchaeological work at the discovery site was hampered by the corps. Site examination was proposed by the plaintiffs and Gary Huckleberry of Washington State University to determine whether the skeleton's deposition was a natural event or an intentional burial.[41] Such an investigation could determine not only the skeleton's stratigraphic location in the bank of the Columbia River but also whether cultural artifacts are associated with the remains, whether unrecovered portions of the skeleton are still in situ, and whether there are recoverable organic materials that could be used for radiocarbon dating to confirm the skeleton's age. After considerable delay, the corps allowed restricted evaluation of the site under its direction, as noted in the Plaintiff's Status Report for 1 January 1998:

> Plaintiffs have objected to the Corps' project and to unreasonable restrictions that were imposed on Dr. Huckleberry and his research team. During Phase 2 of the Corps' project, Dr. Huckleberry's research team was allowed to collect some organic samples for radiocarbon dating and to make observations of some limited sediment exposures at the site. They were not allowed, however, to: (a) excavate a trench as requested in Dr. Huckleberry's permit application; (b) take core drillings at the site; (c) excavate a vertical sediment exposure of appropriate length at the

discovery location and at other locations in the area; or (d) obtain all sediment samples needed for dating purposes and other analyses. Plaintiffs believe that defendants' refusal to allow Dr. Huckleberry's research team to conduct the foregoing activities is inconsistent with sound scientific practices, and will deny plaintiffs access to important information needed to interpret the site and the depositional history of the Kennewick Man skeleton.[42]

In April 1998, in spite of protests from scientists, Congress, and their own geologists, the corps chose to bury the Kennewick site under riprap, soil and more than five hundred tons of boulders, which were airlifted to the riverbank by helicopter. The alleged purpose of this action was to protect the site from erosion and looters, but it also precluded scientific investigation. If the objectivity of science is lost, we will be left with the subjectivity of mythology.

In December 1998 the corps finally released a report of the site's evaluation of December 1997, in which its own geologists recommend that further study of the site is required.

Conclusion

As a result of the Kennewick Man case, a congressional bill (H.R. 2893) was introduced in November 1997, and resubmitted on 28 July 1999, to amend NAGPRA by adding provisions specifically authorizing the study of human remains and other cultural items found on federally administered land. The proposed amendment has been endorsed by the Society for American Archaeology, the Society for Historical Archaeology, the American Association of Physical Anthropologists, and the State Historic Preservation Officers. If ratified, this amendment will provide scientists with the opportunity to study new discoveries like Kennewick Man, as well as specimens in existing museum and federal collections. This suit may help to clarify the points of contention caused by the current wording and may aid in developing an amendment that respects the aims of both scientists and Native Americans. All sectors (museums, universities, federal agencies, Native Americans, and so forth) affected by NAGPRA have had some experience with implementing this complicated law; they have all confronted problems not envisioned by Congress. The time to clarify the legislation through amendment is now, to avoid further conflicts in the future.

Discovering the biological affinities of Kennewick Man is possible but requires thorough examination. According to an editorial in *The Oregonian*, "This find offers an unparalleled opportunity to contribute to our knowledge about the environment, nutrition, health, lifestyles and ancestry of the earliest peoples in the Americas, and to positively touch our modern lives as well."[43] This insight into prehistory, and the story of Kennewick Man's life and death, is his legacy to the citizens of the United States.

Notes

On 30 August 2002, U.S. Magistrate John Jelderks set aside the Department of the Interior's decision to classify the Kennewick Man skeleton as Native American and to give it to a coalition of Columbia River Indian claimants. Jelderks also ruled that the scientists will be allowed to study the skeleton, supporting their contentions that the American past is the common heritage of all Americans and should be open to legitimate scientific research. In addition, he ruled that the United States Army Corps of Engineers violated the National Historic Preservation Act by burying the discovery site.

The opinions and concerns presented in this article represent the personal views of the authors. Alan Schneider, lead attorney for the plaintiffs, helped us interpret the legal procedures and rulings. Dr. Jan Simek helped formulate our assessment of the politics of this case. Editorial assistance and an assessment of the first phase of the government's study were provided by Cleone Hawkinson. Additional editorial guidance was provided by Sandra Schlachtmeyer, Margaret Richardson, and Malcolm Richardson. Robert Ruch prepared the figure. Katie Spiker helped with word processing.

1. *Bonnichsen et al. v. United States*, District of Oregon, CV 96-1481-JE.

2. R. E. Taylor et al., "Radiocarbon Dates of Kennewick Man," *Science* 280 (1998): 1171–72.

3. James C. Chatters, "Encounter with an Ancestor," *Anthropology Newsletter* 38, no. 1 (1997): 9–10.

4. Catherine J. MacMillan, letter to Floyd Johnson, Benton County Coroner, 31 August 1996; and Grover S. Krantz, letter to James Chatters, 2 September 1996.

5. Alan L. Schneider, "NAGPRA and First Americans Studies," *Current Research in the Pleistocene* 12 (1995): 117–23.

6. D. G. Sampson, letter from the chairman of the Umatilla Indian Reservation Board of Trustees to Col. Bartholomew B. Bohn II (United States Army Corps of Engineers, 1996); and Alan L. Schneider, "Kennewick Man Myths," *Anthropology Newsletter* 40, no. 4 (1999): 21–22.

7. D. G. Sampson, "Science Needs to Respect Culture of Indians," *Tri-City Herald*, 30 November 1997, D1.

8. Armand Minthorn, "Ancient Human Remains Need to Be Reburied," *Tri-City Herald*, 27 October 1996, D1.

9. Kenneth L. Feder, "Indians and Archaeologists: Conflicting Views of Myth and Science," *Skeptic* 5, no. 3 (1997): 74–80.

10. Minthorn, "Ancient Human Remains" (note 8).

11. Quoted in George Johnson, "Indian Tribes' Creationists Thwart Archeologists," *New York Times*, 22 October 1996, A1.

12. Terence E. Fifield, James Dixon, and Timothy H. Heaton, "Tribal Involvement in Investigations at 49-PET-408 Prince of Wales Island, Southeast Alaska," *Anthropology Newsletter* 39, no. 5 (1998): 23–24.

13. Repatriation Office, "Total National Museum of Natural History Repatriations as of 29 April 1999," manuscript on file, Repatriation Office, National Museum of Natural History, 1997.

14. Douglas W. Owsley and Jerome C. Rose, eds., *Bioarchaeology of the North Central United States* (Fayetteville: Arkansas Archaeological Survey, 1997).

15. Sue Myster, personal communication, 18 June 1998.

16. Sampson, "Science Needs to Respect Culture" (note 7).

17. Senator Daniel Inouye (D-Hawaii), from the Select Senate Committee on Indian Affairs, *Report on Legislation Providing for the Protection of Native American Graves and the Repatriation of Native American Remains and Cultural Patrimony* (101st Cong., 2d sess., Calendar No. 842, 1990, S. Report 101–473), 4–5.

18. Bruce Babbitt, cited in Daniel Haas, *Federal Archaeology Program, Secretary of the Interior's Report to Congress 1994–95, by Daniel Haas, U.S. Department of the Interior, National Park Service* (Washington, D.C.: Government Printing Office, 1998), inside cover.

19. Don Alan Hall, "Those Rarest of Rare Treasures," *Mammoth Trumpet* 13, no. 1 (1998): 5.

20. David B. Madsen and David Rhode, eds., *Across the West: Human Population Movement and the Expansion of the Numa* (Salt Lake City: Univ. of Utah Press, 1994); and Mark Q. Sutton, "Warfare and Expansion: An Ethnohistoric Perspective on the Numic Spread," *Journal of California and Great Basin Anthropology* 8 (1986): 65–82.

21. Marta M. Lahr, "History in the Bones," *Evolutionary Anthropology* 6, no. 1 (1997): 2–6, esp. 5.

22. D. G. Steele and J. F. Powell, "Peopling of the Americas: Paleobiological Evidence," *Human Biology* 64 (1992): 303–36; and Richard L. Jantz and Douglas W. Owsley, "Pathology, Taphonomy, and Cranial Morphometrics of the Spirit Cave Mummy," *Nevada Historical Society Quarterly* 40 (1997): 62–84.

23. William W. Howells, *Who's Who in Skulls: Ethnic Identification of Crania from Measurements* (Cambridge: Peabody Museum of Archaeology & Ethnology, Harvard University, 1995); and Richard L. Jantz, "Cranial, Postcranial, and Discrete Trait Variation," in Douglas W. Owsley and Jerome C. Rose, eds., *Bioarchaeology of the North Central United States* (Fayetteville: Arkansas Archaeological Survey, 1997), 240–47.

24. Mahalanobis distance is a statistic that measures the distance of a single data point from the sample mean or centroid in the multivariable space. It provides a way of finding points that are far from all the others in a multidimensional space.

25. Jantz and Owsley, "Pathology" (note 22).

26. Duane Meier, quoted in Edie Lau, "Who Were the First Americans? New Finds Challenge View," *Sacramento Bee*, 8 December 1997, A1, A16.

27. R. E. Taylor and D. L. Kirner, letter to the U.S. Army Corps of Engineers, 10 February 1998.

28. Amy L. Ollendorf, *Court Affidavit for USDC No. CV 96-1481, 10 February 1997*, 4.

29. United States Magistrate Judge John Jelderks, *United States District Court Opinion for the District of Oregon, Civil No. 96-1481-JE, 27 June 1997*, 3.

30. Jelderks, *United States District Court Opinion* (note 29), 46.

31. Jelderks, *United States District Court Opinion* (note 29), 47.

32. Jelderks, *United States District Court Opinion* (note 29), 33–34.

33. Douglas W. Owsley, *Report of the Inventory of the Kennewick Skeleton, U.S. District Court, CV 96-1481, 28–29 October 1998*.

34. Alan L. Schneider and Cleone Hawkinson, "Struggle Ends over Kennewick DNA," *Anthropology Newsletter* 40, no. 4 (1999): 20–21.

35. Francis P. McManamon, "K-Man Undergoes Complete Physical," *Anthropology Newsletter* 40, no. 5 (1999): 21–22.

36. Francis P. McManamon et al., *Report on the Non-Destructive Examination, Description, and Analysis of the Human Remains from Columbia Park, Kennewick, Washington*, a special report prepared at the request of the Department of the Interior, 14 October 1999; the full text is posted at http://www.cr.nps.gov/aad/kennewick (22 February 2002). See also Mike Lee, "Report on Kennewick Man Suggests Asian Origin," *Tri-City Herald*, 15 October 1999; posted at http://www.kennewick-man.com/news/101599.html (22 February 2002).

37. For example, see Owsley and Rose, *Bioarchaeology* (note 14).

38. Michael K. Trimble and Thomas B. Meyers, *Saving the Past from the Future: Archaeological Curation in the St. Louis District* (Saint Louis: U.S. Army Corps of Engineers, Saint Louis District, 1991), 9; see also Thomas B. Meyers and Michael K. Trimble, *Archaeological Curation-Needs Assessments Technical Report No. 1* (Saint Louis: U.S. Army Corps of Engineers, Saint Louis District, 1993).

39. National Park Service, *Report to the NAGPRA Review Committee*, 21 April 1999.

40. United States Representative Doc Hastings (R-Washington), cited in "Hastings Seeks to End Battle Over Bones," Congressional News Release, 13 November 1997, Washington, D.C.

41. Gary Huckleberry, application for a federal permit under the Archaeological Resources Protection Act for work at Columbia Park, Benton County, Washington, 26 August 1997; and Alan L. Schneider, letter to Timothy Simmons, Assistant U.S. Attorney, and Daria Zane, United States Department of Justice, 29 July 1997.

42. Alan L. Schneider and Paula A. Barran, Plaintiff's Status Report for 1 January 1998, CV No. USDC CV No. 96-1481 JE, 4–5.

43. "A Teacher for Everyone" (editorial), *The Oregonian*, 1 November 1996, D10.

Cultural Significance and the Kennewick Skeleton: Some Thoughts on the Resolution of Cultural Heritage Disputes

Patty Gerstenblith

A Story

Through the doorway which led from her receptionist-secretary's office into her own, Catherine Morris Perry instantly noticed the box on her desk. It was bulky—perhaps three feet long and almost as high....

"Where'd that come from?" Catherine said, indicating the box.

"Federal Express," Markie [Bailey] said. "I signed for it."

"Am I expecting anything?"

"Not that you told me about..."...

With her free hand Catherine Perry was slicing the tape away with the letter opener. She thought that this box was probably a result of that story in the *Washington Post*. Any time the museum got into the news, it reminded a thousand old ladies of things in the attic that should be saved for posterity. Since she was quoted, one of them had sent this trash to her by name. What would it be? A dusty old butter churn? A set of family albums?

"The other [message] was somebody in the anthropology division. I put her name on the slip. Wants you to call. Said it was about the Indians wanting their skeletons back."

"Right," Catherine said. She pulled open the top flaps. Under them was a copy of the *Washington Post,* folded to expose the story that had quoted her. Part of it was circled in black.

MUSEUM OFFERS COMPROMISE
IN OLD BONE CONTROVERSY

The title irritated Catherine. There had been no compromise. She had simply stated the museum's policy. If an Indian tribe wanted ancestral bones returned, it had only to ask for them and provide some acceptable proof that the bones in question had indeed been taken from a burial ground of the tribe. The entire argument was ridiculous and demeaning.... She glanced at the circled paragraph.

"Mrs. Catherine Perry, an attorney for the museum and its spokesperson on this issue, said the demand by the Paho Society for the reburial of the museum's entire collection of more than 18,000 Native American skeletons was 'simply not possible in light of the museum's purpose.'"

"She said the museum is a research institution as well as a gallery for public display, and that the museum's collection of ancient human bones is a potentially important source of anthropological information. She said that Mr. Highhawk's suggestion that the museum make plaster casts of the skeletons and rebury the originals was not practical 'both because of research needs and because the public has the right to expect authenticity and not be shown mere reproductions.'"

The clause "the right to expect authenticity" was underlined. Catherine Morris Perry frowned at it, sensing criticism. She picked up the newspaper. Under it, atop a sheet of brown wrapping paper, lay an envelope. Her name had been written neatly on it. She opened it and pulled out a single sheet of typing paper. While she read, her idle hand was pulling away the layer of wrapping paper which had separated the envelope from the contents of the box.

Dear Mrs. Perry:

You won't bury the bones of our ancestors because you say the public has the right to expect authenticity in the museum when it comes to look at skeletons. Therefore I am sending you a couple of authentic skeletons of ancestors. I went to the cemetery in the woods behind the Episcopal Church of Saint Luke. I used authentic anthropological methods to locate the burials of authentic white Anglo types … and to make sure they would be perfectly authentic. I chose two whose identities you can personally confirm yourself. I ask that you accept these two skeletons for authentic display to your clients and release the bones of two of my ancestors so that they may be returned to their rightful place in Mother Earth. The names of these two authentic—

Mrs. Bailey was standing beside her now. "Honey," she said, "What's wrong?" Mrs. Bailey paused. "There's bones in that box," she said. "All dirty, too."

Mrs. Morris Perry put the letter on the desk and looked into the box. From underneath a clutter of what seemed to be arm and leg bones, a single empty eye socket stared back at her. She noticed that Mrs. Bailey had picked up the letter. She noticed dirt. Damp ugly little clods scattered on the polished desktop.

"My God," Mrs. Bailey said. "John Neldine Burgoyne. Jane Burgoyne. Weren't those—Aren't these your grandparents?"[1]

Another Story: The Kennewick Skeleton

In July 1996 a skeleton, later dubbed the Kennewick Man, was accidentally discovered in a bank of the Columbia River in the state of Washington.[2] The skeleton is that of a middle-aged man with a stone spearhead embedded in his pelvis. In a brief forensic study of the skull, anthropologists concluded that it displayed "Caucasoid" characteristics,[3] based on measurements of its width, the eye and nose cavities, and the teeth. Radiocarbon dating of bone samples indicates that the skeleton is approximately ninety-three hundred years old. A *New York Times* article reporting the discovery explained that

> in the world of old bones and educated conjecture about the first Americans, the Columbia River skeleton is a riveting discovery. It adds credence to theories that some early inhabitants of North America came from European stock, perhaps migrating across northern Asia and into the Western Hemisphere over a land bridge exposed in the Bering Sea about 12,000 years ago, or earlier, near the end of the last Ice Age.[4]

Following this brief study by anthropologists, the United States Army Corps of Engineers took possession of the skeleton and, pursuant to the procedures of the Native American Graves Protection and Repatriation Act (NAGPRA),[5] published a notice of intent to repatriate it. Among other things, the notice indicated that "the Corps had determined that the remains were of Native American ancestry"; "that the remains had been inadvertently discovered on federal land recognized as the aboriginal land of an Indian tribe;"[6] and "that there is a relationship of shared group identity which can be reasonably traced between the human remains and five Columbia River basin tribes and bands."[7]

Before the corps was able to return the skeleton, however, a group of physical anthropologists filed suit in October 1996 to prevent the skeleton's reburial before they had an opportunity to conduct more extensive studies. In *Bonnichsen et al. v. United States,* the anthropologists claim that the discovery of "a well-preserved skeleton of this antiquity in North America represents a 'rare discovery of national and international significance' that could shed considerable light on the origins of humanity in the Americas."[8] The anthropologists also question whether remains of this age are Native American or if they can be associated with any modern Native American peoples. Furthermore, the scientists claim that the federal government is denying their right, based on the First Amendment, to study the Kennewick skeleton.[9] A second group of plaintiffs, known as the Asatru Folk Assembly, also entered the case. They claim to be descendants of a pre-Christian pagan European group and that the skeleton is ethnically affiliated with them.[10]

Since that time, two lengthy judicial opinions have been written.[11] In June 1997 the Federal District Court for the District of Oregon ruled that the anthropologists have standing to maintain their suit[12] and vacated the decision of the corps to repatriate the skeleton.[13] The holding by the court that the plaintiff-scientists have standing to challenge the government agency's alleged overenforcement of NAGPRA is an interesting aspect of the opinion that has not attracted much legal analysis.[14] Two of the requirements for establishing standing appear not to be met in this case. First, the injury does not seem to be traceable to the defendant's action. If the bones do not belong to the federal government, then not only is the government not denying anything to the plaintiffs but the government does not even have the legal authority to grant such access to the plaintiffs.[15] Second, the injury is not redressable by the relief requested. Even if the government's application of NAGPRA in this case were unconstitutional or otherwise wrong, there is no requirement that the government turn to the particular scientists who filed the suit for study of the skeleton.[16]

The district court remanded the case to the corps for reconsideration of its decision to repatriate the remains and seemed to indicate that the court considered the corps' original decision to have been arbitrary or irrational. The court instructed the corps to consider seventeen issues, which as summarized include

- Are the remains subject to NAGPRA;
- What is meant by terms such as *Native American* and *indigenous;*
- Does NAGPRA apply to the remains or cultural objects from a wave of ancient migration or subpopulation of early Americans that did not survive;
- Is a biological connection or cultural affiliation between the remains and a contemporary Native American tribe required under NAGPRA;
- Are scientific studies necessary to make appropriate determinations and, if so, are they permitted under NAGPRA;
- Are scientific study and repatriation mutually exclusive or can both objectives be accommodated;
- What happens to the remains if no cultural affiliation can be established with an extant tribe;
- Do the plaintiffs have a right under the First Amendment to study the remains; and
- Do the Asatru (nonscientist) plaintiffs have a right to equal protection that is violated by NAGPRA or the corps' decision?

The corps turned to the Department of the Interior for a response to these questions.[17]

In addition, the corps turned over responsibility for the skeleton to the Department of the Interior. Extensive bickering ensued between the Department of the Interior and the plaintiffs over the custody and handling of the skeleton, as well as over formulation of a plan for its study. The Department of the Interior then embarked on studies to determine if the skeleton is Native American and, therefore, subject to NAGPRA.[18] In October 1998 the bones were moved to the Burke Museum of Natural History at the University of Washington, at which time the Department of the Interior appointed a team of scientists that did not include any of the plaintiffs in the *Bonnichsen* case. In February and March 1999, the team conducted the first phase of its study of the skeleton. In early July 1999 the first round of reports was completed, and on 14 October 1999, the report was issued by the Department of the Interior.[19] The report indicated that the closest association of the Kennewick skeleton is to groups from Polynesia and Southeast Asia and to the Ainu of Japan. No close association with Europeans, Africans, or any modern peoples was indicated. The report also mentions that the bones were covered with ochre and showed signs of gnawing, both of which may indicate intentional burial. Subsequent radiocarbon tests securely date the bones to about ninety-two hundred years old.[20] With this conclusive determination that the bones predate the arrival of Europeans in North America, the skeleton is subject to NAGPRA.

The next step was to determine if the bones bear a cultural affiliation with a modern Native American tribe. DNA tests conducted under the auspices of the Department of the Interior in late spring 2000 were unsuccessful in obtaining any DNA that was usable for the purpose of determining genetic affiliation or other information.[21] The Department of the Interior then engaged in a series of other studies for the purpose of determining whether the Kennewick skeleton is culturally affiliated with any modern Native American tribe. The Department of the Interior issued its determination in September 2001 that the Kennewick skeleton is culturally affiliated with the five claimant tribes;[22] this determination will be discussed in greater detail later in this essay. The parties have returned to court, and a judicial decision is now awaited.

Long before a resolution of this specific dispute, the legal contest has spawned additional controversies and is testing the fundamental purposes of NAGPRA. The media's reports of the story of the Kennewick skeleton have become racialized, and the case has become the flash point for a backlash of resentment in the public media about treatment of Native American tribes.[23] In March 1998, at the meetings of the Society for American Archaeology, James Chatters, the first anthropologist to study the skeleton, unveiled his reconstruction of the skull designed to look like the British actor, Patrick Stewart, of *Star Trek* fame. Although he claimed not to have intentionally made the Kennewick skeleton appear to be that of a white person, Chatters had made his plaster reconstruction white in color.[24] This controversy has also sparked a debate within the scholarly community of physical anthropologists as to whether one can even determine race or biological or cultural affinity based on craniometric studies, as the plaintiffs in *Bonnichsen* seem to claim.[25]

In fall 1997 Representative Doc Hastings (R-Washington) introduced a bill to amend the way NAGPRA handles unidentified human remains in order to permit more extensive study.[26] These amendments would have revised NAGPRA to eliminate the determination of ownership of human remains based on classification of aboriginal lands and to allow studies that would establish affiliation "or to obtain scientific, historical, or cultural information" when lineal descendants cannot be identified. At least in the case of cultural items, "studies may be conducted if needed for the completion of a specific scientific study, the outcome of which is reasonably expected to provide significant new information concerning the history or prehistory of the United States."[27] This equation excludes the significance of the cultural item to a claimant Native American group as a competing interest to be balanced against the scientific needs of the United States. This amendment would have caused significant revisions both in NAGPRA's technical mandates and in its fundamental purpose of returning to Native American groups control over their history, their culture, and their identity.

NAGPRA *and the Treatment of Human Burials and Native American Archaeological Materials*

Background

Perhaps the most central notion in the political consciousness of the United States and the understanding of its history is that the United States was founded on pristine land. Fundamental to this myth is the belief that the European explorers and colonists gave birth to their experiment in liberty and democracy on a blank slate — a virgin territory.[28] This empty land offered great promise and opportunity, unsullied by the failings, intolerance, and internecine and interreligious fighting that had plagued European history and that the colonists sought to escape by coming to the New World. A necessary component of this belief in the creation of a New World was that the American continent was empty, and this, in turn, required first the dehumanization and second the elimination of the native population. Despite initial positing of the Native American as Jean-Jacques Rousseau's "noble savage," Native Americans were soon demonized. This dehumanization functioned as a justification for the unilateral acquisition of their land and eradication of their culture.[29]

Interest in the Native American Indian cultures was largely motivated by scientific curiosity about a culture that was considered sometimes exotic, sometimes inferior, but always available for study and exploration. Hand in hand with scientific exploration was the belief in a discontinuity between "ancient" Indians and the Indians living during the eighteenth and nineteenth centuries. The burial mounds and antiquities found on the American continent held considerable fascination for the colonists and pioneers, but these archaeological materials were not thought to be associated with living Native Americans. Irving Hallowell described the attitude of these early investigators as follows:

> The keen interest taken in the antiquities of the New World was not founded on a hope that these remains would illuminate the prehistoric past of the Indians. Instead, American archeology became a fascinating subject in the public mind because it was based on the myth of a vanished race. It was thought that people superior to and distinct from the contemporary living Indians may have occupied this continent prior to them. If so, they must have been some superior "grade" of Indians or have had some close connection with the past civilizations of the Old World. For the white pioneers held the contemporary Indians in low esteem; they were essentially savages.[30]

During the latter part of the nineteenth century, surveys and excavations of Indian mounds throughout the continental United States—particularly in the Southwest—both revealed the beginnings of destruction and looting of sites and stimulated the market for the products of that looting.[31] The scientific community excavated Indian burials to obtain skeletal materials for their collections and to conduct craniometric studies, while antiquities hunters quickly learned the market value of both Indian skeletal remains and associated burial goods, as well as nonburial Indian artifacts.[32] Craniometric studies have left a legacy of mistrust of archaeology in general, and of physical anthropology in particular, by native peoples and the well-founded perception that the purpose of these studies was to prove the inherent inferiority of aboriginal populations.[33]

By the early twentieth century, the growing public interest in Southwest American Indians and the concern of academics over looting and destruction of sites led to two major developments. The first was enactment of the Antiquities Act of 1906,[34] followed by the designation in the same year of Mesa Verde as the first Native American Indian site to be protected as a national monument. A series of federal statutes culminated with enactment of the Archaeological Resources Protection Act (ARPA) in 1979.[35] Although these statutes were admirable attempts to protect archaeological resources in the interest of scientific and anthropological research, they suffered from the defect of failing to take the interests of the Native American communities explicitly into account, and, at least subconsciously, they still treated the Native American cultures as simply a matter of the past. It was not until amendments to the National Historic Preservation Act were made in 1980 that a provision for Native American participation in the process of deciding treatment for their artifacts and ancestral remains was included in these statutory regimes.[36] ARPA increased participation of Native American groups[37] and can now be seen as a foreshadowing of the direction taken by subsequent legislation.

Enactment of NAGPRA

The legal status of the Native American cultural past illustrates the disparate and unequal treatment of different groups within the American legal system.[38] This inequality between the treatment of the human remains of the dominant European-derived culture and that of the Native Americans results from this unresolved clash in cultural values. Native Americans have suffered the desecration of their dead in the interests of science and the antiquities market for over two hundred years. Archaeologists and anthropologists have long studied the Native American civilizations, excavated their archaeological sites, and placed their human and material cultural remains on exhibit and in storage in museums. These practices often failed to recognize that these remains are part of continuing extant cultural and religious traditions. Although state statutes criminalized the desecration of or interference with religious structures, human gravesites, and cemeteries,[39] such statutes were rarely, if ever, applied to the scientific or archaeological study of the graves of Native American cultures.[40] These laws generally require or are interpreted to require that burials had to be in cemeteries or had to be marked in order to receive protection. Native American burials often are solitary or in small groups, do not have headstones, and are not placed in enclosed cemeteries. These laws, therefore, were not applied to prevent or punish casual desecration of Native American burials. This unequal treatment and violation of the religious rights of Native Americans aroused considerable anger, and Native American groups have demanded (and now achieved) significant changes in the legal system.[41]

Increased activism—particularly in the Indian reburial movement, which developed in the 1970s and received recognition and political power in the 1980s—has caused a reevaluation of the protection laws regarding Native American remains.[42] This movement forced changes in the laws of many states so that human remains, burial sites, and sites with religious significance would no longer be treated as suitable subjects for scholarly research and display; instead, they would be regarded as deserving appropriate respect. The changes achieved were far from uniform throughout the various states, and they have engendered considerable controversy. The use of Native American remains and artifacts has long been regarded as the province of those involved with both education and the promotion of tourism, and these groups have tended to oppose vigorously the treatment of Native American human remains as private and religious matters.[43] Following increasing pressure from Native American groups and changes in public perception and attitudes,[44] and after fierce debate and several unsuccessful attempts,[45] Congress followed the voluntary actions of some museums,[46] and the example of some states,[47] and in 1990 enacted NAGPRA.[48]

Purpose and Effect of NAGPRA

NAGPRA represents an attempt to accommodate the competing interests of Native American tribes, scientists (both physical anthropologists and archaeologists), and museums. It focuses primarily on newly discovered materials and human remains and on remains and objects in federal agencies and those museums and universities that receive federal funding. NAGPRA provides immediate restitution of human remains and cultural objects found on federal or tribal lands after 16 November 1990 to lineal descendants or, where those descendants are unknown, to the tribe on whose lands the objects were discovered or with the tribe that "has the closest cultural affiliation with such remains."[49] It is the application of this latter provision that is in dispute in the Kennewick skeleton controversy. NAGPRA also requires museums, universities, and federal agencies to prepare inventories of human remains and associated grave artifacts, as well as less detailed summaries of unassociated funerary objects, sacred objects, and objects of cultural patrimony that are in their collections. These inventories and summaries must identify the cultural and geographical affiliations of these remains and objects to the extent possible, and notices must be sent to those Native American groups reasonably believed to be culturally affiliated. Restitution can be obtained based on the cultural affiliations established in the inventories.[50]

The practical, positive effects of NAGPRA encompass the following:

- The distribution of information regarding museum and agency collections pursuant to the inventory requirements;
- The growing list of objects in museums and federal agencies that are now available for repatriation;
- A better understanding of the cultural diversity embodied in these issues, not only among Native Americans but also among museum professionals and government agencies;
- A better understanding of the collections themselves;
- A closer relationship among all the parties;
- Enrichment of the discipline of anthropology;
- The returning of control of the information to Native Americans;
- The broadening of these questions to the international arena in which repatriation for a variety of cultural materials has become more prevalent; and
- A reduction in trafficking in cultural materials.[51]

Aside from its practical and specific effects, however, NAGPRA is the first comprehensive approach to treating the Native American cultures as living cultures, worthy of respect for both their past contribution to North American society and their continuing vitality.[52] NAGPRA needs to be understood, first and foremost, as civil rights and human rights legislation,[53] protecting the fundamental liberties of the Native American community by recognizing their rights of free exercise of religion and equal protection under the law.[54] NAGPRA's requirement of equality of treatment and its implicit recognition of the Native Americans as living descendants of past cultures have also produced significant psychological and cultural effects. These effects focus on more than the actual repatriation of specific cultural items or even of human remains. The ultimate result is that Native American groups once again have the ability to control their history and their heritage (religious, spiritual, and mythic), which are crucial to the formation of their identity.

Restitution of Prehistoric Human Remains under NAGPRA

The Meaning of Indigenous

Among the questions that the district court magistrate posed in *Bonnichsen,* perhaps the most crucial concern the definitions under the statute of the terms *Native American* and *indigenous.* The statutory definition of Native American is "of, or relating to, a tribe, people, or culture that is indigenous to the United States."[55] The court in the *Bonnichsen* case raised the question of whether the term *Native American* is, therefore, limited by the use of the term *indigenous,* which the dictionary defines as "occurring or living naturally in an area; not introduced; native."[56] According to this dictionary definition, the Native Americans might not be "indigenous" if it were established that the precontact inhabitants of North America migrated from some other continent or even from some other part of the Americas not currently encompassed within the modern political boundaries of the United States. There would then be no indigenous population of the United States to qualify as Native American under NAGPRA and certainly no indigenous population of Hawaii. As the Department of the Interior's memorandum concludes, "[s]uch an anomalous construction would frustrate the fundamental purposes of NAGPRA with respect to Native Hawaiians and perhaps with respect to some or all Indian tribes."[57]

The memorandum of the Department of the Interior resolves this conundrum by reference to other sections of NAGPRA and other federal statutes that refer to Native Hawaiians as indigenous, despite the fact that the term clearly applies to peoples who migrated to the Hawaiian Islands some time between 200 B.C. and A.D. 800. Even within their own understanding of their history, Native Hawaiians believe that they are descended from primarily two groups who migrated first from the Marquesas Islands and second from Tahiti. Thus the statutory use of the word *indigenous* to describe precontact inhabitants of the Hawaiian Islands clarifies that the term *Native American* is intended by NAGPRA to refer to

> human remains and cultural items relating to tribes, peoples, or cultures that resided within the area now encompassed by the United States *prior to the historically documented arrival of European explorers,* irrespective of when a particular group may have begun to reside in this area, and, irrespective of whether some or all of these groups were or were not culturally affiliated or biologically related to present-day Indian tribes.... [T]he term cannot properly be construed so as to exclude descendants of immigrant peoples [emphasis added].[58]

In addition to the dictionary definition of *indigenous* utilized by the district court in *Bonnichsen* and the statutory definition used by the Department of the Interior in its response to the questions posed by the court, one can also turn to the definition proposed by anthropologists. This definition sheds additional light not only on the technical definition but also on the underlying meaning of the word as it is used today: "Indigenous peoples have a past that has included a time of social and political independence. They have a more recent history that chronicles the loss of that independence to colonial states. During this period they were converted into enclaves in nations controlled by others, and they experienced a growing intrusion, often forced, into their lifeways of the cultural and economic ways of the surrounding society."[59]

Perhaps the primary characteristic of indigenous peoples is thus their loss of autonomy and subjugation often through military conquest. This conquest was followed by a process of colonization that treated indigenous peoples as inferior and generally sought to eradicate them in the attempt to legitimate the claims of the colonizers to territorial acquisitions.[60] Just as indigenous peoples are distinguished by their "connections to land...[that] has often been intricate, subtle, and tremendously complex in ways that make the European criteria of ownership seem simplistic,"[61] so they were often forcibly displaced from these lands with the motive of acquisition of territory and the natural resources the land contained.[62]

This understanding is mirrored in the definitions and policy statements of many international and nongovernmental organizations. One such definition is that of the International Labour Organization's Convention 169 of 1989, which defines indigenous peoples as "[p]eoples in independent countries who are regarded as indigenous on account of their descent from the populations which inhabited the country, or a geographical region to which the country belongs, at the time of conquest or colonisation or the establishment of present state boundaries and who, irrespective of their legal status, retain some or all of their own social, economic, cultural and political institutions."[63] All these definitions share the common characteristics that an indigenous group occupied a particular area before contact with and conquest by another group, and that the indigenous group attempts to maintain a distinct culture, based on a variety of factors, including religion, means of livelihood, lifestyle, language, decentralized political institutions, generally organized at the community level; and occupation of ancestral lands.[64]

By these criteria, it would seem self-evident that the Native American tribes of the United States fit the definition of an indigenous population. They were forcibly removed from their ancestral lands by European settlers, a process that broke their traditional links to the land, their ancestors, and their way of life. At different periods of time, teaching and use of their languages were banned or severely discouraged. Today, they often try to maintain a distinct cultural lifestyle, while also attempting to survive within the dominant culture of the United States. Native Americans, therefore, qualify and should be recognized as indigenous peoples.

Determination of Cultural Affiliation

As previously stated, NAGPRA provides for the immediate restitution of newly discovered Native American human remains and cultural materials found on federal or tribal land after the effective date of the statute. NAGPRA establishes a prioritized list of those entitled to ownership or control, beginning with direct lineal descendants. In the absence of a lineal descendant, such remains or objects should be given to the Indian tribe or Native Hawaiian organization on whose tribal land such objects or remains were discovered; the tribe that has the closest cultural affiliation with such remains or objects; or the Indian tribe that is recognized by a final judgment of the Indian Claims Commission or the United States Court of Claims as aboriginally occupying the area in which the objects were discovered.[65]

There are clearly no discernible lineal descendants of the Kennewick skeleton nor is the land where the skeleton was discovered owned by any Native American tribe. At first, it was thought that this land was part of a settled land claim of the Umatilla tribe, but it was subsequently realized that this is not the case.[66] Thus the skeleton could not be repatriated based on a tribe's aboriginal occupation of the land where the skeleton was discovered.[67] The only remaining statutory basis for determining disposition of the skeleton is found in section 3002(a)(2)(B) of NAGPRA, which calls for restitution to the tribe "which has the closest cultural affiliation with such remains." A literal reading of this provision seems to indicate that it is intended only to address the situation in which two or more tribes claim the same skeletal remains, so that the tribe with the "closest cultural affiliation" will prevail. The regulations implementing NAGPRA, however, interpret this provision as requiring any tribe to establish at least some minimal level of cultural affiliation before it is entitled to restitution even in the absence of any conflicting tribal claim.[68] Pursuant to these regulations, it therefore becomes necessary to determine how a modern Native American tribe might establish cultural affiliation with the Kennewick skeleton.

The definition of and tests for establishing cultural affiliation are applicable to several of NAGPRA's provisions. These have raised some of the most difficult problems in understanding NAGPRA, which defines cultural affiliation as "a relationship of shared group identity which can be reasonably traced historically or prehistorically between a present-day Indian tribe or Native Hawaiian organization and an identifiable earlier group."[69] The implementing regulations further clarify the standard by outlining three requirements for establishing cultural affiliation: first, existence of an identifiable and recognized present-day Indian tribe; second, evidence of the existence of an identifiable earlier group, which may be supported by evidence "establish[ing] the identity and cultural characteristics of the earlier group, document[ing] distinct patterns of material culture manufacture and distribution for the earlier group, or establish[ing] the existence of the earlier group as a biologically distinct population"; and, third, "[e]vidence of the existence of a shared group identity that can be reasonably traced between the present-day Indian tribe ... and the earlier group. Evidence to support this requirement must establish that a present-day Indian tribe ... has been identified from prehistoric or historic times to the present as descending from an earlier group."[70]

The statutory definition of cultural affiliation and the various tests incorporated in the statute and its implementing regulations raise two problems that require examination. The first problem is the question of the type of evidence used in establishing cultural affiliation. A tribe can demonstrate cultural affiliation by a preponderance of the evidence "based upon geographical, kinship, biological, archaeological, anthropological, linguistic, folkloric, oral traditional, historical, or other relevant information or expert opinion."[71] This formula mixes different types of evidence, thus setting the stage for a fundamental cultural and legal conflict. This conflict thus pits scientific data, to which Western cultures and their courts are accustomed, against evidence based on oral, folkloric, and religious information, more prevalent in indigenous societies. The dominant cultural attitude in the United States, as represented by the physical anthropologists who are the plaintiffs in the *Bonnichsen* case, would presumably reject a "historical" evaluation based on religious and mythical beliefs, particularly when these conflict with "science."[72] In the search for truth, however, one must decide whose truth is accepted. Particularly when the determination of truth is institutionalized by the majority cultural group, the determination of whose truth, as a product of that culture, is likely to become culturally biased.

A recent decision in Canada, the case of *Delgamuukw v. British Columbia,* validates an approach that attempts to equalize judicial evaluation of both types of evidence. This case involved a claim for self-government in an area of fifty-eight thousand square kilometers in British Columbia brought by hereditary chiefs representing the Gitskan and Wet'suwet'en peoples. The Canadian Supreme Court reversed the trial court's decision that excluded evidence based on oral history. This evidence included the tribes' collections of sacred oral traditions about their ancestors, histories, and territories, and their *kungax,* a spiritual song, dance, or performance that ties them to their land. The Supreme Court stated that a special approach was justified in a determination of aboriginal rights when the trial court failed "to appreciate the evidentiary difficulties inherent in adjudicating aboriginal claims." The court further explained that "those rights are aimed at the reconciliation of the prior occupation of North America by distinctive aboriginal societies with the assertion of Crown sovereignty over Canadian territory." The court needs to achieve that reconciliation by the "bridging of aboriginal and non-aboriginal cultures."[73]

> [A]boriginal rights are truly *sui generis*, and demand a unique approach to the treatment of evidence which accords due weight to the perspectives of Aboriginal peoples.... Notwithstanding the challenges created by the use of oral histories as proof of historical facts, the laws of evidence must be adapted in order that this type of evidence can be accommodated and placed on an equal footing with the types of historical evidence that courts are familiar with, which largely consists of historical documents.[74]

Courts and legislatures in the United States could learn much from the approach adopted by this Canadian decision, particularly in making a factual determination on the question of cultural affiliation.

The ability to dictate the types of evidence that will be used to formulate the "truth," which, in turn, forms the basis for legal conclusions, is itself a significant form of power within any cultural or political structure. Thus the acceptance of only the truth that is derived from the scientists' formulation and the ability to dictate this to minority cultural groups are a form of control over that group. On the one hand, the scientists offer the explanation that their research will benefit all humankind, an argument that reappears frequently in other cultural heritage disputes. Furthermore, they claim that this benefit justifies their unilateral appropriation of cultural and human remains and their control over interpretation of the past through these remains. On the other hand, indigenous groups are in the process of regaining the right to control their own past, and NAGPRA is one of the few examples of a politically won legislative vindication of that right.[75]

The second problem facing the definition of cultural affiliation is inherent in the history of the Native American peoples. Much of the proof of ownership of cultural artifacts in the Anglo-American common law property system is based on ownership of the land where human remains and material culture are found.[76] This form of proof is, however, made particularly difficult when a group of people has been forcibly displaced from its ancestral lands, subjected to intentional policies of cultural eradication, and denied access to both the tangible and intangible remains of its cultural past. The definition of indigenous peoples discussed earlier reinforces the fact that the history of the treatment of Native Americans has made it even more difficult for tribes to establish links with the past over long periods of time. National governments and private interest groups often dictated or encouraged the forced relocation of indigenous populations in order to weaken them and to free up their land and natural resources for commercial exploitation. Such relocation, combined at other times with policies intended to assimilate indigenous populations, may cause a loss of identity, including loss of language and "eradication of cultural phenomena such as kinship systems, ceremonials, and so forth, that had lent coherence to the population."[77]

The difficulties in establishing cultural identity for modern Native Americans are illustrated by the trial of the Mashpee tribe of Wampanoag Indians on Cape Cod, and even more so by the analysis of the trial offered by the anthropologist James Clifford.[78] The issue at trial was whether the Mashpee were a tribe; if so, they could sue for recovery of their tribal lands on Cape Cod. Although the claimants lost their bid for tribal recognition, the legal proceeding forced a reexamination of modern tribal life and the meaning of cultural identity. Clifford points out three elements in the failure of the Mashpees' case. First was the privileging of written historical evidence over oral history, as many of the elements of tribal life would be preserved only in oral evidence. Second was the definition of *culture* or *cultural identity* adopted by the court. This definition saw the disparate facets of Mashpee modern life as an indication that the traditional way of life had died out rather than representing a continual transformation of that way of life in response to interactions with the modern world. The third element was a requirement to demonstrate unbroken cultural continuity from the past to the present, another factor that was made difficult because of a failure to view the complexity of the interactions between distinctive, traditional tribal life and modern life.

Clifford's analysis demonstrates that the criteria of cultural and tribal identity over long periods of time are more intricate than the court's approach to the question. The anthropological understanding of culture has itself become considerably more complex. Rather than static and limited, human culture is now viewed as fluid and based on "a process involving intergroup exchange and continual re-creation of the self."[79] Both the wording of NAGPRA and much of its legislative history seem intended to change the way cultural continuity was defined in the past, as exemplified in the Mashpee trial.[80] It is also clear that, as Clifford stated, culture and cultural affiliation are not determined by biology or genetic factors.[81] Only one tangible object (the spear point) was found with the Kennewick skeleton, and there may be some evidence of intentional burial and the use of ochre on the bones. Other than these indications, virtually the only remaining evidence of cultural affiliation is the oral histories, traditions, and beliefs of the Native American claimants.

The methodology utilized by the Department of the Interior in making its determination of cultural affiliation is similar to that suggested here.[82] The Department of the Interior reviewed geographical, kinship, biological, archaeological, anthropological, linguistic, folkloric, oral tradition, historical, and other types of evidence. It based its conclusion of cultural affiliation primarily on the geographical and oral tradition evidence as establishing a reasonable link between the Kennewick skeleton and the modern claimant tribes.

The Department of the Interior was able to associate the modern claimant tribes with the Plateau culture that existed in the Columbia Plateau region two to three thousand years ago. The Kennewick skeleton is dated to approximately eighty-five hundred to nine thousand years ago in the same region. It was therefore necessary for the Department of the Interior to link the modern tribes to the Kennewick skeleton over a gap of five to eight thousand years, depending on which estimates are used. The difficulty of bridging this gap is apparent. In reaching its conclusion, the Department of the Interior relied primarily on the oral tradition evidence. This evidence lacks any reference to a migration of people into or out of the Columbia Plateau region and indicates continuity in descriptions of and references to the Columbia Plateau's past landscape. Other evidence, such as differences in material culture, seemed to indicate possible cultural discontinuity, while still other evidence, such as mortuary patterns, morphological characteristics, and linguistic evidence, was considered inconclusive. In light of the totality of the circumstances and evidence, the Department of the Interior found sufficient evidence of cultural continuity to satisfy the standard of the preponderance of the evidence.[83]

The conclusion of the Department of the Interior has been criticized, particularly in its determination of cultural affiliation. For example, the Society for American Archaeology points out that former Secretary of the Interior Bruce Babbitt's letter equates "cultural affiliation" with "reasonable cultural connection" and then equates the latter phrase with "cultural continuity."[84] The Society for American Archaeology states that "[b]y substituting these less restrictive terms for the statutory language, the Secretary's decision undermines Congress' effort to balance scientific and Native American interests by limiting repatriation to cases where there is relatively strong connection with a modern tribe."[85] The Society for American Archaeology is also critical of the sufficiency of the evidence on which the conclusion is based that there is a relationship of shared group identity that can be reasonably traced between the claimant tribes and the Kennewick skeleton. The paucity of information from which a conclusion concerning cultural affiliation can be drawn points to the last aspect of NAGPRA that needs to be considered—the disposition of culturally unaffiliated remains.

Disposition of Culturally Unidentifiable Human Remains

If the court disagrees with the Department of the Interior's determination and concludes that the Kennewick skeleton cannot be linked through cultural affiliation or a shared group identity with any extant Native American tribe, then disposition of the skeleton would seem to be governed by section 3002(b) of NAGPRA. This provides that disposition of culturally unidentified Native American human remains will be determined by regulations to be promulgated by the secretary of the interior in consultation with the NAGPRA Review Committee. More than a decade after enactment of NAGPRA, these regulations have not yet been finalized. The committee has offered a set of draft principles of agreement, which are considered a beginning point of discussion of this topic. The notice of these draft principles was published in the *Federal Register*,[86] yet it appears that we are still far from finalization of the regulations that could determine the ultimate fate of culturally unidentifiable human remains.

Even the draft principles do not provide clear guidance to the resolution of such a dispute. The principles state that "[t]he process [should] be primarily in the hands of Native people (as the nearest next of kin)" and that "[r]epatriation is the most reasonable and consistent choice."[87] Furthermore, "[c]ulturally unidentifiable human remains are no less deserving of respect than those for which cultural affiliation can be established."[88] The principles also present four reasons why human remains may be unidentifiable and suggest a variety of resolutions based on these different reasons. Two of the reasons that might apply to the Kennewick skeleton are that no information or insufficient information exists for a determination of cultural affiliation. Yet the proposed resolution for both circumstances is that the unidentified remains "should be speedily repatriated since they have little educational, historical, or scientific value."[89] This assumption, however, seems not to be true of a skeleton such as the Kennewick skeleton. The draft principles do not suggest any model of resolution for remains that are unidentifiable for the third possible reason, that the remains "represent a defined past population, but for which no present day Indian tribe exists."[90] Thus, although the principles seem to display a sensitivity toward the Native American perspective, they do not at this point seem well drafted to address the type of dispute that will center on the Kennewick skeleton if the court concludes that the skeleton is culturally unidentifiable.

Conclusion

The controversy surrounding the Kennewick skeleton is, in reality, a dispute about whether the self-definition of a Native American group should be recognized even when it conflicts with the scientific interests of the dominant cultural and political group in the United States. While the scientific community seems to have conceded control over the recent past to Native American groups, it is still seeking to limit that control by externally imposed and artificial time boundaries.[91] This attempt to remove the distant past from the control of living Native Americans seems similar to nineteenth-century attitudes toward prehistoric remains in North America that were considered the product of some non-Indian, often European-derived, earlier peoples. Such an approach will ultimately limit the self-definition and understanding of history as developed within the Native American community itself, thus divorcing the modern Native Americans from their past. This undermines some of NAGPRA's goals to eliminate the cultural discontinuities between past and present, and to return control over their past and the formation of their cultural identities to the Native American communities.

To some Native Americans, this dispute places their heritage and their religious beliefs in jeopardy. It is against their traditional beliefs to engage in the destructive, scientific study of human remains; rather, these must be reburied as quickly as possible. Furthermore, Native American traditions and history indicate that they have been in North America from the beginning of time.[92] This controversy thus seems to be a retraction of the recognition of Native American control, which was so long contested and only recently won.

The conflict between a group's self-definition and the definition conferred by an external group involves the question of significance. If one adopts a test for restitution of cultural objects based on a determination of cultural significance to the nation or group seeking restitution, who will be the arbiter of that "significance"? While we might advocate a goal that permits each group to determine and control its own cultural identity, there will be inevitable and seemingly irreconcilable clashes where these identities overlap. How does one resolve such a conflict between the group's self-definition of its own cultural identity and the definition of that identity granted by a larger and more powerful external community? The following are three possible principles for resolution.

The first principle is based on the development of international norms as evinced in several declarations and conventions. The Organization of American States (OAS) Proposed American Declaration on the Rights of Indigenous Peoples, prepared by the Inter-American Commission on Human Rights and approved on 26 February 1997, explicitly recognizes the right of indigenous peoples to "freely preserve, express and develop their cultural identity in all its aspects" (article V). Indigenous peoples also have "the right to their cultural integrity, and their historical and archeological heritage, which are important both for their survival as well as for the identity of their members" (article VII, 1).[93] The United Nations Draft Declaration on the Rights of Indigenous Peoples includes the rights of indigenous peoples to the repatriation of human remains (paragraph 13), and states are called on to ensure the protection of and respect for indigenous sacred places, including burial sites.[94]

Another facet of international norms is embodied in agreements such as the United Nations Educational, Scientific and Cultural Organization (UNESCO) Convention on the Means of Prohibiting and Preventing the Illicit Import, Export, and Transfer of Ownership of Cultural Property of 1970,[95] and the International Institute for the Unification of Private Law (UNIDROIT) Convention on Stolen or Illegally Exported Cultural Objects of 1995.[96] Although these conventions primarily address the restitution of stolen and illegally exported cultural objects on an international scale, they also represent a fundamental shift in the power relationships among the economically dominant market nations of Europe and North America, and the archaeologically rich nations of the developing world. Although NAGPRA and these international conventions seem to address different facets of the cultural heritage debate, in fact they all recognize the need to develop respect for different cultures within their original contexts. They also have had a significant effect on the operation and, particularly, the acquisition policies of many American museums, as well as the development of codes of ethical conduct for various scientific and museum organizations.[97]

The second principle is that of fostering cooperation among Native American communities, museums, and scientists. Unfortunately, the legacy of the Kennewick skeleton controversy may become the dissension and disagreement it has exacerbated between the Native American and scientific communities. It is also unfortunate that this case received as much attention in the media, the scientific literature, and the legal literature as it has. The controversy gives the impression that these conflicts are inevitable, but this need not be the case.

In contrast, examples of cooperation between the scientific and Native American communities are becoming more frequent. In fact, the construction of the identities of the Native American, scientific, and museum communities against the backdrop of both the tension and the cooperation that NAGPRA requires has been seen as one of the goals—or at least one of the beneficial incidental effects—of NAGPRA.[98] Examples of cooperation include the increasing number of museums founded by Native American tribes, the staffing of non-native museums with Native Americans,[99] and the collaboration between tribes and archaeologists, who are, more often, Native Americans.[100] Such cooperation has certainly been facilitated by the training of Native American scientists who are able to meld both the scientific and the Native American perspectives in their studies and in their evaluation and explication of the material culture. The oral histories and traditions that can only be found in Native American knowledge often permit the placement of Native American remains into their full cultural context, providing the missing links in the cultural record. This allows a fuller interpretation and understanding of the past than can be achieved through study of only the archaeological record.[101]

The third principle for resolution is to recall the fundamental nature of NAGPRA as civil rights legislation.[102] Throughout most of the past two centuries Native Americans suffered discrimination, denial of the constitutional guarantees of equal protection and free exercise of religion, and, in particular, the mistreatment of their human remains. There is a close nexus between this history of discrimination and the difficulties of establishing cultural affiliation. Resolution of this type of conflict also forces us to confront the question of how a group forms its cultural identity in the context of conflict with surrounding, dominant groups. How can Native American cultural identity formation and its recognition in the United States be divorced from the national history of conquest, subjugation, and official policies of eradication? If the judicial and political power structures of the majority culture are used as decision makers, the response will always privilege the majority culture's statement of what is significant to it. The response, in turn, is to privilege the minority group's own cultural history and memory as the basis for resolving the conflict, at least in the context of historical and persistent discrimination. Thus, issues left unresolved by NAGPRA, such as the disposition of ancient or culturally unaffiliated human remains, need to be resolved by reliance on the philosophical, civil, and political goals of NAGPRA.[103] This leads to the conclusion that control over their past must remain within the Native American communities. This may mean that Western science will have one less skeleton to study.

Notes

On 30 August 2002, U.S. Magistrate John Jelderks overturned the decision of the Department of the Interior that the Kennewick Man bones are protected under the Native American Graves Protection and Repatriation Act (NAGPRA) and must be returned to the tribes. The government has not yet announced whether it will appeal the decision. If it does not, the scientists will be allowed to study the Kennewick Man skeleton before it is returned to the Native American tribes for burial.

I would like to thank Holly Kuschell-Haworth and Kulsum Ameji for their help in preparing this paper and the DePaul University College of Law for its summer research grant support.

1. Tony Hillerman, *Talking God* (New York: Harper & Row, 1991), 1–9.

2. The facts of the case have been widely reported in the media. Two Web sites maintained by newspapers that contain useful and current information about the case are *The Oregonian* at http://www.oregonlive.com/special/kman (22 February 2002) and the *Tri-City Herald*'s Kennewick Man Virtual Interpretive Center at http://www.kennewick-man.com (22 February 2002). The latter site is a particularly good source for newspaper articles recounting the history of this case as well as many relevant legal documents. The mounting legal literature focused on the case includes the following: Douglas W. Ackerman, "Kennewick Man: The Meaning of 'Cultural Affiliation' and 'Major Scientific Benefit' in the Native American Graves Protection and Repatriation Act," *Tulsa Law Journal* 33 (1997): 359–83; Robert W. Lannan, "Anthropology and

Restless Spirits: The Native American Graves Protection and Repatriation Act, and the Unresolved Issues of Prehistoric Human Remains," *Harvard Environmental Law Review* 22 (1998): 369–439; Larry J. Zimmerman and Robert N. Clinton, "Kennewick Man and Native American Graves Protection and Repatriation Act Woes," *International Journal of Cultural Property* 8 (1999): 212–28; Rebecca Tsosie, "Privileging Claims to the Past: Ancient Human Remains and Contemporary Cultural Values," *Arizona State Law Journal* 31 (1999): 583–677; Sherry Hutt and C. Timothy McKeown, "Control of Cultural Property as Human Rights Law," *Arizona State Law Journal* 31 (1999): 363–89, esp. 380–82; and Sarah Harding, "Value, Obligation and Cultural Heritage," *Arizona State Law Journal* 31 (1999): 291–354, esp. 349–52. See also David Hurst Thomas, *Skull Wars: Kennewick Man, Archaeology, and the Battle for Native American Identity* (New York: Basic, 2000).

3. In the language of physical anthropology, the term *Caucasoid* does not mean the same thing as *Caucasian;* it is a nineteenth-century anthropological term that specifies a skeletal type, not an ethnic identification; see Zimmerman and Clinton, "Kennewick Man" (note 2), 213. Many journalists did not understand this and thus reported that this identification indicated that a European-derived racial or ethnic group may have occupied North America as precursors to or in place of the ancestors of modern Native Americans. The chief archaeologist for the National Park Service was quoted as saying that "international interest in Kennewick Man is fueled by a mistaken popular notion that the bones are Caucasian from Western Europe because some of the cranial features have been described with a technical term, 'Caucasoid'"; see Mike Lee, "Despite Tribal Objections, Interior Still Plans to Date Kennewick Man Bones," *Tri-City Herald,* 29 July 1999; story posted at http://www.kennewick-man.com/news/0729991.html (22 February 2002). Ancient southern Asians typically had a "Caucasoid" skeletal structure; see "'Caucasoid' Kennewick Man Bone of Contention," *Seattle Post-Intelligencer,* 28 July 1999, B2.

4. Timothy Egan, "Tribe Stops Study of Bones that Challenge History," *New York Times,* 30 September 1996, A12. The controversy over the Kennewick skeleton has evoked considerable media coverage, including a full-length article in the *New Yorker* magazine; see Douglas Preston, "The Lost Man," *New Yorker,* 16 June 1997, 70–78. The reactions of the media and the perceptions captured in these reports would present an interesting but different study of the public's attitude toward restitution and the implementation of NAGPRA. The archaeological evidence for the geographic origins of the early inhabitants of North America has undergone dramatic changes even during the four years of the Kennewick controversy. See, for example, Michael Kilian, "Europeans Possibly First Americans," *Chicago Tribune,* 6 April 2000, A1.

5. *Native American Graves Protection and Repatriation Act, U.S. Code,* vol. 25, secs. 3001–13 (2002); posted at http://www.cast.uark.edu/other/nps/nagpra (22 February 2002).

6. The Department of the Interior has since concluded "that the site of discovery does not fall within any area recognized as the aboriginal land of any Indian Tribe in a final judgment of the Indian Claims Commission or the United States Court of Federal Claims," although the site is included within lands ceded by the tribes in 1855. See "Federal Defendants' Fourth Quarterly Status Report, July 1, 1998"; posted

at http://www.kennewick-man.com/documents/statusreport.html (22 February 2002).

7. *Bonnichsen v. U.S.*, 969 F. Supp., 614, 618 (D. Or. 1997).

8. *Bonnichsen v. U.S.*, 969 F. Supp. at 618.

9. The courts have not otherwise recognized that the First Amendment to the United States Constitution establishes the right to study; it seems the only relevant analogy, which raises different problems, would be the rights of access created by the Freedom of Information Act. The plaintiffs' claim that the skeleton is similar to a book that they have the right to read is not only legally questionable but doubtless offensive to many Native Americans; see Zimmerman and Clinton, "Kennewick Man" (note 2), 221.

10. Controversy has also surrounded this group of plaintiffs. Information is available at the Web site maintained by the Asatru Folk Assembly at http://www.runestone. org/n_e_.html (22 February 2002). Although some of the media, particularly the *New York Times*, reported that an organization that monitors racist organizations has linked some current and former members of the Asatru Folk Assembly with neo-Nazi and white supremacist organizations, this has been vehemently denied by the Asatru themselves; see http://www.webcom.com/lstead/race.html (22 February 2002). See also Timothy Egan, "Old Skull Gets White Looks, Stirring Dispute," *New York Times*, 2 April 1998, A12. The Asatru subsequently withdrew from the case; see Mike Lee, "Asatru Give Up Kennewick Man Battle," *Tri-City Herald*, 14 January 2000; posted at http://www.kennewick-man.com/news/0114001.html (22 February 2002).

11. *Bonnichsen v. U.S.*, 969 F. Supp. 614 (D. Or. 1997); and *Bonnichsen v. U.S.*, 969 F. Supp. 628 (D. Or. 1997).

12. *Bonnichsen v. U.S.*, 969 F. Supp. at 637.

13. *Bonnichsen v. U.S.*, 969 F. Supp. at 645. The magistrate remanded to the United States Army Corps of Engineers for further consideration.

14. The United States Supreme Court has tended to limit the ability of individuals to challenge federal agency actions in recent years. An interesting contrast is presented in a subsequent decision, *Idrogo and Americans for Repatriation of Geronimo v. U.S. Army*, 18 F. Supp. 2d 25 (D. D.C. 1998), in which a group demanding reburial of the remains of the Indian leader Geronimo was denied standing under NAGPRA. The Court set out the following basic requirements for establishing standing: "the plaintiffs must show injury in fact that is fairly traceable to the defendant's action and redressable by the relief requested," citing a long line of Supreme Court decisions that have denied standing to those who claim injury due to government agency decisions that are primarily directed at others, including *Allen v. Wright*, 468 U.S. 737, 756 (1984); *Whitmore v. Arkansas*, 495 U.S. 149, 155 (1990); *Lujan v. Defenders of Wildlife*, 504 U.S. 555, 560 (1992); and *Warth v. Seldin*, 422 U.S. 490, 508 (1975); see *Idrogo and Americans for Repatriation of Geronimo v. U.S. Army*, 18 F. Supp. 2d at 27. In *Idrogo* the court held that the plaintiffs did not have standing because "only direct descendants of Native American remains and affiliated tribal organizations stand to be injured by violations of the Act"; see *Idrogo and Americans for Repatriation of Geronimo v. U.S. Army*, 18 F. Supp. 2d at 27. It is perhaps ironic that the case for standing seemed stronger for the Asatru plaintiffs because standing for a claim brought under the Equal Protection Clause is generally broader than that for a claim challenging government agency action under the First Amendment.

15. See Zimmerman and Clinton, "Kennewick Man" (note 2), 221.

16. See note 14. Further discussion of the standing aspect of the case falls outside the scope of this paper.

17. See notes 57–58 and accompanying text.

18. Studies for the purpose of determining cultural affiliation were approved in the case *Na Iwi O Na Kupuna O Mokapu v. Dalton*, 894 F. Supp. 1397, 1415 (D. Haw. 1995), although this case involved NAGPRA's provisions pertaining to human remains held in a museum.

19. Francis P. McManamon et al., *Report on the Non-Destructive Examination, Description, and Analysis of the Human Remains from Columbia Park, Kennewick, Washington,* a special report prepared at the request of the Department of the Interior, October 1999; the full text is posted at http://www.cr.nps.gov/aad/kennewick (22 February 2002). See also Mike Lee, "Report on Kennewick Man Suggests Asian Origin," *Tri-City Herald,* 15 October 1999; posted at http://www.kennewick-man.com/news/101599.html (22 February 2002).

20. See Mike Lee, "Lab Tests Support Age of Kennewick Man," *Tri-City Herald,* 13 January 2000; posted at http://www.kennewick-man.com/news/011300.html (22 February 2002). Leaders of the Native American tribes in the area opposed the radiocarbon studies because of their destructive nature; see Lee, "Despite Tribal Objections" (note 3).

21. See *Report on the DNA Testing Results of the Kennewick Human Remains from Columbia Park, Kennewick, Washington,* posted at http://www.cr.nps.gov/aad/Kennewick/index.htm (22 February 2002). See Mike Lee, "Government Releases Plans for More Tests of Old Bones," *Tri-City Herald,* 11 April 2000; posted at http://www.kennewick-man.com/news/041100.html (22 February 2002). The tribes also objected to the DNA tests; see Mike Lee, "Tribes Call DNA Decision 'Dangerous Precedent,'" *Tri-City Herald,* 19 February 2000; posted at http://www.kennewick-man.com/news/-021900.html (22 February 2002).

22. See *Letter from Secretary of the Interior Bruce Babbitt to Secretary of the Army Louis Caldera Regarding Disposition of the Kennewick Human Remains* (21 September 2000) with the following enclosures: "Determination That the Kennewick Human Skeletal Remains are 'Native American' for the Purposes of the Native American Graves Protection and Repatriation Act (NAGPRA): Memorandum from the Departmental Consulting Archeologist to the Assistant Secretary, Fish and Wildlife and Parks"; "Comparison between Studies Initiated by the Department of the Interior on the Kennewick Human Remains and Those Requested and Recommended by Plaintiffs (*Bonnichsen et al. v. United States*)"; "Human Culture in the Southeastern Columbia Plateau, 9500–9000 B.P. and Cultural Affiliation with Present-Day Tribes: A Summary of the Evidence, Department of the Interior"; "NAGPRA and the Disposition of the Kennewick Human Remains: Memorandum from the Solicitor to the Secretary of the Interior"; and the "Cultural Affiliation Report." These documents are available at http://www.cr.nps.gov/aad/kennewick/index.htm (18 June 2002).

23. An example of this is a broadcast of *60 Minutes* on 25 October 1998, which somehow linked the Kennewick controversy with the rights of tribes to conduct gambling and casinos on reservation lands. For discussion of the program, see Zimmerman and Clinton, "Kennewick Man" (note 2), 227 n. 24.

24. Chatters stated that when "he had tried to visualize the skull, the 'Star Trek' star [was] what most strongly came to mind"; see Egan, "Old Skull Gets White Looks" (note 10). See also Mike Lee, "Tri-Citians Sculpt Theoretical Look for Kennewick Man," *Tri-City Herald*, 10 February 1998; posted at http://www.kennewick-man.com/news/021098.html (22 February 2002).

25. See Zimmerman and Clinton, "Kennewick Man" (note 2), 216.

26. *NAGPRA Amendment*, 105th Cong., 1st sess., 1997, H.R. 2893. The text of the proposed bill is posted at http://www.saa.org/repatriation/lobby/h2893_ih.html (22 February 2002). Testimony presented at the congressional hearings held in June 1998 is available at http://www.kennewick-man.com/documents/testimony/index.html (22 February 2002). The position of the Society for American Archaeology regarding these proposed revisions is posted at http://www.saa.org/repatriation/lobby/hr2893_analysis. html (22 February 2002). The proposed amendments are discussed by Lannan, "Anthropology and Restless Spirits" (note 2), 422–23.

27. *NAGPRA Amendment*, 105th Cong., 1st sess., 1997, H.R. 2893.

28. For discussion of the grand narrative of American history incorporating this myth, see Dane Morrison, "In Whose Hands Is the Telling of the Tale?" in idem, ed., *American Indian Studies: An Interdisciplinary Approach to Contemporary Issues* (New York: Peter Lang, 1997), 10–13.

29. The Native Americans' status as heathens served as a justification under contemporary understandings of international law for the British wars of conquest against them beginning as early as the mid-sixteenth century. At this time, Alberico Gentili proposed in his *De iure belli* that "Europeans could lawfully wage war against normatively divergent peoples who violated Eurocentrically conceived natural law"; quoted in Robert A. Williams Jr., *The American Indian in Western Legal Thought: The Discourses of Conquest* (New York: Oxford Univ. Press, 1990), 195–96. Williams's book (*The American Indian in Western Legal Thought*, 193–225) also provides a history of the development of British legal, philosophical, and religious justifications during the sixteenth and seventeenth centuries for the conquest and eradication of Native Americans based on their status as heathens and aliens. The primary justification for Chief Justice John Marshall's decision in *Johnson v. M'Intosh*, 21 U.S. (8 Wheat.) 543 (1823), vesting title to the North American lands in the European powers and their successor, the United States government, was that the native population differed so radically that it could not be assimilated into the dominant, European-derived culture of North America. Chief Justice Marshall acknowledged that conquered peoples are ordinarily allowed to retain their property rights and that little distinction should be made between the new and the old occupants, as the latter are gradually incorporated into the former. He justified different treatment for the Native Americans, however, in the following passage: "But the tribes of Indians inhabiting this country were fierce savages, whose occupation was war, and whose subsistence was drawn chiefly from the forest. To leave them in possession of their country, was to leave the country a wilderness; to govern them as a distinct people, was impossible, because they were as brave and as high spirited as they were fierce, and were ready to repel by arms every attempt on their independence" 21 U.S. at 590. For the changing legal status and treatment of Native Americans under the law of the United States, see, for example, Dean B. Suagee,

"Human Rights and the Cultural Heritage of Indian Tribes in the United States," *International Journal of Cultural Property* 8 (1999): 51–56; and Augie Fleras and Jean Leonard Elliott, *The "Nations Within": Aboriginal-State Relations in Canada, the United States, and New Zealand* (Toronto: Oxford Univ. Press, 1992), 128–69.

30. A. Irving Hallowell, "The Beginnings of Anthropology in America," in idem, *Contributions to Anthropology: Selected Papers of A. Irving Hallowell* (Chicago: Univ. of Chicago Press, 1976), 36, 114.

31. This interest in scientific study was evidenced, for example, by the founding of the Smithsonian Institution in 1846, which, in the same year, supported its first excavation of Indian mounds. Throughout the late nineteenth century, pothunters looted large numbers of ancient dwelling sites and cemeteries for personal gain. Some, such as the Wetherill brothers, profited personally and outfitted major museums — including the American Museum of Natural History in New York — from their collections; see Kristine Olson Rogers, "Visigoths Revisited: The Prosecution of Archaeological Resource Thieves, Traffickers, and Vandals," *Journal of Environmental Law and Litigation* 2 (1987): 47–105, 51; and Ronald F. Lee, *The Antiquities Act of 1906*, gov. doc. no. I 29.2.An8/2 (Washington, D.C.: Office of History and Historic Architecture, Eastern Service Center, 1970), 29; the entire text is posted at http://www.cr.nps.gov/ aad/pubs (22 February 2002). For the history of the development of American archaeology and the struggles among the various academic, museum, and governmental institutions, see Robert H. McLaughlin, "The American Archaeological Record: Authority to Dig, Power to Interpret," *International Journal of Cultural Property* 7 (1998): 342–75.

32. See, for example, James Riding In, "Without Ethics and Morality: A Historical Overview of Imperial Archaeology and American Indians," *Arizona State Law Journal* 24 (1992): 11–34, esp. 17–23; and Jack F. Trope and Walter R. Echo-Hawk, "The Native American Graves Protection and Repatriation Act: Background and Legislative History," *Arizona State Law Journal* 24 (1992): 35–73, esp. 39–43. See also Margaret B. Bowman, "The Reburial of Native American Skeletal Remains: Approaches to the Resolution of a Conflict," *Harvard Environmental Law Review* 13 (1989): 147–208, esp. 149, who estimated that American museum collections included approximately three hundred thousand human remains. Government action exacerbated the situation. Many of the skeletal remains in the Smithsonian Institution were obtained under a United States Surgeon General's order of 1867 to collect Native American Indian crania for research. Native American Indian remains were routinely viewed as archaeological resources and scientific specimens rather than as human remains. For example, in the mid-1870s, the Pawnee were forcibly moved four hundred miles south by the government, away from their tribal lands and cemeteries, which non-Indian settlers quickly plundered; see Rita Sabina Mandosa, "Another Promise Broken: Reexamining the National Policy of the American Indian Religious Freedom Act," *Federal Bar News and Journal* 40 (1993): 109–15, esp. 112.

33. See D. Gareth Jones and Robyn J. Harris, "Archeological Human Remains: Scientific, Cultural, and Ethical Considerations," *Current Anthropology* 39 (1998): 253–65, esp. 260–62; and Dan L. Monroe, "The Politics of Repatriation," in Dane Morrison, ed., *American Indian Studies: An Interdisciplinary Approach to Contemporary Issues* (New York: Peter Lang, 1997), 391–401. Monroe explains that Samuel

Morton, known as the "father of physical anthropology," concluded that "Native Americans had smaller brains than Caucasians" and were therefore "less intelligent" and had "less aptitude for civilization." Monroe also notes that Morton claimed that "Indians had an 'eccentric' and 'peculiar' moral constitution in which 'wildness' was an indelible trait" ("Politics of Repatriation," 392–93).

34. *Preservation of American Antiquities Act*, ch. 3060, sec. 2, 34 Stat. 225 (1906); codified as amended, *U.S. Code*, vol. 16, secs. 431–458a (2002). Passage of the act was also intended to protect Mount Vernon; see Marilyn Phelan, "A Synopsis of the Laws Protecting Our Cultural Heritage," *New England Law Review* 28 (1993): 63–108, esp. 67. This statute is discussed in great detail in Lee, *Antiquities Act* (note 31).

35. *Archaeological Resources Protection Act*, *U.S. Code*, vol. 16, secs. 470aa–470mm (2002).

36. *National Historic Preservation Act*, *U.S. Code*, vol. 16, secs. 470–470w–6 (2002). Although NHPA calls for only limited Native American participation, the amendments of 1980 included Indian tribes among those to be consulted in furtherance of NHPA policies; see H. Barry Holt, "Archeological Preservation on Indian Lands: Conflicts and Dilemmas in Applying the National Historic Preservation Act," *Environmental Law* 15 (1985): 413–53, esp. 431. Both state and federal statutes seeking to protect archaeological sites and to encourage their scientific exploration are not necessarily viewed as positive by Native American groups, since the latter prefer to emphasize private knowledge of sites and noninterference with them; see Holt, "Archaeological Preservation" (this note), 428. The role of tribes in implementing NHPA was further expanded in its amendments of 1992; see Dean B. Suagee, "Cultural Rights, Biodiversity and the Indigenous Heritage of Indian Tribes in the United States," in Halina Niec, ed., *Cultural Rights and Wrongs: A Collection of Essays in Commemoration of the Fiftieth Anniversary of the Universal Declaration of Human Rights* (Paris: UNESCO, 1998), 81, 100–1.

37. ARPA required consent of the Native American owners before archaeological excavation on Native American–owned land was permitted; see *Archaeological Resources Protection Act* (note 35), *U.S. Code*, vol. 16, sec. 470cc(g); and Holt, "Archaeological Preservation" (note 36), 415. This legislation called for the preservation of sites to be done in partnership with Indian tribes.

38. The treatment of these types of remains poses a three-way struggle among Native American groups, the museum and archaeological community, and the pothunters and antiquities traders. While the first two are somewhat in concert in seeking protection for remains in situ, they are bitterly opposed on the questions of whether remains should be excavated and what should be done with remains that were previously excavated. On the one hand, the museum and archaeological communities believe that research and display are important parts of the process of understanding history and that there is much additional scientific information to be derived from the Native American remains under their control; see, for example, John E. Peterson, "Dance of the Dead: A Legal Tango for Control of Native American Skeletal Remains," *American Indian Law Review* 15 (1990): 115, 119. On the other hand, as one commentator has noted, "the cultural curation of mingled remains of various individuals [by museums] does not suggest reverence for the contents"; H. Marcus

Price III, *Disputing the Dead: U.S. Law on Aboriginal Remains and Grave Goods* (Columbia: Univ. of Missouri Press, 1991), 16. See also Gene A. Marsh, "Walking the Spirit Trail: Repatriation and Protection of Native American Remains and Sacred Cultural Items," *Arizona State Law Journal* 24 (1992): 79, 92 (noting the conflict between Native Americans and the archaeological and museum communities in that some Native Americans believe that "any form of archaeological study at any site constitutes desecration"). Native American groups have also argued that curation violates their rights to religious freedom because some tribes believe that the spirits of their dead cannot rest until their remains are reinterred; see Marsh, "Walking the Spirit Trail" (this note), 84. For discussion of the role of NAGPRA in mediating the formation of identities among Native American groups and museum professionals, see Morris A. Fred, "Law and Identity: Negotiating Meaning in the Native American Graves Protection and Repatriation Act," *International Journal of Cultural Property* 6 (1997): 199–229.

39. See, for example, *Colorado Revised Statutes Annotated* (West 2002), sec. 18–9–113(1)(b), making such desecration a class-one misdemeanor. *Desecration* is defined as "defacing, damaging, polluting, or otherwise physically mistreating in a way that the defendant knows will outrage the sensibilities of persons likely to observe or discover his action or its result"; see *Colorado Revised Statutes* (this note), sec. 18–9–113(2). See also *Massachusetts General Laws Annotated* (West 2002), ch. 266, sec. 127A, which punishes the intentional or wanton destruction, defacement, or injury to a religious structure or places to bury or memorialize the dead by a fine up to $2,000 or three times the value of the property destroyed, whichever is greater, or imprisonment up to two and one-half years, or both; if the damage or loss exceeds $5,000, then a person may be punished by a fine up to three times the value of property destroyed, or imprisonment up to five years, or both. The disinterment of a human body has been a criminal act in Massachusetts since at least 1814; today, it is punishable by imprisonment in the state prison for no more than three years or in jail for no more than two and one-half years, or by a fine of not more than $4,000; see *Massachusetts General Laws Annotated*, ch. 272, sec. 71.

40. Part of the reason for this lay in statutory wording, which restricted protection to cemeteries and marked burials. For example, a Massachusetts case decided in 1966 held that although an Indian settlement and skeleton had been found in a particular location, the location was not considered a "burial ground." The conclusion that it was a burial ground would have protected it under the statutory provisions for ancient burial sites; see *Town of Sudbury v. Dept. of Public Utilities*, 351 Mass. 214, 218; N.E. 2d 415 (1966). *Massachusetts General Laws Annotated* (note 39), ch. 114, sec. 17, prohibits a town from appropriating to any use other than as a burial ground any tract that has been used as a burial place for more than one hundred years. This provision was amended in 1983 so that a "burial place" would specifically include "unmarked burial grounds known or suspected to contain the remains of one or more American Indians"; see *Massachusetts General Laws Annotated* (note 39), St. 1983, ch. 659, sec. 6. See also *Newman v. State*, 174 So. 2d 479, 483 (Fla. Ct. App. 1965), which held that the removal of a Seminole Indian skull did not constitute the wanton and malicious disturbance of the contents of a tomb, and *Wana the Bear v. Community Construction, Inc.*,

180 Cal. Rptr. 423, 426–27 (Cal. Ct. App. 1982), which refused to enjoin commercial development of an Indian burial ground because it had failed to attain protected status as a cemetery under a statute of 1873, because the cemetery had previously been "abandoned" after the Miwoks were driven out of the area between 1850 and 1870. One state court has recognized that Native American burials were not, in fact, abandoned when a tribe was forcibly relocated; see *Charrier v. Bell*, 496 So. 2d 601 (La. Ct. App. 1986), *cert. denied*, 498 So. 2d 753 (La. 1986).

41. This dichotomy in treatment was recognized in many of the recent legislative enactments, such as the statement of legislative purpose for the Florida statute of 1987 regarding unmarked human burials: "It is the intent of the Legislature that all human burials and human skeletal remains be accorded equal treatment and respect based upon common human dignity without reference to ethnic origin, cultural background, or religious affiliation"; *Florida Statutes Annotated* (West 2002), sec. 872.05(1). The legislative findings for the Nebraska statute recognize that prior law, although purporting to protect human burial sites, did not "provide equal and adequate protection or incentives to assure preservation of all human burial sites in this state"; see *Revised Statutes of Nebraska Annotated* (Michie 2002), sec. 12–1202(3).

42. See Tamara L. Bray, "Repatriation, Power Relations and the Politics of the Past," *Antiquity* 70 (1995): 440–43; Riding In, "Without Ethics and Morality" (note 32), 30; and Lannan, "Anthropology and Restless Spirits" (note 2), 394–95. Through educational activities and political action, the Indian reburial movement has achieved a greater degree of burial protection for Native American grave sites. Since the 1970s, a number of states have passed legislation aimed at preventing the future storage of disinterred Indian remains in laboratories, universities, and other facilities. For discussion of Indian political activism in the 1970s and 1980s, see Richard J. Perry, *From Time Immemorial: Indigenous Peoples and State Systems* (Austin: Univ. of Texas Press, 1996), 119.

43. For a discussion of the conflicts between the religious rights of Native American groups and the scientific and museum communities, see Walter R. Echo-Hawk, "Museum Rights vs. Indian Rights: Guidelines for Assessing Competing Legal Interests in Native Cultural Resources," *New York University Review of Law and Social Change* 14 (1986): 437–53.

44. The five-hundredth anniversary of Christopher Columbus's voyages sparked debate concerning their effect on the indigenous peoples of North America, while movies such as *Dances with Wolves* (1990) showed the public a different view of the lives of Plains Indians from that traditionally portrayed by Hollywood; see Leonard DuBoff, "Protecting Native American Culture," *Cardoza Arts and Entertainment Law Journal* 11 (1992): 43–58, 53.

45. Legislation was introduced in Congress in 1986, Senate hearings were held in 1988, and both the Native American Burial Site Preservation Act and the Native American Grave and Burial Protection Act were introduced and defeated in 1989. It was also in 1989, however, that the National Museum of the American Indian Act took the first step toward restitution by establishing a separate museum to house the Smithsonian's Native American collection and to begin the process of restoring some remains to Native American groups; *National Museum of the American Indian Act, U.S. Code*, vol. 20, sec. 80q–9 (1994). See June Camille Bush Raines, "One Is Missing: Native

American Graves Protection and Repatriation Act: An Overview and Analysis," *American Indian Law Review* 17 (1992): 639–64, 651–52; and Trope and Echo-Hawk, "Native American Graves" (note 32), 54–58.

46. For example, in 1978 the Zuni tribe successfully persuaded the Denver Art Museum to return a war god, and in 1989 Stanford University agreed to return more than five hundred Ohlone Indian remains to their descendants for reburial; see DuBoff, "Protecting Native American Culture" (note 44), 48–49.

47. While thirty-four states had enacted unmarked burial protective legislation, only five states had enacted restitution statutes; see David J. Harris, "Respect for the Living and Respect for the Dead: Return of Indian and Other Native American Burial Remains," *Washington University Journal of Urban and Contemporary Law* 39 (1991): 195–224; and also Trope and Echo-Hawk, "Native American Graves" (note 32), 52–54.

48. *Native American Graves Protection and Repatriation Act* (note 5), *U.S. Code*, vol. 25, sec. 3001–3013. For the extensive literature concerning NAGPRA, see the annotated bibliography in Nancy Carol Carter, "Native American Graves Protection and Repatriation Act: Law, Analysis, and Context," *International Journal of Cultural Property* 8 (1999): 285–306.

49. *Native American Graves Protection and Repatriation Act* (note 5), sec. 3002(a).

50. See *Native American Graves Protection and Repatriation Act* (note 5), sec. 3003 (regarding the inventory of human remains and associated funerary objects); sec. 3004 (regarding summaries of unassociated funerary objects, sacred objects, and objects of cultural patrimony); sec. 3005 (regarding the repatriation of human remains and cultural items). All of these terms are defined in the *Native American Graves Protection and Repatriation Act* (note 5), sec. 3001. These provisions of NAGPRA requiring the preparation of inventories and summaries and the restitution of Native American remains and objects in collections have generally received more attention in both the legal and general literature, as well as in litigation, than have the provisions of NAGPRA pertaining to newly discovered remains and objects. For discussion of the Review Committee and court cases involving these provisions, see James A. R. Nafziger and Rebecca J. Dobkins, "The Native American Graves Protection and Repatriation Act in Its First Decade," *International Journal of Cultural Property* 8 (1999): 77–107, 94–98.

51. See Timothy McKeown, "Keynote Address" (paper presented at the conference "Law and the Sacred: Native American Repatriation," Social Sciences Division, University of Chicago, 24 October 1997). Several convictions under NAGPRA have been accomplished, and NAGPRA itself was upheld as constitutional despite a claim of vagueness in the appeal of one of these convictions; see *United States v. Corrow,* 941 F. Supp. 1553 (D.N.M. 1996), *aff'd,* 119 F.3d 796 (10th Cir. 1997).

52. See, for example, Rennard Strickland, "Implementing the National Policy of Understanding, Preserving, and Safeguarding the Heritage of Indian Peoples and Native Hawaiians: Human Rights, Sacred Objects, and Cultural Patrimony," *Arizona State Law Journal* 24 (1992): 175–91. Strickland comments (pp. 179–80),

An important threshold consideration…is the recognition that Native Americans and Hawaiians…are legal, living cultures with vital ongoing lifeways rooted in a rich traditional heritage.... NAGPRA recognizes that Native peoples are not themselves museum objects of dead cultures or even isolated remnants of quaint lost tribes; they are members of ongoing governmental, social, economic, religious, and political units. Native peoples are free under the law to define themselves and their lifeways.

Strickland (pp. 180–81, 189–90) notes that NAGPRA utilizes Native American concepts in its legal definitions, as well as returning initiative and responsibility to the Native American community to protect its own heritage.

53. NAGPRA was recognized in its legislative history as "first and foremost, human rights legislation." When NAGPRA was passed by the Senate, Senator Daniel Inouye (D–Hawaii) stated, "In light of the important role that death and burial rites play in native American cultures, it is all the more offensive that the civil rights of America's first citizens have been so flagrantly violated for the past century.... [T]he bill before us is not about the validity of museums or the value of scientific inquiry. Rather, it is about human rights"; see Trope and Echo-Hawk, "Native American Graves" (note 32), 59. See also Nafziger and Dobkins, "Native American Graves" (note 50), 81; and Sherry Hutt, "Native American Cultural Property Law — Human Rights Legislation," *Arizona Attorney* 34 (1998): 18–21.

The Report of the Panel for a National Dialogue on Museum/Native American Relations (28 February 1990) stated in its general principles:

[H]uman rights should be the paramount principle where claims are made by Native American groups that have a cultural affiliation with remains and other materials. Such human rights include religious, cultural, and group survival rights, as understood within the context of U.S. and international standards of human rights and rights of self-determination.... In far too many instances, the human rights of Native American nations and people have been violated in the past through the collection, display and other use of human remains and cultural materials without Native American consent and in ways inconsistent with Native American traditions and religions.

Quoted from the report as reprinted in "Symposium: The Native American Graves Protection and Repatriation Act of 1990 and State Reparation-Related Legislation," *Arizona State Law Journal* 24 (1992): 487–500, esp. 487, 494. The panel was, however, divided as to whether claims by groups that do not have a cultural affiliation to the remains and objects at issue involved the same level of human rights principles.

54. The continuing need for recognition of these rights is, unfortunately, still apparent, as this inequality was perpetuated as recently as 1998 in a decision of the Utah Court of Appeals affirming the dismissal of felony charges for grave desecration brought against a physician who regularly took his family on picnic outings to dig up Native American burials. Both the trial court and later the court of appeals dismissed the prosecution on the grounds that the state's laws prohibiting desecration of cemeteries were not intended to apply to individual burials, such as those used by Native Americans; see *Utah v. Redd,* 954 P.2d 230 (Utah Ct. App. 1998). The Utah Supreme Court ultimately reversed, holding that the lower court's interpretation of the statute

did not serve the public policy in encouraging interment and discouraging interference with burials. Yet its decision was based on the policy of not interfering with or dismembering dead bodies, rather than on an explicit recognition that Native American burials should be protected by the same burial protection legislation that applies to nonnative burials; see *State v. Redd*, 992 P.2d 986 (Utah 1999). This case demonstrates one of the shortcomings of NAGPRA in that it applies only to burials on federal or tribal lands, and not all states have adopted comparable legislation even for burials located on public land. Furthermore, burials located on private land would likely receive protection in only about half of the states.

55. *Native American Graves Protection and Repatriation Act* (note 5), *U.S. Code*, vol. 25, sec. 3001(9).

56. *Bonnichsen v. U.S.*, 969 F. Supp. at 651 and n. 24.

57. Letter from Francis P. McManamon to Lieutenant Colonel Curtis, 23 December 1997; posted at http://www.kennewick-man.com/documents/mcmanamonletter.html (26 February 2002).

58. Letter from McManamon to Curtis (note 57).

59. Thomas C. Greaves, "Indigenous Peoples," in David Levinson and Melvin Ember, eds., *Encyclopedia of Cultural Anthropology* (New York: Henry Holt, 1996), 2:635–37.

60. "A significant dimension of the identity of the populations correctly designated as 'indigenous' derives from a particular history of settlement and usurpation"; André Béteille, "The Idea of Indigenous People," *Current Anthropology* 39 (1998): 187–92, esp. 188. For similar definitions focusing on indigenous peoples' attachment to the land and their descent from preinvasion inhabitants of these lands, see S. James Anaya, *Indigenous Peoples in International Law* (New York: Oxford Univ. Press, 1996), 3–4; and Siegfried Wiessner, "Rights and Status of Indigenous Peoples: A Global Comparative and International Legal Analysis," *Harvard Human Rights Journal* 12 (1999): 57–128, esp. 58. Wiessner notes the paradox in the definitions of indigenous peoples and the Court's discussion in *Bonnichsen v. U.S.* To avoid the problems raised by the Court's definition, Wiessner would eliminate the emphasis on priority in time and suggests the following definition (p. 115):

> Indigenous communities are thus best conceived of as peoples traditionally regarded, and self-defined, as descendants of the original inhabitants of lands with which they share a strong, often spiritual bond. These people are, and desire to be, culturally, socially and/or economically distinct from the dominant groups in society, at the hands of which they have suffered, in past or present, a pervasive pattern of subjugation, marginalization, dispossession, exclusion and discrimination.

61. Perry, *From Time Immemorial* (note 42), 8.

62. As Perry, *From Time Immemorial* (note 42), 9, comments, "Ways to weaken local indigenous peoples might involve dispersing them or relocating them collectively, which frees their land or other resources for exploitation by others."

63. Quoted in Douglas E. Sanders, "Indigenous Peoples: Issues of Definition," *International Journal of Cultural Property* 8 (1999): 4–13, 5. Sanders also discusses the definitions offered in the studies of the U.N. Sub-Commission on Prevention of

Discrimination and Protection of Minorities in 1983, the Working Group on Indigenous Populations, the World Bank, and the work of various individual scholars; neither the United Nations Draft Declaration on the Rights of Indigenous Peoples nor the Proposed American Declaration on the Rights of Indigenous Peoples offers a definition.

64. See, for example, Julian Burger, *Report from the Frontier: The State of the World's Indigenous Peoples* (Cambridge, Mass.: Cultural Survival, 1987), 6–11.

65. *Native American Graves Protection and Repatriation Act* (note 5), sec. 3002(a). The relevant text of this section is as follows:

Sec. 3002. Ownership

(a) Native American human remains and objects

The ownership or control of Native American cultural items which are excavated or discovered on Federal or tribal lands after November 16, 1990, shall be (with priority given in the order listed)—

(1) in the case of Native American human remains and associated funerary objects, in the lineal descendants of the Native American; or

(2) in any case in which such lineal descendants cannot be ascertained...

(A) in the Indian tribe or Native Hawaiian organization on whose tribal land such objects or remains were discovered;

(B) in the Indian tribe or Native Hawaiian organization which has the closest cultural affiliation with such remains or objects and which, upon notice, states a claim for such remains or objects; or

(C) if the cultural affiliation of the objects cannot be reasonably ascertained and if the objects were discovered on Federal land that is recognized by a final judgment of the Indian Claims Commission or the United States Court of Claims as the aboriginal land of some Indian tribe—

(1) in the Indian tribe that is recognized as aboriginally occupying the area in which the objects were discovered, if upon notice, such tribe states a claim for such remains or objects; or

(2) if it can be shown by a preponderance of the evidence that a different tribe has a stronger cultural relationship with the remains or objects than the tribe or organization specified in paragraph (1), in the Indian tribe that has the strongest demonstrated relationship, if upon notice, such tribe states a claim for such remains or objects.

66. See note 6.

67. See Ackerman, "Kennewick Man" (note 2), 366.

68. See Lannan, "Anthropology and Restless Spirits" (note 2), 403–4, and n. 223.

69. *Native American Graves Protection and Repatriation Act* (note 5), 3001(2). In his extensive study of the legislative history of these NAGPRA provisions, Lannan concludes that Congress "soften[ed] its requirement for a cultural relationship between a set of remains and a Native American claimant to them.... The standard finally enacted in NAGPRA allows a more nebulous 'relationship of shared group identity,' and requires only that this relationship be 'reasonably traced' between remains and the claimant tribe"; Lannan, "Anthropology and Restless Spirits" (note 2), 429–30. The Senate committee report stated:

Claimants do not have to establish "cultural affiliation" with scientific certainty.... Where human remains and funerary objects are concerned, the committee is aware that it may be extremely difficult, unfair or even impossible in many instances for claimants to show an absolute continuity from present day Indian tribes to older, prehistoric remains without some reasonable gaps in the historic or prehistoric record. In such instances, a finding of cultural affiliation should be based upon an overall evaluation of the totality of the circumstances and evidence pertaining to the connection between the claimant and the material being claimed and should not be precluded solely because of gaps in the record.

Senate Select Committee on Indian Affairs, *Report to Accompany S. 1980,* 101st Cong., 2d sess., 1990, S. Rept. 101–473, 4, 8, 9; posted at http:// www.cast.uark.edu/ other/nps/nagpra/DOCS/lgm002.html (26 February 2002); quoted in Lannan, "Anthropology and Restless Spirits" (note 2), 419.

70. Francis P. McManamon, Timothy McKeown, and Lars Hanslin, "NAGPRA Regulations," *Federal Register* 60 (4 December 1995): 62168.

71. *Native American Graves Protection and Repatriation Act* (note 5), sec. 3005(a)(4).

72. Many commentators have noted the apparently irreconcilable worldviews of Native Americans and the dominant Anglo-American society; see, for example, Ackerman, "Kennewick Man" (note 2), 373–81; and Strickland, "Implementing the National Policy" (note 52), 181.

73. *Delgamuukw v. British Columbia* [1997] 3 Supreme Court Reports 1010, 1065–66.

74. *Delgamuukw v. British Columbia* [1997] 3 Supreme Court Reports 1010, 1066–69.

The question of acceptance of traditional knowledge by Western courts is well discussed in an article on the *Delgamuukw* decision by Catherine E. Bell and Robert K. Paterson, "Aboriginal Rights to Cultural Property in Canada," *International Journal of Cultural Property* 8 (1999): 167–211. They write (p. 176):

Although Canadian courts will admit oral history, judges are reluctant to give weight to oral histories which consist of out of court statements passed through successive generations of Aboriginal peoples. Accepting the truth of these statements runs contrary to the hearsay rule which maintains that out of court statements cannot be admitted as evidence of the truth of the content of such statements. This reluctance is also fueled by concerns about the frailty of the human memory, the content of oral histories and judicial understandings of truth which require the separation of historical facts from what Aboriginals perceive to be legends, stories or myths, cultural bias in favour of written and physical evidence, and rules of evidence which assume the truth of ancient documents.

In *Delgamuukw,* however, the Canadian Supreme Court held that the courts must "come to terms with oral histories of Aboriginal societies" and that oral histories could only be questioned for reasons that are not inherent in all such histories; see Bell and Paterson, "Aboriginal Rights" (this note), 176. For extended discussion of the treatment of Aboriginals in Canada, see, for example, Michael Asch, *Home and Native Land:*

Aboriginal Rights and the Canadian Constitution (Vancouver: Univ. of British Columbia Press, 1993); Perry, *From Time Immemorial* (note 42), 124–60; and Fleras and Elliott, "*Nations Within*" (note 29), 9–125.

75. See Jones and Harris, "Archeological Human Remains" (note 33), 260; see also Teresa Olwick Grose, "Reading the Bones: Information Content, Value, and Ownership Issues Raised by the Native American Graves Protection and Repatriation Act," *Journal of the American Society for Information Science* 47 (1996): 630.

76. Human skeletal remains were not considered subject to private ownership under common law property principles. On the one hand, the deceased's next of kin have rights to the remains for the purpose of burial. On the other hand, particularly nonfunerary objects embedded in the ground were considered owned by the owner of the land, unless these rights were altered by statute; see Patty Gerstenblith, "Identity and Cultural Property: The Protection of Cultural Property in the United States," *Boston University Law Review* 75 (1995): 559–688, esp. 645–47. The fact that Native Americans were forcibly moved from their lands means that it is significantly more difficult for them to establish claims to their material culture and to their ancestors' human remains.

77. Perry, *From Time Immemorial* (note 42), 9. United States federal policy toward the Native Americans has vacillated among protection, eradication, and assimilation; see Suagee, "Human Rights" (note 29), 54–56.

78. *Mashpee Tribe v. Town of Mashpee,* 447 F. Supp. 940 (D.C. Mass. 1978), *aff'd sub nom. Mashpee Tribe v. New Seabury Corp.,* 592 F.2d 575 (1st Cir. 1979), *cert. denied, Mashpee v. Mashpee Tribe,* 444 U.S. 866 (1979). James Clifford, "Identity in Mashpee," in idem, *The Predicament of Culture: Twentieth-Century Ethnography, Literature, and Art* (Cambridge: Harvard Univ. Press, 1988), 227, 336–44. See also United States Commission on Civil Rights, *Indian Tribes: A Continuing Quest for Survival: A Report* (Washington, D.C.: United States Commission on Civil Rights, 1981), 112–15.

79. Nafziger and Dobkins, "Native American Graves" (note 50), 86–87. The authors point out (p. 87) that "it is ironic that, just when anthropological theory and Native peoples themselves are seeing cultural identity as fluid and contextually constructed, NAGPRA potentially insists that it be determined and fixed in time and space. Issues of cultural affiliation therefore represent a paradoxical dimension of NAGPRA." Bray points out that Native American groups are being forced to define themselves in static categories, frozen at the time of contact with Western Europe and imposed on them by the state. Rather, cultural identity should be viewed "as a subjective process in which individuals and groups identify themselves and others within the framework of specific social and political situations for specific purposes"; see Bray, "Repatriation" (note 42), 443.

80. See note 69. The House Committee's final report describes the standard in NAGPRA as based on the "totality of the circumstances" and allows "some reasonable gaps" in the record; see House Committee on Interior and Insular Affairs, *Report to Accompany H.R. 5237,* 101st Cong., 2d sess., 1990, H.R. Rep. 101–877, 17; posted at http://www.cast.uark.edu/products/NAGPRA/DOCS/lgm001.html (26 February 2002); quoted in Lannan, "Anthropology and Restless Spirits" (note 2), 430 n. 361.

81. Clifford, "Identity in Mashpee" (note 78), 337. The government's decision to conduct DNA tests on the bones may be (and has been) considerably criticized. A representative of the tribes involved in the dispute over the Kennewick skeleton stated, "According to our belief system, the action of destructive DNA testing...would reduce our identity to a series of genetic code"; see Lee, "Tribes Call DNA Decision" (note 21). George Annas, founder of the Law, Medicine and Ethics Program at Boston University, stated that "ethical standards demand that invasive scientific procedures on dead people require consent of the family, which in this case is disputed. 'Mere scientific curiosity' is an insufficient justification,...especially because there is 'no clear consensus' on the relative value of the information that could be obtained"; see Lee, "Tribes Call DNA Decision" (note 21). The principal danger of such DNA testing is that it may lead to the conclusion that culture and identity are premised on biological and genetic factors—a conclusion that, based on observance of modern cultures, seems patently false.

82. This description of the determination of the Department of the Interior is based on the Letter from Babbitt to Caldera (note 22).

83. The Department of the Interior concluded that disposition of the Kennewick skeleton to the claimant tribes could also be premised on a claim based on aboriginal occupation under *U.S. Code*, vol. 25, sec. 3002(a)(2)(C)(1). This conclusion is based on a thorough review of final judgments of the Indian Claims Commission (ICC) and the United States Court of Claims relating to the land where the Kennewick skeleton was found. Disposition under this section of NAGPRA may not be precluded when an ICC final judgment did not specifically delineate aboriginal territory because of a voluntary settlement agreement. The ICC had determined that several Indian tribes, including the Umatilla and Nez Percé, used and occupied the area where the Kennewick skeleton was found. In a subsequent final judgment pursuant to a compromise settlement, these lands were not delineated as aboriginal territory of the Umatilla. Nonetheless, the ICC's prior determination supports disposition of the skeleton to the claimant tribes under section 3002(a)(2)(C)(1); Letter from Babbitt to Caldera (note 22).

84. Society for American Archaeology, "Society for American Archaeology Position Paper on the Secretary of the Interior's September 21, 2000, Determination of Cultural Affiliation for Kennewick Man" (14 October 2000); posted at http://www.saa.org/repatriation/lobby/kennewickc8.html (26 February 2002).

85. Society for American Archaeology, "Position Paper" (note 84).

86. Department of Interior, National Park Service, Notice, "Notice of Draft Principles of Agreement Regarding the Disposition of Culturally Unidentifiable Human Remains—Extended Date for Comments," *Federal Register* 64, no. 145 (29 July 1999): 41135–36; posted at http://www.cast.uark.edu/other/nps/nagpra/nagpra.dat/rcrec003.html (26 February 2002).

87. Department of Interior, "Notice of Draft Principles" (note 86), 41136 [sec. A(4)(a and b)].

88. Department of Interior, "Notice of Draft Principles" (note 86), 41136 [sec. C(1)(a)].

89. Department of Interior, "Notice of Draft Principles" (note 86), 41136 [sec. C(2)(b)].

90. Department of Interior, "Notice of Draft Principles" (note 86), 41136 [sec. B(3)(b)].

91. In suggesting that the older remains belong to the scientific realm, it has been argued that "at the recent end of this range [of age of skeletal remains], one is dealing with spiritual and cultural values similar to those of contemporary societies; at the remote end, the relevant values have to do with their significance for global history"; see Jones and Harris, "Archeological Human Remains" (note 33), 254.

92. See George Johnson, "Indian Tribes' Creationists Thwart Archeologists," *New York Times*, 22 October 1996, A1, where Sebastian LeBeau, repatriation officer for the Cheyenne River Sioux, a Lakota tribe based in Eagle Butte, South Dakota, explained, "We never asked science to make a determination as to our origins. We know where we came from. We are the descendants of the Buffalo people. They came from inside the earth after supernatural spirits prepared this world for humankind to live here." In the same *New York Times* article, Larry Benallie, a tribal archaeologist for the Navajo Nation, stated, "There's a real feeling that we've been here forever. The Bering Strait theory makes logical sense, but it doesn't override the traditional belief at all. That comes first."

93. Siegfried Wiessner, "The Proposed American Declaration on the Rights of Indigenous Peoples," *International Journal of Cultural Property* 6 (1997): 356–63. The text of this declaration by the Organization of American States (OAS) follows Wiessner's article (pp. 364–75); it is also posted at http://www.cidh.oas.org/Indigenous. htm (26 February 2002).

94. See the United Nations Draft Declaration on the Rights of Indigenous Peoples (1994), UN doc. sym. E/CN.4/SUB.2/1994/2/Add.1; as reprinted in Halina Niec, ed., *Cultural Rights and Wrongs: A Collection of Essays in Commemoration of the Fiftieth Anniversary of the Universal Declaration of Human Rights* (Paris: UNESCO, 1998), app. A, 191, 194.

95. For the UNESCO Convention on the Means of Prohibiting and Preventing the Illicit Import, Export, and Transfer of Ownership of Cultural Property, adopted by the General Conference of UNESCO on 17 November 1970, entry in force 24 April 1972, see *United Nations Treaty Series* 823 (1972): 231; and *International Legal Materials* 10 (1971): 289; also posted at http://exchanges.state.gov/education/culprop/unesco01. html (26 February 2002).

96. For the Unidroit Convention on Stolen or Illegally Exported Cultural Objects, 24 June 1995, see *Revue de droit uniforme = Uniform Law Rev.*, n.s., 1 (1996): 110; also posted at http://www.unidroit.org/english/conventions/c-cult.htm (26 February 2002).

97. The parallel between the UNESCO Convention of 1970 and NAGPRA has been noted by others, such as Grose, "Reading the Bones" (note 75), 625; Willard L. Boyd, "Museums as Centers of Controversy," *Daedalus* 128, no. 3 (1999): 185–228, esp. 197–98; and James D. Nason, "Beyond Repatriation: Cultural Policy and Practice for the Twenty-first Century," in Bruce Ziff and Pratima V. Rao, eds., *Borrowed Power: Essays on Cultural Appropriation* (New Brunswick: Rutgers Univ. Press, 1997), 291, 306–8.

98. Fred, "Law and Identity" (note 38). Perhaps the most prominent example of

cooperation is the new National Museum of the American Indian, which is part of the Smithsonian Institution.

99. For examples of such museums, see Karen Coody Cooper, "Museums and American Indians: Ambivalent Partners," in Dane Morrison, ed., *American Indian Studies: An Interdisciplinary Approach to Contemporary Issues* (New York: Peter Lang, 1997), 403. For a discussion of the particular practices adopted by the new Smithsonian National Museum of the American Indian, see Craig Howe, "Sovereignty and Cultural Property Policy in Museums" (paper presented at the Winter Quarter 2000 Workshop "Property Rights and Museum Practice," Cultural Policy Center, University of Chicago, 13 January 2000); also posted at http://culturalpolicy.uchicago.edu/workshop/howe.html (26 February 2002).

100. Tom Paulson, "Sifting through the Ages; Other Digs Prove Federal Law Can Work," *Seattle Post-Intelligencer,* 13 October 1998, B1.

101. See, for example, Bray, "Repatriation" (note 42), 441; and Elizabeth A. Sackler, "The Ethics of Collecting," *International Journal of Cultural Property* 7 (1998): 133–35.

102. In the Letter from Babbitt to Caldera (note 22), the Department of the Interior characterized NAGPRA as "Indian legislation" based on the statutory purpose to protect Native American burial sites and NAGPRA's recognition of the "unique legal relationship between the United States and Indian tribes." This status would indicate that any ambiguities in the statutory language should be resolved liberally in favor of Indian interests. This characterization of NAGPRA adds support for an approach that would vindicate Native American interests in cases in which the statute is unclear, the statute has failed to provide for a specific exigency (such as the disposition of culturally unidentifiable remains), or a determination of cultural affiliation is particularly difficult.

103. Bray, "Repatriation" (note 42), 442.

Part III

Legislating the Intangible

Selling Grandma: Commodification of the Sacred through Intellectual Property Rights

Darrell Addison Posey

The Sacred Balance

Indigenous and traditional peoples have increasingly become the focus of scientific research aimed at the development of new products or the improvement of medicines, agricultural products, body and skin preparations, natural oils, essences, dyes, and insecticides.[1] They have long been targets for expropriation of their music, art, crafts, and images. Trade has removed materials, ideas, expressions of culture, and even human genes from their local social and spiritual contexts to convert them into objects for global commodification. In addition to showing disrespect for other cultures, this violates basic human rights.

Although conservation and management practices are highly pragmatic, indigenous and traditional peoples generally view this knowledge as emanating from a *spiritual* base. All creation is sacred, and the sacred and secular are inseparable. Spirituality is the highest form of consciousness, and spiritual consciousness is the highest form of awareness. In this sense a dimension of traditional knowledge is not *local* knowledge but knowledge of the *universal* as expressed in the local. In indigenous and local cultures, experts exist who are peculiarly aware of the organizing principles of nature, sometimes described as entities, spirits, or natural law. Thus, knowledge of the environment depends not only on the relationship between humans and nature but also between the visible world and the invisible spirit world. According to the Ghanaian writer Kofi Asare Opoku, the distinctive feature of traditional African religion is that it is "A way of life, [with] the purpose of ... order[ing] our relationship with our fellow men and with our environment, both spiritual and physical. At the root of it is a quest for harmony between man, the spirit world, nature, and society."[2] The unseen is, therefore, as much a part of reality as that which is seen—the spiritual is as much a part of reality as the material. In fact, there is a complementary relationship between the two, with the spiritual being more powerful than the material. The community is of the dead as well as the living. Further, in nature, behind visible objects lie essences, or powers, that constitute the true nature of those objects.

Indigenous and traditional peoples frequently view themselves as guardians and stewards of nature. Harmony and equilibrium among components of the cosmos are central concepts in most cosmologies. Agriculture, for example, can provide "balance for well-being" through relationships not only among people but also in nature and deities. In this concept, the blessing of a new field is not mere spectacle but an inseparable part of life, where the highest value is harmony with the earth. Most traditions recognize linkages among health, diet, properties of different foods and medicinal plants, and horticultural and natural resource management practices—all within a highly articulated cosmological and social context.[3] Thus, the plant, animal, or crystal that an ethnopharmacologist may want to collect could, in fact, encompass, contain, or be the manifestation of the ancestral spirit—even the healer's grandmother.

Local knowledge embraces information about location, movements, and other factors explaining spatial patterns and timing in the ecosystem, including sequences of events, cycles, and trends. Direct links with the land are fundamental, and obligations to maintain those connections form the core of individual and group identity. Nowhere is this more apparent than with the "dreaming places" of the Aboriginal peoples of Australia. As James Galarrwuy Yunupingu, chairperson of the Northern Land Council, explains, "My land is mine only because I came in spirit from that land, and so did my ancestors of the same land.... My land is my foundation."[4]

Laurie Anne Whitt, professor of philosophy and founder of the Native American Association at Michigan Technological University, observes that the Cherokee see knowledge itself as being an integral part of the earth; thus, a proposed dam would not just flood the land but also destroy the medicines and the knowledge of the medicines associated with the land.[5] This perception that land and knowledge are bound together, that the natural world is spiritually replete, is present in a statement made by Alice Benally in the 1980s. Facing removal from Big Mountain in Arizona, this Navajo woman noted, "If we are to make our offerings at a new place, the spiritual beings would not know us. We would not know the mountains or the significance of them. We would not know the land and the land would not know us.... We would not know the sacred places.... If we were to go on top of an unfamiliar mountain we would not know the life forms that dwell there."[6]

The same is true for the Mazatecs of southern Mexico, whose shamans and *curanderos* (healers) confer with the plant spirits in order to heal: successful curers must learn, above all else, to listen to the plants talk.[7] For many groups, these communications come through the transformative powers of altered states or trances.[8] Don Hilde, a Pucallpa healer, notes, "I did not have a teacher to help me learn about plants, but visions have taught me many things. They even instruct me as to which pharmaceutical medicines to use."[9]

These links between life, land, and society are identified by the Canadian environmentalist David Suzuki as the "sacred balance."[10] According to Suzuki, science, with its quantum mechanics methods, can never address the universe as a whole; and it certainly can never adequately describe the holism of indigenous knowledge and belief. In fact, science is far behind in the environmental movement. It still sees nature as objects (*components* of biodiversity is the term used in the Convention on Biological Diversity of 1992) for human use and exploitation. Technology has used the banner of scientific "objectivity" to mask the moral and ethical issues that emerge from such a functionalist anthropocentric philosophy. This is made clear in British anthropologist Marilyn Strathern's discussion of the ethical dilemmas raised (or avoided) when embryos are "decontextualized" as human beings to become "objects" of scientific research.[11]

"Components" of Nature in Extended Society

The many "components" of nature for indigenous peoples become an extension not just of the geographical world but also of human society. This is fundamentally difficult for Western society to understand, since the extension of "self" is not through nature but through "hard technology."[12] For indigenous peoples, "natural models" may even serve as templates for social organization, political thought, and modes of subsistence. This also implies radical differences in concepts of time and space. "Myths" and "folklore" have been analyzed for their structural, metalinguistic, and symbolic components and have even been shown to regulate ecological as well as social cycles. They have, perhaps, been less studied as sounding boards for cultural change. Consider, for example, a myth of the Kayapó Indians of Brazil, "The Journey to Become a Shaman."[13] It is exemplary of how oral tradition works to explain ecological-social relationships and changes that occur within them. The myth, dealing with the transformation of the *wayanga* (shaman), is as follows:

> Listen! Those who become sick from strong fevers lie in death's position; they lie as though they are dead. The truly great ones, the truly strong person who is a *wayanga*, shows the sick how to leave their bodies. They leave through their insides. They pass through their insides and come to be in the form of a stone. Their bodies lie as in death, but beyond they are then transformed into an armadillo. As an armadillo, they assume good, strong health and they pass through the other side, over there (pointing to the east).
>
> Then they become a bat and fly—*ko, ko, ko, ko, ko*...(the noise of flying).
>
> Then they go further beyond in the form of a dove. They fly like a dove—*ku, ku, ku, ku*...(the sound of a dove's flight). They join the other *wayangas* and all go together.
>
> "Where will we go? What is the way? Go to the east, way over there." *Ku, ku, ku, ku*...
>
> And way over there is a spider's web.... Some go round and round near the spider's web and they just sit permanently. The true and ancient shamans must teach them how to fly through the web. But those who have not been shown how, try to break through the web and the web grabs their wings thusly (the narrator wraps his arms around his shoulders). They just hang in the web and die. Their bodies are carried by their relatives and are buried without waiting, for the spider's web has entangled them, wrapped up their wings, and they are dead.

Those who have been caused to know themselves, however, go around the spider web. They sit on the mountain seat of the shamans and sing like the dove—*tu, tu, tu, tu*...They acquire the knowledge of the ancestors. They speak to the spirits of all the animals and of the ancestors. They know (all).

They then return (to their bodies). They return to their homes. They enter and they breathe.

And the others say: He arrived! He arrived! He arrived! He arrived!

And the women all wail: *Ayayikakraykyerekune.*[14]

(And the shaman says) "Do not bury me, I am still alive. I am a *wayanga*. I am now one who can cure: I am the one who smokes the powerful pipe. I know how to go through my body and under my head. I am a *wayanga*.

The story is centered around the ability of the *wayanga* to leave his or her body (*ka*) and transform into other physical forms. Energy (*karon*) can be stored temporarily in rocks, but in the end it gets transformed into armadillos, doves, or bats. In the myth, the spider's web represents the barrier between the visible and invisible worlds. Armadillos are persistent animals that know to burrow under the web; doves are powerful flyers that can break through the barrier with ease; while bats are such skillful fliers that they maneuver through the strands. The sounds of the flight by doves and bats represent the different frequencies that are imparted by their vibrations. Frequencies have associated sounds and colors. Just to analyze the variations in frequencies of bee sounds would require discussing the fifty-two different folk species of stingless bees, each of which has a distinctive sound and curative properties.

The most powerful shamans can transform themselves into not just one but all types of animals. Once they have reached the other side of the spider's web, after they have passed through the endless dark chasm, they enter into the spectral frequencies of different light (or colors). There is a different spectral frequency for each animal (*mry-karon*). The general term for undifferentiated energy is *karon*. Defined energies are given distinctive modifiers (*x-karon*), where *x* might be *mry* for animals, *tep* for fish, *kwen* for birds, and so forth.

Some shamans only learn the secrets of a few animals and their energies, while others "know all" (in the words of the myth). They have learned about all the spectral frequencies and their respective animal energies. On return to their bodies, *wayanga* begin to "work with" (*nhipex*) the animal energies encountered in their transformation. The basis of such work is to maintain a balance between animal and human energies. Eating the meat of, coming in contact with, or even dreaming about animals can cause an imbalance in these energies, as can, of course, a well-elaborated list of antisocial actions. *Wayanga* use a great variety of techniques for restoring balance (they can also create imbalances—*kane*—that lead to sickness), but plants are the most common "mediators" that manipulate this balance.[15]

Plants themselves have energies (*karon*) but do not have distinctive energies or spirits (*x-karon*), per se, except for some of the plants believed to aid in conception, *mekrakindja* (lit. "child-want-thing"). These plants have very powerful spirits and cause the user to dream of a child's conception. Men and women use these dreaming plants, although men are usually the ones who first "conceive," that is, first "see" (*kra pumunh*) the child in a dream.[16]

Other plants also have spirits (that is, defined energies or *x-karon*), especially the *metykdja* (poison plants), the *meudjy* (witchcraft plants), and the most deadly and powerful *pitu* (no direct translation). These plants cause drastic alterations to human beings, such as death, paralysis, blindness, insanity, and abortion. Even less-powerful plants have qualities that can either harm or help the balance between human and animal energies (*me-karon* and *mry-karon*)—indeed it appears that all plants have curative values.

The Kayapó respect both plants and animals, since their energies are keys to the health of Kayapó society. Permission is asked of the *mry-karon* when taking the life of an animal, and songs of appreciation are offered to the spirits of the dead animals. Likewise, annual rituals extol the importance of plants and instill a great sense of respect for their overall role in the socioecological balance.[17] The Kayapó do not doubt that their existence and their health are dependent on plants, animals, and the forces of nature.

Normally spirits of the dead pass easily into the otherworld *(mekaron nhon pyka)* and continue their existence in what is roughly the mirror image of what goes on in this world. *Wayanga* who are "deceased" (they never really die, for they have already died and just disappear and reappear) live in a special cave in the mountains, thus the reference in the myth about their stone seats. Spirits of dead animals also go to the otherworld. Devoted pets are sometimes killed and buried with their "owners" at death, so that the human spirit will not be so lonely (some Kayapó say that dogs are buried with their owners because the dogs can help the human spirit find its way to the otherworld). Those who attempt a shamanistic transformation and do not succeed have a more tragic end, however. Their spirits are lost forever in the spider's web. There is disagreement among the Kayapó as to what this really means, but there is no question that it is the worst possible fate. There is little wonder why only a small number of the Kayapó ever try to become a *wayanga*.

Kwyra-ka, one of my shaman mentors, showed great concern when the first coffin arrived in Gorotire and his nephew was buried in it instead of in the traditional manner. The Kayapó traditionally bury the body in a crouched position in deep, round pits, covered with logs and soil. Until recently, secondary burial was practiced four days after principal burial. This allowed time for the spirit to return to the body in case the "dead" person was only on a shamanistic journey. Kwyra-ka anguished over the possibility that the soul of the child would not be able to escape from the casket to the otherworld. Likewise, Kwyra-ka and the *wayanga* Beptopoop have expressed their concern about the plants taken during ethnobotanical surveys to be pressed and dried in herbaria. If the plants were kept in such closed, sterile places, would their spirits be trapped, thereby creating an energy imbalance and putting the Kayapó, as well as those who "kept" the specimens, in danger? Like the casket containing the small child, would the energy not become imprisoned, thereby blocking the "natural" cycles? Even deeper concerns are expressed about the massive quantities of plants that would have to be collected to provide the oils, essences, colorings, and the like for commercialization of plant products. The *wayanga* ask, Has anyone ever consulted the plants? Would the dreaming that is necessary for conception of healthy children be jeopardized? Would the plants stop mediating between the human and animal *karons*, thereby leading to loss of ancient cures and provoking new diseases?

For Kayapó elders, these are fundamental questions; however, to me these unpredictable dilemmas were not immediately obvious. The central concepts of ecological management are deeply embedded and codified in Kayapó myths, from which environmental and social change can also be measured. It is important to realize, however, that the forces or energies exemplified in myths are not historical in the Western sense: in Kayapó myths, time may be cyclical, spiral, or multidimensional. No matter how hard historical ecologists try, the lineality of time and space that pervades our categories of interpretation will never capture the nonlineality of some indigenous ecological concepts.

Recognizing Indigenous and Local Communities

Western science may have invented the words *nature, biodiversity,* and *sustainability,* but it certainly did not initiate the concepts. Indigenous, traditional, and local communities have utilized and conserved a vast diversity of plants, animals, and ecosystems since the advent of *Homo sapiens.* Furthermore, human beings have molded environments through their conscious and unconscious activities for millennia—to the extent that it is often impossible to separate nature from culture.

It was recently "discovered" that cultural landscapes include those of Aboriginal peoples, who were trading seeds, dividing tubers, and propagating domesticated and nondomesticated plant species one hundred thousand years before the term *sustainable development* was coined. Sacred sites acted as conservation areas for vital water sources and individual species by restricting access and behavior. Traditional technologies, including fire use, were part of extremely sophisticated systems that shaped and maintained the balance of vegetation and wildlife. Decline of fire management and loss of sacred sites when Aboriginal peoples were centralized into settlements led to rapid decline of mammals throughout the regions.[18]

Another example of cultural landscapes are the *apete* (forest islands) of the Kayapó.[19] Kayapó practices of planting and transplanting within and among many ecological zones indicate the degree to which indigenous presence has modified Amazonia. Extensive plantations of fruit and nut trees, as well as *apete* created in savanna, force scientists to reevaluate what have often hastily and erroneously been considered "natural" Amazonian landscapes. The Kayapó's techniques of constructing *apete* show the degree to which this Amazon group can create and manipulate microenvironments within and between ecozones to actually increase biological diversity. Such ecological engineering requires detailed knowledge of soil fertility, microclimatic properties, and plant varietal qualities, as well as of the interrelationships among components of a human-modified ecological community. Successful *apete* are dependent on knowledge of not just the immediate properties but also the long-term successional relationships that change as the forest islands mature and grow. Since many plants are specifically grown to attract useful animals, the complexity of the management problem greatly increases: *apete* are managed both as agroforestry units and as game reserves. The Kayapó's knowledge of *apete* formation and succession offers invaluable insights into processes of forestation in savanna and reforestation in denuded areas.

The Kagore Shona people of Zimbabwe have sacred sites, burial grounds, and other sites of special historical significance deeply embedded in the landscape,[20] but outsiders often cannot recognize them, even during land-use planning exercises. There is also evidence that presumed "wild" forests are actually managed landscapes. Forests are more often peoples' backyards, not the wildernesses assumed by outsiders. In societies with no written language or monumental edifices, hills, mountains, and valleys become the libraries and cathedrals that reflect cultural achievement.[21] For the Dineh (Navajo), the Mountain of the South (Tsoodzil) fastens the earth to the sky through lightning, rain, and rainbows.[22] In Nepal, there are sacred mountain groves.[23] It is difficult for outsiders to understand that entire mountains may be sacred to people like the Apache,[24] while certain parts of mountains, such as sacred groves, are holy for groups such as the Khumbu of Nepal.

Sacred groves are, in fact, one of the most common types of cultural landscapes.[25] The "dragon hills" of Yunan Province, China, are kept intact because of their sacred nature.[26] Likewise, some groves in Ghana are linked to burial grounds and spirits of the ancestors that protect the forests that surround them.[27] Similar groves are reported in Ivory Coast and Benin.[28] Sacred groves in India are extensive and are well known in literature.[29] Wells and springs are also frequently considered holy, and the areas around them are often specially protected from disturbance. Wellsprings have been described as the "soul of the Hopi people," representing their very identity.[30] Oases can also be sacred places for people like the Maasai and Fulani, pastoralists whose lives literally depend on these protected areas during severe droughts.[31]

Ecologist Thomas Schaaf has proposed an environmental conservation strategy based on preservation of sacred groves and other holy places, an idea that has been considered by the United Nations Educational, Scientific and Cultural Organization (UNESCO) and other organizations.[32] The social anthropologist Laura Rival warns, however, that there is no guarantee that beliefs about sacred places will continue indefinitely; thus, conservation plans hinged on the concepts of protective spirits and deities should be considered with caution.[33]

A failure to recognize anthropogenic, or human-modified, landscapes has blinded outsiders to the management practices of indigenous peoples and local communities.[34] Many so-called pristine landscapes are in fact cultural landscapes, either created or modified by human activity (such as natural forest management, cultivation, and the use of fire). This is more than semantics. "Wild" and "wilderness" imply that these landscapes and resources are the result of "nature" and, as such, have no owners—they are the "common heritage of all humankind." This has come to mean that local communities have no tenurial or ownership rights and, thus, their lands, territories, and resources are "free" to others just for the taking. This is why indigenous peoples have come to oppose the use of "wilderness" and "wild" to refer to the regions in which they now or once lived. This is expressed in an Aboriginal Resolution from the Ecopolitics IX Conference of 1995 in Darwin, Australia: "Ecopolitics IX reiterates the unacceptability of the term 'wilderness' and related concepts such as wild resources, food, etc. as it is popularised. The term has the connotations of *terra nullius* [empty or unowned land and resources] and as such all concerned people and organisations should look for alternative terminology which does not exclude indigenous history and meaning."[35] Cultural landscapes and their links to conservation of biological diversity are now recognized under the UNESCO Convention Concerning the Protection of the World Cultural and Natural Heritage (the so-called World Heritage Convention) of 1972. A new category of World Heritage Site, the "cultural landscape" takes into consideration "the complex interrelationships between man and nature in the construction, formation and evolution of landscapes."[36] The first cultural landscape World Heritage Site was Tongariro National Park, a sacred region for the Maori people of New Zealand that was included in the World Heritage List because of its centrality in Maori beliefs.[37] UNESCO is developing other new projects to help local communities conserve and protect sacred places.[38]

The Convention on Biological Diversity of 1992 is one of the major international forces in recognizing the role of indigenous and local communities in in situ conservation. The preamble recognizes the "close and traditional dependence of many indigenous and local communities embodying traditional lifestyles on biological resources, and the desirability of sharing equitably benefits arising from the use of traditional knowledge, innovations and practices relevant to the conservation of biological diversity and the sustainable use of its components."[39]

Among the obligations spelled out for the signatories to the Convention on Biological Diversity is the following provision:

> Each Contracting Party shall, as far as possible and as appropriate:...(j) Subject to its national legislation, respect, preserve and maintain knowledge, innovations and practices of indigenous and local communities embodying traditional lifestyles relevant for the conservation and sustainable use of biological diversity and promote the wider application with the approval and involvement of the holders of such knowledge, innovations and practices and encourage the equitable sharing of the benefits arising from the utilization of such knowledge, innovations and practices.

The Convention on Biological Diversity also enshrines the importance of customary practice in biodiversity conservation and calls for protection of and equitable benefit sharing from the use and application of "traditional technologies."[40] Environmental law experts Lyle Glowka and Françoise Burhenne-Guilmin warn that the word *traditional* can imply restriction of the Convention on Biological Diversity only to those embodying traditional lifestyles, keeping in mind that the concept can easily be misinterpreted to mean "frozen in time."[41] Ecological activists Winin Pereira and Anil K. Gupta claim, however, that "it is the traditional methods of research and application, not always particular pieces of knowledge" that persist in a tradition of invention and innovation.[42] Technological changes do not simply lead to modernization and loss of traditional practice but rather provide additional inputs into vibrant, adaptive, and adapting holistic systems of management and conservation.

"Traditional knowledge, innovations, and practices" are often referred to by scientists as traditional ecological knowledge (TEK), which is far more than a simple compilation of facts.[43] It is the basis for local-level decision making in areas of contemporary life, including natural-resource management, nutrition, food preparation, health, education, and community and social organization.[44] TEK is holistic, inherently dynamic, and constantly evolving through experimentation, innovation, fresh insight, and external stimuli.[45] In addition, TEK is transmitted in many ways. Mostly this is accomplished through repeated practice, such as in an apprenticeship with elders and specialists. For example, Marilyn Walker has sketched how the "collective memory" of the Tlingit of the Northwest Coast of North America is embedded in basketry, with oral tradition playing a critical role in this transmission,[46] while Reimar Schefold and Gerard Persoon have described how knowledge is transmitted in Sumatra through songs,[47] and Alistair McIntosh has documented the "psychospiritual" effect of social upheaval in Celtic culture and shown how poetry and music serve to register the resulting devastation of communities and biodiversity.[48] By extension, it seems obvious that poems and music provide important remedies and pathways for environmental restoration.

One of the most important areas in which TEK plays a major role is in traditional medicines and health systems. Health-policy researcher Gerard Bodeker sketches some exemplary systems—such as traditional Hindu (Ayurvedic) and traditional Chinese medicines—whose cosmologies define *dis-ease* as a "breaking of the interconnectedness of life."[49] A fundamental concept in traditional health systems is that of balance between mind and body, given that both are linked to community, local environments, and the universe.[50] As Rippling Water Woman, a member of the Pelican Lake Cree Nation and past president of the Aboriginal Nurses Association of Canada, says: "I have gained an understanding that the relationship a healer has with the environment is a reflection of the depth of understanding achieved of the personal relationship with all creation."[51] This connectedness is a main reason why medicines cannot be so easily "extracted" from their "knowers" or their social contexts.[52]

Of course, these medical concepts can be radically different from Western ones,[53] making evaluation of efficacy—not to mention global application—very difficult.[54] Medicinal plant qualities also vary considerably depending on when and where they are collected.[55] It is also important to remember that the distinctions among medicine, food, and health are Western distinctions. For many indigenous and traditional peoples, foods serve as medicines and vice versa; in fact, the Western division of the two makes little sense to many traditional peoples.[56] Above all else, healthy ecosystems are critical to healthy societies and individuals, because humanity and nature are one; they are not in opposition to each other.[57]

Equity and Rights

Recognition by the Convention on Biological Diversity of the contributions of indigenous and traditional peoples to maintaining biological diversity may be a major political advance; however, there are major dangers. Once TEK or genetic materials leave the societies in which they are embedded, there are few national safeguards and virtually no international laws that afford protection for community "knowledge, innovations, and practices." Many countries do not even recognize the right of indigenous peoples to exist, let alone grant them self-determination, land rights, or control over their traditional resources.[58]

The Indigenous and Tribal Peoples Convention (Convention 169) adopted by the International Labour Organization (ILO) in 1989 is the only legally binding international instrument specifically intended to protect indigenous and tribal peoples. Convention 169 supports community ownership and local control of lands and resources. It does not, however, cover the numerous traditional and peasant groups that are also critical in conservation of the diversity of agricultural, medicinal, and nondomesticated resources. To date, the convention has only fourteen national signatories and provides little more than a baseline for debates on indigenous rights.[59] The same bleak news comes from an analysis of intellectual property rights laws, which were established to protect individual inventions and inventors—not the ancient folklore and collective TEK of indigenous and local communities. Even if intellectual property rights were secured for communities, differential access to patents, copyright, know-how, and trade-secret laws and lawyers would generally price them out of any effective registry, monitoring, or litigation using such instruments.[60] In general, intellectual property rights are considered inadequate and inappropriate for protecting the traditional ecological knowledge and collective resources of indigenous and traditional peoples because they

- recognize individual, not collective rights
- require a specific act of "invention"
- simplify ownership regimes

- stimulate commercialization
- recognize only market values
- are subject to economic powers and manipulation
- are difficult to monitor and enforce
- are expensive, complicated, and time consuming

The World Trade Organization's General Agreement on Tariff and Trade (GATT) contains no explicit reference to the knowledge and genetic resources of traditional peoples, although it does provide for states to develop sui generis systems for plant protection.[61] Governments and nongovernmental and peoples' organizations are pouring considerable intellectual energy into defining what new alternative models of protection would include.[62] There is skepticism, however, that this sui generis option will be adequate to provide any significant alternatives to existing intellectual property rights.[63] One glimmer of hope comes from the Convention on Biological Diversity's decision to implement an "intersessional process" to evaluate the inadequacies of intellectual property rights and develop guidelines and principles for governments seeking advice on access and transfer legislation to protect traditional communities.[64]

This decision provides exciting opportunities for many countries and peoples to engage in a historic debate. United Nations agencies have been reluctant to discuss the "integrated systems of rights" that link environment, trade, and human rights; however, agreements among the Convention on Biological Diversity, the United Nations' Food and Agriculture Organization, and the World Trade Organization now guarantee broad consultations on sui generis systems and community intellectual property rights among the World Intellectual Property Organization, United Nations Environment Program, United Nations Development Program, United Nations Commission on Trade and Development, United Nations Center for Human Rights in Geneva, UNESCO, ILO, and others. It will take the creative and imaginative input of all these groups—and many more—to meet the complicated challenge of devising new systems of national and international laws that support and enhance cultural and biological diversity.

Many of the principles of sui generis systems of rights have already been established in international conventions such as the Convention on Biological Diversity and the ILO's Convention 169, as well as by major human rights agreements such as the International Covenant on Civil and Political Rights; the International Covenant on Economic, Social, and Cultural Rights; and, of course, the Universal Declaration of Human Rights.[65] For indigenous peoples, the Draft Declaration of Rights of Indigenous Peoples is the most important statement of basic requirements for adequate rights and protection. Over nearly two decades, the Draft Declaration was developed by hundreds of indigenous representatives to the United Nations Working Group on Indigenous Populations. It is broad ranging, thorough, and reflects one of the most transparent and democratic processes yet to be seen in the United Nations.

The process itself and many of the principles established will undoubtedly serve as models for traditional societies and local communities seeking greater recognition of rights. Among the principles affirmed by the Draft Declaration of Rights of Indigenous Populations are the following:

- Right to self-determination, representation, and full participation
- Recognition of existing treaty arrangements with indigenous peoples
- Right to determine own citizenry and obligations of citizenship
- Right to collective, as well as individual, human rights
- Right to live in freedom, peace, and security without military intervention or involvement
- Right to religious freedom and protection of sacred sites and objects, including ecosystems, plants, and animals
- Right to restitution and redress for cultural, intellectual, religious, or spiritual property that is taken or used without authorization
- Right to free and informed consent (prior informed consent)
- Right to control access and exert ownership over plants, animals, and minerals vital to their cultures
- Right to own, develop, control, and use the lands and territories, including the total environment of the air, lands, waters, coastal seas, sea-ice, flora, fauna, and other resources that they have traditionally owned or otherwise occupied or used
- Right to special measures to control, develop, and protect their sciences, technologies, and cultural manifestations, including human and other resources, seeds, medicines, knowledge of the properties of fauna and flora, oral traditions, literatures, designs, and visual and performing arts
- Right to just and fair compensation for any such activities that have adverse environmental, economic, social, cultural, or spiritual impact.[66]

The Global Balance Sheet

Although international efforts to recognize indigenous, traditional, and local communities are welcome and positive, they are pitted against enormous economic and market forces that propel globalization of trade. Critiques of globalization are numerous[67] and point to at least two major shortcomings: first, value is imputed to information and resources only when they enter external markets; and, second, expenditures do not reflect actual environmental and social costs. This means that existing values recognized by local communities are ignored, despite knowledge that local biodiversity provides essential elements for survival (food, shelter, medicine, and so on). It also means that the knowledge and managed resources of indigenous and traditional peoples are both ascribed no value and assumed to be free for the taking. This perception has been called "intellectual *terra nullius*" (empty land), after the concept that allowed colonial powers to expropriate "discovered" land for their empires. Corporations and states still defend this morally vacuous concept because it facilitates the "biopiracy" of local folk varieties of crops, traditional medicines, and useful species.

Scientists, too, have been accomplices to such raids by publishing data they know will be catapulted into the public domain and gleaned by "bioprospectors" seeking new products. They have also perpetuated the "intellectual *terra nullius*" concept by declaring useful local plants as "wild" and entire ecosystems as "wildernesses," often despite knowing that these have been molded, managed, and protected by human populations for millennia. It is also common for scientists to declare areas and resources wild through ignorance — or negligence — without even basic investigations into archaeological or historical records or into actual human management practices. The result is to declare the biodiversity of a site as "natural," thereby transferring it to the public domain. Once public, communities are stripped of all rights to their traditional resources.

It is little wonder, then, that indigenous groups in the Pacific region have declared a moratorium on all scientific research until protection of traditional knowledge and genetic resources can be guaranteed to local communities by scientists. The "moratorium movement" began with the Mataatua Declaration of 1993, which stated that "a moratorium on any further commercialisation of indigenous medicinal plants and human genetic materials must be declared until indigenous communities have developed appropriate protection mechanisms."[68] The Mataatua Declaration, in turn, influenced the Final Statement of the Consultation on Indigenous Peoples' Knowledge and Intellectual Property Rights held in Suva, Fiji, in 1995, which includes the following in its "plan of action":

> 2. Call for a moratorium on bioprospecting in the Pacific and urge indigenous peoples not to cooperate in bioprospecting activities until appropriate protection mechanisms are in place
>   1. Bioprospecting as a term needs to be clearly defined to exclude indigenous peoples' customary harvesting practices.
>   2. Assert that in situ conservation by indigenous peoples is the best method to conserve and protect biological diversity and indigenous knowledge, and encourage its implementation by indigenous communities and all relevant bodies.
>   3. Encourage indigenous peoples to maintain and expand our knowledge of local biological resources.[69]

To allay these deep concerns, many scientific and professional organizations are developing codes of conduct and standards of practice to guide research, health, educational, and conservation projects with indigenous and local communities.[70]

One of the most extensive is that of the International Society for Ethnobiology, which undertook a ten-year consultation with indigenous and traditional peoples — as well as with its extensive international membership — to establish "principles for equitable partnerships."[71] The main objective of the process was to establish terms under which collaboration and joint research between ethnobiologists and communities could proceed based on trust, transparency, and mutual concerns. A list of these principles is as follows:

Principle of self-determination. This principle recognizes that indigenous peoples have a right to self-determination (or local determination for traditional and local communities) and that researchers shall as appropriate acknowledge and respect such rights. Culture and language are intrinsically connected to land and territory, and cultural and linguistic diversity are inextricably linked to biological diversity; therefore, the principle of self-determination includes: (1) the right to control land and territory; (2) the right to sacred places; (3) the right to own, to determine the use of, and to accreditation, protection, and compensation for knowledge; (4) the right of access to traditional resources; (5) the right to preserve and protect local languages, symbols, and modes of expression; and (6) the right to self-definition.

Principle of inalienability. This principle recognizes the inalienable rights of indigenous peoples and local communities in relation to their traditional lands, territories, forests, fisheries, and other natural resources. These rights are both individual and collective, with local peoples determining which ownership regimes are appropriate.

Principle of minimum impact. This principle recognizes the duty of scientists and researchers to ensure that their research and activities have minimum impact on local communities.

Principle of full disclosure. This principle recognizes that it is important for the indigenous and traditional peoples, and local communities, to have disclosed to them, in a transparent manner, the manner in which the research is to be undertaken, how information is to be gathered, the ultimate purpose for which such information is to be used, and by whom it is to be used.

Principle of prior informed consent and veto. This principle recognizes that the prior informed consent of all peoples and their communities must be obtained before any research is undertaken. Indigenous peoples, traditional societies, and local communities have the right to veto any program, project, or study that involves them.

Principle of confidentiality. This principle recognizes that indigenous peoples, traditional societies, and local communities, at their sole discretion, have the right to exclude from publication and/or keep confidential any information concerning their culture, traditions, mythologies, or spiritual beliefs, and states that such confidentiality will be observed by researchers and other potential users. Indigenous and traditional peoples also have the right to privacy and anonymity.

Principle of active participation. This principle recognizes the critical importance of local communities to be active participants in all phases of the project from inception to completion.

Principle of respect. This principle recognizes the necessity for Western researchers to respect the integrity of the culture, traditions, and relationship of indigenous and traditional peoples with their natural world and to avoid the application of ethnocentric conceptions and standards.

Principle of active protection. This principle recognizes the importance of researchers taking active measures to protect and enhance the relationship of local communities with their environment and to thereby promote the maintenance of cultural and biological diversity.

Principle of good faith. This principle recognizes that researchers and others having access to knowledge of indigenous peoples, traditional societies, and local communities will at all times conduct themselves with the utmost good faith.

Principle of compensation. This principle recognizes that local communities should be fairly, appropriately, and adequately remunerated or compensated for access and use of their knowledge and information.

Principle of restitution. This principle recognizes that where as a result of research being undertaken, there are adverse consequences and disruptions to local communities, all those responsible for undertaking the research will make appropriate restitution and compensation.

Principle of reciprocity. This principle recognizes the inherent value to Western science and humankind in general of gaining access to knowledge of indigenous peoples, traditional societies, and local communities as well as the desirability of reciprocating that contribution.

Principle of equitable sharing. This principle recognizes the right of local communities to share in the benefits from products or publications developed from access to and use of their knowledge, and the duty of scientists and researchers to equitably share these benefits with indigenous peoples.

Conclusion

Increases in bioprospecting for new products using traditional knowledge and genetic resources, combined with heightened awareness by indigenous and local communities of how their resources are being exploited, have provoked something of a global ethical crisis. Commodification of collective resources—often of a secret or sacred nature—is not only an expression of disrespect for local culture but a violation of religious principles and human rights. The "decontextualization" of the "components" of biodiversity or local culture results in the unauthorized extraction of inalienable information and materials. This ignores the "sacred balance" of life and violates the kinship relationships that indigenous and traditional peoples maintain with their "extended family" of all living things. Outsiders have also ignored the historical impacts of communities on ecosystems, forgetting that the "wild" landscapes and resources actually belong to the peoples who have managed and conserved them. This affects medicines and healing, since the materia medica may take its healing force from the earth—and certainly medical plants are affected by the times at which they are selected and the places from which they come.

There are some admirable efforts in international processes, such as the implementation of the Convention of Biological Diversity and the ILO's Convention 169, but there is now general agreement that new and additional instruments will be necessary if we are to adequately protect traditional ecological and medical knowledge systems. It is unclear how these sui generis systems will emerge, but concerned scientists and professionals must not wait for a political solution. Codes of conduct and standards of practice are needed now to counter the growing distrust of and animosity toward research and conservation efforts that indigenous and local peoples are, rightfully, beginning to express.

Notes

1. The definition of *indigenous* is problematic in many parts of the world. In his *Study of the Problem of Discrimination against Indigenous Populations,* vol. 5, Conclusions, Proposals and Recommendations, UN sales no. E.86.XIV.3 (New York: United Nations, 1987), 29, para. 380, Special Rapporteur José R. Martínez Cobo of the United Nation's Sub-Commission on Prevention of Discrimination and Protection of Minorities offered the following definition:

Indigenous communities, peoples and nations are those which, having a historical continuity with pre-invasion and pre-colonial societies that have developed on their territories, consider themselves distinct from other sectors of the societies now prevailing in those territories, or parts of them. They form at present the nondominant sector of society and are determined to preserve, develop, and transmit to future generations their ancestral territories, and their ethnic identity, as the basis of their continued existence as peoples, in accordance with their own cultural patterns, social institutions, and legal systems.

This historical continuity may consist of the continuation, for an extended period reaching into the present, of one or more of the following factors:
(a) occupation of ancestral lands, or at least of part of them;
(b) common ancestry with the original occupants of these lands;
(c) culture in general, or in specific manifestations (such as religion, living under a tribal system, membership of an Indigenous community, dress, means of livelihood, life-style, etc.);
(d) language (whether used as the only language, as mother tongue, as the habitual means of communication at home or in the family, or as the main, preferred, habitual, general or normal language);
(e) residence in certain parts of the country, or in certain regions of the world;
(f) other relevant factors.

The International Labour Organization (ILO), in article 1 of its Convention 169 Indigenous and Tribal Peoples Convention (1989), identifies indigenous peoples as:

(a) tribal peoples in countries whose social, cultural and economic conditions distinguish them from other sections of the national community, and whose status is regulated wholly or partially by their own customs or traditions or by special laws or regulations.

(b) peoples in countries who are regarded by themselves or others as indigenous on account of their descent from the populations which inhabited the country, or a geographical region to which the country belongs, at the time of conquest or colonisation or the establishment of present state boundaries and who, irrespective of their legal status, retain, or wish to retain, some or all of their own social, economic, spiritual, cultural and political characteristics and institutions.

A fundamental principle established by the ILO's Convention 169 is that "self-identification as indigenous or tribal shall be regarded as a fundamental criterion for determining the groups to which the provisions of this convention apply." This principle is upheld by all indigenous groups, who, as the Final Statement from the UNDP Consultation on Indigenous Peoples' Knowledge and Intellectual Property Rights, Suva, April 1995, states: "We assert our inherent right to define who we are. We do not approve of any other definition." The full text of Convention 169 is posted at http://ilolex.ilo.ch:1567/cgi-lex/convde.pl?query=C169&query0=169&submit=Display (4 April 2002); the full text of the Final Statement is posted at http://users.ox.ac.uk/~wgtrr/suva.htm (4 April 2002).

Indigenous peoples insist that they be recognized as "peoples," not "people." The "s" is very important, because it denotes not just the basic human rights to which all individuals are entitled but also land, territorial, and collective rights, subsumed under the right to self-determination. In contrast, terms such as *people, populations,* and *minorities* implicitly deny territorial rights.

The term *traditional* is also problematic. A submission made on 15 January 1996 by the Four Directions Council of Canada to the Executive Secretary of the Convention on Biological Diversity argues that this term should not to be used to constrain local innovation and cultural chance: "What is 'traditional' about traditional knowledge is not its antiquity, but the way it is acquired and used. In other words, the social process of learning and sharing knowledge, which is unique to each indigenous culture, lies at the very heart of its 'traditionality.' Much of this knowledge is actually quite new, but it has a social meaning, and legal character, entirely unlike other knowledge"; as quoted in Conference of the Parties to the Convention on Biological Diversity, Subsidiary Body on Scientific, Technical and Technological Advice (2d meeting: 2–6 September 1996, Montreal), "Knowledge, Innovations and Practices of Indigenous and Local Communities: Note by the Secretariat," para. 78; the full text is available at http://www.biodiv.org/doc/meetings/sbstta/sbstta-02/official/sbstta-02-07-en.pdf (4 April 2002). Traditional livelihood systems, therefore, are constantly adapting to changing social, economic, and environmental conditions. They are dynamic but—no matter the changes—embrace principles of sustainability; see J. Baird Callicott, *In Defense of the Land Ethic: Essays in Environmental Philosophy* (Albany: State Univ. of New York Press, 1989); Linda Clarkson, Vern Morrissette, and Gabriel Regallet, *Our Responsibility to the Seventh Generation: Indigenous Peoples and Sustainable Development* (Winnipeg: International Institute for Sustainable Development, 1992); Robert Earle Johannes and Kenneth Ruddle, "Human Interactions in Tropical and Marine Areas: Lessons from Traditional Resource Use," in Andrew Price and Sarah Humphrey, eds.,

Application of the Biosphere Reserve Concept to Coastal Marine Areas: Papers Presented at the UNESCO/IUCN *San Francisco Workshop of 14–20 August 1989* (Gland, Switzerland: IUCN with UNESCO, 1993), 19–25; John Bierhorst, *The Way of the Earth: Native America and the Environment* (New York: Morrow, 1994); and Darrell A. Posey and Graham Dutfield, *Beyond Intellectual Property: Toward Traditional Resource Rights for Indigenous Peoples and Local Communities* (Ottawa: International Development Research Centre, 1996).

2. Kofi Asare Opoku, *West African Traditional Religion* (Accra: FEP International Private, 1978), 13.

3. See, for example, Stephen Hugh-Jones, "'Food' and 'Drugs' in North-West Amazonia," in Darrell A. Posey, ed., *Cultural and Spiritual Values of Biodiversity* (London: ITDG Publishing, 1999), 278–80.

4. As quoted in Australian Catholic Social Justice Council, "Recognition: The Way Forward," in *Native Title Report, January–June 1994: Report of the Aboriginal and Torres Strait Islander Social Justice Commissioner to the Minister for Aboriginal and Torres Strait Islander Affairs* (Canberra: Australian Government Publishing Service, 1994), vi; also see David Bennett, "Stepping from the Diagram: Australian Aboriginal Cultural and Spiritual Values Relating to Biodiversity," in Darrell A. Posey, ed., *Cultural and Spiritual Values of Biodiversity* (London: ITDG Publishing, 1999), 102–5.

5. Laurie Anne Whitt, "Metaphor and Power in Indigenous and Western Knowledge Systems," in Darrell A. Posey, ed., *Cultural and Spiritual Values of Biodiversity* (London: ITDG Publishing, 1999), 69–72.

6. Affidavit of Alice Benally, ¶56, at 248, *Jenny Manybeads et al. v. U.S.,* 730 F. Supp. 1515 (D. Ariz. 1989) (civ. no. 88-410); as cited in Laurie Anne Whitt et al., "Belonging to Land: Indigenous Knowledge Systems and the Natural World," *Oklahoma City University Law Review* 26 (2001): 702.

7. See Francisco Montes, "Spirit, Story and Medicine: Sachamama—An Example of the Ancient Beings of the Amazon Rainforest," ed. and trans. Kathleen Harrison, in Darrell A. Posey, ed., *Cultural and Spiritual Values of Biodiversity* (London: ITDG Publishing, 1999), 276, box 6.4.

8. See, for example, Glenn Shepard's account of Machiguenga shamanism, "Shamanism and Diversity: A Machiguenga Perspective," in Darrell A. Posey, ed., *Cultural and Spiritual Values of Biodiversity* (London: ITDG Publishing, 1999), 93–95.

9. Quoted in Marlene Dobkin de Rios, *Amazon Healer: The Life and Times of an Urban Shaman* (Dorset, England: Prism, 1992), 146; see Francoise Barbira-Freedman, "'Vegetalismo' and the Perception of Biodiversity: Shamanic Values in the Peruvian Upper Amazon," in Darrell A. Posey, ed., *Cultural and Spiritual Values of Biodiversity* (London: ITDG Publishing, 1999), 277–78.

10. David Suzuki, "Finding a New Story," in Darrell A. Posey, ed., *Cultural and Spiritual Values of Biodiversity* (London: ITDG Publishing, 1999), 72–73.

11. Marilyn Strathern, "Potential Property: Intellectual Rights and Property in Persons," *Social Anthropology* 4 (1996): 17–32.

12. See Evelyn Martin, "The Last Mountain," *American Forests* 99, nos. 3–4 (1993): 44–47, 54.

13. See Darrell A. Posey, "The Journey to Become a Shaman: A Narrative of Sacred

Transition of the Kayapó Indians of Brazil," *Latin American Indian Literatures* 7, no. 1 (1983): 13–19.

14. This phrase has no direct translation. It roughly means "He has arrived!" For more information on the details of this myth, see Posey, "The Journey to Become a Shaman" (note 13).

15. See Darrell A. Posey and Elaine Elisabetsky, "Conceito de animais e seus espíritos em relação a doenças e cura entre os indios Kayapó da Aldeia Gorotire," *Boletim do Museu Paraense Emílio Goeldi: Série antropologia* 7 (1991): 21–36.

16. See Darrell A. Posey and Elaine Elisabetsky, "Use of Contraceptive and Related Plants by the Kayapo Indians (Brazil)," *Journal of Ethnopharmacology* 26 (1989): 299–316.

17. See Posey, "The Journey to Become a Shaman" (note 13).

18. See R. Sultan, D. Craig, and H. Ross, "Aboriginal Joint Management of Australian National Parks: Uluru-kata Tjuta," in IUCN Inter-Commission Task Force on Indigenous Peoples, *Indigenous Peoples and Sustainability: Cases and Actions* (Gland, Switzerland: IUCN Indigenous Peoples and Conservation Initiative, 1997), 326–38.

19. See Darrell A. Posey, "Indigenous Management of Tropical Forest Ecosystems: The Case of the Kayapó Indians of the Brazilian Amazon," *Agroforestry Systems* 3 (1985): 139–58; Darrell A. Posey, "Cultivating the Forests of the Amazon: Science of the Mebengokre," *Orion Nature Quarterly* 9, no. 3 (1990): 16–23; and Darrell A. Posey, "The Kayapó: The Role of Intellectual Property in Resource Management in the Brazilian Amazon," in IUCN Inter-Commission Task Force on Indigenous Peoples, *Indigenous Peoples and Sustainability: Cases and Actions* (Gland, Switzerland: IUCN Indigenous Peoples and Conservation Initiative, 1997), 240–54.

20. See Z. Z. Matowanyika, "Resource Management and the Shona People in Rural Zimbabwe," in IUCN Inter-Commission Task Force on Indigenous Peoples, *Indigenous Peoples and Sustainability: Cases and Actions* (Gland, Switzerland: IUCN Indigenous Peoples and Conservation Initiative, 1997), 257–66.

21. See Edwin Bernbaum, "Introduction: Mountains: The Heights of Biodiversity," in Darrell A. Posey, ed., *Cultural and Spiritual Values of Biodiversity* (London: ITDG Publishing, 1999), 327–32.

22. See Washington Matthews, "Navaho Legends Collected and Translated," *American Folklore Society* 5 (1897): 5.

23. See Stanley F. Stevens, *Claiming the High Ground: Sherpas, Subsistence, and Environmental Change in the Highest Himalaya* (Berkeley: Univ. of California Press, 1993).

24. See Martin, "The Last Mountain" (note 12), 47.

25. See Sarah A. Laird, "Forests, Culture and Conservation," in Darrell A. Posey, ed., *Cultural and Spiritual Values of Biodiversity* (London: ITDG Publishing, 1999), 347–58.

26. See Pei Shengji, "The Holy Hills of the Dai," in Darrell A. Posey, ed., *Cultural and Spiritual Values of Biodiversity* (London: ITDG Publishing, 1999), 381–82.

27. See Julia Falconer, "Non-Timber Forest Products in Southern Ghana: Traditional and Cultural Forest Values," in Darrell A. Posey, ed., *Cultural and Spiritual Values of Biodiversity* (London: ITDG Publishing, 1999), 366–70; and M. M. Iwu,

"Symbols and Selectivity in Traditional African Medicine," in Darrell A. Posey, ed., *Cultural and Spiritual Values of Biodiversity* (London: ITDG Publishing, 1999), 370–71.

28. See Jeanne Zoundjihekpon and Bernadette Dossou-Glehouenou, "Cultural and Spiritual Values of Biodiversity in West Africa: The Case of Benin and Côte d'Ivoire," in Darrell A. Posey, ed., *Cultural and Spiritual Values of Biodiversity* (London: ITDG Publishing, 1999), 370–72.

29. See E. Bharucha, "Cultural and Spiritual Values Related to the Conservation of Biodiversity in the Sacred Groves of the Western Ghats in Maharashtra," in Darrell A. Posey, ed., *Cultural and Spiritual Values of Biodiversity* (London: ITDG Publishing, 1999), 382–85; and V. D. Vartak and M. Gadgil, "Studies on Sacred Groves along Western Ghats from Maharashtra and Goa: Role of Beliefs and Folklores," in Sudhanshu K. Jain, ed., *Glimpses of Indian Ethnobotany* (New Delhi: Oxford Univ. Press, 1981), 272–78.

30. See Peter Whiteley and Vernon Masayesva, "The Use and Abuse of Aquifers: Can the Hopi Indians Survive Multinational Mining?" in John M. Donahue and Barbara Rose Johnston, eds., *Water, Culture, and Power: Local Struggles in a Global Context* (Washington, D.C.: Island, 1998), 9–34.

31. See Paul Chambers, "Introduction: Aquatic and Marine Biodiversity," in Darrell A. Posey, ed., *Cultural and Spiritual Values of Biodiversity* (London: ITDG Publishing, 1999), 399–402.

32. Thomas Schaaf, "Environmental Conservation Based on Sacred Sites," in Darrell A. Posey, ed., *Cultural and Spiritual Values of Biodiversity* (London: ITDG Publishing, 1999), 341–42. See also Jo Edwards and Martin Palmer, eds., *Holy Ground: The Guide to Faith and Ecology* (Yelvertoft, Australia: Pilkington, 1997); Martin Palmer and Tjalling Halbertsma, "Sacred Mountains of China," in Darrell A. Posey, ed., *Cultural and Spiritual Values of Biodiversity* (London: ITDG Publishing, 1999), 337–38; and Terrence Hay-Edie, "Landscape Perception and Sensory Emplacement," in Darrell A. Posey, ed., *Cultural and Spiritual Values of Biodiversity* (London: ITDG Publishing, 1999), 246–49.

33. Laura Rival, "Trees and the Symbolism of Life in Indigenous Cosmologies," in Darrell A. Posey, ed., *Cultural and Spiritual Values of Biodiversity* (London: ITDG Publishing, 1999), 358–62.

34. See W. M. Denevan, "The Pristine Myth: The Landscape of the Americas in 1492," *Annals of the Association of American Geographers* 82, no. 3 (1992): 369–85; and Arturo Gomez-Pompa and Andrea Kaus, "Taming the Wilderness Myth," *BioScience* 42, no. 4 (1992): 271–79.

35. *Ecopolitics IX: Conference Papers and Resolutions, Northern Territory University, Darwin, 1–3 September 1995* (Casuarina, Australia: Northern Land Council, 1996), 166, no. 1.

36. "Conserving Outstanding Cultural Landscapes," *World Heritage Newsletter*, no. 2 (1993); posted at http://www.unesco.org/whc/news/2newsen.htm (4 April 2002). See also UNESCO General Conference (17th session, 1972), Convention Concerning the Protection of the World Cultural and Natural Heritage, doc. code WHC.2001/WS/2; the full text is posted at http://www.unesco.org/whc/world_he.htm (4 April 2002).

37. See M. Rössler, "Tongariro: First Cultural Landscape on the World Heritage List," *World Heritage Newsletter,* no. 4 (1993): 15.

38. Hay-Edie, "Landscape Perception" (note 32).

39. The Convention on Biological Diversity was developed under the auspices of the United Nations Environment Programme (UNEP) and entered into force on 29 December 1993; the full text is posted at http://www.biodiv.org/convention/articles.asp (4 April 2002).

40. Convention on Biological Diversity (note 39), arts. 8(j), 10(c), 18(4).

41. Lyle Glowka, Françoise Burhenne-Guilmin, and Hugh Synge, in collaboration with Jeffrey A. McNeely and Lothar Günding, *A Guide to the Convention on Biological Diversity,* IUCN environmental policy and law paper, no. 30 (Gland, Switzerland: IUCN, 1994).

42. Winin Pereira and Anil K. Gupta, "A Dialogue on Indigenous Knowledge," *Honey Bee: A Newsletter of Creativity and Innovation at the Grassroots* (Ahmedabad, India) 4, no. 4 (1993): 6.

43. See M. Gadgil, F. Berkes, and C. Folke, "Indigenous Knowledge for Biodiversity Conservation," *Ambio* 22 (1993): 151–56; and Martha Johnson, ed., *Lore: Capturing Traditional Environmental Knowledge* (Ottawa: Dene Cultural Institute, International Development Research Centre, 1992).

44. See D. Michael Warren, L. Jan Slikkerveer, and David Brokensha, eds., *The Cultural Dimension of Development: Indigenous Knowledge Systems* (London: Intermediate Technology, 1995).

45. See Peter Knudtson and David T. Suzuki, *Wisdom of the Elders: Honouring Sacred Visions of Nature* (Toronto: Stoddart, 1992).

46. Marilyn Walker, "Basketry and Biodiversity in the Pacific Northwest," in Darrell A. Posey, ed., *Cultural and Spiritual Values of Biodiversity* (London: ITDG Publishing, 1999), 86–88.

47. Reimar Schefold and Gerard Persoon, "Nature in Songs, Songs in Nature: Texts from Siberut, West Sumatra, Indonesia," in Darrell A. Posey, ed., *Cultural and Spiritual Values of Biodiversity* (London: ITDG Publishing, 1999), 105–12.

48. Alastair McIntosh, "Psychospiritual Effects of Biodiversity Loss in Celtic Culture and Its Contemporary Geopoetic Restoration," in Darrell A. Posey, ed., *Cultural and Spiritual Values of Biodiversity* (London: ITDG Publishing, 1999), 480–83.

49. Gerard Bodeker, "Traditional Health Systems," in Darrell A. Posey, ed., *Cultural and Spiritual Values of Biodiversity* (London: ITDG Publishing, 1999), 263–67.

50. See Darshan Shankar, "Cultural and Political Dimensions of Bioprospecting," in Darrell A. Posey, ed., *Cultural and Spiritual Values of Biodiversity* (London: ITDG Publishing, 1999), 534–35; and Bhanumathi Natarajan, "Traditional Knowledge, Culture and Resource Rights: The Case of *Tulasi,*" in Darrell A. Posey, ed., *Cultural and Spiritual Values of Biodiversity* (London: ITDG Publishing, 1999), 268–70.

51. Quoted in Lea Bill, "Learning to Connect Spirit, Mind, Body and Heart to the Environment: A Healer's Perspective," in Darrell A. Posey, ed., *Cultural and Spiritual Values of Biodiversity* (London: ITDG Publishing, 1999), 272–73.

52. See Olive Tumwesigye, "Bumetha Rukararwe: Integrating Modern and Traditional Health Care in South-West Uganda," *Journal of Alternative and Complementary*

Medicine 2, no. 3 (1996): 373–76; and Olive Tumwesigye, "Bumetha Rukararwe: Integrating Modern and Traditional Health Care in South-West Uganda," in Darrell A. Posey, ed., *Cultural and Spiritual Values of Biodiversity* (London: ITDG Publishing, 1999), 265, box 6.1.

53. See Elois Ann Berlin and Brent Berlin, "General Overview of Maya Ethnomedicine," in Darrell A. Posey, ed., *Cultural and Spiritual Values of Biodiversity* (London: ITDG Publishing, 1999), 273–75.

54. See Michael J. Balick et al., "Ethnopharmacological Studies and Biological Conservation in Belize: Valuation Studies," in Darrell A. Posey, ed., *Cultural and Spiritual Values of Biodiversity* (London: ITDG Publishing, 1999), 275–77.

55. See Balick et al., "Ethnopharmacological Studies" (note 54).

56. See Elisabeth Motte-Florac, Serge Bahuchet, and Jacqueline M. C. Thomas, "The Role of Food in the Therapeutics of the Aka Pygmies of the Central African Republic," in Darrell A. Posey, ed., *Cultural and Spiritual Values of Biodiversity* (London: ITDG Publishing, 1999), 280–82; and Hugh-Jones, "'Food' and 'Drugs'" (note 3).

57. See Iwu, "Symbols and Selectivity" (note 27).

58. See Andrew Gray, "Indigenous Peoples, Their Environments and Territories," in Darrell A. Posey, ed., *Cultural and Spiritual Values of Biodiversity* (London: ITDG Publishing, 1999), 61–66.

59. See Russell Lawrence Barsh, "An Advocate's Guide to the Convention on Indigenous and Tribal Peoples," *Oklahoma City University Law Review* 15 (1990): 209–53. There are now, according to *World Factbook 2002*, 191 independent states; according to the ILO Web site, the fourteen states that have ratified Convention 169 are Argentina (the most recent signatory, in July 2000), Bolivia, Colombia, Costa Rica, Denmark, Ecuador, Fiji, Guatemala, Honduras, Mexico, Netherlands, Norway, Paraguay, and Peru.

60. See Posey and Dutfield, *Beyond Intellectual Property* (note 1), esp. chap. 8.

61. World Trade Organization, Agreement on Trade-Related Aspects of Intellectual Property Rights (TRIPS), art. 27(3)(b); the full text is posted at http://www.wto.org/english/tratop_e/trips_e/t_agm0_e.htm (4 April 2002). The agreement is Annex 1C of the Marrakesh Agreement Establishing the World Trade Organization, signed 15 April 1994.

62. See Dan Leskien and Michael Flitner, *Intellectual Property Rights and Plant Genetic Resources: Options for a Sui Generis System* (Rome: International Plant Genetic Resources Institute, 1997).

63. See C. Montecinos, "*Sui Generis* — A Dead End Alley," *Seedling* 13, no. 4 (1996): 19–28.

64. See Decision III/14, "Implementation of Article 8(j)," in *The Biodiversity Agenda: Decisions from the Third Meeting of the Conference of the Parties to the Convention on Biological Diversity, Buenos Aires, Argentina, 4–15 November 1996*, 2d ed. (New York: United Nations, 1997), 49–50.

65. See Tom Greaves, ed., *Intellectual Property Rights for Indigenous Peoples: A Sourcebook* (Oklahoma City: Society for Applied Anthropology, 1994); Leo van der Vlist, ed., *Voices of the Earth: Indigenous Peoples, New Partners and the Right to Self-*

Determination in Practice: Proceedings of the Conference (Amsterdam: International Books, Netherlands Centre for Indigenous Peoples, 1994); and Posey and Dutfield, *Beyond Intellectual Property* (note 1).

66. The full text of the Draft Declaration of Rights of Indigenous Peoples is posted at http://www.treatycouncil.org/new_page_51.htm (4 April 2002).

67. For example, David C. Korten, *When Corporations Rule the World* (London: Earthscan, 1995).

68. The Mataatua Declaration on Cultural and Intellectual Property Rights of Indigenous Peoples was passed by the plenary of the First International Conference on the Cultural and Intellectual Property Rights of Indigenous Peoples, convened by the Nine Tribes of Mataatua in the Bay of Plenty region of Aotearoa, New Zealand, 12–18 June 1993; the full text is posted at http://www.ankn.uaf.edu/mataatua.html (4 April 2002). I am quoting from recommendation 2.8.

69. Final Statement from the UNDP Consultation (note 1).

70. A summary of some of these can be found in A. B. Cunningham, *Ethics, Ethnobiological Research, and Biodiversity* (Gland, Switzerland: WWF — World Wildlife Fund for Nature, 1993); Darrell Posey, "Indigenous Peoples and Traditional Resource Rights: A Basis for Equitable Relationships?" (paper commissioned by the Green College Centre for Environmental Policy and Understanding, Oxford, England, 1995); and Posey and Dutfield, *Beyond Intellectual Property* (note 1). The Convention on Biological Diversity Web site lists and provides links to similar documents developed by a range of organizations; see http://www.biodiv.org/programmes/socio-eco/traditional/instruments.asp (4 April 2002).

71. A. B. Cunningham, *Ethics, Biodiversity, and New Natural Products Development,* sec. 9; posted at http://www.rbgkew.org.uk/peopleplants/dp/dp2 (4 April 2002). The International Society for Ethnobiology's Code of Ethics (1998) is posted at http://guallart.dac.uga.edu/ISE/SocEth.html (4 April 2002).

The Stones Resung:
Ethnomusicology and Cultural Property

Hélène La Rue

Music has always been a shared pleasure and delight. Descriptions of music and music making are found in many of the earliest of travelers' tales and in the stories of fabled voyages. In the recent past this pleasure was shared by those musicians and scholars who heard and were inspired by the new musical styles of cultural traditions unfamiliar to them. It was the advent of sound recording and the development of computer technology, together with the ability to manipulate recorded sound and the growth of the commercial saleability of world music, that presented new dilemmas. Music, particularly when recorded, has since become a valuable commodity: at the same time it is both a cultural treasure and a highly saleable resource — one that is increasingly easy to misuse.

This essay is concerned with issues arising from the use and reuse of recorded sound. The development of modern methods of digitalizing and sampling sound has led to the popularity of new styles of music based on the computerized manipulation of prerecorded sound. As a result, new demands have been created for richer, more varied palettes of instrumental timbre and musical styles. Sources for these new types of sound and effect have frequently been found outside European music and its more conventional instrumentarium. Traditional copyright law, even for music, has been based on the music of literate traditions, and until now there has been no need to consider the aural tradition or to take into account the act of performance itself. It is because of the new developments of the use of recorded sound that new laws are now being devised. For example, the World International Property Organization (WIPO), originally created to work for the protection of the written word and material culture, has turned its efforts to new fields, including the protection of musical and performance copyrights. The following is a brief history of international musical contacts and a look at how this has developed into the interest in and use of what is known today as "world music." I shall also outline some of the dangers involved in using other peoples' musical heritage and chronicle the history of the attempts of organizations such as WIPO and the United Nations Educational, Scientific and Cultural Organization (UNESCO) to combat it.

The issues involved are not simple. The making of field recordings is no longer the province of the ethnomusicologist; increasingly, it is that of commercial recording companies. It is not only the material being recorded today but also historic recordings in archives that present their own problems of ownership and commitments of care. How are historic recordings to be managed, and how should this resource be used? To whom do these recordings truly belong? Should they be made public?

A Short Background to the Present Problem

Two things are credited with inspiring the development of the study of world musics: Thomas Alva Edison's invention of the phonograph in 1877 and the rapid development of sound recording as a scientific tool that could be used for the analysis of music. In addition, ethnomusicology was developed as a science. Before sound recording, the only method a musician or scholar could use to preserve music from the aural tradition was to write it down with the cooperation and patience of the performers themselves. No matter how hard a musician tries, even the most meticulous repetition of a piece of music will vary each time it is played. The recording machine liberated musicians from the tiresome repetition necessary for the listening scholar to make an accurate transcription. It also enabled even those unskilled in musical transcription to collect music as a part of their fieldwork. Their field recordings were then taken back to museums and sound archives where specialists transcribed them.

In the 1960s and 1970s the development of analog and digital synthesizers led to new possibilities in the use of recorded sound. During the 1980s the growth of the commercial sales of many traditional musical styles, marketed as world music, and the popularity of the exotic musical sound became a rising market as instrument sounds were sampled and sold as tracks on CD-ROMs designed for use in home sound studios.[1] In this chapter, I briefly explore this fascination with and use of those musics that have inspired the world music sales. Most of these styles originate from outside the Western musical canon, whether classical or popular. I will also discuss some of the issues that are increasingly involved in the process. These issues are now being dealt with at legal levels, and the legal response to these problems is also of interest. The situation is as follows: we now have over one hundred years of recorded sound and new technology that simplifies even further the recording process. Despite these advances, the rights of many musicians, particularly those outside the Western unionized traditions, do not appear to be considered in an equitable way.

It is because of the new ease of recording that there has been an increase in the insensitive use of recorded music, so that now not only are the notes and melodies of the music reused but the actual performance is distributed as well. Performance has been abused in another powerful way: recordings are made without the knowledge of the performer and subsequently used in a commercial release, or the recorded music is sampled, once again used without the performer's knowledge or consent. In general, there has been little sensitivity to this issue; in fact, material recorded in this way is even used at times in education programs in schools in the United Kingdom. Thus, it is necessary to begin by exploring briefly the history of musical contact.

New Encounters — New Musics

From the first accounts of encounters between European travelers and the inhabitants of the new worlds they discovered, there are descriptions of the music heard and of occasions during which music was shared and performances exchanged. Historically, traveling musicians have themselves been a source of both entertainment and information; in fact, the sharing of music and musical styles must be as old as human society itself.

The earliest accounts of music are generally simple descriptions without any attempts made of the music's notation.[2] In the past, musical styles would have traveled with those who performed them, foreign musicians being employed in royal courts, such as the women musicians who worked in the court of the emperor of China. European travelers and merchants who traveled by sea always had musicians with them. Before the invention of the system of signaling with flags at sea the trumpet was used — trumpeters having a system of known calls used to signal between ships. Few expeditions went to sea without enough persons skilled in the use of the trumpet to cover each watch.[3] Other musicians would make up the crew of a ship; they were very important in keeping up the morale of those on board, helping them to while away the journey's long, tedious hours by providing entertainment.[4] Captain James Cook describes hearing music and a musical evening in which his ship's musicians played.[5] In fact, merchants trading abroad would sometimes take these musicians on shore with them to entertain their customers.[6]

Of course, the European travelers brought this music back to Europe, although not without altering the music being composed. A fragment of sheet music with two Chinese melodies arranged for the pianoforte or harpsichord shows how melodies notated in 1793, during the mission of Lord Macartney, the first British emissary to China, were changed to suit the English ear.[7] During the period in which chinoiserie was all the rage in England, it would be surprising if a taste for the exotic in music did not also accompany it. In Austria Mozart was writing music in the Turkish manner for a piano with a built-in percussive device that enabled Turkish-style sound effects.[8]

It was not until the nineteenth century that musicians from other traditions themselves traveled in any number to Europe.[9] The first musicians who were to make their mark in Europe were those who came for the international exhibitions. European composers who heard music new to them at these exhibitions were often profoundly influenced by the encounter. It was at the Exposition Universelle de 1889 in Paris that Claude Debussy first heard a Javanese gamelan (orchestra). Some years later, in writing to a friend, Debussy described the effect that this music had on him: "22 January 1895, Remember the music of Java which contained every nuance, even the ones we no longer have names for. There tonic and dominant have become empty shadows of use only to stupid children."[10]

Debussy's "Pagodas" from the piano suite *Estampes* (1903) is always singled out as the piece of music that most displays the effect that hearing Javanese music and tonalities had on the composer. This experience altered his perception of tonality and timbre so profoundly that it remained a fundamental influence on his chordal and tonal writing until the end of his life. In writing about the impression that gamelan music had on Debussy, the ethnomusicologist Neil Sorrell says that "the key word is *influence,* with its suggestion of bringing about a change of course. With Debussy a much more fruitful word would be *confirmation.* It seems far more plausible that what he heard in 1889 confirmed what he had, at least subconsciously, always felt about music, and this experience went far deeper than a desire to imitate something new and exotic."[11]

In the late nineteenth century, music scholars were well aware of the new studies that were opened up as a result of the phonogram. Jaap Kunst, who coined the term *ethnomusicology,* had no doubts about the central role played by the invention of recorded sound:

> Ethnomusicology could never have grown into an independent science if the gramophone had not been invented. Only then was it possible to record the musical expressions of foreign races and peoples objectively; it was no longer necessary to make do with notations made by ear on the spot, which notations, however well-intended, usually fell short in every respect—i.e., both rhythmically and as regards pitch. And in addition it now became possible to incorporate the style of performance—that extremely important element—into the subject matter of the investigation.[12]

Phonogram archives, established in the United States and Europe, acted as central reservation points for the wax cylinders made by both anthropologists and musicians in the field. Scholars worldwide began to make recordings for the purpose of studying the music at leisure after their fieldwork. One of these, Frances Densmore, who worked for more than forty years collecting Native American music, was well aware both of the importance of the phonogram as a tool and of its limitations: "My work, as you know, is the recording of Indian songs and transcribing them as nearly possible in our notation, so that the eye can get an impression that the ear does not receive while listening to the song."[13]

It is interesting to note that Densmore's wax cylinder recordings were most useful as an aid to notating an accurate arrangement of the song rather than as a record of the performer's rendition of it. She describes those recordings she considered too poor for use for transcription as "seconds" that are not worth preserving.

Recordings or Transcriptions

Even in the early years of the twentieth century there were still musicians for whom the preferred method was to transcribe the music directly from the performer. One of these was Cecil Sharp, the well-known collector of English folk songs. Sharp was renowned for the incredible speed and accuracy with which he made his transcriptions from live performance. He disliked mechanical recording devices, and on the rare occasion that he did use one, he credited the machine with saving his life from a jealous husband:

> Cecil Sharp's collecting was, of course, done before the days of the tape-recorder and he used to take down the tune in ordinary staff notation and then write out the words. Occasionally he used a phonograph, but he did not much like it, as he thought it made the singer self-conscious. However, on one occasion the phonograph was the means of saving his life — or so he said. He was noting songs by phonograph from a gypsy woman in a caravan, when suddenly she stopped singing and, turning deathly white, announced that she heard her husband approaching and as he was of a jealous disposition she was afraid he would kill Mr. Sharp. Cecil Sharp did not want to be killed, and there was nothing for it but to present a bold face. Opening the caravan door, he shouted to the man: "A happy Christmas to you. Stop a moment and listen. I've got your wife's voice in a box." The man listened to the record of his wife's song and was so amazed and delighted that he forgot to kill Cecil Sharp, and instead they became great friends.[14]

It was by the date of Sharp's work (1899–1924) that questions began to be raised as to the ownership of the songs that he collected. His opinion was quite unequivocal; for him, the song as sung remained the property of the singer, while the transcribed work was the property of the scholar. Another scholar could just as easily go to the same singer and transcribe the song for himself. In doing so they may even have found that they had a rather different version from the first performance: "The law protects the product of the man's brain, not the thing on which he exercises his wits.... A collector who takes down a song from a folk-singer has an exclusive right to his *copy* of that song.... It is always open to someone else to go...to the same source, exercise the same skill and so obtain a right to *his* copy."[15]

Certain types of music remain notoriously difficult to record — one example being that of the Indonesia gamelan. The first commercial recordings of Balinese gamelan were made in 1928.[16] These recordings demonstrate a number of the problems associated with contemporary recording technology on the 78 rpm disk. First, the length of the music recorded had to be limited to the amount of time possible on one side of a 78 rpm disk — a mere three minutes. In Indonesia Walter Spies was responsible for directing efforts by the Odeon and Beka record companies, and because of his keenness to have a representative selection of the gamelan's sound, the albums feature examples of a broad range of musical genres. The companies both hoped that their release would help to stimulate a local market; however, as might have been expected, no one was interested when there was still such a wealth of live music to be enjoyed. Colin McPhee made one of the rare purchases of these albums, and he was to hear these recordings for the first time when a friend brought them back from Bali in 1929. While listening to them, he was inspired to conduct research in Bali.[17] During his subsequent research, McPhee transcribed the gamelan music for piano.

Works such as McPhee's piano transcriptions are sometimes criticized as examples of colonial appropriation; however, in this case I would argue that his work was in the same tradition as that of Cecil Sharp. Recording techniques during McPhee's lifetime could only give a poor reproduction of the distinctive musical elements of Balinese music such as the acoustical spacing. This acoustical effect, which provides the genre with its particular character, is still difficult to reproduce even with today's sophisticated modern sound-recording methods and machinery. It is because of these limitations that McPhee did not use the recorder to enable his transcriptions; the method he used was to have the musicians play Balinese gamelan instruments next to his Steinway grand piano. According to Edward Herbst, "As musicians would play a phrase, McPhee would try to repeat it on the piano, going back and forth until all were satisfied, after which he would transcribe the music onto paper."[18] The resulting transcriptions were not an effort to reproduce a non-Western form played by Western instruments; rather, they were intended to be an introduction to this musical style. Herbst writes, "These works are evidence that McPhee was an astute listener who had the skill and feeling to communicate to pianists something of what he heard, enriching the piano repertoire. Indeed, it is not Balinese gamelan, but a pianist's and Western flutist's reflection of it."[19] McPhee's aim in making the recordings, to introduce the music he enjoyed to new audiences, was clearly stated on the record sleeve: "The object of the present album is to introduce, through the medium of Western instruments, this exotic music, too little known in other parts of the world."[20]

In contrast with this is the more recent work of David Fanshawe, who traveled extensively in Africa to make a series of recordings on which his composition *African Sanctus* was based. This work demonstrates a move away from the cooperative work as seen above among McPhee and the Balinese musicians. As with McPhee, non-Western musical styles provided inspiration for Fanshawe's compositions. He records in the field, not only because he wants more people to enjoy the wonderful music he hears but also as an aid to his composition. Here there is a difference, however, as Fanshawe is sampling the actual performance he heard. The field recordings he makes are sufficient for use when he mixes them with a live performance of his own composition, which is possible due to developments in the technology of recording music. In addition to *African Sanctus,* Fanshawe wrote a book of the same name that chronicled his search for music to inspire his own composition. He also made a compilation of original recordings from his travels, which he sold commercially. In the book he describes how he made one of the tracks included on the released compilation of fieldwork recordings:

I heard fantastic singing like some modern composer only much better — it got nearer — I climbed up a steep bush-covered hill and entered the compound of a village. Climbing over stone walls and knocking a barking dog for six with my foot plus a stone, I jumped into a hole beside the hut and peeped over the top. Already the recorder was running.

Like the Omda, four men in a trance sat on a mat swaying from side to side, and the most extraordinary singing came out of them. I crept forward and, unnoticed, placed my microphones on a small tripod right in the middle of them. . . .

I found my batteries were flat [and hurried back concerned that they may have stopped singing]. . . .

I needn't have worried. The four men on the prayer mat carried on all night and never even knew I had been there.[21]

This extract shows Fanshawe to be operating worlds away from the cooperative methods used by McPhee. Whether or not anyone in authority has given Fanshawe permission to record, the recording of people without their knowledge, particularly at such a private moment, and then releasing it commercially, seems insensitive as well as unethical. These legal implications will be discussed below.

The Ends of Recording

This brief overview of the explorers, travelers, musicians, and scholars who were interested in the new music that they heard or the traditional music that they wished to preserve shows that until the last quarter of the twentieth century, recorded sound was used as an aid to the study of new musical styles. Often these new musical styles were introduced to the wider public through transcription rather than through the actual recordings of performances made in the field. This was mainly due to an unsatisfactory standard of sound reproduction. In the last two decades of the twentieth century, we have witnessed a growth in the number of people interested in world music as well as in the number of students going out into the field. Ethnomusicology has stimulated the foundation of a number of societies worldwide and its own academic literature, while ethnomusicologists are increasingly more aware of the impact that they can make on indigenous musics and musical styles. A survey of the current academic literature offering advice to student ethnomusicologists about to embark on fieldwork and make field recordings for the first time demonstrates that this is still an area in which insufficient weight is given to the possible implications of the recordings made or the difficulties that may arise concerning their use in the future.

Training for the New Technologies

In the training of new scholars and within the academic discipline as a whole, there needs to be a greater awareness of the implications of the ethnomusicologist's work. It is important that those embarking on fieldwork are first taught the implications of recording various material, as well as any implication of its future use. Laws are not yet in place that fully address the problems of copyright and ownership, and the questions of whether ownership belongs to the performer or the recorder and whether the music itself belongs to a group of people in the form of cultural property remains open.[22]

The problems that face those in charge of archive recordings are manifold.[23] Many requests to copy material come from students who need recorded examples to use in presentations and lectures. Permission to use the recordings has to be given by the copyright holders, and contacting the copyright holders can be extremely complicated. The recorders may themselves be working in the field faraway from contact, and they may neglect to make note of the performers' names. Janet Topp-Fargion, curator of the International Music Collection of the British Library National Sound Archive, writes as follows:

> It is essential for the archive to be able to point such users in the direction for obtaining permissions, and documentation on copyright and ownership needs to be in place. How can the archive ensure that this documentation is so, and that it can be maintained and updated over time? In what contexts can copies be made without reference to copyright owners? And where reference must be made, how can the process be made more straightforward? The archive relies on the researcher/ recordist, but how can we ensure we maintain contact? How can we be sure the appropriate agreements with artists represented on the recordings were and still are in place? Furthermore, plans for future ownership and administration of a collection need to be made. Suggestions in the YTM [*Yearbook for Traditional Music*] articles puts the responsibility on ethnomusicologists, including watchdog functions within, but many recordists are not ethnomusicologists and don't necessarily have institutional backgrounds.[24]

Of the literature giving guidelines for good practice in fieldwork, *A Manual for Documentation, Fieldwork and Preservation for Ethnomusicologists* (1994) was designed as a basic introduction to ethnomusicology and to fieldwork. In the introduction it highlights the ethnomusicologist's responsibilities:

> Ethnomusicologists are part of a process whereby musical traditions all over the world are recorded, documented, studied, written about, and made accessible to new audiences. We are not the only people doing this, but our goals are scholarship and understanding, and the time frame within which we should be thinking is longer than that of most other people carrying recorders and talking about music. The results of our work are often useful and sometimes highly significant to the peoples whose musics we have studied—sometimes decades after we made the recordings. Furthermore, as ethnomusicologists, we have obligations not only to ourselves and to our institutions, but to the traditions we study and the people from whom we learn.[25]

Much of the advice concerning preparation before fieldwork concentrates on the possible use of the recordings afterward.[26] A whole section that is thorough and clear is devoted to ethical and legal considerations;[27] the section is closed by two pages, "Depositing Fieldwork Materials in Archives." This piece introduces those who are new to the field to some of the considerations concerning the use of their material later, the need for good storage, and the reasons for contracts to be drawn up between the archive and fieldworker and between the fieldworker and subjects recorded.

In the Norton Grove handbook *Ethnomusicology,* Mark Slobin gives a series of cases illustrating possible ethical issues that can occur. In case three, which concerns record royalties, he discusses the complexity of the royalty rights issue:

> This is an area of extremely grey ethical consideration in which it is hard to presuppose a solution without a great deal of contextual information. Most ethnomusicologists would probably feel that the rapport with the particular musician is the major factor here, rather than a uniform policy on royalties. Two or three solutions might be needed for different musicians from varied locales or local status levels. The question of whether the record was premeditated or evolved as a project after fieldwork makes some difference here. There are roving pseudo- or quasi-ethnomusicologists who have muddied these waters by producing records after the most casual of contact with local musicians without informing them of the intention to market their music; such behaviour would probably be universally condemned in the discipline.[28]

The quotation from Fanshawe's book discussed earlier is worth considering once again. In it, Fanshawe is describing an occasion when he made a recording by stealth, intentionally creeping up on his subjects who were praying in their own home. I believe that what compounds this insensitivity is the fact that the actual recording was made (and continues to be) available commercially and that the music, book, and recordings have been made use of in public education and continue to be performed in university and school settings.[29] This example does not present a model of good practice to students involved in the study and performance of Fanshawe's work. Fanshawe's behavior has become a particularly sensitive issue due to the amount of exposure *African Sanctus* has received from establishment channels. The BBC television program *Music Machine* introduced it as one of the useful compilations and compositions for educators to use in class.[30]

The Development of World Music

Interest in recordings of what is now known as world music has grown steadily since the 1970s, when *African Sanctus* was first performed. Until the 1980s such music was classified as "folk," "exotic," and "ethnic." The invention of the term *world music* is described in *World Music: The Rough Guide:*

> World Music as a concept is less than a decade old. The name was dreamed up in 1987 by the heads of a number of small London-based record labels who found their releases from African, Latin American and other international artists were not finding rack space because records stores had no obvious place to put them. And so

the world music tag was hit upon, initially as a month-long marketing campaign to impress on the music shops, the critics, and buyers that here were sounds worth listening to. The name stuck, however, and was swiftly adopted at record stores and festivals, in magazines and books, on both sides of the Atlantic. The Germans caught on, too, coining the more lively weltbeat.[31]

The creation of a title now used as a section heading in all music shops has made the recordings easier to find, and the incorporation of world music styles and performance in popular releases has in turn increased its attraction. Add to this commercial desirability the interest in indigenous cultures by the New Age movement, and suddenly recordings of world music have become viable commercial commodities.

The New Age and Old Tradition

The music and traditions of the native peoples of the United States are now very popular among New Age audiences. This interest in Native American traditions by the various New Age groups has resulted in the issue of a number of recordings purporting to be by native artists. The compilation *Sacred Spirit: Chants and Dances of the Native Americans* is a good example both of the type of music produced for this market, and of the style of language used to market the CD, as is seen on the Web site advertising it:

> From its moody musical content to its striking packaging, *Sacred Spirit* represents a most unusual artistic experience. Combining ancient Native American ceremonial chants with modern instrumental arrangements, the album's eleven tracks progress through a cycle of celebration, growth, wisdom, reverence, and rebirth.
>
> The music focuses on authentic vocal chants sung by Native American performers, with each chant's meaning and content reflected in the song's English subtitle. Beginning with "Intro & Prelude," *Sacred Spirit* takes the listener on a journey through the timeless Native American cultural heritage.[32]

Both the term *authentic* and the phrase "Native American performers" recur as a leitmotiv, as does the concept of the music's antiquity: "Featuring authentic performances in accordance with tribal rituals, an undeniable power and spirituality infuses the unique collection. Almost all vocal recordings have been gleaned from extensive tribal archives with the guidance of several Native Americans—in particular, Jard Gorbohay, whose contributions to this album have been invaluable."[33]

Nowhere on the record sleeve, however, are the names of the "Native American performers" who played on the original recordings. This boxed set of CDs caused outrage among the Native American community. One result of *Sacred Spirit* was the A Line in the Sand Web site. At this site one can find clearly expressed the grievances felt as a result of the production of the *Sacred Spirit* CD:

The album producer, Claus Zundel, is also the composer, lyricist and arranger. The entire 6.25% of the album proceeds which is [*sic*] usually split by these people. In this case, all goes to Mr. Zundel, who bills himself as The Fearsome Brave on the album cover material. The only true Native American connection with the album comes from a set of Native American chants that were mixed over the "ambient and techno" music that forms the base of the album. The "rights" to these chants were purchased 3 years ago for approximately $2000 from the Recorded Anthology of American Music, a non-profit-making foundation in New York. This foundation has its own record label, New World Records. They collect authentic "roots" music; their products are usually used in schools and colleges. The four tribes from whose music these chants come had each negotiated their own terms with New World Records, sometimes for a flat fee and in other cases for royalties. At the time of these negotiations there was no prospect of a hit record in sight. Apparently the costs of producing the album were minimal.[34]

The Use of the Internet

The Internet has become the most popular medium for expressing publicly any reactions to such productions as the CD called *Sacred Spirit*. Arlie Neskahi, one of the contributors to the A Line in the Sand Web site, expresses at his Rainbow Walker Web site his outrage with what he calls the "fraudulent" abuse of traditional music. He states how easy it is to be fooled by the names and credentials of the artists and makes three suggestions:

1. All non-native performed recordings should be labeled "NATIVE INFLUENCED or NATIVE INSPIRED." I could live with that, I might even set up a page to that effect someday. It would be less confusing to me.
2. OR, non-native musicians let people publically know their ethnic background so there is no mistake.
3. Finally, I suggest that all Native musicians put their tribal identity on their releases.[35]

Zundel's compilation was released in 1998 under the name *Native American Collection*.[36] Once again, no credit was given to the musicians of the original recordings. This time, however, there is very little text, and in contrast to the earlier release, perhaps as a result of Neskahi's suggestion, the description on the CD is that the music is "inspired by the legendary Red Indian Tribes."

Music Performance and Recording as Cultural Property

Concerns about matters of ownership and abuse of cultural property led to the foundation of the WIPO, which was established by a convention signed at Stockholm on 14 July 1967. The convention went into force in 1970, and by 1974, WIPO was one of the sixteen specialized agencies of the United Nations. The agency grew rapidly. In 2002, 178 states were members of WIPO (membership is open to any state that is a member of the Paris Union for the

Protection of Industrial Property or the Bern Union for the Protection of Literary and Artistic Works). WIPO describes itself as

> an international organization dedicated to helping to ensure that the rights of creators and owners of intellectual property are protected worldwide and that inventors and authors are, thus, recognized and rewarded for their ingenuity. This international protection acts as a spur to human creativity, pushing forward the boundaries of science and technology and enriching the world of literature and the arts. By providing a stable environment for the marketing of intellectual property products, it also oils the wheels of international trade.[37]

The role that WIPO plays is described as follows: "responsible for the promotion of the protection of intellectual property throughout the world through cooperation among States, and for the administration of various multilateral treaties dealing with the legal and administrative aspects of intellectual property."[38]

WIPO also explains that the two areas it covers are issues of industrial property and copyright. The term *copyright,* in reference to music, is further explained as "musical works: whether serious or light; songs, choruses, operas, musicals, operettas; if for instruments, whether for one instrument (solos), a few instruments (sonatas, chamber music, etc.) or many (bands, orchestras);"[39] with an additional section that also applies to the music industry:

> In certain countries, mainly in countries with common law legal traditions, the notion 'copyright' has a wider meaning than 'author's rights' and, in addition to literary and artistic works, also extends to the producers of sound recordings (phonograms, whether disks or tapes), to the broadcasters of broadcasts and the creators of distinctive typographical arrangements of publications.[40]

It is because the copyright laws are so firmly rooted in Western concepts of composition, transmission, and styles that the current problem exists, along with the subsequent need to protect indigenous musics, which derive not from a literary but from an aural tradition. During the 1990s there was a steady growth in the number of working parties and agreements cooperating internationally to tackle the problems of the use of sound recordings. These have been drawn up both as a result of local initiatives and as a result of international directives. In the main these documents concentrate on the cultural ownership of objects, traditions, and ritual, many of which include music and performance.

The most recent initiatives are a result of the close collaboration between WIPO and UNESCO. Access to most national copyright laws is now easily available through the UNESCO Web site.[41] The laws do still cover music and performance that have already been published in written form. These laws all demonstrate their origination from societies that have notated musics with known authorship. For the first time, copyright law is beginning to take into consideration those musical works that belong to a group's "folklore" or cultural heritage and are part of an aural tradition. This has now become the central problem that the new initiatives are attempting to resolve.

Indeed certain local pronouncements actually exclude music. One example of this is the United States' Protection for Products of Indian Arts and Craftsmanship, a rule that adopts regulations to carry out the Indian Arts and Crafts Act of 1990, which built on an act of 1935.[42] This earlier act adopted criminal penalties for selling goods misrepresented as having been produced by Native Americans. In the public comments received before the rule was adopted, the issue of what made something a "product" was raised, and music was specifically excluded from the regulations.

> Several comments stated that the definition of Indian product should be more inclusive. One comment stated that the definition should be broad enough to include the work of musicians, actors, and writers.... The final regulations do not adopt these comments. In keeping with the Indian Arts and Crafts Board's organic legislation, its primary mission, and the Congressional intent of the Act, the Board has determined in the final regulations that the Act applies to Indian arts and crafts and not to all products generally. However, what constitutes an Indian art or craft product is potentially very broad.[43]

This certainly provides a loophole through which Zundel and others have been able to proceed with impunity.

The Limitations of Copyright Protection

As a result of increasing concern at a formal level, more and more legal time has been spent discussing the issues, especially those concerning traditional music and its performance. Throughout the 1990s a number of edicts and declarations were published. As a result of increased anxiety in the Pacific region, the Mataatua Declaration on Cultural and Intellectual Property Rights of Indigenous Peoples was published in 1993.[44] In the last few years the pace of the discussion has quickened with the buildup toward the Pacific area meeting of WIPO and UNESCO in 2000. Local initiatives such as the bill proposed by the Western Samoan government on 9 June 1998 were ratified:

> A copyright amendment bill has been introduced to stop a growing number of Samoan artists from reaping significant financial rewards by plagiarizing both local and overseas music, then crediting the work as their own.
>
> It also is increasingly common for music retailers to duplicate large numbers of legitimate audio cassettes. The pirated copies then are sold openly at the same price as the original product, generating significant retail profits.
>
> Deputy Prime Minister Tuilaepa Malielegaoi says both practices are unfair and unethical and the government is going to bring them to a halt.
>
> The government-proposed copyright amendment bill is expected to become law within a week, with pirated tapes to be confiscated and destroyed by police.[45]

It is interesting that the edict not only concerned Samoan music but also the piracy of "overseas" music, and it may well be that American initiatives to stamp out the piracy of music recordings worldwide is stimulating matching efforts on the part of those in whose countries pirate copies of recordings are readily available. These issues prompted discussion, on 16 June 1998, by the American Samoan lawmakers.[46]

The year 1999 was one of conferences and discussions leading toward the 2000–2001 biennium of the UNESCO General Conference. The application of the 1989 UNESCO Recommendation on Safeguarding of Traditional Culture and Folklore was presented at a seminar held by the Secretariat of the Pacific Community on 11 and 12 February 1999 in Nouméa, New Caldonia. The results of this seminar were reported during the UNESCO Symposium on the Protection of Traditional Knowledge and Expressions of Indigenous Cultures in the Pacific Islands, which was held at Nouméa from 15 to 19 February 1999.[47] After an international conference in Washington, D.C., in June 1999, the thirtieth session of the General Conference asked the director general of UNESCO to "carry out a preliminary study on the advisability of regulating internationally, through a new standard-setting instrument, the protection of traditional culture and folklore." At its thirty-first session, the General Conference decided that "this question should be regulated by means of an international convention" and invited the director general to offer a preliminary draft for such a convention at the thirty-second session.[48]

The Archive at the Cutting Edge

Archives have an increasing burden in this field, not only to proceed sensitively but also to allow access to early recordings. As a result of over a century of fieldwork recordings, considerable sound archives now exist. Archivists and curators are now presented with the tremendous tasks of managing this material to enable scholarly access and using sensitively material that may include recordings made at rituals now considered too private to be heard by the general and unassociated listener. In the case of sound recordings, the return of material is not difficult. Making copies and holding these copies both in the country of origin and in an international archive is highly desirable and might ensure their longevity. This course of action does, however, put a great burden of responsibility on the archives, not only morally but also financially, as a copying program is not cheap.

It may be that archived recordings should have a greater public than just those engaged in scholarly research. The music may well be of commercial interest, finding a market because of its historicity or sentimental associations in its country of origin. Another question then arises: Should the original performers have a right to any revenue produced? In many cases, tracking down the performer of the historic recording—or even any of the performer's surviving relatives—is no easy matter. One institutional project to make available archival recordings is the Endangered Music Project initiated by the Library of Congress in collaboration with the musician Mickey Hart, which is the first in a series of digitally remastered field recordings from the Library of Congress' vast Archive of Folk Culture. Many of the cultural traditions practiced by the people on these recordings are in danger of extinction. Others have vanished altogether, leaving only the songs behind. *The Spirit Cries,* compiled by Mickey Hart, was recorded within the rainforests of South America and the Caribbean by Kenneth Bilby.... Proceeds from the sale of this recording will be used to support the performers, their cultural traditions and produce future releases.[49]

Using the proceeds from the recording to pay the performers — or their descendants — is a step toward a more equitable use of the music. If the names of the performers were not recorded, and there is no way to trace their relatives, at least funds can be sent to aid projects in which the original participating cultural group might benefit.

The Conscience of Contemporary Musicians

It is also to be hoped that Western musicians who enjoy and profit by contact with other musicians might reimburse them by sharing a proportion of the royalties gained from released recordings. Encouragingly, there are several recent initiatives put into place by musicians to enable indigenous music to become what is sometimes referred to as a completely sustainable resource. One such initiative is that of the musician Martin Cradick, who traveled to the Central African Rain Forest and recorded the music of the Baka people. This work led to two commercial recordings: *Spirit of the Forest,* which is a compilation of Cradick's own music influenced profoundly by the music of the Baka; and *Heart of the Forest,* which is a compilation of recordings of Baka music made during visits to the area by Cradick and his colleagues.[50]

Spirit of the Forest uses samples of music from the Baka themselves. It is interesting to note that Martin Cradick went back to visit the Baka with his first cuts of their music, to play it to them and to see how they reacted to it. The disk was only released with the Baka's approval. Of the distribution of royalties, Cradick writes in the liner notes that "all performance and compositional royalties due to the Baka for this Album (*Heart of the Forest*) will be collected for them to use to protect their forest and to develop in a sustainable way without losing their knowledge and culture. While the forest stands their way of life is secure within it, but while the forest is under threat from logging and encroachment on their lands, so too is their survival."[51]

Much remains to be done to secure equitable use of recorded music and performance. New developments in the technology of computer-generated sound and manipulation make performance all the more easy to record and moreover to record without the knowledge of the musician. Sadly it appears that the only way to protect the rights of musicians and performers is through legal intervention. It is hoped that the WIPO and UNESCO initiatives will eventually provide such protection. It is also to be hoped that with this protection the joy in shared music and the consequent richness of the exchange of ideas and influences will continue to exist and inspire.

Notes

1. For a brief history of the synthesizer and developments of new related musical styles, see Paul Théberge, *Any Sound You Can Imagine: Making Music/Consuming Technology* (Hanover, N.H.: Wesleyan Univ. Press/University Press of New England, 1997).

2. For accounts of the descriptions made by early travelers, see *The Garland Encyclopedia of World Music*, vol. 1, *Africa*, ed. Ruth M. Stone (New York: Garland, 1998), 74–99; and *The Garland Encyclopedia of World Music*, vol. 9, *Australia and the Pacific Islands*, ed. Adrienne L. Kaeppler and Jacob W. Love (New York: Garland, 1998), 7–52.

3. Elizabeth Story Donno, *An Elizabethan in 1582: The Diary of Richard Madox, Fellow of All Souls* (London: Hakluyt Society, 1976), 122.

4. Richard Madox describes a celebration of Christmas in the course of his journey to the Spice Islands when "placing the trays and food on the table, we were entertayned with a musical concert"; see Story Donno, *An Elizabethan in 1582* (note 3), 273.

5. Johann Reinhold Forster, *The Resolution Journal of Johann Reinhold Forster, 1772–1775*, ed. Michael E. Hoare (London: Hakluyt Society, 1982), 3:378.

6. See, for instance, a seventeenth-century Japanese screen in the Musée du Louvre that shows a European merchant making a transaction with Japanese clients while three European musicians play. The merchant's ship is in the background.

7. K[arl] Kambra, *Two Chinese Songs, "Moo-lee-Chwa" and "Higho Highau," for the Pianoforte or Harpsichord* (London: n.p., n.d.).

8. For an account of the ways in which Western composers have used "exotic elements," see Jonathan Bellman, ed., *The Exotic in Western Music* (Boston: Northeastern Univ. Press, 1998).

9. For a survey of the exhibitions and festivals that brought musicians to Europe and the United States, see Curtis M. Hinsley, "The World as Marketplace: Commodification of the Exotic at the World's Columbian Exposition, Chicago, 1893," in Ivan Karp and Steven D. Lavine, eds., *Exhibiting Cultures: The Poetics and Politics of Museum Display* (Washington, D.C.: Smithsonian Institution Press, 1991), 344–65.

10. Claude Debussy, *Debussy Letters*, ed. François Lesure and Roger Nichols, trans. Roger Nichols (Cambridge: Harvard Univ. Press, 1987), 76.

11. Neil Sorrell, *A Guide to the Gamelan* (London: Faber & Faber, 1990), 3.

12. Jaap Kunst, *Ethnomusicology: A Study of Its Nature, Its Problems, Methods and Representative Personalities, to Which Is Added a Bibliography* (reprint, 3d much enl. ed. of *Musicologica* and 2d ed. of the supplement, The Hague: Martinus Nijhoff, 1974), 12.

13. Frances Densmore, "The Music of the American Indian" (paper presented to the Department of Sociology and Anthropology, University of Florida, 31 March 1954).

14. Maud Karpeles, *Cecil Sharp: His Life and Work* (London: Routledge & Kegan Paul, 1967), 41.

15. Karpeles, *Cecil Sharp* (note 14), 56.

16. These recordings, which were made by the companies Odeon and Beka, are described in Andrew Toth, comp., *Recordings of the Traditional Music of Bali and Lombok* (N.p.: Society for Ethnomusicology, 1980), 16–17. They have been reissued by

Arbiter Records on *The Roots of Gamelan: The First Recordings: Bali, 1928, New York, 1941*, World Arbiter 2001.

17. Colin McPhee, *A House in Bali* (New York: John Day, 1946; reprint, Singapore: Oxford Univ. Press, 1986), 72.

18. Edward Herbst, liner notes to *The Roots of Gamelan: The First Recordings: Bali, 1928, New York, 1941*, World Arbiter 2001, 19; currently the notes are posted at http://www.arbiterrecords.com/notes/2001notes.html (19 February 2002).

19. Herbst, liner notes to *The Roots of Gamelan* (note 18), 22.

20. *The Music of Bali,* transcribed and arranged by Colin McPhee, performed by Colin McPhee, Benjamin Britten, and Georges Barrère, Schirmer's Library of Recorded Music, set no. 17 (three 78 rpm analog sound disks, first issued in 1941).

21. David Fanshawe, *African Sanctus: A Story of Travel and Music* (London: Collins & Harvill, 1975), 137.

22. The *Yearbook for Traditional Music* 28 (1996) concentrated on the problems of copyright and ownership; see the articles by Steven Feld, "Pygmy POP: A Genealogy of Schizophonic Mimesis," 1–35; Hugo Zemp, "The/An Ethnomusicologist and the Record Business," 6–56; Sherylle Mills, "Indigenous Music and the Law: An Analysis of National and International Legislation," 57–86; and Anthony Seeger, "Ethnomusicologists, Archives, Professional Organizations, and the Shifting Ethics of Intellectual Property," 87–105.

23. See John B. Post and M. R. Foster, *Copyright: A Handbook for Archivists* (London: Society of Archivists, 1992).

24. Janet Topp-Fargion, personal communication, March 1998.

25. *A Manual for Documentation Fieldwork and Preservation for Ethnomusicologists* (Bloomington, Ind.: Society for Ethnomusicology, 1994), 4.

26. *Manual for Documentation* (note 25), 10.

27. *Manual for Documentation* (note 25), 53–58.

28. Mark Slobin, "Ethical Issues," in Helen Myers, ed., *Ethnomusicology: An Introduction* (New York: W. W. Norton, 1992), 334.

29. The University of Puget Sound Web page, advertising a performance of *African Sanctus* to be held 1 and 2 May 1999, reads: "A universal work who's [*sic*] impact is immediate, the message of 'African Sanctus' is simple — peace, goodwill and understanding between nations. 'African Sanctus' is a choral and archival work; an unorthodox setting of the Latin Mass harmonized with authentic traditional African music recorded by David Fanshawe, a British composer and explorer, on his now legendary journeys up the river Nile"; see http://www.ups.edu/news/releases/african_sanctus.htm (19 February 2002).

30. "Sacred Music from Different Cultures Is Imaginatively Fused in *African Sanctus*"; posted on the BBC *Music Machine* Web page at http://www.bbc.co.uk/music_machine/50/index2.html (1 April 1999).

31. See the introduction to Simon Broughteon et al., eds., *World Music: The Rough Guide* (London: Rough Guides, 1994), unpaginated.

32. *Sacred Spirit: Chants and Dances of the Native Americans,* Virgin Records compact disk 72438-40945-2-2. For the marketing material, see http://www.virginrecords.com/artists/VR.cgi?ARTIST_NAME=Sacred (1 April 1999).

33. Http://www.virginrecords.com/artists/VR.cgi?ARTIST_NAME=Sacred (1 April 1999).

34. Http://www.hanksville.org/sand/site.html (19 February 2002).

35. Http://www.rainbowwalker.net (6 March 2002).

36. Released in 1998 as a boxed set of three compact disks, *Native American Collection*, Castle Pulse (UK) PBXCD 317, is described in a subtitle on the slipcase as "A stunning collection of music and chants inspired by the legendary Red Indian Tribes."

37. See the section entitled "An Organization for the Future" at http://www.wipo.int/about-wipo/en (26 February 2002).

38. Http://www.wipo.int/eng/newindex/meetings/1998/indip/pdf/rt98_4a.pdf-25.0kB-wipo/indip/rt/98/4a:11 (18 June 2002).

39. Http://www.wipo.int/about-ip/en/iprm/index.htm (18 June 2002).

40. Http://www.wipo.int/eng/newindex/intellct.htm (1 April 1999).

41. Http://www.unesco.org/culture/copy/index.shtml (18 June 2002).

42. Indian Arts and Crafts Board, Rule, "Indian Arts and Crafts Act of 1990, Public Law 101-644," *Federal Register* 61, no. 204 (21 October 1996): 54551–56; posted at http://www.artnatam.com/law.html (19 February 2002).

43. See "Definition of Indian Product, Section 309.2(d)," in Indian Arts and Crafts Board, "Indian Arts and Crafts Act" (note 42).

44. The Mataatua Declaration on Cultural and Intellectual Property Rights of Indigenous Peoples, June 1993; posted at http://linux.soc.uu.se/~jorge/indgen/Mataatua.html (19 February 2002).

45. "Samoan Government Wants to Stop Music Piracy" (Apia, Samoa, 9 June 1998; PACNEWS/Ioane), *Pacific Islands Report,* 11 June 1998; posted at http://166.122.164.43/archive/1998/june/06-11-03.htm (19 February 2002).

46. "American Samoa House Speaker Considers Plagiarism and Piracy Laws" (Pago Pago, American Samoa, 16 June 1998; Samoa News), *Pacific Islands Report,* 22 June 1998; posted at http://166.122.164.43/archive/1998/june/06-22-06.htm (19 February 2002).

47. See Secrétariat de la Communauté du Pacifique, "Symposium sur la protection des savoirs traditionnels et des expressions des cultures traditionnelles et populaires dans les îles du Pacifique (Nouméa, Nouvelle-Calédonie, 15–19 février 1999): Rapport"; posted at http://www.spc.int/Culture/site_pac/documents/Symposium/rapport/rapport-symposium-99.htm (11 March 2002), which includes a section entitled "Rapport du séminaire sur l'application de la recommandation UNESCO sur la culture traditionnelle et populaire dans le Pacifique Sud, qui s'est tenu les 11 et 12 février 1999 à la CPS."

48. See Resolution 25.B.2 in UNESCO General Conference (30th session, 1999), *Records of the General Conference*, vol. 1, *Resolutions*, doc. code 30 C/Resolutions; and UNESCO General Conference (31st session, 2001), "Preparation of a New International Standard-Setting Instrument for the Safeguarding of the Intangible Cultural Heritage," doc. code 31 C/43.

49. Liner notes to *The Spirit Cries: Music from the Rainforests of South America and the Caribbean,* produced by Mickey Hart and Alan Jabbour, Rykodisc RCD 10250.

50. *Heart of the Forest: The Music of the Baka Forest People of Southeast Came-roon*, recorded by Martin Cradick and Jeremy Avis, Hannibal Records HNCD 1378; and Martin Cradick, *Spirit of the Forest: Baka Beyond*, performed by Martin Cradick and Baka forest people, Hannibal Records HNCD 1377.

51. Martin Cradick, liner notes to *Heart of the Forest: The Music of the Baka Forest People of Southeast Cameroon*, recorded by Martin Cradick and Jeremy Avis, Hannibal Records HNCD 1378.

More than Skin Deep:
Ta Moko Today

Ngahuia Te Awekotuku

Taia o moko, hai hoa matenga mou. You may lose your most valuable property through misfortune in various ways. You may lose your house, your *patupounamu*, your wife, and other treasures—you may be robbed of all your most prized possessions, but of your moko you cannot be deprived. Except by death. It will be your ornament and your companion until your last day.

—Netana Rakuraku[1]

Te Ao Tawhito: *Ancient Times*

Ta Moko, an ancient Pacific art form in which the Maori excelled, involves tattooing patterns on much of the body. Men were tattooed from the waist to the knees; occasionally on the shoulders, neck, and throat; and most emphatically across the entire face. Women were typically adorned on the chin, abdomen, thighs, calves, and back. Density of application varied from tribe to tribe; some women, usually war leaders, had tattoos covering their faces, similar to men's. Unlike other Pacific tattooing cultures, the Maori tradition had one unique feature: the engraved face, in which the skin was cicatriced and colored, chiseled into a boldly textured relief.

According to British ethnohistorian Peter Gatherole, "*Moko* was remarkable because the designs were normally cut into the skin of the face with chisels, not punctured with needle-combs as was the usual case with Maori body tattoo—and indeed with tattooing elsewhere in Oceania. This carving technique obviously links *moko* with wood and other forms of Maori carving."[2] This was first commented on by Joseph Banks, like the artist Sydney Parkinson (fig. 1) a member of the *Endeavour* crew, who recorded in March 1770 that "their faces are the most remarkable, on them they by some art unknown to me dig furrows in their faces a line deep at least and as broad, the edges of which are often indented and most perfectly black."[3]

According to the early-nineteenth-century visitor Augustus Earle, *Ta Moko* was recognized for its artistry and grace:

The art of tattooing has been brought to such perfection here, that whenever we have seen a New Zealander whose skin is thus ornamented, we have admired him. It is looked upon as answering the same purposes as clothes. When a chief throws off his mats, he seems as proud of displaying the beautiful ornaments figured on his skin as a first rate exquisite is in exhibiting himself in his last fashionable attire.[4]

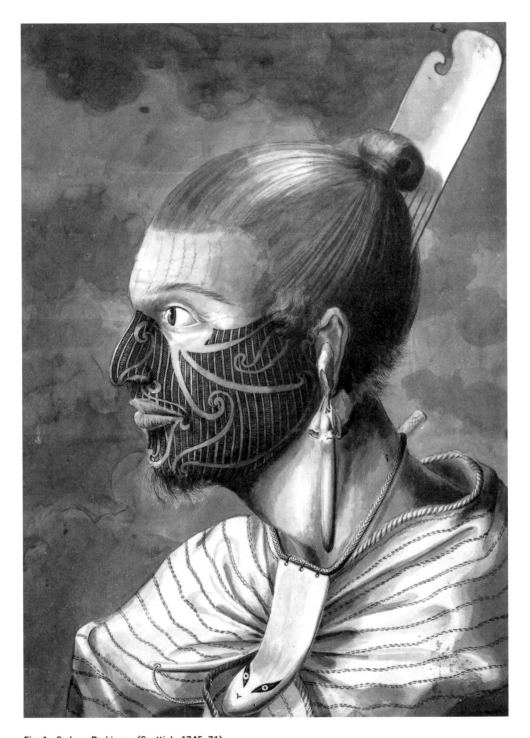

Fig. 1. Sydney Parkinson (Scottish, 1745–71)
Portrait of a New Zeland Man
New Zealand (Bay of Islands), 1769, pen and wash, 39.4 × 29.8 cm (15 1/2 × 11 3/4 in.)
London, British Library

The tattooed face most of all fascinated the newcomers to the islands of Aotearoa (New Zealand). As distinctive and unforgettable personal emblems, they were inscribed on deeds of sale and other official documents, including Te Tiriti o Waitangi (The Treaty of Waitangi), which was signed in February 1840 at Waitangi by a convocation of Maori chiefs and Governor Hobson, who represented Queen Victoria. This treaty is recognized as the constitutional basis of the New Zealand state.

Oftentimes, the tattooed face survived long after death through the artistry of preservation and the genius of Maori mortuary practice. In an issue of the *Victorian Naturalist* published in 1891, T. Steel wrote that "occasionally, in the case of individuals who had distinguished themselves as warriors or wise leaders of their people, the heads were preserved intact with the flesh, and were regarded with great veneration and respect."[5] This is endorsed by another commentator, Robert McNab, who wrote in 1907 that "they were kept with the peaceful and domestic purpose in providing mementoes to keep green the memories of warriors passed away."[6]

While *upoko tuhi* (preserved heads) are not the focus of this paper, it is interesting to note that the heads of enemy chiefs were reviled, collected, abused, and—according to Banks's journal for March 1770—actually purchased. An old man approached the *Endeavour* with "six or seven heads," very lifelike, in his canoe. Banks recorded,

> He was very jealous of shewing them. One I bought tho much against the inclinations of its owner, for tho he likd the price I offerd he hestitated much to send it up, yet having taken the price I insisted either to have that returnd or the head given, but could not prevail until I enforc'd my threats by shewing Him a musquet on which he chose to part with the head rather than the price he had got, which was pair of old Drawers of very white linnen.[7]

From this grisly beginning, the trade escalated. Soon used clothing was abandoned as currency and was replaced by firearms. A government order issued by Governor Darling of New South Wales in 1831 put a halt to "this disgusting traffic.... the scandal and prejudice which it cannot fail to raise against the name and character of British traders in a country with which it has become highly important to cultivate feelings of natural good will" of the natives.[8] This was shortly followed by an act that imposed a £40 fine and ordered the publication of the names of those concerned.

About two hundred *upoko tuhi* are known to have been exported at this time—about half that number have been repatriated back to Aotearoa and the stewardship of the Museum of New Zealand Te Papa Tongarewa. The dialogue about bringing the rest of them home continues.

Te Ao Hurihuri: *The Nineteenth Century*
With traders of flax and firearms, Christian missionaries were welcomed into Maori communities by entrepreneurial leaders who valued the new weaponry,

the prospect of literacy, and the opportunity for military expansion. According to John Liddiard Nicholas, a missionary who visited New Zealand in 1814 and 1815, these self-righteous newcomers perceived the art of *Ta Moko* as ungodly, pagan, and demonic, as a "heathenish badge of their forefathers," and its demise was eagerly encouraged. Nicholas continues, "It is hoped that this barbarous practice will be abolished in time among the New Zealanders, and that the missionaries will exert all the influence they are possessed of to dissuade them from it."[9] At the same time, it was being recorded for the voyeuristic sensibilities of European readers.

One notable example is found in the writings of the nineteenth-century explorer, botanist, and cartographer Jules-Sébastien-César Dumont d'Urville:

> The chief Tuao showed me his wife while she was in the act of receiving the completion of her moko on the shoulders. Half her back was already incised with deeply cut designs, similar to those which adorned the faces of Coro-Coro's relatives, and a female slave was engaged in decorating the other side of the back with designs of like taste. The unfortunate woman was lying on her chest, and seemed to be suffering greatly, while the blood gushed forth abundantly from her shoulders. Still she did not even utter a sigh, and looked at me merrily with the greatest composure, as did the woman who was operating upon her. Tuao himself seemed to glory in the new honour his wife was receiving by these decorations.[10]

Another writer comments further in 1859 that "tattooing is going out of fashion, partly from the influence of the missionaries, who described it as the Devil's Art, but chiefly from the example of the settlers."[11]

By the 1860s, the art itself was in decline; few *tohunga* (highly trained practitioners) of *Ta Moko* remained, and they worked only in regions of active antisettler resistance, where warriors sustained the rituals and aesthetics of Tu Matauenga, the Maori god of war. Women, however, continued to endure the chisels of albatross bone—and later metal, and then bound needle clusters—until the 1950s.

In July 1774 Omai, a Tahitian nobleman from the Society Islands, arrived in Portsmouth, England, with the English explorer Tobias Furneaux, on the *Adventure*. Omai was regarded as a unique trophy, a noble savage incarnate. A charming young man familiar with the courtly rituals of another culture, which prepared him well for his coming encounters, he was introduced to King George III and Queen Charlotte at Kew Gardens near London. From there, he made a sensational tour of the best drawing rooms of London. His tattooed body and gracefully decorated hands caused a brief flurry of indelible fashion on bourgeois and aristocratic skin.[12] Ironically, for some Europeans, and many of them gentry as well as scoundrels (and probably both), their own ornamented skin became an immediate, collectible, and erotic curiosity. From the fashionable lady with a flower blossom drawn discreetly on her breast to the heavily tattooed sailor home from the sea, the most remarkable body marking was that of John Rutherford.

Originally from Bristol, England, Rutherford went to sea as a youth and came to New Zealand on the brig *Agnes*. This ship was attacked in the Poverty Bay area in March 1818, and Rutherford was captured and marked during his first few weeks of bondage. He remained with his captors until his escape in January 1826 and worked as a tattooed man in various circuses when he returned to England. Rutherford's portrait reveals extensive Maori facial and hip adornment as well as a range of Malay and Hawaiian body work. One wonders when and how he acquired these markings. Did he collect some designs in the Malay Archipelago and even more in Hawaii, before he met the *tohunga Ta Moko* of the Maori? If so, could this explain why he was spared the fate of many of his crewmates, and also why he was later subjected to *Ta Moko* himself?[13] Rutherford was probably one of the first fully tattooed white males to be seen in the British Isles for many centuries; he may indeed have been the first modern primitive.

The Emergence of the Modern Primitive

From Polynesian and Japanese pricking and puncturing techniques, a new technology developed with the patenting of New York City tattooist Samuel Reilly's first electric machine in 1891. Western tattoo with its anchors, pierced hearts, daggers, sailing ships, eagles, crucifixes, stars, patriotic flags, bluebirds, snakes, and naked ladies found its niche and flourished. The popularity of tattooing was fanned by successive wars, and in the last thirty years it has been utilized by a massive traveling public. Many went forth in search of the "primitive," and their journeys often led to finding the primitive within themselves, and their subsequent compulsion to "change the world" often prompted them to set about changing what they did have the power to change: their own bodies. They found another frontier to explore—that of the Western human body. As two apostles of this movement, Vivian Vale and Andrea Juno, observe:

> In this postmodern epoch in which all the art of the past has been assimilated, consumerized, advertised and replicated, the last artistic territory resisting cooptation remains the Human Body. For a tattoo is more than a painting on skin . . . it is a true poetic creation, and always more than meets the eye. As a tattoo is grounded on living skin, so its essence emotes a poignancy unique to the mortal human condition.[14]

Ta Moko is thus perceived as part of "the art of the past"—a commodity assimilated, consumerized, advertised, and replicated.

Is it really? And by whom?

Leo Zulueta, of Los Angeles, is celebrated internationally as a great tattoo artist. He discovered the beauty of ancient tribal forms, particularly those of Sarawak in Borneo. According to Zulueta, he is "really . . . carrying a torch for those ancient designs. But I'm afraid that those traditions are dying out where they originated; the original peoples have no interest in preserving them. They'd rather have a ghetto blaster and a jeep and a pack of Marlboro cigarettes. The western encroachment has triumphed—all the old men having primitive style tattoos are dead…this is why I really feel strongly about preserving these ancient designs."[15]

Having condemned American consumerism, Zulueta then "saves" the art form by consuming it himself and offering it—with an appropriately lofty remittance—for actual consumption. Nevertheless, he remains conscious "that there's quite a bit of spirituality behind a lot of these tribal designs… they might contain talismans for the future or perhaps encode some cryptic knowledge…but if they're not preserved, we'll never know!"[16] For a native such as myself, perhaps the "we" to whom Zulueta refers is someone that was never meant to know. Some meanings should remain secret, even at the risk of their loss. But does he know that? Possibly.

Some years ago, a popular tattoo magazine presented an image of a unique white American male. He had a beautifully cut *kauae moko,* a Maori woman's chin design, as well as complex rafter patterning on his body.[17] I vowed that one day I would meet and challenge him. While I was in London in 1996 I met Ron Athey, a performance artist, choreographer, and dancer engaged in stretching the limits of the human body. Athey was performing at the Institute for Contemporary Art, where I approached him, introduced myself as Maori, and courteously asked him if he was aware of what he had on his skin (fig. 2). His reaction both intrigued and insulted me. He inquired how much Maori blood I had and claimed he did not know that there were any of us still around. I was astonished at this and instantly regretted the absence of a video or audio recorder to record such odd assumptions. He then exclaimed, with real warmth and sincerity, that his body work paid homage to the artistic genius of the Maori people, who had one of the "greatest design traditions in the world." I could hardly disagree, and I found myself enjoying his company but also wondering whether we needed or even appreciated his affirmation. More to the point, I wondered what my proudly ornamented grandaunts (fig. 3) would have to say about—and to—Athey with regard to their art.

Much of the body markings covering Athey were created by London-based tattoo artist Alex Binney. As an artist, Binney claims the right to take forms from wherever he looks, for art surrounds us and is universal. For many indigenous peoples in the Fourth World, however, this is just another form of pillaging, of extracting the spirit of a tribal people to sate the culturally malnourished appetites of the decadent and industrial West, whose people believe they are justified to do so.

Conversely, in the Pacific, practitioners of the enduring magnificence of the Samoan *tatau* (tattoo) offer a gracious yet different perspective. At a lecture held at Victoria University in Wellington, New Zealand, in August 1998, the late Su'a Paulo Sulu'ape reflected, "I think that the time is right that we should share—so the art can be appreciated, because it's not something that we can put on the wall for the rest of the world to see and enjoy. It has to be there, to be seen."[18]

A small number of Maori artists concur with this—some advise makeup

Fig. 2. American performance artist Ron Athey at Torture Garden, London, 1995
Chin tattoo by Jill Jordan, Los Angeles; photograph by jeremychaplin@netscapeonline.co.uk

Fig. 3. Georgina and Eileen, the Maori "twin guides" of Whakarewarewa Thermal Reserve, Rotorua region, New Zealand, ca. 1930

artists in the film industry and create designs such as those appearing in *The Piano* (1993), *Once Were Warriors* (1995), and other New Zealand films. Others inscribe their work on celebrity wearers such as British pop star Robbie Williams, whose *moko* tells the story of his life, using Maori myth and symbolism inked on by a Maori artist. Many Maori artists deplore such practice, however, condemning it as a betrayal of the art itself, no different from the cultural exploitation and mimicry of French clothing designer Paco Rabanne's 1998 early spring collection, which featured a "Maori Wedding Costume" (in metal and leather); Thierry Muegler's eccentric sartorial borrowings; and soccer star Eric Cantona's painted warrior sneer on the cover of *GQ*.[19]

The reality nevertheless remains; whether we, the Maori, favor that reality, the images are there to be seen, interpreted, and consumed by everyone. Furthermore, these images will not disappear, although a leading contemporary *tohunga Ta Moko* of the Tai Rawhiti region observes "What they do is tattoo. And what we do is *Ta Moko*. And they are not the same."[20] One wonders why not? What is the distinction?

Te Ao Whakahirahira: *Times of Pride*

> It's a powerful statement, because it's there forever. Once you've done it, you've
> made the commitment. What more appropriate way to commit yourself to
> *tikanga* Maori than to get a *moko*?
>
> —Amster Reedy[21]

In the first decades of the twentieth century, for various reasons only Maori women wore *Ta Moko*, including the marking of a significant event in tribal history, the death of a leading chief, and the birth of a first grandchild. Often women were inscribed in groups, as the *tohunga Ta Moko* were itinerant specialists who traveled from place to place, invited and eagerly anticipated. Tawera of the Tuhoe people and Tama Poata from Tai Rawhiti were the most celebrated specialists but also working were a few notable women, including Kuhukuhu of Waikato and Hikapuhi of Te Arawa. They used self-fashioned metal chisels and needle clusters and concocted their pigments from soot and Indian ink, occasionally mixing both. In some instances, women returned to have their chin adornment revitalized or completely recut if it had faded over time. The last few were done in the 1950s, by the enduring practitioners of that transitional period. Like many of their clients, the artists were dying; it seemed as though the art might die out as well. The social landscape of Aotearoa was changing, too. The Maori people shifted from a struggling rural village environment into the booming post-war opportunities in the city. Thousands migrated to the large metropolitan centers for work and education; and fitting in, or at least appearing to do so, became important.

As that generation of practitioners and proud bearers of *Ta Moko*, a few brave and determined souls—all elderly women and one man in his thirties— approached European-style tattoo artists for traditional body markings, including, in the late 1970s, New Zealand artists such as Roger Ingerton of Wellington, a designer of consummate artistry and style, and Merv O'Connor of Auckland, a canny technician whose work covers three or even four generations. The Maori world, therefore, has never been bereft of the tattooed face. There has always been at least one such face at *marae* (ceremonial sites) in the country.

There has always been the compulsion to imprint the skin—Maori youth just do it, methodically slicing themselves with slivers of razor blade, poking themselves with sewing needles, or jabbing their skin in precise designs with a sharpened compass point. This is not considered self-mutilation or defiant posturing but a compulsion that comes from a place deep within. Schoolteachers or others may not understand the compulsion, but the children's parents usually do, fingering their own faded tracings of half a lifetime ago.

For years, body markings have been an emblem of gang membership and an expression of urbanized, or criminal, Maori identity. Much gang or prison work is covered by clothing—long sleeves, gloves, and scarves; now, however, for a variety of reasons, *Ta Moko* is highly visible and applauded once again. Members of the international and national tattoo fraternities, including O'Connor and Ingerton, have also contributed to the skill base and technology of this revival. Their decision to undertake facial marking was courageous and, for Maori, very meaningful. Through their work, the tattooed face (*te mata ora*) remained in view.

By 1990, European practitioners were increasingly involved in body markings. For example, Jan and Birthe Christiansen of Denmark and Henk Schiffmacher of the Netherlands visited aspiring Maori artists, contributed to workshops on *marae,* and stayed in the Maori community for many months.[22] Some outreach has also occurred with Paulo and Petelo Sulu'ape, Samoan brothers who are the premier traditional artists of the Pacific and heirs to an unbroken family practice that has existed for one thousand years. Paulo was based in New Zealand and gave workshops in the Maori community and demonstrations at public events until his sudden death in 1999. In the late 1990s, there were still about twenty Maori practitioners engaged in commercial *Ta Moko,* working from shops or their own home studios; a comparable number of practitioners work in the tribal environment. Considerable movement takes place between the commercially and tribally based groups, and most artists undertake some ritual observation during the actual process of *Ta Moko,* commencing either with prayer or chant. Music, usually chosen by the client and often performed by his or her supporters, is played throughout the operation.

There are many practitioners working on a casual basis, such as in prisons and gangs, who may go on to become employed as commercial tattooists. Contemporary artists recognize the prison and gang legacy, which has helped to continue the practice to this day, not unlike the rare individuals who sought out facial adornment in the 1970s and 1980s despite public reaction and distaste. *Ta Moko* has become a significant and potent symbol within contemporary Maori life; it challenges the non-Maori observer and celebrates the survival of

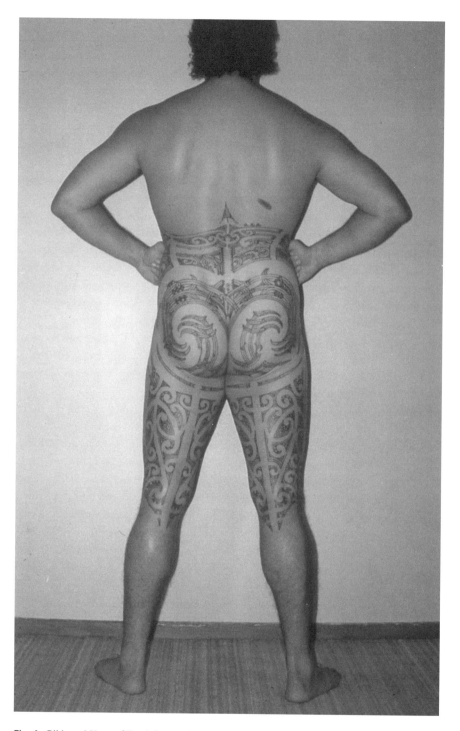

Fig. 4. Rikirangi Moeau (Maori, Rongowhakaata Tribe), Turanga nui a Kiwa, Gisborne district, New Zealand, 1999
Puhoro and *raperape* designed and inscribed by Derek Lardelli (Maori, Te Aitanga a Hauiti Tribe) of the Te Toi Houkura (Maori Arts Program), Tai Rawhiti Polytechnic, Gisborne, New Zealand

an art form that was supposedly extinct, or near to it. It is literally "in your face." The Maori consider *Ta Moko* as a treasure to be respected, conserved, and celebrated as a visible assertion of tribal heritage, political activism, and kinship networks; as a pictorial remembrance of important events like birth, death, partnership, triumph, and recovery; and as a commitment to our warrior culture. Derek Lardelli, an artist of Te Aitanga (a Hauiti people), reflects, "It is ours. It is the living face. It is about life."[23] This is endorsed by his colleague Te Rangkaihoro, who says, "The more people see it and get it, the better, for it must come alive again among all Maori, for our children, for all of us."[24] The patterns that are made on skin today, based on centuries-old images (fig. 4), will carry and protect the people into the future.

Deirdre Nehua, the granddaughter of Ina Te Papatahi who was one of the favorite portrait models of artist Charles F. Goldie (New Zealand, 1870–1947), writes of her experience, "And now it is over, and I have the *moko kauae*. And the *moko*, I know, is a symbol not of an ending, but a beginning. The *tohunga Ta Moko* says, 'Kua mutu.' It is done.... I return from Motu Kowhai. My journey into a new world is about to begin."[25] For Maori, *Ta Moko* is much more than an art form. It is an ancestral legacy, a statement of resilience and survival. It is a gift from the ancestors and should be treated carefully, respectfully, and gratefully. It should not be abused, exploited, or commodified. It is about pride, about potential. It is about the people. Moana Maniapoto, a Maori lyricist and lawyer, sings

I wear my pride upon my skin
My pride is been here within
I wear my strength upon my face
Comes from another time and place
Bet you didn't know that every line
Has a message for me?
Did you know that?[26]

Notes

1. Netana Rakuraku of Tuhoe, as told to James Cowan, in James Cowan, "Maori Tattooing Survivals—Some Notes on Moko," *Journal of the Polynesian Society* 30 (1921): 241–45.

2. Peter Gatherole, "Contexts of Maori *Moko*," in Arnold Rubin, ed., *Marks of Civilization: Artistic Transformations of the Human Body* (Los Angeles: Museum of Cultural History, University of California, Los Angeles, 1988), 171–78.

3. Joseph Banks, *The Endeavour Journal of Joseph Banks, 1768–1771*, ed. J. C. Beaglehole (Sydney: Public Library of New South Wales, 1962; 2d ed., 1963), 2:13.

4. Augustus Earle, *A Narrative of a Nine Months' Residence in New Zealand in 1827* (London: Longman, 1832), 113.

5. T. Steel, "Maori Preserved Heads of New Zealand," *Victorian Naturalist* 8 (1891): 105.

6. Robert McNab, *Murihiku and the Southern Islands* (Invercargill, New Zealand: Wilson Smith, 1907), 158.

7. Banks, *The Endeavour Journal* (note 3), 2:31.

8. Cited in Horatio G. Robley, *Moko; or, Maori Tattooing* (London: Chapman & Hall, 1896; reprinted 1969, 1987), 180.

9. John Liddiard Nicholas, *Narrative of a Voyage to New Zealand, Performed in the Years 1814 and 1815, in Company with the Rev. Samuel Marsden* (London: James Black, 1817), 1:360–61.

10. Jules-Sébastien-César Dumont d'Urville, in Horatio G. Robley, *Moko; or, Maori Tattooing* (London: Chapman & Hall, 1896; reprint, Wellington: A. H. & A. W. Reed, 1969; reprint, [Auckland]: Southern Reprints, 1987), 39–41.

11. Arthur S. Thomson, *The Story of New Zealand: Past and Present, Savage and Civilized.* (London: John Murray, 1859), 1:77–78.

12. E. H. McCormick, *Omai: Pacific Envoy* (Auckland: Auckland Univ. Press, 1977).

13. James Drummond, ed., *John Rutherford: The White Chief, A Story of Adventure in New Zealand* (Christchurch: Whitcombe & Tombs, 1908).

14. Vivian Vale and Andrea Juno, *Modern Primitives: An Investigation of Contemporary Adornment and Ritual* (San Francisco: RE/Search Publications, 1989), 5.

15. Leo Zulueta, as quoted in Vale and Juno, *Modern Primitives* (note 14), 99.

16. Leo Zulueta, as quoted in Vale and Juno, *Modern Primitives* (note 14), 99.

17. Conversation with Ron Athey at the Institute for Contemporary Art, London, 26 November 1995.

18. Su'a Paulo Sulu'ape, Samoan Studies, Lecture Series, Victoria University of Wellington, "O le Tatau: Tattoo of Samoa," 26 August 1998.

19. For *moko* in the movie *The Piano*, see Annie Goldson, "Piano Lessons," in Jonathan Dennis and Jan Bierenga, eds., *Film in Aotearoa New Zealand* (Wellington: Victoria Univ. Press, 1996); and in the movie *Once Were Warriors*, see "Movie Tattoos Spark Race Office Probe," *Sunday Star-Times* (Auckland), 29 May 1994, A3. For Robbie Williams's *moko*, see Robbie Williams and Mark McCrum, *Somebody Someday* (London: Ebury, 2001), 247. For its use by Thierry Mugler, see "Fashion Designer's Moko Trick Angers Maori," *Wanganui Chronicle*, 25 January 1999, 9; and for its use by Paco Rabanne, see "Moko Use Rude," *Evening Post* (Wellington), 23 January 1999, 5. Eric Cantona appeared on the cover of the January 1998 issue of *GQ*.

20. Derek Lardelli, *Ta Moko* demonstration at the International Festival of the Arts, Wellington, 14 March 1998.

21. Amster Reedy, "Tattoos are Back!" *Mana: Maori News Magazine for All New Zealanders* 2 (April–May 1993): 6.

22. Henk Schiffmacher, *1000 Tattoos* (Cologne: Taschen, 1996).

23. See Lardelli, *Ta Moko* demonstration (note 20).

24. Conversation with Te Rangkaihoro at Oparure Marae, Te Kuiti, April 1996.

25. Deirdre Nehua, "Three Women," in Witi Ihimaera, ed., *Growing up Maori* (Auckland: Tandem, 1998), 97.

26. From Moana Maniapoto, "Moko," available on Moana and the Moa Hunters' CD *Rua*, Tangata Records TANGD532. Quoted by permission.

Part IV

Righting Representations

The New Negro Displayed: Self-Ownership, Proprietary Sites/Sights, and the Bonds/Bounds of Race

Marlon B. Ross

It seems absurd to suggest that a race can claim proprietary rights and, therefore, a sort of copyright on the public reproduction and distribution of images pertaining to itself. The history of intellectual property is, most frequently, constructed as a progress in which prerogatives once held solely by the Crown gradually transfer to printers and publishers. Eventually, then, unlike a privilege granted to merchants by the state, intellectual property becomes a foundational economic right, protected and policed by the state, enabling private individuals to profit in a fair market from the original ideas and images that they solely create.[1] As Alfred C. Yen and others have pointed out, there is an intrinsic conflict in copyright law and history between the property rights of the individual author and the educational benefit of the public at large.[2] In copyright theory, this intrinsic conflict is normally conceptualized as one between the individual, who can own property, and the "public domain," a collective utopia in which property is hypothetically suspended. Thomas Streeter writes, "Copyright law matured in the classical era of liberalism, which formally enshrined the ideal of the abstract individual freely exercising his or her creative capacity protected by a neutral system of natural rights, the most important of which was the right of property."[3] Against these more definitely defined individual rights, rhetorically the amorphous "public domain" is usually equated with the nonpropertied general welfare of the common people of a particular nation-state or, more generously, with the larger welfare of the undifferentiated global community as a whole. To identify intellectual property with race, racial history, and the construction of racial collectivity seems counterintuitive at the least, possessing a basis neither in constitutional and statutory law nor in social organization, neither in the sacred property rights of the private individual nor in the public interest of a nonpropertied concept of "the encouragement of learning," a phrase used in many early copyright statutes.[4] A gap exists in this binary logic of intellectual property rights by bringing attention to the collective property value invested in the cultural-historical operation of race in the United States. I propose that race marks categories that determine who is legally allowed and culturally endowed to hold certain kinds of property, intellectual and otherwise, as much as it is also a category that marks the bonds and bounds of property itself; that is, who gets included and excluded from the right to determine the value of the intellectual properties of others.

When we examine the racial history of the United States, we discover that what might be called "copyright in race" constitutes a crucial site of cultural contest. Although it is not conceptualized in law as such, at issue in United States history has been exactly the rights of one race to invent, construe, and distribute images of another race in ways that are seen as distorting the properties and injuring the property value of that race. These racial intellectual property disputes involve scenes of specific white and black authors battling over the authenticity of their racial compositions as printed products; they also involve scenes of civil claimants competing for the public authority to create, reproduce, and own knowledge concerning what constitutes proper racial properties, valuations, and boundaries.[5] As the legal theorist Patricia J. Williams has ably demonstrated, race in the United States is first and foremost a property relation constituting the privilege—or lack thereof—of belonging to a particular ruling group, whose membership defines who can participate fully within the nation-state by determining who possesses the rights to vote, work, shop, reside, and attend school according to the "free" private consumption of such liberties. In a nation-state where political rights are property rights based in a market economy, and where the market itself is defined by racial and sexual characteristics and boundaries, citizenship itself becomes a property relation.[6] In the United States, to belong to a particular race is to possess copyright in that race; the right to turn a profit—or not—on the reputation credited to that race; the right to image the race in particular ways; the right to hold property, invest in, and profit from one's racial "stock"—pun intended—in particular ways. Historically, the right to belong to the white race has been represented by the liberty to defame publicly without any sort of legal, political, or social liability the whole black race as naturally inferior, a liberty based on the assumption of white superiority and thus in the natural authority of belonging to the Anglo-Saxon brotherhood.[7] In challenging this racial liberty, some African Americans and their allies have claimed their right not only to full citizenship but also to the integrity of their own racial property. In effect, they claim a right to invent and image the race to which they belong—that is, the race whose creative experience and intellectual property they own—as they see fit.[8]

Unless this question of racial copyright appears merely to be name-calling, we should briefly remind ourselves of the actual civil and property rights at stake in belonging to one race rather than another, and thus the legal and de facto rights at stake in determining who has the power to attribute racial properties by reproducing authoritative images of a race in public discourse. In the *Dred Scott v. Sandford* decision of 1857, the United States Supreme Court ruled that African Americans are "so far inferior, that they had no rights which the white man was bound to respect; and that the negro might justly and lawfully be reduced to slavery for his benefit."[9] When the highest court of a nation establishes property in persons as a matter of property in race to be the basis for determining individual rights within the state, it necessarily follows that individuals of the constitutionally inferior race have no legal recourse for challenging any other property rights. In other words, the *Dred Scott* decision gave to white men the right to determine the proper value of black bodies and of the black race as a whole by legally preempting claims by African Americans to possessing a property interest in their own bodies. The Thirteenth and Fourteenth Amendments to the United States Constitution (dated 1865 and 1868) outlawed "involuntary servitude" and granted citizenship regardless of previous condition of servitude; however, these Civil War–era amendments did not fundamentally alter the rights of property in race. In the *Plessy v. Ferguson* decision of 1896, lawyers for the plaintiff, Homer Plessy, argued against the Louisiana statute enforcing "separate but equal" accommodations on intrastate railroads, a statute that caused their client to be seated in the Jim Crow car against his will. As a "mixed-blood"—a French-speaking Creole, he was one-eighth African and seven-eighths European "blood" with no "discernible" trace of an African phenotype—Homer Plessy, through his attorneys, claimed that "the Louisiana law deprived him of a reputation as a white man and thus took away property without due process of law."[10] Plessy's lead attorney, Albion W. Tourgée, pointedly asked this question of the Court: "Six-sevenths of the population are white. Nineteen-twentieths of the property of the country is owned by white people.... Under these conditions, is it possible to conclude that the *reputation of being white* is not property? Indeed, is it not the most valuable sort of property, being the master-key that unlocks the golden door of opportunity?"[11] Although the majority upheld the Jim Crow "separate but equal" statute of Louisiana, codifying it effectively as the law for any state so desiring such, the Supreme Court readily conceded Tourgée's argument that whiteness constitutes property not accessible to people of African descent. Writing for the majority, Justice Henry Billings Brown, a northerner, unflinchingly accepted the cold logic of property in race: "If he be a white man and assigned to a colored coach, he may have his action for damages against the company for being deprived of his so called property. Upon the other hand, if he be a colored man and be so assigned, he has been deprived of no property, since he is not lawfully entitled to the reputation of being a white man."[12] By confirming the different property values of the (artificially binary) races, *Plessy v. Ferguson* makes two things clear. First, rather than being an arbitrary determination by law, race is reaffirmed constitutionally as a categorical classification of marketable property value, and, second, by exempting the legal possibilities for mulattos to cross over into the higher value of whiteness, the Court provided only one legal alternative for African American race leaders, whose ranks were filled predominantly with "mixed-blood" individuals with lighter skin. The only way to raise the property value of individuals within the black race would be to raise the property value of the race itself.

The Court's *Plessy* ruling is patently self-contradictory. On the one hand, it assigns a separate and, therefore, different property value to each race. On the other hand, it affirms that each race should receive equal treatment despite these differing property values. On the one hand, this difference in property value results from the customarily unusual treatment of each race. That is, blacks have less property value (including the fact that they can own less property) solely *because* they have been treated unequally. On the other hand, the Court uses this difference in property value resulting from unequal treatment to justify that different treatment. Clearly, as long as the property values are considered different, then there is no basis for equal treatment, and yet the Court pretends that treatment can be simultaneously equal and different. The difficult problem was how to prove the equal property value of the race. Indeed, how did one determine the value of a race in the first place? Was it merely a matter of the amount of money and material goods owned by the members of the race? Booker T. Washington took the *Plessy* decision literally, as evident in the famous phrases that echo from his address at the Atlanta Exposition of 1895. The races could remain separate "in all things that are purely social," while the black race gradually accumulates the "material prosperity" to deserve the same treatment under law. Washington's solution entailed the attempt to increase the amount of property owned by members of the race by training blacks for profitable enterprise and labor within the industrial national economy. As Washington's critics understood, as long as Jim Crow strictures were sanctioned by the state, blacks would never have equal access to capital and labor in the industrial economy and, therefore, never achieve their proportionate amount of material prosperity, no matter how equally or better skilled as entrepreneurs and laborers. As Washington himself surely understood as a master of the public marketing of his own image, property value is determined as much by the packaging of a commodity as by any definite, intrinsic worth of material accumulation. To increase the value of the race through savvy marketing would be far easier than gaining access to capital and fair wages in the industrial economy, and, in any case, no industrial strategy could succeed without a strong marketing strategy. Whether black leaders were in or against Washington's camp, the only way that they could begin to claim their equal property value was to increase the market value—and thus the social, political, and economic worth—of the race over time.

For all practical purposes, *Plessy v. Ferguson* remained the law of the land until 1954, when the Supreme Court reversed itself in the *Brown v. Board of Education* decision. Accordingly from the 1890s until after World War II, a primary strategy of racial uplift for African Americans remained to raise the property value of the race by increasing its market value. In practical terms, this strategy entailed, among other things, a massive media campaign to reshape the public image of the race by insisting on the development of what leading African Americans called the "New Negro." To gain the racial authority to invent and market the public image of the New Negro, black uplifters had to claim a sort of racial copyright; that is, they persistently had to wrestle away from whites their customary liberty of determining how the black race

Fig. 1. Advertisement for the opening of D. W. Griffith's
The Birth of a Nation (1915) in New York City
From *New York Times,* 28 February 1915, sec. 7, p. 6

should be imaged and valued; how expert knowledge on the race should be gleaned, mediated, and distributed; and who should possess ultimate responsibility for determining the standards of such expertise. With the establishment of the first modern biracial uplift organization in 1909, the National Association for the Advancement of Colored People (NAACP), African Americans and their allies began a systematic campaign to police the public image of the race, especially as distributed in modern media such as newspapers, commercial advertising, mass-manufactured and mass-marketed books, and, perhaps most powerfully, the new movie industry. One of the most financially lucrative and politically effective efforts came only five years after the founding of the NAACP with the fight to prevent advertising and screening of *The Birth of a Nation* (1915), a propaganda film that portrayed the role of African Americans during Reconstruction in a vicious, sinister light (fig. 1).[13] Given that lynchings of blacks occurred immediately following the movie's screening in many places, the NAACP was willing to sacrifice so-called freedom of speech to keep the movie out of theaters—a difficult task considering that President Woodrow Wilson, Supreme Court Chief Justice Edward White, and a number of congressmen had already enthusiastically endorsed the movie after private screenings.[14] This fight over what proved to be the most success-ful movie up to that time helped to define the national identity of the NAACP, and it set a precedent for the crucial role of visual media in the battle over racial copyright. What *The Birth of a Nation* controversy made clear is that the struggle of the NAACP against the film's writer, director, and producer, D. W. Griffith, was also a struggle between the license of a white individual to invent whatever stories (that is, lies) he so desired about African Americans versus the right of black people to censor that image as one libelous toward not any particular individual within the race but toward the race itself.

In his book entitled *The New Negro* (1916), William Pickens, one of the black leaders of the NAACP, theorized the need for an ongoing advertising campaign on behalf of the New Negro.[15] Rather than a well-scrubbed uni-form body of self-sacrificing petit bourgeois rural teachers, family farmers, skilled laborers, and small-time entrepreneurs envisioned by Booker T. Wash-ington's policies, Pickens's vision of the New Negro captured the self-interest of a varied, versatile, multilayered mass body, rubbing shoulders with the advance guard of modernity and assimilating what he called the "whiter light" of civilization through sheer contact with it. Subtitling the enlarged edi-tion (1923) of his autobiography *The Autobiography of a "New Negro,"* Pickens was instrumental in marketing the New Negro concept to a mass public of whites and migrant blacks.[16] The old view of the Negro, according to Pickens, fixes his status and value in the rural South in order to bind him to the land as a commodity based in an agrarian economy of mercantile trade, unskilled manual labor, and parochial folkways—a sort of commodification of black bodies that perpetuates the property relation of slavery. The newer view of the Negro mobilizes the mass body in order to raise the race to the status and value of self-activating and self-monitoring *agents* in a market economy of urban and urbane exchange. In his polemical *The New Negro,* Pickens writes:

> Suppose we consider the city Negro from the standpoint of his own interests. Would it be better for the American Negro if all Negroes stayed in the rural districts and none went to the cities? The Negro as a whole has been advertised in his worst phase, but the city Negro, being under the whiter light of the centers of civilization, has had his baser and uglier traits more than exaggerated. Most of what the world has been told about him is half truth.[17]

In the "whiter light of the centers of civilization," African Americans come under heightened scrutiny, but closer attention does not guarantee a more accurate representation of the race. The *only* guarantee of an accurate and fair self-image is the right to make that image according to the self-conscious self-interest of the race. What Pickens proposes and enacts in *The New Negro,* then, is a modern advertising campaign in which the New Negro becomes new through gaining control of the circulation of his own image in the media machines of the urban centers, such as publishing houses, magazines, newspapers, and advertising concerns. Describing the tactics of this media campaign, Pickens remarks:

> Conditions will be described from different viewpoints, without unnecessary repetition. The condition of the American Negro is hardly sufficiently known to the members of his own race.... But along with the great advance which the Negro can be expected to make in the United States in the next fifty years, every few years should see a book up to date on the general subject of "The Renaissance of the Negro Race" or "The New Negro."[18]

Renewing the Negro is an ongoing process of mediating that image through the voice of African Americans while preventing, policing, and protesting any infringement on that voice made by whites in their customary license to defame the race. It is because modern mass media are always seeking to exploit and expand into new markets that they create an unprecedented opening in which urbanizing African Americans can reshape themselves as a viable market, thus enhancing their value as economic agents and overcoming their customary status as commodified objects of labor. In seizing the opportunity provided by modern mass media, African Americans can redraw the boundaries that segregate them from control of their market value while recasting the slave chains tying black individuals to their race into bonds of consolidated strength. In the foreword to his novella *The Vengeance of the Gods* (1922), Pickens spells out how the need of each race to invent and reproduce its self-image grows out of a sort of Darwinian competition for survival and superiority among the races:

> Colored people often complain that in American literature the Negro characters are made either hideous or undesirable or unheroic. The colored people did not make that literature. People do not present another race as beautiful and heroic, unless that race is far removed from them in time or space; or unless, as in the case of the white man and the American Indian, the stronger race has killed off the weaker and removed it as a rival....
>
> If the Negro wants to be idealized in a world where the Negro is a considerable potential factor, he must idealize himself,—or else he must expect a sorry role in every tale.... It is not simply that the white story teller *will not* do full justice to the humanity of the black race; he *cannot*. A race must present its own case and ennoble its own ideals.[19]

The cultural campaign for racial self-interest that Pickens theorizes is enacted historically in a variety of ways through a variety of genres and media, from the public relations work done by biracial organizations like the NAACP and the National Urban League to the establishment of black urban sociology as the dominant scientific discourse on the identity of the black race. Here, however, it is important to focus on two competing theories of racial iconography; more specifically, I want to contrast two conflicting but complementary iconographic projects. One is embodied in Booker T. Washington's practice of displaying the surface of bourgeois materialism at a glance through the visual proof of the senses, an iconographic practice that dominates uplift strategy from the turn of the twentieth century to around 1915. The other is embodied in Alain Leroy Locke's advocacy of an internalized race genius whose spiritual integrity can be glimpsed only by going beneath the skin surface through the psychological insight of modernist artistic experimentation, a practice that successfully challenged Bookerite materialism during the New Negro renaissance of the 1920s.

Henry Louis Gates Jr. pinpoints the way in which the claim to being a New Negro must be constantly repeated throughout African American history: "A paradox of this sort of self-willed beginning is that its 'success' depends fundamentally upon self-negation, a turning away from the 'Old Negro' and the labyrinthine memory of black enslavement and toward the register of a 'New Negro,' an irresistible spontaneously generated black and sufficient self."[20] In effect, each generation repudiates the name, political strategy, persona, and bodily self-representation of the previous one in a bid to claim a certain kind of progress. "It is a bold and audacious act of language," Gates continues, "signifying the will to power, to dare to recreate a race by renaming it, despite the dubiousness of the venture."[21] The "new" epithet cannot merely be made as a feat of language and figuration, as Gates argues. Instead, it must be backed up with action, including momentous, news-making political activity; self-consciously advertised daily discipline; constant institution building and rebuilding; perpetual reinvention of racialized discourses as concepts and images of the race become fossilized and stagnant; and most importantly for our purposes, perpetual authoritative reinventions and reimagings of the race in mass media. Washington was a master of all these strategies in his invention and perpetuation of the institutional apparatuses comprising the "Tuskegee Machine." Early on, Washington and his allies collaborated on a mass-market campaign in their compilation of 1900 aptly entitled *A New Negro for a New Century* (fig. 2). Although cataloged under Washington's signature, the book is a compendium of the work done by leading black writers on the history of the race in America. The purpose of the book was to assert the cumulative achievement of African Americans from slavery to the present and to establish the specific progressive makeup of the Bookerite New Negro on the verge of the new century.[22] When Pickens asserts in *The New Negro* that "every few years should see a book up to date on the general subject of 'The Renaissance of the Negro Race' or 'The New Negro,'" we can see how he is revising this precursor text, *A New Negro for a New Century,* whose title page screams in all capital letters: "*AN ACCURATE AND UP-TO-DATE RECORD OF THE UPWARD STRUGGLES OF THE NEGRO RACE.*" One should not underestimate the racial aggression suggested by the adjectives "accurate," "up-to-date," and "upward." Similar to Martin Robison Delany's *The Condition, Elevation, Emigration, and Destiny of the Colored People of the United States* (1852), and others like it published

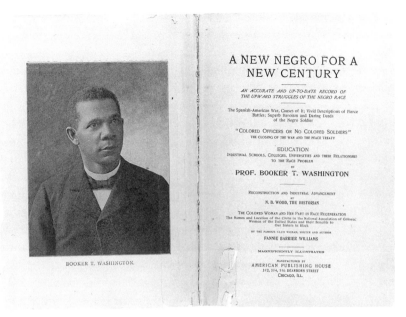

Fig. 2. Title spread for Booker T. Washington, *A New Negro for a New Century* (1900)

Fig. 3. Title spread for William J. Simmons, *Men of Mark: Eminent, Progressive and Rising* (1887)

in the nineteenth century, *A New Negro for a New Century* is engaged in an ongoing propaganda battle over who, whites or blacks, has the right to determine the nature of the race.[23] What is new about *A New Negro for a New Century* is its unprecedented emphasis on realistic photographic portraiture as a strategy for relaying over a series of repeated glances the accumulative material status of the race under the accommodationist ideology of Washington's Tuskegee Machine. It was not the first book to use the visual strategy of eminent-man portraiture; in 1887 the Reverend William J. Simmons published *Men of Mark: Eminent, Progressive and Rising,* an encyclopedia containing brief biographies with selected accompanying visual sketches of the leading men of the Negro race.[24] A visual sketch of Simmons graces the frontispiece to the volume (fig. 3), and a verbal sketch of the author by the Reverend Henry M. Turner introduces the series. Rather than using a chronological or alphabetical method, the book lists the biographies in an arbitrary manner.[25] Using the format of an encyclopedia, *Men of Mark* largely avoids any overt ideological orientation, and thus it does not achieve, or strive for, the narrative and visual coherence of propagandistic purpose set out by the solidly Bookerite *A New Negro for a New Century.*

The anthologists of *A New Negro for a New Century* perhaps see their strongest evidence for the rise of a New Negro in this visual proof, the photographs selected for admiration and emulation. In the post-Reconstruction period, photography itself became a battleground, as New Negroes attempt to exploit its technology for the purposes of displaying the successes of the race. According to Kevin K. Gaines, "Because photography was crucial in transmitting stereotypes, African Americans found the medium well suited for trying to refute negrophobic caricatures. In addition, black painters, illustrators, and sculptors, along with writers of fiction, produced antiracist narratives and iconography featuring ideal types of bourgeois black manhood and womanhood."[26] The visual evidence of these post-Reconstruction New Negro books indicates that great care was taken in selecting these "ideal types" for photographic subjects, and some attention was also paid to the placement of photographs in the volumes. As Gates points out, "Booker T. Washington's portrait forms the frontispiece of the volume, while Mrs. Washington's portrait concludes the book, thus standing as framing symbols of the idea of progress."[27] This framing symbolism of "Booker T. Washington" (see fig. 2) and "Mrs. Booker T. Washington" (fig. 4) also embodies the demand for the New Negro patriarch to take care of his own racial household in league with a strong supporting matriarch.[28] Furthermore, it enacts a normalizing gesture, making the Negro race into a respectable Victorian family. While equating the more problematic construct of the black race with the highly accommodating image of a settled, middle-class American family, the visual gallery of the volume also captures Washington's belief that the best proof of black people's progress and growing acceptance as American citizens will be the evidence of the senses, the external display of respectability through material commodities, bodily cleanliness, and transparent self-discipline.[29] The photographs provide

Fig. 4. Mrs. Booker T. Washington
From Booker T. Washington, *A New Negro for a New Century*
(Chicago: American Publishing House, 1900), 425

Fig. 5. Charles E. Young
From Booker T. Washington, *A New Negro for a New Century*
(Chicago: American Publishing House, 1900), 13

such evidence of the senses in the clothes, postures, and physiognomy of the black people displayed. Trying to identify black men with the most conventional poses of masculine heroics, the first part of the volume is devoted to the black man's bravery in historic wars, focusing especially on the very recent Spanish-Cuban-American War. Intermingled within the chapters on the war are pictures of Cuban and Black American officers. Charles E. Young (fig. 5), an officer who served in the war, is the first photo after Washington's portrait. It stands out as the only photograph to present a full-body view: Lieutenant Young is in full dress uniform, with cape, hat, gloves, and ceremonial saber. Such a dashing display, bordering on a dandy figure, is exactly the kind of appearance that New Negro men needed to assert but that could easily, under the wrong circumstances, provoke a violent reaction from white onlookers. In fact, black men in military uniform were frequently the target of white mobs during the Spanish-Cuban-American War, World War I, and World War II. All the other photos and sketches are bust shots, almost all of them frontal—suggesting the integrity of character that comes with directness and that can be read phrenologically by the shape of the head. In other words, the focus is not on the body per se, but rather on the physiognomy of the "head," which was seen as the true source of character.[30] In this way, the gallery of photographs attempts to avoid the insinuations associated with the display of the black body as the embodiment of backward savagery. These black countenances are supposed to present self-evident proof against those who similarly display black physiques to illustrate the physical, intellectual, and moral inferiority of African peoples. Ironically, however, it is the "outer" covering of clothing, grooming, hairstyles, and facial expressions that really has to communicate the newness of these Negro figures. The "interior" character represented by the dignified heads themselves can always be too easily misread as racially regressive, simply because they *are* "negroid" heads, or at least they are identified as such by their inclusion in this volume on the New Negro.

Following the gallery of officers are *male* writers, lawyers, physicians, elected officials, founders, educators, scholars, scientists, bureaucrats, and successful entrepreneurs. The photographs are chosen as much for the impression made by the dress, posture, countenance, and demeanor of the subjects as for their accomplishments. This is observable in the photograph of Alexander Miles (fig. 6), whose caption reads that he was "one of the Founders of the City of Duluth, Minnesota." Like the four-line caption listing his accomplishments, the mane of whiskers flaring around his mouth gives testimony to Miles's daring frontier achievements. Likewise, the photo of Professor W. S. Scaraborough (fig. 7) displays his tidier, softer beard, which seems in line with his more sedentary accomplishments of having written "a Greek Grammar and many treatises on Greek." Although at first glance it might seem that such a dignified scholarly pose would appear innocuous or perhaps even effete to a white onlooker, such was not at all the case at the turn of the century. For the same reason that Washington forbade his teachers at Tuskegee from carrying books in public, the costume and demeanor of an

Fig. 6. Alexander Miles
From Booker T. Washington, *A New Negro for a New Century*
(Chicago: American Publishing House, 1900), 55

Fig. 7. W. S. Scaraborough
From Booker T. Washington, *A New Negro for a New Century*
(Chicago: American Publishing House, 1900), 89

educated gentleman of the world could be very dangerous for a Negro man to wear in the wrong sites. As Washington noted in his very popular autobiography, *Up from Slavery* (1901): "The white people who questioned the wisdom of starting this new school [at Tuskegee] had in their minds pictures of what was called the educated Negro, with high hat, imitation gold eye-glasses, a showy walking-stick, kid gloves, fancy boots, and what not—in a word, a man who was determined to live by his wits."[31] In the coming decade, the heavyweight boxing champ Jack Johnson would come to represent exactly such an image, as photographs of him attest. Furthermore, as Johnson reconfirmed, it is a small step from wearing such clothes to marrying white men's daughters. Because the same accessories that signal manly success also signal the arrival of an uppity Negro who needs to be put in his place, Bookerite photography had to walk a very fine line between such easily projected arrogance and the image of aspiring but unassuming racial worth. Through portraiture that displays determined middle-class formality while also bearing a countenance of understated uniformity, *A New Negro for a New Century* is nonetheless eager to show the versatility of masculine accomplishment, for communicating authentic manly leadership in United States civilization at the turn of the twentieth century required cultivating the bold demeanor of frontier aggression and the finer capacity for delicacy in highest culture.

As Carole Marks has noted, the degree of a person's urbanity could be quickly typed by dress during this period.[32] All the subjects in the photos are from (or aspire to appear as though they are from) the same social rank; therefore, no significant differences in dress exist based on geographic region and degree of rusticity. In fact, the overwhelming uniformity in dress is supposed to indicate the consolidation of New Negro aspiration and achievement transcending sectionalism and demographics. The racial implications of this familiar hyperformality in the photos can easily get lost in history if one forgets that this style of portraiture is not "natural" but evolves as a "realistic" way of portraying the authority and respectability of solidly middle-class late-Victorian patriarchs. This realistic style of photography asserts class and gender norms so quietly and yet so forcefully that we can easily overlook how historically fabricated is the masculine attire of dark suit, white shirt, and simple cravat—a uniform no less than the ones worn by the military officers—and how culturally situated is the posture of spine stiffened, shoulders broadened, chin slightly tilted up, eyes locked, face absolutely sober. Unlike the smirk on Jack Johnson's face in myriad photographs of the boxer, there are no smiling portraits of either men or women in *A New Negro for a New Century*. In this period, not only does the convention of formal portraiture forbid the smile as flippant and disrespectful but also, in terms of racist stereotyping for African Americans, the smile too easily slips into either the darky grin or the uppity sneer. The sobriety of clinched lips, slightly frowning, is supposed to communicate the seriousness and high-mindedness of these race leaders.

The choice of isolated, individual portraits also might easily go unnoticed because they are so familiar to us. Except for the portrait of Anna J. Cooper in a conventional pose at her desk,[33] all the photos are abstract and without context. They do not bespeak the subjects' success by relating them to their houses, parlors, families, places of work, or instruments of their professions. The abstract, autonomous individualism connoted in their isolation from context, however, seems contradicted by the uniformity of their social and self-expressive representations. In *Progress of a Race* (1925), the authors extend this Bookerite logic of bourgeois materialist iconography, following through with the injunction to update the Negro's progress perpetually by associating New Negroes with the mastery of commodified objects in the most graphic manner. *Progress of a Race,* in addition to isolated portraits similar to those in *A New Negro,* includes contextual photographs.[34] Robert S. Abbott (fig. 8), the editor of the very popular and lucrative *Chicago Defender,* is shown "on active duty" at the wheel of his shiny new automobile. Another photograph revises the isolated portrait style by inserting a picture of the eight-story building owned by a "wealthy Chicago Banker" at the bottom of his eminent-man portrait. As Jesse Binga literally towers over the inset of his eight-story bank (fig. 9), we come to appreciate the magnitude of his accomplishment. *Progress of a Race* gallery contains many photographs of impressive exteriors and interiors of buildings built and owned by African Americans, and group shots of professionals, soldiers, and students "on active duty" at their work. Despite such extensions of the New Negro iconography through trick photography, *Progress of a Race* stays true to the spirit of its Bookerite-materialist predecessors.

That Washington-era New Negroes put great stock in this style of photography as a crucial vehicle for communicating the proper features of the New Negro can be ascertained from Washington's own response to a book by a white Englishman whom he felt failed to use racial photography fairly. Sir Harry Johnston, a British explorer, anthropologist, and geographer who wrote almost a dozen books on Africa, published his own book on the "New World Negro" in 1910.[35] *The Negro in the New World* provides a historical and geographical survey of the distribution of Africans in the ancient and modern eras, and it makes an assessment of the successes and failures of the Negro to adapt to the "advanced" civilizations of the New World before and after enslavement. In his review for the *Journal of the African Society,* Washington praised Johnston's book, noting how it names the Hampton-Tuskegee model as the best answer to the problem of civilizing the New World Negro. Given that Johnston was a very involved, influential, and even heroic patron of Negro causes, it is not surprising that Washington would both agree to review the book and treat it so favorably in the review. Significantly, the only fault that Washington finds with the book is its choice of photographic subjects used to illustrate the Negro's "representative types":

> Although I am not an anthropologist and for this reason cannot presume to discuss the first chapter of the book which deals with the anthropology of the Negro, yet it

Fig. 8. Robert S. Abbott
From John William Gibson, James Lawrence Nichols, and
William Henry Crogman, *Progress of a Race* (Washington,
D.C.: A. Jenkins, 1925), 130

Fig. 9. Jesse Binga
From John William Gibson, James Lawrence Nichols, and
William Henry Crogman, *Progress of a Race* (Washington,
D.C.: A. Jenkins, 1925), 230

appears to me that in some instances much more representative types could have been given. For example, the picture of the Kru man from the Kru Coast, Liberia, as representing the typical Negro will, I am afraid, be misleading to the average reader, in that the type here shown does not represent that to which the present Negro race is tending, but rather that away from which it is tending. I think that the anthropological section, in fact the whole book, could have been made much more valuable, if there had been more pictures showing the types toward which the Negro is tending.[36]

The photographs become a lightning rod in Washington's review, provoking a correspondence between him and Johnston on the question of such visual (mis)representation, and, in addition, the intellectual misappropriation of racial character. In his characteristically respectful way, Washington is going out on a limb to challenge a white man whose authority on African peoples is supposed to be unsurpassed. While presenting an opportunity for Washington's own propagandizing for the authentic physical features of the representative Negro type, the review politely but assertively sets out Washington's—and thus the black race's—intellectual ownership of what determines the properties and boundaries of New Negro progress.

What does Washington object to in the photograph of the Kru man captioned *The Typical Negro: A Kru Man from the Kru Coast, Liberia* (fig. 10) at the beginning of Johnston's *The Negro in the New World?* Clearly, he would find objectionable the nakedness of the man and perhaps his hair, which might be perceived as unkempt because it is untreated by African American–style trimming and hair relaxers. How does one "tend" away from the physical features of the Kru man except through miscegenation, a strategy that Washington obviously cannot condone in print and would not condone in any case, although he admits that he himself is the product of such an illicit bond across race? Basing racial uplift on this kind of visual representation necessarily confuses one kind of physical proof (the material signs of wealth in the West) with another kind (physical features), thus reenacting exactly what the Bookerite New Negroes are attempting to transcend, the bases of merit in physical attributes like skin color and facial physiognomy. Washington clearly believes that the racial picture presented in the photographs is more important than the text for "the average reader." In fact, it is almost as if Washington has not read Johnston's text, not even the caption beneath the picture (as Johnston himself points out in his letter to Washington). The first chapter of Johnston's book provides a typical social Darwinist explanation of the relations among the four racial "sub-species," offering a photo gallery of the most representative "types." Johnston puts forward the familiar racist ethnology so popular during the period by comparatively elaborating in great detail all the putative physical differences among the races, not neglecting the other senses besides sight. About the African's smell, he writes that "a striking peculiarity of the African Negro is the musk or goat-like smell exhaled from the sweat, more especially from the axillary and inguinal glands.... It is practically absent from many Africans who keep their bodies constantly washed."[37] Like Washington in his obsession with cleanliness as a sign of racial advancement, Johnston is attempting to draw a distinct line (in this case by obvious smell) between the "typical" Negro of old and the newer Negro, who reaps the benefits of European culture. The purpose of the first chapter is, of course, to hierarchize the races in order to place the Negro in his anthropological context at the bottom of civilization before moving on to explain how he is faring in the New World. Given this fact, clearly laid out in the text, Washington should not be surprised by Johnston's use of pictures that represent the Negro in his "primitive" state. Johnston's conclusion concerning the capacity for Africans to raise themselves up from the bottom is absolutely clear. Quoting from one of his previous books, he writes the following about the "pure" Negro type in the heart of Africa:

> He is a fine animal, but in his wild state exhibits a stunted mind and a dull content with his surroundings which induces mental stagnation, cessation of all upward progress, and even a retrogression towards the brute. In some respects the tendency of the negro for several centuries past has been an actually retrograde one. As we come to read the unwritten history of Africa by researches into languages, manners, customs, traditions, we seem to see a backward rather than a forward movement going on for some thousand years past, a return towards the savage and even the brute. I can believe it possible that had Tropical Africa been more isolated from contact with the rest of the world and cut off from the immigration of the Arab and the European, the purely negro races, left to themselves, so far from advancing towards a higher type of humanity, might have actually reverted by regress to a type no longer human, just as those great apes lingering in the dense forests of Western Africa have become in many respects degraded types that have known better days of larger brains, smaller tusks, and stouter legs.[38]

Johnston's photograph *The Typical Negro,* then, is totally in keeping with his historical and anthropological narrative in the text, for it is supposed to represent the pure Negro's apish reversion. Washington no doubt found the narrative itself offensive but was willing to let it go unchallenged. It is also possible that he felt the best way to attack it was by challenging the visual representation, with its power to speak more graphically than a thousand words.

A Kru Man from the Kru Coast, Liberia, presents exactly the opposite image of what Washington desired and had propagated in *A New Negro for a New Century*. The naked torso, suggesting a naked or slightly covered lower body, is intended to communicate savagery, as are the Negroid facial features, which Johnston has gone into great detail to explain as the markers of primitive Africanness. In case anyone is blind to the contrast, on the next pages Johnston includes photographic comparisons. *The Caucasian Type: An Englishman: Early Twentieth Century* (fig. 11) and *The Caucasian Type: An Anglo-Saxon American (W. Plumer, an Anti-Slavery Reformer of the Middle Nineteenth Century)* (fig. 12) provide the at-a-glance evidence. Exhibiting

Fig. 10. *The Typical Negro: A Kru Man from the Kru Coast, Liberia*
From Harry H. Johnston, *The Negro in the New World* (London: Methuen, 1910), 3

Fig. 11. *The Caucasian Type: An Englishman: Early Twentieth Century*
From Harry H. Johnston, *The Negro in the New World* (London: Methuen, 1910), 4

Fig. 12. *The Caucasian Type: An Anglo-Saxon American (W. Plumer, an Anti-Slavery Reformer of the Middle Nineteenth Century)*
From Harry H. Johnston, *The Negro in the New World* (London: Methuen, 1910), 6

**Fig. 13. *The Unregenerate Type of Slavery Days:
A Virginian Negro***
From Harry H. Johnston, *The Negro in the New World*
(London: Methuen, 1910), 369

Fig. 14. *A Real Negro Minstrel, Louisiana*
From Harry H. Johnston, *The Negro in the New World*
(London: Methuen, 1910), 392

Fig. 15. *A Negro Student of Hampton*
From Harry H. Johnston, *The Negro in the New World*
(London: Methuen, 1910), 393

exactly the same styles of clothing, postures, mannerisms, and countenances already examined in the Bookerite New Negro galleries, the Englishman and the American Caucasian type (who seem to be equivalent) give the final proof of how the African, if left to his own devices, will retrogress into "a type no longer human," for it is contact with white civilization that raises the Negro to new heights (and a new racial type) in the New World. When Johnston turns to the Negro in the United States in the final chapters of his book, he again offends Washington's photographic sensibility by initiating chapter 15, "Slavery in the Southern States: II," with a photograph captioned *The Unregenerate Type of Slavery Days: A Virginian Negro* (fig. 13). The tattered clothes; the uncombed, untrimmed hair and beard; and the minstrel smile communicate his "unregenerate" nature to the viewer. In chapter 16, "The Education of the Negro," Johnston does present other images. He juxtaposes *A Real Negro Minstrel, Louisiana* (fig. 14) with *A Negro Student of Hampton* (fig. 15) to demonstrate what progress the Hampton-Tuskegee model makes in training up the Negro to civilized status. Thus, he includes many photos of New Negroes, including W. E. B. Du Bois, George Washington Carver, octoroons at Tuskegee, Lewis Adams, some prosperous Negro farmers, and, of course, Washington himself. Given the number of respectable Negroes pictured, Washington's criticism of Johnston's choice of photographic images has to result from the fact that *any other kind* of image is given space at all.

Johnston's letter to Washington justifying his selection of photographs shows to what extent Johnston's racism prevents him from grasping Washington's point. Johnston patronizingly lectures Washington on the importance of showing "the Negro at his worst":

> You call attention to my having given in the first chapter pictures of exaggerated negro types, exaggerated as regards their development of muscle and their homeliness of feature, and you seem to resent this a little. But my object was (as I think I explained in the text) not only to show the question in all its bearings, but to illustrate extreme features as well. For example, in my portraits of a typical Englishman and a typical Anglo-Saxon American, I selected faces altogether exceptional [and] remarkable for their beauty of outline or for the spirituality they conveyed, in order to show the White man at his best. I also wished to show the Negro at his worst, or, let us say, at his least developed; *not* from malice, but in some way to explain and partially excuse the White man's attitude of mind towards him in the unreasonable guise in which it often appears. Perhaps, also, I illustrated the best types of Anglo-Saxon to explain why the Negro has on the whole been so forgiving and so ready, over and over again, to "put up with" the White man.[39]

It could not have escaped Washington how Johnston equates the typical European with the "exceptional," the "remarkable," "beauty," and "spirituality." Just as Johnston shows the European only "at his best," Washington wants the Negro to be shown likewise. Fighting on "the White man's" turf, it would be difficult for Washington to win this argument, for under such terms the handsome "Kru Man from the Kru Coast" will always be an "exaggerated" instance of "homeliness" and overdeveloped animal muscle. Complicating the argument, Johnston also turns Washington's issue from a sociopolitical one to a purely aesthetic one: "But if you had looked through all my illustrations… you would have seen that I strive over and over again, in regard to Africa as well as to America, to photograph the Negro and Negroid at their *best*. You will find in that same book some pictures of negroes or negroids which for physical beauty stand very nearly in rivalry with the White man."[40] In Washington's response to Johnston's letter, he seems to want to put the issue to rest, but he does so diplomatically by pointing up the relative nature of such aesthetics: "Of course, it is a matter of one's personal judgment only as to whether he likes or does not like that kind of thing."[41]

The incentive of photography in presenting evidence of the senses at a glance has, ironically, the distinct disadvantage of immobilizing the image of the New Negro over a period of time. Portraiture—whether visual or verbal—halts the narrative of progress by fixing the image in a particular historical moment. Johnston's photograph of a naked, muscled African man fixes the supposedly retrograde race in time, as the Kru man's color, physiognomy, and nakedness cannot capture his backward movement toward "the brute" or "a type no longer human." The temporally frozen nature of the photograph instead can only capture the implication of that retrogression in one particular moment of time before that regress is completed. Similarly, Washington's gallery in *A New Negro for a New Century* attaches Negro achievement to a particular aesthetic in a particular moment of time; it cannot capture the actual progress that is signaled by the adjective "new." The sober solidity of Washington's photographs, while gesturing the uniform and immovable stability of racial achievement, might be seen to work *against* the idea of social and economic *mobility*—the guiding principle of the race's perpetual struggle, renewal, and upward climb. Although some readers might be inspired to strive toward this stolid status captured in the Bookerite photographs, others could easily be intimidated or bemused. While one can emulate the expression of the countenance, can one emulate the upward movement that brought about the self-expression? More damaging to this photographic notion of the New Negro is the probability of the image's quick obsolescence, falling into anachronism even before it can be effectively emulated. By the time the book is packaged, have the newer breed of Negroes moved on to another narrative, another place, another fashion, another facial demeanor, another political stance? Are they now smiling?

In his landmark anthology about the Harlem Renaissance, *The New Negro: An Interpretation* (1925), Alain Leroy Locke repudiates the iconographic tradition fixed in realistic, dour Victorian portraiture by Washington and his colleagues.[42] Locke repackages the New Negro to show that "[s]eparate as it may be in color and substance, the culture of the Negro is of a pattern integral with the times and with its cultural setting."[43] In other

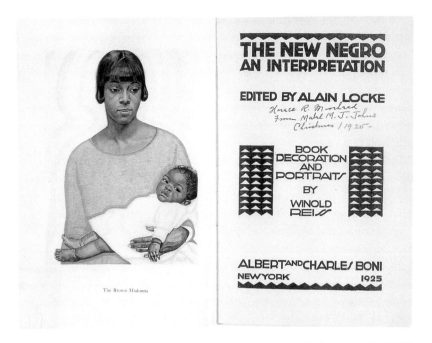

Fig. 16. Title spread for Alain Leroy Locke, ed., *The New Negro: An Interpretation* (1925)
The Brown Madonna and book decoration by Winold Reiss (German, 1886–1953)

words, New Negro culture is quintessentially modern, but not in Washington's sense of quickly progressing apparatuses of modern industry and enterprise; rather in the sense of urban and urbane spiritual, psychological, emotional, and artistic modernity. Against Washington, Locke turns the discourse of New Negrodom away from the evidence of the senses, away from an accumulative display of material and physical endowments, and toward the concept of "the race-gift as a vast spiritual endowment from which our best developments have come and must come."[44] This means that he explicitly associates the New Negro with the artistic experimentation of high modernism, with its tendency to value abstraction and artistic expressionism over figurative or photographic realism, and with its emphasis on Freudian creative and Jungian collective consciousness.[45] Locke's belief in cosmopolitanism leads him to authorize an anthology in which African Americans are ready to place their own view of themselves unapologetically next to white points of view on the race. This cosmopolitan view of the New Negro contradicts Washington's image of newness as a patriarchal, parochial family romance. By taking the New Negro movement out of the proper household, Locke attempts to place it in the pluralistic streets, in the midst of the hustle and bustle of the masses. As a result, not only does Locke welcome white contributors to *The New Negro*, including most prominently the German-born artist

Winold Reiss, who designed the book's decorative art and its title page (fig. 16); he also authorizes visual representations of common people, including sketches of Harlem's jazz culture. Ironically, this side-by-side vision of the masses and the Harlem or New Negro Renaissance's Talented Tenth only serves to reaffirm the black elite's leadership of those masses in this uplift enterprise, just as the presence of white authorities on the black race further serves to legitimate the worldly sophistication and progressive integration of the black contributors.[46]

No longer an external matter of demonstrating technical mimicry, the New Negro claims modernity by resisting the surface issues arising from controversies of black skin color, dialect, and physiognomy. Locke writes that "the artistic problem of the Young Negro has not been so much that of acquiring an outer mastery of form and technique as that of achieving an inner mastery of mood and spirit."[47] It is the inner life of the Negro that measures advancement, and only by representing the innerness of this inner life can the New Negro be glimpsed. Locke's *The New Negro* takes this problem of internal versus external representation of the race quite literally. There are no realistic photographs offering visual proof of the success accrued by African Americans contributing to the volume. The capacity for such material success must be taken for granted. "There is ample evidence of a New Negro in the latest phases of social change and progress," he says, "but still more in the internal world of the Negro mind and spirit." He continues:

> Of all the voluminous literature on the Negro, so much is mere external view and commentary that we may warrantably say that nine-tenths of it is *about* the Negro rather than of him, so that it is the Negro problem rather than the Negro that is known and mooted in the general mind. We turn therefore in the other direction to the elements of truest social portraiture, and discover in the artistic self-expression of the Negro to-day a new figure on the national canvas and a new force in the foreground of affairs.[48]

Throughout his own contributions to *The New Negro*, Locke puns on these notions of visual representation as a way of suggesting that a focus on what the Negro looks like — whether in terms of whites' minstrel caricatures or blacks' impersonation of white bourgeois posing for the camera — can no longer be tolerated.

In rejecting the bourgeois realism of photography for the iconoclastic inwardness of modernist art, Locke sees himself as pushing African American representation forward to "the legacy of the ancestral arts." Like the Old World European, the Old World African possesses a high civilization — represented by the achievement of his art: disciplined, abstract, laconic, fatalistic, and thus sophisticated. The modernity of African culture — as opposed to the lagging aspect of African American (and thus also American) culture — is indicated by a prescient modernist *aesthetic* in African arts. As Locke characterizes the African aesthetic, it counters everything we associate with the

Fig. 17. *Benin Bronze (Berlin Ethnological Museum)*
From Alain Leroy Locke, ed., *The New Negro: An Interpretation*
(New York: Albert & Charles Boni, 1925), 265

middle-class showy material accumulation advocated by Washington,[49] stressing instead emotional, spiritual, formal, and material restraint. The circumstances of enslavement and second-class citizenship, Locke argues, have
alienated African Americans from this disciplined ancestral aesthetic; the fact
of this African prescience, however, lays ground for the emergence of African
Americans themselves into the spotlight of American and global modernity. In
Locke's essay "The Legacy of the Ancestral Arts," the gallery of African ceremonial masks and sculptures brings the countenance of the African back into
sight, not through the brutality of the clumsy camera lasciviously eyeing the
muscular forms and "homely" features of the Kru man in Johnston's *Negro in
the New World*. The bronze sculpture from Benin (fig. 17) captures the kind
of aesthetic that Locke wants African American artists to emulate. What
makes the Benin sculpture of a head different from the distorting minstrel
mask forced on African Americans on the stage, in literary and filmic representation, and sometimes in the everyday life of Jim Crow? Both the sculpture
and the Jim Crow mask display a round, soft face; large, bulging eyes; fleshy,
flat nose; and frozen, upturned mouth. The bronze, however, does not construct these features through historical experience in the United States, and

thus the proportions can hold together within a different aesthetic *because* it is in a different sociohistorical context. The aesthetic of the Benin sculpture transcends Jim Crow because it was produced by an African artist in his or her own native media and according to an artistic tradition untouched by Jim Crow. It is the historical presence of Africa's continuous traditions despite colonialism that structures the sophisticated aesthetic unity of the Benin sculpture; it is the *absence* of this cultural historical continuity that haunts the African American artist. For the African American with eyes to see, the bronze sculpture can reallocate the features of the face, can reroute them through a different pair of cultural-historical eyes. Certainly, no one would mistake the noble Benin head for a minstrel mask, Locke would insist.

The word that Locke prefers in describing the classical austerity of the African arts is "stylized." Style, for Locke, is the opposite of mangling distortion. Style is not the difference between bulging eyes and sedate ones, between a flat nose and a long, sharp one. Instead, it is a matter of how these features are treated, distributed, and formalized within the historically continuous artistic medium. The self-expression found in these African arts indicates the refined "objectivity" — Locke's word — that African artists possess in interpreting their own figures. It also provides an "objective" position from which to view African physiognomy for African American artists whose visions have been previously clouded by generations of internalized self-loathing and externalized masking: "The Negro physiognomy must be freshly and objectively conceived on its own patterns if it is ever to be seriously and importantly interpreted," Locke observes. "Art must discover and reveal the beauty which prejudice and caricature have overlaid. And all vital art discovers beauty and opens our eyes to that which previously we could not see."[50] The African countenance, presented through the stylized "race genius" of Africa's "self-expression," becomes a sight of civilized beauty. For the African, the dignified face set in bronze is a continuous (ancestral) lineage; for the European, European American, and African American, it is "iconoclastic" (another of Locke's favorite words), a break with the stilted past.

It is not that Locke altogether abandons pictorial representation in this flight from a Bookerite materialist ethos. Alongside the abstract book decorations designed by Winold Reiss and the expressionist "symbolic sketches" by Reiss's famous African American student, Aaron Douglas, the portraits in *The New Negro* are as crucial as the photographs in the Bookerite texts. The volume evinces what Locke calls "cultural reciprocity," which we might define as the demand for an ideal "equivalence" (Locke's word) in the inevitable exchange of values and practices that occurs wherever distinct cultural groups meet.[51] Reiss's modernist decorations are clearly influenced by African designs (see fig. 16), and Douglas's symbolic sketches are in turn influenced by Reiss as well as by the African ancestral arts (see fig. 17). Presumably Reiss will, in turn, be influenced by his student's designs. Africa returns to the African American through the mediation of Europe; as a result, the African American becomes the prototypical genius of cultural reciprocity.[52] Ironically, it is an

Old World coalition—Europeans restocking their depleted culture by appropriating high African style—that comes to the rescue of a provincial, stagnant New World aesthetic. This attribution of Locke credits European artists with the rediscovery of the African aesthetic. This helps to explain why Locke goes to Reiss when he decides to include New World Negro portraits in the volume. Although he intersperses some drawings by Douglas and others, he commissions Reiss to do the decorative designs and portraits for the book, which gives to the European artist equal billing with Locke on the title page. He explains that Reiss's work for the volume "has been deliberately conceived and executed as a path-breaking guide and encouragement to this new foray of the younger Negro artists. In idiom, technical treatment and objective social angle, it is a bold iconoclastic break with the current traditions that have grown up about the Negro subject in American art."[53] Aware of the awkwardness implied in this statement, he then nuances it in an attempt to eliminate the aura of old patronage: "It is not meant to dictate a style to the young Negro artist, but to point to the lesson that contemporary European art has already learned—that any vital artistic expression of the Negro theme and subject in art must break through the stereotypes to a new style, a distinctive fresh technique, and some sort of characteristic idiom."[54] Locke, however, cannot so easily dismiss the vicious entanglements of old-fashioned patronage, especially given Reiss's own cultural-historical point of view, evident in the aesthetic of the graphics as well as informed by the artist's biographical relation to the subject of his art. Reiss had emigrated to the United States only twelve years previous to becoming Locke's New Negro artist par excellence. Reiss's fresh European point of view derives as much from his own European romantic ideology of primitivism as from any artistic breakthrough. In an interview conducted by John Hylan Hemingway, Tjark Reiss (Winold's son) said, "He came to America...to paint Indians.... He thought there'd be Indians waiting on the dock in New York."[55] Funded by Reiss's wealthy wife, the trip to the New World was intended to provide the young artist economic and artistic opportunities less competitive than in the Old World. In other words, just as European American modernists went slumming in Harlem for artistic inspiration, so Reiss goes slumming in America in search of an exotic Otherness to stimulate his art. As Jeffrey Stewart points out, the European romantic tradition out of which Reiss comes is "as stereotypic as the American" tradition that he supposedly breaks through.[56]

Despite Locke's attachment to internalizing tropes of "soul," "character," "spirit," and "psychology," neither he nor Reiss can completely overcome the ideology of racial "types" nor the tyranny of the external eye. The color of the Negro skin as an aesthetic object for Reiss is entangled with anthropological notions of racial types and personal notions of the exotic nature of African skin color. At best, therefore, Reiss's art reveals the "truth" inside the type and the beauty of its form, rather than exploding type itself. Perhaps what attracts Locke to Reiss's New Negro portraits is a combination of "naturalistic accuracy and individuality" associated with realistic photographic portraiture.

Setting off this realism, however, is a highly stylized figuration, which seems to comment on the constructed nature of the familiar photographic-artistic portrait pose. One can witness this fusion (or tension) at work in Reiss's portrait of Alain Locke in *The New Negro* (fig. 18). Just as Washington presides over earlier New Negro anthologies, so Locke's presides over this one.[57] In all of the Reiss portraits, the head and hands of the subjects are in stark color, whereas the rest of the drawing—the clothes being most prominent—is in delicate black and white. On the one hand, the physical features—head and hand—appear photographically realistic, as if a montage has been created with the three-dimensional photograph of face and hands mounted on the two-dimensional drawing of the clothed body. On the other hand, the portrait is highly stylized in that the face and hands float almost surrealistically on the white canvas. Inverting the Bookerite logic of the earlier New Negro volumes, where urbane clothing marks the rise of true men, here it is not the clothing that makes the man but the man who makes the clothing. Nevertheless, as it seems to suggest the reality of the person or personality—what Locke calls the "individuality" and the "psychology"—above the façade of the clothing, the portrait also highlights the texture and coloring of the skin. As surely as the picture says that this is a man to be respected and admired equally with white men, the portrait also seems to bespeak Reiss's interest in this *Negro* man as a subject due to the beautiful aesthetic qualities of the color and texture of the skin. It is the vibrancy of the color (the luscious brown of the skin and the muted red of the lips) that brings vitality to the portrait against the unreal black and white of the Western costume. What Jeffrey Stewart notes of the Paul Robeson portrait is equally true of the others: "It seems as if Robeson is emerging from whiteness wearing white culture in the form of Western clothing."[58] Or it could be the other way around: the face and hands become the mask and gloves of minstrelsy, ironically shining out in living color—the exotic against a field of drab black-and-white Westernness. Reiss's portrait of Roland Hayes (fig. 19) even more clearly announces the idea that a racial type is being studied by a patron from another civilization.[59] The head floats on a white canvas and appears to be detached from its body; it looks like a death mask, except that the eyes are open and penetrating. It also looks like an African ceremonial mask except that the head's features are realistically (almost surrealistically) rendered, not laconic, stylized, or abstract in any sense. Despite the modernity announced by his respect for his black subjects and by his experimental, stylized treatment of forms and color, Reiss's portraits of New World Negroes still present an overall impression of racial type that reveals a fascination with the tension between the subjects' black skin and their fashionable Western attire.

Reiss has clearly studied the African art held in private and public collections in the United States. His use of the mask as a movable abstraction of the face—as a way to arrest the objectifiable features of the face—is a modernist insight borrowed or stolen from the ancestral arts as surely as the African sacred emblems amassing in the private and public collections of Americans

Fig. 18. Winold Reiss (German, 1886–1953)
Alain Locke
From Alain Leroy Locke, ed., *The New Negro: An Interpretation*
(New York: Albert & Charles Boni, 1925), facing p. 6

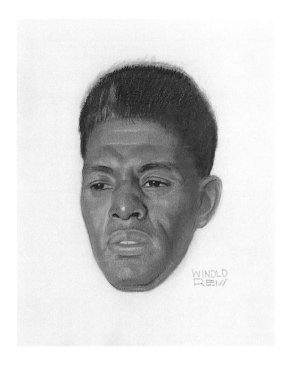

The CRISIS

NOVEMBER, 1926   15 Cents a Copy

Fig. 19. Winold Reiss (German, 1886–1953)
Roland Hayes (1887–1976), Singer
United States, ca. 1924, pastel on artist board, 49.4 × 40.6
cm (19 7/16 × 16 in.)
Washington, D.C., Smithsonian Institution, National Portrait
Gallery

Fig. 20. Front cover of *The Crisis* (November 1926)
Portrait head by Aaron Douglas (American, 1899–1979)

are bought off or stolen from colonized African peoples. More to the point, many of the African masks on which Locke himself retrains his African American eyes are accessible to him only because a wealthy white American, Alfred Barnes, has parlayed his interest in European modernism by relocating these objects to America. Locke may think that the inner life of art can transcend the superficial and brutal petit bourgeois economics of commodity accumulation represented in Bookerite photography. In reality, however, his own cosmopolitanism — and that of his modernist colleagues — is just as reliant on such material expropriation.

In attempting to use the African mask as a cultural resource, African American artists since the New Negro Renaissance have been very much aware of the questions raised concerning the ideology of cultural expropriation. Aaron Douglas, in using a death-mask design similar to Reiss's Roland Hayes mask, begins to unpack this issue by recomposing the African mask back through American and African American history and culture. Featured on the cover of the November 1926 issue of *The Crisis* (fig. 20), Douglas's portrait head de-exoticizes the colors of the face by muting them. Rather than the fortunate play of color that Reiss exploits in his fascination with the sunny warmth of African pigmentation, Douglas hardens the face/mask into a sculptural, almost stony, silence. This silence is so deafening that it reminds us of the human death always immanent in the religious meaning of the African mask. This stony silence also reminds us of how the depiction of African (American) features can so easily turn from celebration of the exotic and otherworldly into the awful brutalities and absences historically perpetrated against the real human faces of blackness. Douglas half-closes the eyes, making them vacant and thus more similar to the function of an African religious mask, which reveals the mystery by concealing the personality of the body that wears the skin. Do those eyes hold the profundity of historical knowledge or the emptiness of a hard history? More abstract than Reiss's surreal beheading of Roland Hayes, Douglas's head seems suspended between form and found object, between life and death, a somber gray that is lost between black and white and that seems to hide a face behind a mute, mysterious facade. Perhaps a critical commentary on Reiss's self-confident extravagance, Douglas's mask seems to wrench out of his white master's hands the "breakthrough" form that Locke wants to insist the European master has made. If so, Douglas is reminding viewers of the external surface of the palpable skin that the European has insisted on making a fetish. Remarking on the skin's obstinate opaqueness, Douglas turns Reiss's and Locke's artistic breakthrough against itself. We cannot see through to the "soul," "character," "spirit," "personality," and "psychology" muffled behind that face mask of skin. Only the material surface evinces itself.

As the African mask has become a touchstone for the development of African American art into the contemporary moment, black artists like Marianetta Porter have continued to use the idea of the mask to raise questions concerning cultural appropriation and reciprocity, asking to what degree African Americans can "own" a sense of collective identity through the ancient cultural resources of Africa. In Locke's time, African icons like traditional masks were still newly acquired things wrenched out of context and redeployed as "art objects" in the avant-garde European and American art circuit by wealthy collectors and galleries. Whereas Locke eagerly relies on icons expropriated and thus radically displaced from their "native" African contexts, contemporary artists like Porter live in a time when travel to the continent is much more accessible to African Americans generally, and to black artists and academics in particular. Able to see materials in their contexts, including the famous slave castles at Elmira, Porter does not necessarily need to bring back objects with her in order to assimilate and transpose them into postmodern African American experience. As she explains an artistic statement, she is strongly influenced by a trip to Ghana in summer 1994, and her work frequently engages "a number of visual interpretations that seek to draw a correlation between memory and modern African American life."[60] Unlike Locke, Porter also inhabits a moment when the African ancestral arts have long been ensconced in the history and aesthetics of modern art, as they have become prominently displayed in elite museums, in standard art-history books, and in the canonical curriculum of art schools across the world. Rather than a novelty in that word's truest sense, African artwork has become a mainstay of the American art market, and as such it presents to an artist like Porter not so much a problem of promoting a new aesthetic as one of defamiliarizing a curious cliché that paradoxically has retained in its provenance the aura of exotic, primitive, savage resource — still very much in the Western lexicon of the African Other. Douglas comments on Reiss's appropriation by self-consciously rerouting the African mask through the half-closed eyes of a hardened African American face that is imperturbable to cross-racial seduction. Although Porter takes her face masks in a contrary direction — toward the slickness that can be elicited from hardwood — she nonetheless makes a similarly subtle aesthetic-ideological statement, for slick surfaces can impede the eye's racial desire in no less a way than angular ones. Reading Porter's postmodern work through Douglas, Locke, and Washington, we find how the passion for fashioning New Negroes out of durably appropriated ancestral arts does not terminate in the 1920s New Negro Renaissance moment.

In her sculptural triptych of personas *#1, #2, and #3* (fig. 21), Porter, similar to Douglas, works against the material medium itself to present the mask as a genuinely false facade. Just as Douglas exploits paper and pencil to create a hard sculptural look suggestive of a detachable face that hides a profoundly unknowable mask, so Porter exploits the traditional African media of hardwood (basswood, mahogany, and walnut, respectively) to suggest a human face transcendently hidden in every masking facade. Porter gives us three masks in one to emphasize how the face is always a variation on a theme, all face masks possessing the same universal structure but with radically different forms. As triplets, the three face masks also play on questions of visual replication in a postmodern age of digital reproduction. Porter seems to suggest

Fig. 21. Marianetta Porter (American, b. 1953)
Persona #1, Persona #2, Persona #3
1997, basswood, 40.6 × 15.2 × 2.5 cm (16 × 6 × 1 in.); mahogany, 38.1 × 17.8 × 2.5 cm
(15 × 7 × 1 in.); walnut, 45.7 × 17.8 × 2.5 cm (18 × 7 × 1 in.)
Michigan, Collection of Marianetta Porter

how old media must seek to inhabit the faces of uniquely New Negroes, how aesthetically renewable media always seek to mold new stereotypes of familiar black faces. Each of the modern black face masks composes "African" features in wittily unsettling ways. Where Africa begins and African America ends in these playful portraits is far beyond visual reckoning, or any other kind of reckoning.

Persona #1 reminds us that the display of the face is always somebody's fashion, in some sense a self-fashioning of the self's other face in the mirror. The mask is the replica of a generalized face, just as this particular mask replicates the notion of African masks in general. At yet another level, the persona (which is itself a notion of replication) is an image that implicates the mask in the trends of art as fashion, creation as makeup, self-expression as self-performance. Is the head covered by an African wrap, a stylish black woman's hat, or an urban black man's rebellious, fashion-making bandanna? If *Persona #1* subtly encodes the seduction of fashion, *Persona #2* just as subtly encodes the defensive aggressions of the warrior's shield. Moving from the creamy lightness of basswood to the burnished moodiness of mahogany, we also seem to move from one skin tone to another, with all their incipient cultural implications. *Persona #2* exaggerates flaring hair, bulging eyes, and flat nose only to taper off in the slightest hint of lips, diminished like the lines of the face to the triangulated point of an abstract chin. When the closed-off face becomes a warrior's shield, civilization becomes "tribal" in the same way that the abstract features of the human head can be turned into the insinuations of jungle savagery. Just as *Persona #2* exaggerates the flat, angular geometry of the black face, so its wavy strands standing on end above the head suggest the anatomy of Negro hair. Whether styled or scared upright, the hair recalls the passing fashions of working with the hair as a cultural history of racial self-expression and self-defensiveness. Porter's artfulness here almost wants to make us forget the minstrel caricature that distorts the African American face in similar ways, but it does so by going the opposite direction of dour Bookerite photographic realism.

Persona #3 seems so much blunter—in every sense—that it almost tricks us into thinking that it simulates the "African" face more realistically. Although it is no less abstract than *Persona #1* or *Persona #2*, it feels less an abstraction, for the hair, eyes, nose, and mouth replicate what we have come to expect in a drawing of the black face. These attributes seem properly proportioned in relation to one another and to the structure of the face, but this is, of course, deceptive. As Locke attempted to use the classic proportions of the African ancestral arts against such racist propaganda, Porter more subtly comments on the cultural mysteries of natural beauty as racial construction. Does the persona, in fact, sport an Afro or "natural," that African American statement of Black Pride? The grain of the walnut, including the knots, recalls the artfully constructed nature of the face mask, as well as the historical ambivalence of skin tone in a color-struck society.

As personae, these face masks conjure the ancient masks worn in dramatic performance in the ceremonies of the "classical" Greeks, as well as in the ancestral dances dramatizing the acts of African gods. The boundaries between masculine and feminine, black and white, African and African American, modern and ancestral, native use and displaced fetish, cartoon and classic, fashion and art, knotted wood and dimpled flesh no longer hold us, although we insist on making such boundaries because they are so ambiguously (not) there. If Porter has brought Locke's theory and Douglas's practice into the novelty of postmodern play, she has also issued a timely commentary on the artistic inappropriateness of cultural boundaries, but without ever leaving behind the necessity of cultural binding as the pressure for an ongoing racial inheritance, not just for African Americans but for everyone in their differently converging historical trajectories.

In the end, Locke's New Negro project of stylized modernity must reveal its obsolescence as rapidly as Washington's investment in realistic Victorian portraiture. Indeed, Locke's ideal of the moment—European continental expressionist modernism mediated through Africa's classical forms—cannot evade "the external view." If we could see to the inside of these men and women behind the veiling masks—if we could see their insides—we would not need the physical features at all, nor our eyes with which to "see" in the first place. To the extent that modernism's claim to probe the psychological depths of the individual through visual imagery is based on a metaphor of sight as "*in*sight," to that extent Locke's new vision of the Negro is also a metaphor. This does not mean that he has failed to see anew. It simply means that the New Negro he sees into can be no more transparent than the old Negro whose features always brought attention to the sheer externality of racial attributes. Whereas Bookerite photographic sight asserts that the subjects are Negro in color and social consolidation only, for in every other way they are quickly rising United States moderns, Locke's *in*sight into the New Negro raises the unintended question of whether the soul—the genius of the race—itself possesses racial attributes. It is only by following these New Negro trends back and forth across time and space that we come to recognize the impossibility of answering the persistent question that Locke himself asks in his essay "Who and What Is '*Negro*'?" (1942). "The fallacy of the 'new' as of the 'older' thinking," Locke writes, "is that there is a type Negro who, either qualitatively or quantitatively, is the type symbol of the entire group. To break arbitrary stereotypes it is necessary perhaps to bring forward counter-stereotypes, but none are adequate substitutes for the whole truth. There is, in brief, no '*The Negro*.'"[61] There are no adequate substitutes for the whole truth of race, but, as the cultural history of racial copyright reveals, in the end all we have are inadequate substitutes, the masks in place of the faces, for race itself constructs the myth that there can be a whole truth, one that is able to be possessed and reproduced by the voice of one group or another.

Notes

1. On this concept of the progress of intellectual property, see John Feather, *Publishing, Piracy, and Politics: An Historical Study of Copyright in Britain* (New York: Mansell, 1994); Martha Woodmansee, "The Genius and the Copyright: Economic and Legal Conditions of the Emergence of the 'Author,'" *Eighteenth-Century Studies* 17 (1984): 425–48; Mark Rose, "The Author as Proprietor: *Donaldson v. Becket* and the Genealogy of Modern Authorship," *Representations* 23 (1988): 51–85; and the various essays in Martha Woodmansee and Peter Jaszi, eds., *The Construction of Authorship: Textual Appropriation in Law and Literature* (Durham: Duke Univ. Press, 1994).

2. Yen writes: "Authorship is possible only when future authors have the ability to borrow from those who have created before them. If too much of each work is reserved as private property through copyright, future would-be authors will find it impossible to create. Society would presumably suffer from the decreased production of creative works. Proper construction of our copyright law therefore depends on striking a socially acceptable balance between the interests of authors and the public"; see Alfred C. Yen, "The Interdisciplinary Future of Copyright Theory," in Martha Woodmansee and Peter Jaszi, eds., *The Construction of Authorship: Textual Appropriation in Law and Literature* (Durham: Duke Univ. Press, 1994), 159–60.

3. Thomas Streeter, "Broadcast Copyright and the Bureaucratization of Property," in Martha Woodmansee and Peter Jaszi, eds., *The Construction of Authorship: Textual Appropriation in Law and Literature* (Durham: Duke Univ. Press, 1994), 306.

4. The 1710 Statute of Anne was entitled "An Act for the Encouragement of Learning, by Vesting the Copies of Printed Books in the Authors or Purchasers of Such Copies, during the Times Therein Mentioned"; see Mark Rose, "The Author in Court: *Pope v. Curll* (1741)," in Martha Woodmansee and Peter Jaszi, eds., *The Construction of Authorship: Textual Appropriation in Law and Literature* (Durham: Duke Univ. Press, 1994), 213; and Feather, *Publishing, Piracy, and Politics* (note 1), 60–61, 122.

5. When taken up as a matter of law, these issues inevitably get articulated in terms of freedom of speech, censorship, and civil rights, rather than as what I am calling racial copyright. Most recently, the courts, including the United States Supreme Court, have been embroiled in determining whether municipalities and educational institutions can create ordinances and policies protecting whole groups — most popularly construed as races — from being addressed in ways that many find offensive. The question of whether there is a right and of who has the right to use the epithet "nigger" sums up this debate. Generally, the epithet is seen as off-limits only when used by non-blacks in reference to African Americans. Even though some groups of African Americans frequently use this epithet in referring to one another, African Americans' use of it among themselves has *not* been a legal issue exactly because of racial copyright, the right of African Americans to produce and reproduce a public image of themselves as they see fit. The epithet is commonly understood as a word created by the white race in order to sustain their rightful ownership of the black race, a property relation that still holds power in the usage of the word long after the abolition of legal enslavement. According to Clarence Major, one etymology of the word takes it back to the Germanic verb "'nicking,' as in nicking a coin; a 'niggler' clips and files gold coins"; see Clarence Major, ed., *Juba to Jive: A Dictionary of African American Slang* (New York: Penguin, 1994), 319; originally published as *Dictionary of Afro-American Slang* (New York: International Publishers, 1970). I find this etymology especially intriguing given the attempt to objectify African American people in terms of property, which was the intention of the original usage of the epithet in the United States.

6. Patricia J. Williams, *The Alchemy of Race and Rights: Diary of a Law Professor* (Cambridge: Harvard Univ. Press, 1991), 15–43, 221–24. Williams points out, for instance, that in *Buckley v. Valeo* (1976), the Supreme Court "held not only that it is undesirable to constrain the expenditure of money in political elections, but that such expenditure *is speech*" (p. 29).

7. According to the logic of the market, during legal Jim Crow (1896–1954) any black person attempting to defame the white race in print would simply not be given access to the means of production, reproduction, and distribution. And in cases where African Americans managed to garner these economic instruments for themselves, limits on what could be said were enforced legally and extralegally through threat of job loss and physical violence against those producing and reading the material, including the destruction of printing presses owned by African Americans. An excellent example of this "market" process at work is provided by what happened to Ida B. Wells-Barnett's publishing enterprise, the newspaper *Free Speech and Headlight,* located in

Memphis, Tennessee, after she attacked the actions of white mobs and called on African Americans to leave the city en masse; see Alfreda M. Duster, ed., *Crusade for Justice: The Autobiography of Ida B. Wells* (Chicago: Univ. of Chicago Press, 1970), 47–67.

8. By the time of the Black Power movement and the post–Civil Rights period of the late 1960s, it had become a commonplace idea that a person's race should give her or him a natural right to invent and reproduce knowledge about that race not available to those of other races. Bringing this idea into focus is the controversy over William Styron's book, *The Confessions of Nat Turner* (New York: Random House, 1966), in which the white author depicts the black cultural hero in historically undocumented ways. See the enraged response to this racial defamation recorded in John Henrik Clarke, ed., *William Styron's Nat Turner: Ten Black Writers Respond* (Boston: Beacon, 1968). Consider the representative language that Lerone Bennett Jr. uses in his contribution to the collection: "We are not quibbling here over footnotes in scholarly journals. We are objecting to something more insidious, more dangerous. *We are objecting to a deliberate attempt to steal the meaning of a man's life.* And that attempt must be condemned in the name of the man whose name has been illicitly appropriated for a dubious literary adventure"; see Lerone Bennett Jr., "Nat's Last White Man," in John Henrik Clarke, ed., *William Styron's Nat Turner: Ten Black Writers Respond* (Boston: Beacon, 1968), 5 (italics in original).

9. Quoted in Williams, *The Alchemy of Race* (note 6), 162.

10. Brook Thomas, ed., *Plessy v. Ferguson: A Brief History with Documents* (Boston: Bedford, 1997), 30. Plessy's lawyers actually exploited a barrage of sometimes conflicting arguments in addition to this one.

11. Quoted in Thomas, *Plessy v. Ferguson* (note 10), 30 (italics and ellipsis in original).

12. Thomas, *Plessy v. Ferguson* (note 10), 48.

13. *The Birth of a Nation* (originally titled *The Clansman*), directed and produced by D. W. Griffith, screenplay by Griffith and Frank E. Woods, based on novels by Thomas Dixon, 1915. On the racial history of this film, see Thomas Cripps, *Slow Fade to Black: The Negro in American Film, 1900–1942* (New York: Oxford Univ. Press, 1993), 41–69.

14. Wilson, White, and the congressmen had ties to the Ku Klux Klan, which the movie presented in a heroic light. On the history of the NAACP involvement in attempting to censor this movie, see David Levering Lewis, *W. E. B. DuBois: Biography of a Race, 1868–1919* (New York: Henry Holt, 1993), 506–9; Charles Flint Kellogg, *NAACP: A History of the National Association for the Advancement of Colored People*, vol. 1, *1909–1920* (Baltimore: Johns Hopkins Univ. Press, 1967), 121; and Carolyn Wedin, *Inheritors of the Spirit: Mary White Ovington and the Founding of the NAACP* (New York: John Wiley, 1998), 148–55. This fight was ongoing into the 1930s. The most notable successes in getting the movie banned, at least temporarily, were in the cities of Chicago and Boston and in the states of Ohio and Kansas. In addition to fighting the film in the print media, by political lobbying, and with mass marches and rallies, the NAACP attempted to raise funds to produce a counter-propaganda movie entitled *Lincoln's Dream* but never succeeded in getting it produced; see Wedin, *Inheritors of the Spirit* (this note), 152–54.

15. William Pickens, *The New Negro: His Political, Civil, and Mental Status; and Related Essays* (New York: Neale, 1916; reprint, New York: AMS Press, 1969). Very influential in the early history of the NAACP, William Pickens (1881–1954) is now largely (and unfortunately) forgotten in the annals of African American and United States history. He burst on the scene in 1903, when he won a Yale University oratory contest while a student there. He then returned to the South to teach at Talladega College in Alabama, where as a student he had first attracted the attention of white patrons before moving on to Yale. After teaching at Wiley College and becoming dean and then vice president of Morgan College in Baltimore, Pickens accepted the position as the national field secretary for the NAACP in 1920. He is credited with helping to enlarge the membership of the organization, especially in the South, through his exceptional oratorical skills. In addition to publishing *The New Negro*, two autobiographical volumes (*The Heir of Slaves: An Autobiography* in 1911 and its updated version in 1923, *Bursting Bonds*), and the novel *The Vengeance of the Gods* (1922), Pickens was a popular syndicated columnist for black newspapers at the height of the black press's influence. On Pickens's life, see Sheldon Avery, *Up from Washington: William Pickens and the Negro Struggle for Equality, 1900–1954* (Newark: Univ. of Delaware Press, 1989).

16. William Pickens, *Bursting Bonds: Enlarged Edition, The Heir of Slaves: The Autobiography of a "New Negro,"* ed. William L. Andrews (Bloomington: Indiana Univ. Press, 1991).

17. Pickens, *The New Negro* (note 15), 161. Although Pickens associates urbane civilization with whiteness here, he significantly relativizes this association by using the comparative *whiter*. Following Pickens's curious coinage of this term, I use the term *whiter* throughout this essay to indicate the relative and mixed nature of these categories in the volatile atmosphere of image-conscious, market-driven, urbanizing, racially jumbled metropolitan centers. Just as civilization in these places could no longer be seen as purely or wholly white, so patronage could no longer be so easily assumed as the act of a superior white person generously lifting up an inferior non-white—the dominant discourse of progressive political and social movements in the United States from the pre–Civil War anti-slavery campaigns to the Bookerite post-Reconstruction policies. In New Negro discourse the question becomes how African Americans have contributed to a broadened and modernized civilization, rather than how civilization can lift African Americans out of the mire of slavery, servility, and sharecropping peonage. Pickens is clearly referring in part to urban sociology when he speaks of the exaggerated portrait of African American migrants "bruited abroad."

18. Pickens, *Bursting Bonds* (note 16), 15.

19. William Pickens, *The Vengeance of the Gods, and Three Other Stories of Real American Color Line Life* (Philadelphia: A.M.E. Book Concern, 1922; reprint, Freeport, N.Y.: Books for Libraries Press, 1972), 7.

20. Henry Louis Gates Jr., "The Trope of a New Negro and the Reconstruction of the Image of the Black," *Representations* no. 24 (1988): 132.

21. Gates Jr., "The Trope of a New Negro" (note 20), 132.

22. Booker T. Washington et al., *A New Negro for a New Century* (Chicago: American Publishing House, 1900; reprint, Miami: Mnemosyne, 1969). Although *A*

New Negro is usually attributed to Washington, it is actually a variously authored anthology that borrows material from a variety of other works. Washington's name is given predominance on the title page, as though he is the primary author, probably for prestige and to aid in marketing the book and its image of newer Negro progress. I speak of the book as a product of Washington throughout because it is so clearly in line with his ideology.

23. Martin Robison Delany, *The Condition, Elevation, Emigration, and Destiny of the Colored People of the United States* (Philadelphia: M. R. Delany, 1852; reprint, New York: Arno, 1968).

24. William J. Simmons, *Men of Mark: Eminent, Progressive and Rising* (Cleveland: George M. Rewell, 1887; reprint, New York: Arno, 1968).

25. Simmons's *Men of Mark* (note 24) begins with a visual sketch and an unusually long biography of Frederick Douglass, clearly judging him the most prominent African American man of all time. The encyclopedia includes martyrs to the race like Denmark Vesey and Nat Turner, as well as the first martyr of the American War for Independence, Crispus Attucks, "A Negro whose Blood was given for Liberty" (p. 11); it extends as far as Europe by including Alexandre Dumas, "Distinguished French Negro" (p. 19), as well as scores of politicians, ministers, lawyers, doctors, soldiers, businessmen, scholars, educators, musicians, artists, and writers, many of whom have now been long forgotten but whose middle-class accomplishments at the time represented spectacular signs of the "eminent, progressive and rising" character of the race as a whole.

26. Kevin K. Gaines, *Uplifting the Race: Black Leadership, Politics, and Culture in the Twentieth Century* (Chapel Hill: Univ. of North Carolina Press, 1996), 68.

27. Gates Jr., "The Trope of a New Negro" (note 20), 138.

28. The photograph is of Margaret Murray Washington, Washington's third wife and the "lady" or vice principal of Tuskegee Institute.

29. Simmons's *Men of Mark* (note 24) also places great store in the sketches of its subjects: "The illustrations are many, and have been presented so that the reader may see the characters face to face," Simmons writes (p. 9).

30. Although I do think that the compilers of *A New Negro* (note 22) chose this style of photography with self-conscious calculation, even if this is not the case, their selection of photographed subjects suggests an intuitive understanding of the connotative meanings resonating in this iconographic tradition in portraiture.

31. Booker T. Washington, *Up from Slavery: An Autobiography* (Garden City, N.J.: Doubleday, Page, 1901), 119.

32. Marks provides illustrative photos of differing styles in the rural South, the urban South, and the urban North to suggest the prevalence of migrants from the urban South to the North; see Carole Marks, *Farewell–We're Good and Gone: The Great Black Migration* (Bloomington: Indiana Univ. Press, 1989), 102–4.

33. Washington et al., *A New Negro* (note 22), 385.

34. John William Gibson, *Progress of a Race; or, The Remarkable Advancement of the American Negro, from the Bondage of Slavery, Ignorance, and Poverty to the Freedom of Citizenship, Intelligence, Affluence, Honor and Trust,* rev. J. L. Nichols and William H. Crogman (Naperville, Ill.: J. L. Nichols, 1920). The publishing history of this volume is quite complicated—it went through several editions under various titles and

with various authors and publishers. Editions published between 1897 and 1912 include an introduction by Booker T. Washington and his portrait heads the book, but in the later editions, published between 1920 and 1929, Washington's portrait and introduction are superceded by the words and picture of his successor, Robert Russa Moton.

35. Harry H. Johnston, *The Negro in the New World* (London: Methuen, 1910). Henry Hamilton Johnston (1858–1927), the son of a wealthy insurance businessman, first traveled to North Africa (Tunisia) in 1879, to west central Africa in 1882 to try his luck as a painter and linguist, and then to East Africa and Mount Kilimanjaro, after which he became known as Kilimanjaro Johnston, spending the rest of his life as a colonialist promoter of Britain's profitable interest in the continent. An admirer of David Livingstone, Cecil Rhodes, and Henry M. Stanley, who befriended him, he pursued a career as an explorer, missionary, artist, soldier, novelist, amateur anthropologist, geographer, linguist, botanist, zoologist, and colonial administrator. Johnston traveled to the United States and the West Indies in winter 1908–9 in preparation for his book, *The Negro in the New World*. According to Johnston's biographer, Roland Oliver, "The initiative for his journey had come from President Theodore Roosevelt, who shared a surprising number of his many interests, who knew and admired his writings, and who wanted his assistance in planning the East African holiday which he was to take on laying down the presidency in 1909. With such a sponsor, invitations to lecture arrived in shoals, and a judicious selection easily covered all the expenses of the trip." Oliver suggests about Johnston's trip, "After his visit to America Johnston's anti-racialist propaganda began to assume a new note of urgency and of prophetic warning"; see Roland A. Oliver, *Sir Harry Johnston and the Scramble for Africa* (London: Chatto & Windus, 1964), 350–51. Considered a liberal among the African colonialists, Johnston saw himself as promoting knowledge of and respect for African "races" (for he more generously thought of Africa as containing many distinguishable races), for he believed the continent had legitimate cultures, though predictably he considered these cultures retrograde and much less civilized than those of Europe.

36. Booker T. Washington, "The Negro in the New World," reprinted in Louis R. Harlan, Geraldine McTigue, and N. E. Woodruff, eds., *The Booker T. Washington Papers*, vol. 10, *1909–1912* (Urbana: Univ. of Illinois Press, 1972–81), 567.

37. Johnston, *The Negro in the New World* (note 35), 11.

38. Johnston, *The Negro in the New World* (note 35), 13–14.

39. Washington, "The Negro in the New World" (note 36), 571.

40. Washington, "The Negro in the New World" (note 36), 571–72 (emphasis in original).

41. Washington, "The Negro in the New World" (note 36), 526 (emphasis in original).

42. Alain Leroy Locke, ed., *The New Negro: An Interpretation* (New York: Albert & Charles Boni, 1925). Born Arthur Locke in Philadelphia in 1885 into a middle-class family of free Northern lineage, Alain Leroy Locke (the name he chose and became known by) possessed forebears who had been teachers and missionaries. His father (who died in 1891) had served as private secretary to O. O. Howard and as an accountant in the Freedman's Bureau, before receiving his law degree from Howard University, and returning to Philadelphia to work as a clerk for the United States Post Office.

Locke's mother worked as a teacher to support the family; after he moved to Washington, D.C., she lived with her son until her death in 1922. Locke studied philosophy at Harvard University (1904–8) and was named the first African American Rhodes scholar, at Hertford College, Oxford (1908–10), as well as at the Friedrich-Wilhelms-Universität zu Berlin (1910–11). He served as an instructor at Howard (1912–16), returning to Harvard for his doctorate (1916–17, awarded 1918). Locke was chair of Howard's philosophy department from 1917 to 1925, when he, along with other African American professors, was fired by the university in order to calm protests over the disparity between the salaries of black and white faculty. It is during this brief period of leave from Howard that Locke became more active in the New Negro Renaissance as an editor, reviewer, critic, theorist, and patron, compiling the *Survey Graphic Magazine*'s March 1925 special issue on Negro culture, out of which came his anthology *The New Negro: An Interpretation* (this note). Rehired by Howard in 1928, Locke served as chair of philosophy until his death in 1954. Although he is still best known for *The New Negro*, Locke was a prolific reviewer, writing annual reviews of Negro literature for *Opportunity*, as well as articles, essays, and reviews for other journals on African art and culture, African American culture, adult education (in which he became passionately involved in the 1930s), and academic philosophy. At Howard he had a large impact on the curriculum of the liberal arts college beyond the teaching of philosophy. Locke was the teacher of a large number of students, including E. Franklin Frazier, who later achieved great success and credited Locke with playing a significant role in his intellectual development. For biographical information on Locke, see Leonard Harris, "Rendering the Text," in Alain Locke, *The Philosophy of Alain Locke: Harlem Renaissance and Beyond*, ed. Leonard Harris (Philadelphia: Temple Univ. Press, 1989), 3–8; Eugene C. Holmes, "Alain Leroy Locke: A Sketch," *Phylon* 20 (1959): 82–89; William M. Brewer, "Alain Leroy Locke," *Negro History Bulletin* 18 (1954): 26, 32; and Jeffrey C. Stewart, ed., *The Critical Temper of Alain Locke: A Selection of His Essays on Art and Culture* (New York: Garland, 1983), 3.

43. My discussion of Locke's philosophy of the New Negro draws on all of the essays he contributed to *The New Negro* (note 42): the "Foreword" (pp. ix–xi); the lead essay, also entitled "The New Negro" (pp. 3–16); "Negro Youth Speaks" (pp. 47–53), the essay introducing the largest, and clearly in his eyes the most important, section of the same name; "The Negro Spirituals" (pp. 199–213); and his art-historical piece on the modernity and sophistication of African art, "The Legacy of the Ancestral Arts" (pp. 254–77).

44. Locke, "Negro Youth Speaks" (note 43), 47.

45. Concerning the influence of Carl Jung and Sigmund Freud on Locke, see Johnny Washington, *A Journey into the Philosophy of Alain Locke* (Westport, Ill.: Greenwood, 1994), 34, 131–34.

46. The term *Talented Tenth* originates with the early writing of W. E. B. Du Bois, who argues that one-tenth of the black population possessing greater access to formal education, professional vocations, decent salaries (and thus to middle-class pretensions), had an obligation to serve and lift up the black masses who lacked such resources. Similar to Washington, Du Bois also argues that representations of the race should focus on this middle-class group rather than on the black masses, whose images

were most frequently stereotyped as racially representative in dominant white media. See W. E. B. Du Bois, *The Souls of Black Folk* (New York: Viking Penguin, 1989; originally published in 1903), 74–90; and idem, *The Philadelphia Negro: A Social Study* (Philadelphia: Univ. of Pennsylvania Press, 1996; originally published in 1899), 309–21. Although Locke is influenced by Du Bois's idea of the Talented Tenth, he also wants to credit the black masses with greater initiative and autonomy than the Du Boisian concept allows. As Washington notes, "On the one hand, he maintained that the aesthetic tastes of the Black masses lacked refinement and, on the other, he insisted that the Black masses were the repository of cultural and spiritual energy, from which the artist must draw in order to produce culture"; see Johnny Washington, *Alain Locke and Philosophy: A Quest for Cultural Pluralism* (Westport, Ill.: Greenwood, 1986), 168. For another superb reading of Locke's ambivalence toward the black masses in his ideal of the urban racial community, see Charles Scruggs, *The Sage in Harlem: H. L. Mencken and the Black Writers of the 1920s* (Baltimore: Johns Hopkins Univ. Press, 1984), 92–102. Locke's ambivalence is captured in this statement: "No sane observer, however sympathetic to the new trend, would contend that the great masses are articulate as yet, but they stir, they move, they are more than physically restless"; see Locke, *The New Negro* (note 42), 7.

47. Locke, "Negro Youth Speaks" (note 43), 48.

48. Locke, *The New Negro* (note 42), ix.

49. This bourgeois aesthetic of exuberant accumulation and comfort can still be glimpsed in Washington's house, the Oaks, on the campus of Tuskegee University. Of note is how Washington displayed in his study the furniture, pictures, paintings, books, and gifts from famous patrons.

50. Locke, "The Legacy of Ancestral Arts" (note 43), 264.

51. Alain Locke, "Unity through Diversity: A Baha'í Principle" and "The Contribution of Race to Culture," both reprinted in his *The Philosophy of Alain Locke: Harlem Renaissance and Beyond,* ed. Leonard Harris (Philadelphia: Temple Univ. Press, 1989), 134–38, 202–6.

52. Houston A. Baker Jr. persuasively points to the combination of "marronage, masses, and modernism" coming together in Locke's anthology "in a striking, even an aggressive manner." He points to the ways in which *The New Negro* conceptualizes its contributors' aspirations as "coextensive with global strivings" and the migrant black mass as "a marooned society or nation existing on the frontiers or margins of *all* American promise, profit, and modes of production"; see Houston A. Baker Jr., *Modernism and the Harlem Renaissance* (Chicago: Univ. of Chicago Press, 1987), 79, 74, 77 (emphasis in original).

53. Winold Reiss was the art editor of *Survey Graphic Magazine* and as such was responsible for the expressionist designs of the special issue, *Harlem: Mecca of the New Negro* (vol. 6, no. 6 [1925]; reprint, Baltimore: Black Classic Press, 1980), out of which Locke's *The New Negro* grew.

54. Locke, "The Legacy of Ancestral Arts" (note 43), 266.

55. As quoted in John Hemingway, "An Immigrant Artist Captured the Faces of the New World," *Smithsonian* (November 1989), 172–83.

56. Jeffrey C. Stewart [a.k.a. Jeffrey C. Smith], *To Color America: Portraits by*

Winold Reiss (Washington, D.C.: Smithsonian Institution Press, 1989), 50.

57. Actually, Reiss's drawing *The Brown Madonna* presides over the volume. This portrait recalls neither a medieval Christian allegory nor a Victorian domestic scene. Like the other anonymous portraits of women, it seems instead to elicit an inviting feminine aesthetic sphere with a subtle erotic flavor.

58. Stewart, *To Color America* (note 56), 49.

59. The drawing of Hayes was used as the cover of the Harlem special issue of *Survey Graphic Magazine* (note 42).

60. 60. Marianetta Porter, artistic statement written for *Facing Forward, Looking Back*, an exhibition at the Matrix Gallery, Ann Arbor, Michigan, in 1997.

61. Alain Locke, "Who and What Is 'Negro'?," *Opportunity*, 20 (1942): 36–41, 83–87; reprinted in Locke, *The Philosophy of Alain Locke: Harlem Renaissance and Beyond*, ed. Leonard Harris (Philadelphia: Temple Univ. Press, 1989), 209–28.

The Birth of Whose Nation?
The Competing Claims of National and Ethnic Identity and the "Banning" of *Huckleberry Finn*

Jonathan Arac

According to the sociologist Paul Gilroy in *Against Race*, his challenging new attempt at "imagining political culture beyond the color line," a defining anxiety of our present moment is "the emphasis on culture as a form of property to be owned rather than lived."[1] As the historian Elazar Barkan has argued, in the burgeoning discussions and debates provoked by these anxieties, a key term has been cultural *appropriation*.[2] Yet the negative connotation with which this term has been weighted is somewhat puzzling. It is not nearly so negative a term as *expropriation*. Appropriation focuses on the beneficiary of the process, expropriation on the loser; and I have a far warmer fellow feeling for someone who likes something (and so appropriates it) than for someone who takes it away from someone else (expropriates it).

These issues of appropriation and expropriation bear on the history of debates concerning a great American novel, for Mark Twain's *The Adventures of Huckleberry Finn* is implicated in a process of cross-cultural transactions that may not be so benign as give-and-take. For nearly a century in the United States, beginning in the 1830s, blackface minstrelsy was a widely popular form of entertainment. It allowed many white people to make a living by rendering their impressions of art forms and cultural practices that had originated with African Americans, who were denied access to the financial rewards a white audience could provide. Eric Lott's study of blackface minstrelsy transforms the terms *appropriation* and *expropriation*, with straightforward power, into *love* and *theft*. In the 1970s, Ralph Ellison wrote with relief that in the United States the age of cultural expropriation was over: "We've reached a stage of general freedom in which it is no longer possible to take the products of a slave or an illiterate artist without legal consequence."[3] But the love and theft that produced minstrelsy also made possible the art of *Huckleberry Finn*, as Ellison had pointed out in "Change the Joke and Slip the Yoke" (1958), in which he identified Twain's figure of the fugitive slave Jim as "fitted into the outlines of the minstrel tradition."[4]

It causes trouble to this day that Twain's novel, first published in 1885, a product of radically unequal relations of power, has been widely taken as an icon of American identity, as the book that "we have embraced as most expressive of who we really are."[5] Who is meant by "we," and what, exactly, is real? Some Americans gain a desired identity by this process, but at a cost to other Americans.

Writing for an interdisciplinary and global audience requires establishing a few fundamental facts about *Huckleberry Finn* as a cultural object in the United States. To this end, I present a recent moment of controversy in my former home state of Pennsylvania, and after rather rapidly sketching this incident, then reprise the issues, both on a larger scale and in more detail.[6]

Huckleberry Finn is the most widely known work of American literature, both the most admired and the most loved. In the United States, there is no nationally mandated curriculum, yet this book is taught in most schools across the nation. In recent decades it has been widely claimed by teachers and scholars as a weapon against racism in the classroom. For them it has become an idol of interracial goodwill. This educational role is the focus of my inquiry; that is why I put the word *banning* in quotation marks in the title of this essay. Most of what is imagined to be the defense against the banning of *Huckleberry Finn* is in fact argument over its place in the schools. It is not a First Amendment, free speech issue, but a question of educational policy.

In February 1998, as part of what is "Black History Month" in the United States, the Pennsylvania state chapter of the National Association for the Advancement of Colored People (NAACP) put forward a resolution requesting schools not to make *Huckleberry Finn* required reading.[7] The NAACP has targeted it as racially offensive. How can this be? The answer lies in the explosive powers of the term *nigger*.

Twain's novel is a bold experiment because it is told in the voice of Huck, a poorly educated preteen boy of the 1840s. He has grown up in Missouri amid a system of slavery in which some white people owned African Americans as property. Slavery was part of his world, and he uses the offensive term *nigger* hundreds of times.[8] In fact, the reader can scarcely read one page without encountering it. Huck uses this word, which is associated with the domination of whites over blacks; yet Huck helps Jim, who is fleeing from slavery. Huck's deeds are better than his words; while his words are the book's strength, they also pose an obstacle to many readers. This is the difficulty of irony. As literary scholars have long recognized, irony cannot be reliably controlled, for it always depends on differences in position.[9]

The NAACP does not want to ban the book; rather, it wants to change the way educators and parents think about it. The NAACP does not say that the book, or Mark Twain, is racist. It says that the book makes for bad classroom experiences.

Why did *Huckleberry Finn* become the most widely taught American book in postsecondary schools at all grade levels? It is a tremendously funny book, but that has never been enough to win a place in the classroom canon. School boards demand higher values than pleasure. It has long been loved by millions of readers, but only in the last fifty years have large numbers of critics, scholars, and teachers called it the greatest American novel and attached to it high moral meaning. For many readers in positions of authority, *Huckleberry Finn* seemed morally great because it showed a white person overcoming the prejudices of his background. This seemed a very important model for the schoolroom, because in the years after World War II the Allied triumph over Nazi racism fueled the wish to bring about racial equality in the United States.

For many liberal teachers and writers, *Huckleberry Finn* symbolized the ideals of the Civil Rights movement. For many African Americans, however, it has seemed wrong that the classroom model for racial equality should be a white person who uses racially offensive language. Once *Huckleberry Finn* became an idol of interracial goodwill, it also became a target for criticism and protest by African Americans. This pattern has occurred often in the last twenty years and has been widely discussed in newspapers and broadcast media.

The cultural and educational establishment have accorded great value to Twain's novel. Against this, the recent NAACP initiative argues that *Huckleberry Finn* should not hold a place as the highest example of American excellence, as it does in many curricula. For the last two decades, attempts like those of the NAACP have regularly been met by fierce opposition. If the book symbolizes America's moral excellence, then it hurts to have it questioned. Because *Huckleberry Finn* has become an idol, its defenders, inadvertently but regularly, make inaccurate and misleading statements. They have lost contact with the book itself and recall only an idealized memory.

When the Associated Press learned of the NAACP's initiative, it contacted the Office for Intellectual Freedom at the American Library Association. The director of this office defended the book, claiming that "Jim's name is Nigger Jim in the book because that's exactly what he would have been called at the time."[10] She is, however, completely wrong about Jim's name. In *Huckleberry Finn*, Jim is called Jim. It is only innumerable cultural authorities, such as the *New York Times*, Harvard professors, Pulitzer Prize–winning historians, and Twain scholars in *TLS*, the *Times Literary Supplement*, as recently as 1996 who call him "Nigger Jim."[11] Idolatry of the book has successfully taught one lesson: that it is acceptable to use the word — after all, America's greatest novel uses it.

The way *Huckleberry Finn* has been taught, written about, and discussed since the 1950s has allowed many teachers, writers, and directors of intellectual freedom to believe, wrongly, that there was once a time in the United States when *nigger* was not a term meant to wound and humiliate. The historian Edward Ayers, in his Pulitzer Prize–winning study of Southern life after Reconstruction, recounts this etiquette lesson from a memoir. A white youngster referred to a respected black man as "Mr. Jones." His aunt corrected him: "Robert Jones is a nigger. You don't say 'mister' when you speak of a nigger. You don't say 'Mr. Jones,' you say 'nigger Jones.'"[12] The term was clearly understood as a weapon to keep whites on top. Mark Twain showed sensitivity to this issue in keeping Jim simply "Jim," and yet humiliation is still felt when African American students are made to swallow the term hundreds of times in order to pass an English course.

Nonetheless, *Huckleberry Finn* appears in almost every curriculum. A scholarly survey in the early 1990s indicates that *Huckleberry Finn* was required reading in more than 70 percent of American high schools.[13] This means, among other things, that each year taxpayers pay for scores of thousands of copies of *Huckleberry Finn*. Only Shakespeare was more often required reading, and then only if all his plays are added together. *Huckleberry Finn* was required far more than any particular play of Shakespeare, more than any other work of American literature, more than any other work of fiction, or any other long work in any genre. I have coined a term to denote this extraordinary standing: *hypercanonization*.

Huckleberry Finn was widely bought, read, and loved from its first publication in 1885, but it was slow to make its way into schools. It is not obvious that it set a good example, for its title character, hero, and narrator, Huck, is shy of schooling and his speech is not an example of proper grammar, either in its syntax or its vocabulary. Shortly after its publication in 1850, *The Scarlet Letter* became the first still-canonical work of American literature to be taught in high school because its prose was decorous and its morality repressive. In contrast, it was not until after World War II that *Huckleberry Finn* became a national cultural property in this sense.

Almost as soon as it entered the classroom, *Huckleberry Finn* became an object of controversy. Ever since the 1954 decision of the Supreme Court *Brown v. The Board of Education* struck down racial segregation in the schools and gave the legitimacy of national policy to the presence of African Americans in classrooms with whites, there have been protests by African Americans against requiring a book whose language is saturated in the single most symbolically offensive term in the American vocabulary — *nigger*. *Huckleberry Finn* has become both an idol and a target.

Mark Twain died in 1910, and in 1920 the new model intellectual Van Wyck Brooks, a Harvard contemporary of T. S. Eliot, authored a psychobiographical cultural critique, *The Ordeal of Mark Twain*, which suggested that Twain should be left behind as America matured. Measured against the work of Jonathan Swift, Voltaire, or even Charles Dickens, Brooks argued, Twain did not achieve a major body of satiric art. In Brooks's analysis, Twain had failed to keep his outsider's radical perspective and was too eager to be accepted by the dominant, genteel, corporate culture. For Brooks, because Twain was so widely read and loved, he served as an apt symptom for diagnosis of the national malady.

To answer Brooks involved a judgment of American culture as well as of Twain. Bernard DeVoto provided this in *Mark Twain's America* of 1932, which concludes with an admonitory memento. As opposed to the optative mood that motivates Brooks, whose America was still to be wished into existence, DeVoto asserted a past perfect indicative: "There is, remember, such an entity. It seems necessary to explain that America has existed, has had a past."[14] DeVoto was a figure in American letters and scholarship who still is not reckoned at his full consequence. From 1935 until his death in 1955, he wrote a column called the "Editor's Easy Chair" for *Harper's Magazine;* before being denied tenure at Harvard, he had contributed to the founding of its doctoral program in American civilization in 1937; and he was a Pulitzer Prize–winning and best-selling historian of the American frontier in the 1940s. He was the first real scholar of Twain, and he made crucial contributions to the process by which Mark Twain was converted from private intellectual property to national cultural property.

Samuel L. Clemens was the first to recognize Mark Twain as a matter of property: "Mark Twain" is not simply Clemens's pen name but a registered trademark. During the years that he was writing *Huckleberry Finn,* Twain was also actively involved in arguing for international copyright agreements that would protect authors from what was called "piracy," the unauthorized but legal reproduction and mass sale of their works in cheap editions by publishers who paid no royalties to the authors. The gaps in international copyright allowed British works to be appropriated by American publishers and allowed Canadian publishers to export pirated editions of Twain into the United States.[15]

In December 1881 Twain traveled to Canada to establish a Canadian copyright for *The Prince and the Pauper,* and he spoke bitingly about the oddities in regulation of verbal property. He looked forward to the time when, "in the eye of the law," literary property "will be as sacred as whiskey, or any other of the necessaries of life." He explained that the identity of whiskey was guarded by the law but that the identity of literature was not: "If you steal another man's label to advertise your own brand of whiskey with, you will be heavily fined . . . for violating that trademark." Moreover, "if you steal the whiskey without the trademark, you go to jail." However, in the existing state of law, you would be free to steal them both "if you could prove that the whiskey was literature." And by the same token, Twain speculated, literature might be treated with greater respect by the law if only "a body could . . . get drunk on it."[16]

To this day, scholars of Twain include a remarkable credit line in their archivally based publications (and note in the first line of what follows that the key term is indeed *words,* not a misprint for *works*):

> Mark Twain's previously unpublished words quoted here are copyright [date] by Edward J. Willi and Manufacturers Hanover Trust Company as Trustees of the Mark Twain Foundation, which reserves all reproduction or dramatization rights in every medium. Quotation is made with the permission of the University of California Press and Dr. Robert H. Hirst, General Editor of the Mark Twain Project. Each quotation is identified by an asterisk (*).[17]

The little stars spattered in a scholar's text are the merit badges for having found good words of Twain's never before published, and in turn they mark the growth of the foundation's legally certified property.

A key moment in transforming Twain from private to state property occurred in the middle of this century, when the University of California undertook the guardianship of the Mark Twain Papers. The materials of the literary estate were deposited at Berkeley in 1949, and when Clemens's last survivor, daughter Clara Clemens Samossoud, died in 1962, they were bequeathed to the University of California.[18] Shortly thereafter, the University of California and its press began the prodigious editorial and publication project that is, for instance, bringing out Twain's correspondence at a rate of about one volume per year of his adulthood. As a mark of the national cultural stakes, this editorial project has been "supported, without interruption, since 1967" by grants from the National Endowment for the Humanities, an agency itself established only as recently as 1965.[19]

Before this current national public system began, and after the death of Albert Bigelow Paine in 1937, who had been Twain's Boswell—interviewer and authorized biographer—the papers were in the care of DeVoto, literary executor of Samuel Clemens's estate, for nearly a decade. DeVoto's edited selection from manuscript autobiographical papers, *Mark Twain in Eruption* (1940), and a documentary critical study of manuscripts of Twain's fiction, *Mark Twain at Work* (1942), are two books that still have currency. Both arose from DeVoto's labors in the archives.

The trustees of the Twain estate, however, had in mind to cash in their property more directly, and they kept instructing DeVoto to appraise the value of the materials. In January 1944, he wrote the estate's lawyer a letter that laid the foundations for current academic scholarship on Twain. Two things are immediately evident in this letter. First, it argues strongly and persuasively for the value of the archive as capital rather than as commodity, as a resource from which money may be made not by its being sold but by the productive use to which it may be put. Second, he argues that this capitalization of the archive will bring in greater income than would its sale. In retrospect, he may have been wrong about this for two reasons: because of the immense growth in price for celebrity memorabilia and because the Twain Foundation does not necessarily receive the payoff from the kind of work that DeVoto envisioned and that has, in fact, come to pass. The following is what he wrote:

> Over the years, it seems to me, by far the greatest asset is the sale of Mark Twain's books and of such subsidiary rights in them as movie, radio, etc. Compared with this, the value of our collection is slight, even if you realize $100,000 from it (as you wouldn't). Our main job is what may be called institutional advertising—the spread of discussion of Mark Twain in order to maintain and increase the sale of his books. Thus, if I were to go on and complete the edition of letters and make the edition of notebooks as our original plan called for, both books would sell well and go on selling. Both would make 10 to 20 thousand dollars in themselves. But far more important would be the fact that they would lead old readers to buy Mark's books and create new readers who would also buy them. You have made $8,000 in royalties from *Mark Twain in Eruption*, which I edited, and in the end will make twice that. But in the end also you will make four times $8,000 from the sale of Mark Twain's

books which would not have been sold except for the stimulation of old readers and the creation of new readers by *Mark Twain in Eruption*.

Similarly with the books I have written and may yet write—and the books which other qualified students may write about Mark Twain, the institutional advertising which such books will create will be of great and in fact indispensable value. In fact, if Mark Twain is to go on selling, he must go on being discussed, and if he is to be discussed books about him, especially controversial books, must continue to be written.

That is the one prime reason for keeping our collection together as a unit—so that I and other qualified students can use it for the writing of books about Mark Twain.[20]

DeVoto's logic still proves powerful. The most successfully controversial scholarly work about Mark Twain in my lifetime—Shelley Fisher Fishkin's book *Was Huck Black?* (1993)—led immediately into an immense book-selling project. To attract new and old readers alike, this project offers at a modest price a set of twenty-nine well-made clothbound facsimiles of the American first editions of Twain's books, all published in his lifetime and now out of copyright, with introductions by notable literary figures and scholarly afterwords by an honor roll of Twainians, all under the general editorship of Professor Fishkin and under the imprint of the world's greatest brand name for scholarship: Oxford University Press.

The publication of DeVoto's massive cultural history, *Mark Twain's America*, published in 1932 and still in print, won him the standing that brought him the Twain papers. The title plays with the double sense of the genitive case. DeVoto provides the American context that he argues, explains Twain, but he also makes the case for Twain's possession of America. For DeVoto, Twain "more completely than any other writer, took part in the American experience."[21] As the scholar Louis J. Budd has detailed, by the later years of Twain's life, he was widely known to American journalists as "our" Mark Twain, and caricaturists imaged him in the iconography of the national figuration his birthname echoed, Uncle Sam.[22] DeVoto contributed the scholarly goods to make the connection of the man and nation endure beyond Samuel Clemens's death. Since DeVoto, scholars and journalists have unhesitatingly, repetitiously, praised *Huckleberry Finn* by characterizing it as "quintessentially American."[23]

For DeVoto, it was an important feature of the Americanness of both Twain and *Huckleberry Finn* that America included the cultural contributions of its enslaved population. In the sixty years between *Mark Twain's America* and *Was Huck Black?*, no scholarly book did more than DeVoto's to emphasize the theme of Fishkin's book: that the character of Twain's accomplishment depended on what he took from African Americans.

Here are some of DeVoto's formulations on this matter: "Slavery as an institution and Negroes as sharers of the scene are organic in the community to which [Twain's] novels are devoted. It is a whole community; the effect is totality.... Sam Clemens grew up among Negroes; the fact is important for Mark Twain...[for] much that is fruitful in his art springs from the slaves." The "two facets of democracy" included not only the "idyll" of river, forest, and prairie and the "rush and clamor" of America's development but also "the melancholy, the music, the laughter, the terror, and the magic of the slaves." DeVoto saw Twain's art as what we now call hybrid, drawing from established British culture, from marginal religious sectarians, and from black culture. As he put it, "engraftments from Africa, England, and the Apocalypse... are part of the American experience here, as nowhere else, given existence in literature."[24]

Fishkin orients her argument in relation to Ellison, the most widely admired African American novelist and cultural critic of his generation. He believed in the ideal of integration as opposed to separatist Black Power and drew theoretical and historical emphases similar to DeVoto's from Constance Rourke's pathbreaking study of popular culture, *American Humor: A Study of the National Character* (1931), which was published the year before *Mark Twain's America*.[25] Fishkin's use of Ellison not only allows her an effective rhetorical stance in answering African Americans who object to Twain but also allows her to claim *Huckleberry Finn* for American patriotism without confronting the language of empire that is so important for DeVoto. For DeVoto, the America that emerged from the Civil War had been deeply changed from the entity that entered the war; using the terms of Roman and French history, he saw it as a shift from republic to empire, and as a shift carrying cultural consequence. As he put it, "Emerson is the classic literary man of the First Republic," and "Mark Twain was the classic writer of the Empire that succeeded it."[26]

Although DeVoto considered *Huckleberry Finn* Twain's greatest work, the one most fully expressive of Twain's America, he has very little to say of the work itself. In this respect, however erudite, his work remains a kind of middlebrow appreciation. Something more was needed to make *Huckleberry Finn* the work it has become—not simply beloved to readers, not just "quintessentially American," but also a work amenable to the resources of the most advanced modes of criticism, which already by the rise of New Criticism in the 1930s had begun to mean the close analysis of specific passages.

Lionel Trilling, the most influential American literary intellectual of the Cold War, began the final stage of work that made *Huckleberry Finn* the hypercanonical object it has become. The first college textbook edition of Twain's novel appeared in 1948 with Trilling's introduction. For ten years Trilling had been teaching a general education course on great books of the Western tradition, from Homer to Goethe, and his hyperbolic praise of *Huckleberry Finn* is undergirded by comparisons to Homer, Sophocles, and Molière. Trilling's key move, however, was to endow the work with a moral authority it had never before been understood to possess, a moral authority that made it appropriate for the schoolroom by the test of Trilling's model, Matthew Arnold: it could be shown to offer a "criticism of life."[27]

In chapter 31 of *Huckleberry Finn*, Huck is nagged by his conscience, which urges him to write to Miss Watson, who held legal title to Jim as property, telling her how to recover her chattel. His conscience warns him of the infernal punishments awaiting disobedience. Huck drafts the letter but finds he can't bring himself to send it. He tears it up, saying, "All right, then, I'll *go* to hell." Trilling was the first to name this scene as the book's "great moral crisis." He claims of this sequence that "no one who reads thoughtfully the dialectic of Huck's great moral crisis will ever again be wholly able to accept without some question and some irony the assumptions of the respectable morality by which he lives."[28] For this reason, Trilling asserts, the book is indeed "subversive," just as had been feared by the libraries that initially refused to carry it. So *Huckleberry Finn* was now both quintessentially American and also a work of what Trilling would later call "the adversary culture,"[29] suitable simultaneously for patriotic reassurance and for high-brow strenuosity.

Fishkin combines DeVoto's sense of the essential Americanness of *Huckleberry Finn*, as amplified by Ellison, together with Trilling's praise for the book as being "subversive."[30] For she believes that, in demonstrating the role of "African American voices" in the book's language, she has given scholarly grounding to the white liberal belief that has been crucial to Huck's role in the schools; namely, that it presents an importantly progressive model for American race relations. As she put it in a newspaper interview of 1995, "It's a weapon in the battle against racism that we can't afford to take out of our classrooms."[31] This belief that the mere presence of *Huckleberry Finn* will have a specific, predictable, beneficial effect is part of the structure that I call "idolatry."

Not all cultural authorities participate in hypercanonization or idolatry. Wayne Booth, who is not an Americanist, judged of *Huckleberry Finn*, with the rigor of someone pursuing a theoretical argument, that "few readers if any have ever learned from [it] that slavery is bad." He emphasized, in contrast to Trilling's claim for subversion, that *Huckleberry Finn* does not "teach . . . us a truth we did not know before" nor is it "an effective attack on slavery." Whatever "messages" there may be, he argued, "are in fact brought by most readers to the passage, not derived from it." The achievement of the book, in his analysis, is made possible by what the reader, implied author, and author already hold in common: "the convictions shared by Samuel L. Clemens, Mark Twain, and every successful reader." In Booth's reading, when Huck decides, "All right, then, I'll *go* to hell," the result is "wonderfully warm moral comedy."[32]

But Booth's argumentative scrupulousness prepared for a further lowering in the pitch of what he was willing to claim for *Huckleberry Finn*. His generalizations concerned *few* readers, *most* readers, and *successful* readers. But clearly, by his analysis, in cases where there are not well-shared "convictions," the interaction of text and reader will not be successful. When *Huckleberry Finn* is required in schools, the hope for warmth and intimacy in the reader's response sometimes dissolves not into laughter but into anger, because the cultural stakes are so much higher. For years Booth remembered with nagging puzzlement the African American colleague who had refused to continue teaching *Huckleberry Finn* in the required first-year humanities course at the University of Chicago. Booth's seriousness finally made this refusal the starting point for a book exploring the "ethics of fiction." Booth summarizes the gist of his colleague Paul Moses's case: "The way Mark Twain portrays Jim is so offensive to me that I get angry in class, and I can't get all those liberal white kids to understand why I'm angry."[33] More than twenty years later, Booth got the point.

Booth's colleague Paul Moses had raised his protest in 1963; Booth's acknowledgment that there was a strong ethical case for Moses's critique appeared in 1988, and yet authorities still repeat their claims for the obligatory classroom value of *Huckleberry Finn*. To this day, a significant number of African Americans are compelled to resist the structure of idolatry, to protest the book's role, and thereby to dissociate themselves from the national consensus that it is supposed to represent. The actual character and terms of the protests do not indicate a strong assertion of "ethnic identity" in the sense of calling for a distinctive alternative culture. Rather, they seem to be calling the wishfulness of white, liberal beliefs back to reality by insisting, "This book does not do the work you claim; it is not making an America where we can happily live together."

Let me cite a letter to the *New York Times* in response to its editorial asserting the merits of *Huckleberry Finn* against a protest in 1982: "I still recall the anger and pain I felt as my white classmates read aloud the word 'nigger.' . . . I wanted to sink into my seat. Some of the whites snickered, others giggled. I can recall nothing of the literary merits of this work that you term the 'greatest of all American novels.' I only recall the sense of relief I felt when I would flip ahead a few pages and see that the word 'nigger' would not be read that hour."[34]

Does the established public response to such concerns take them seriously? It seems that the major newspaper of the Pennsylvania state capital does not. In response to the NAACP recommendation of 1998 that *Huckleberry Finn* not be required, the front-page headline was offensively dismissive: "Group Tries to Sell 'Huck Finn' Up the River."[35] In this headline the NAACP is deprived of its character and history and reduced to the anonymity of any group, and the history of slavery in the United States, as well as the meaning of Twain's book, is mocked by the reversal of a key metaphor. For an enslaved human being to be sold southward *down* the river—as Jim, in *Huckleberry Finn,* is threatened with—was a terrible thing because it meant separation from friends and family and exposure to even more severe conditions of forced labor. To forget this meaning, to think that for slaves the bad direction was "up" the river, is a contemptuous, and contemptible, amnesia. Perhaps it also inadvertently reveals what has often been remarked: in the United States today the worst problems of race relations may be northward.

To the extent that challenges to *Huckleberry Finn*'s obligatory primacy are taken seriously, they seem to be taken only as threats rather than as opportunities for serious dialogue. To judge from the newspaper headlines that mark these incidents, one would think that what in Black Power days was called "mau-mauing" was taking place. In summer 1995 a workshop for teachers was held at the museum housed in the mansion that Twain built in Hartford, Connecticut. The *Pittsburgh Post-Gazette* reported "Mark Twain Museum Mounts 'Huckleberry Finn' Defense," and the *New York Times* ran the following headline: "Huck Finn 101; or, How to Teach Twain without Fear." The *Pittsburgh Post-Gazette* cast the workshop as "coming to the rescue" of beleaguered teachers, and the *New York Times* explains that "for the lovers of Mark Twain, the event is a pre-emptive effort to bolster the nerve of teachers."[36]

I do not support this logic, which insists that the book must be rescued from African American parents and students for their own good and, therefore, targets them for preemptive cultural strikes. If we take seriously Trilling's foundational claim that *Huckleberry Finn* teaches us to challenge the moral certainties of the culture that formed us, then we should be willing to contemplate the possibility that *Huckleberry Finn* itself may not be entitled to so central a role in our culture as it has been asked to play. It may be as limited in its way as Huck's conscience was when it defended slavery. In his own time, Twain was far more committed to human equality than were most of his contemporaries, and he was vastly better informed about and admiring of African American contributions to culture in the United States. *Huckleberry Finn* has made millions laugh and is a brilliant experiment in style. There are effective ways to teach it, but too many schools require it because they think it is good for race relations. Instead of authorities telling students and parents who disagree that they are bad readers, I think it would be preferable to mount a genuine debate over what counteracts racism in the classroom.

Ellison greatly admired *Huckleberry Finn*, but he did not accept the principle that a black audience had no right to pass judgment on works produced by whites, especially when those works had the tendency to make whites feel complacent about participating in progressive race relations. In a 1949 review essay, discussing four liberal films, he warned against "the temptation toward self-congratulation which comes from seeing these films and sharing in their emotional release." Ellison urged, "as an antidote to the sentimentality of these films," that they be seen "in predominantly Negro audiences, for here, when the action goes phony, one will hear derisive laughter, not sobs."[37] *Huckleberry Finn* is a stronger work than Elia Kazan's *Pinky* (1949), the best of the four films Ellison was discussing, but it is being asked to serve many of the same purposes, and cultural authorities would be well advised to subject *Huckleberry Finn*, in earnest, to a version of Ellison's touchstone.

Notes

1. Paul Gilroy, *Against Race: Imagining Political Culture beyond the Color Line* (Cambridge: Harvard Univ. Press, 2000), 24.

2. For a valuable conspectus, see the section entitled "Cultural Appropriation" in Elazar Barkan, "Collecting Culture: Crimes and Criticism," *American Literary History* 10, no. 4 (1998): 759–63.

3. Eric Lott, *Love and Theft: Blackface Minstrelsy and the American Working Class* (New York: Oxford Univ. Press, 1993); and Ralph Ellison, "Going to the Territory," in idem, *The Collected Essays of Ralph Ellison,* ed. John F. Callahan (New York: Modern Library, 1995), 611. In Ellison, "The Little Man at Chehaw Station," in idem, *The Collected Essays of Ralph Ellison*, ed. John F. Callahan (New York: Modern Library, 1995), 510–12, the author defines the "process of cultural appropriation" as the means by which "Englishmen, Europeans, Africans, and Asians became Americans."

4. See Ralph Ellison, "Change the Joke and Slip the Yoke," in idem, *The Collected Essays of Ralph Ellison,* ed. John F. Callahan (New York: Modern Library, 1995), 104.

5. Shelley Fisher Fishkin, *Was Huck Black? Mark Twain and African-American Voices* (New York: Oxford Univ. Press, 1993), 144 (see the last words of the text).

6. I draw here on analyses that are detailed and elaborated in Jonathan Arac, *Huckleberry Finn as Idol and Target: The Functions of Criticism in Our Time* (Madison: Univ. of Wisconsin Press, 1997).

7. "NAACP Wants Huck Out of Classrooms," *Pittsburgh Post-Gazette,* 3 February 1998, B6.

8. Respected scholars place the actual number at 213. See James S. Leonard, Thomas A. Tenney, and Thadious M. Davis, eds., *Satire or Evasion? Black Perspectives on Huckleberry Finn* (Durham: Duke Univ. Press, 1992), 231 (editors' note).

9. Wayne Booth's classic study of "stable irony," *A Rhetoric of Irony* (Chicago: Univ. of Chicago Press, 1974), requires a scrupulous limitation of the questions to be pursued in order to achieve its illuminating simplifications.

10. "NAACP Wants Huck Out of Classrooms" (note 7).

11. For citations, see Arac, *Idol and Target* (note 6), 22, 24–29, 34, 78–80.

12. Edward L. Ayers, *The Promise of the New South: Life after Reconstruction* (New York: Oxford Univ. Press, 1992), 132.

13. Arthur N. Applebee, "Stability and Change in the High-School Canon," *English Journal* 81, no. 5 (1992): 27–32.

14. Bernard DeVoto, *Mark Twain's America* (Boston: Little, Brown, 1932), 321.

15. For details, see Victor A. Doyno, *Writing Huck Finn: Mark Twain's Creative Process* (Philadelphia: Univ. of Pennsylvania Press, 1991), 184–98.

16. Quoted in Paul Fatout, ed., *Mark Twain Speaking* (Iowa City: Univ. of Iowa Press, 1976), 158.

17. I take this boilerplate from the copyright page of Doyno, *Writing Huck Finn* (note 15).

18. This information comes from the description of the archive on the Web site of the Mark Twain Papers and Project, Bancroft Library, University of California, Berkeley, at http://bancroft.berkeley.edu (22 February 2002).

19. The quotation is drawn from the description of "The Edition" at the Mark Twain Papers and Project Web site (note 18).

20. Quoted in Wallace Stegner, ed., *The Letters of Bernard DeVoto* (Garden City, N.Y.: Doubleday, 1975), 97.

21. DeVoto, *Mark Twain's America* (note 14), 321.

22. Louis J. Budd, *Our Mark Twain: The Making of His Public Personality* (Philadelphia: Univ. of Pennsylvania Press, 1983).

23. For references to some examples, ranging from Norman Podhoretz in the *New York Times* in 1959 to the *Washington Post* in the 1990s, see Arac, *Idol and Target* (note 6), 3, 10, 81.

24. Quotations in this paragraph are from DeVoto, *Mark Twain's America* (note 14), 66, 77, 294, 306.

25. Ellison cites Rourke, for example, in "Society, Morality, and the Novel" (1957), "Change the Joke and Slip the Yoke" (1958), and a review essay on Leroi Jones's *Blues People* (1964); see Ellison, *Collected Essays* (note 3), 103, 287, 703, 718.

26. Bernard DeVoto, *Forays and Rebuttals* (Boston: Little, Brown, 1936), 357.

27. Matthew Arnold, "Wordsworth" (1879), in Lionel Trilling, ed., *The Portable Matthew Arnold* (New York: Viking, 1949), 343.

28. Lionel Trilling, "*Huckleberry Finn*" (1948), in idem, *The Liberal Imagination: Essays on Literature and Society* (New York: Viking, 1950; reprint, Garden City, N.Y.: Doubleday, 1953), 108.

29. Lionel Trilling, *Beyond Culture: Essays on Literature and Learning* (New York: Viking, 1965), xii–xviii.

30. Fishkin, *Was Huck Black?* (note 5), 144.

31. *Pittsburgh Post-Gazette*, 20 July 1995, A5.

32. Booth, *Rhetoric of Irony* (note 9), 141.

33. Wayne Booth, *The Company We Keep: An Ethics of Fiction* (Berkeley: Univ. of California Press, 1988), 3. See also his full discussion of *Huckleberry Finn* in the same volume, 457–78.

34. Allan B. Ballard, letter to the *New York Times*, 9 May 1982.

35. Harrisburg (Pa.) *Patriot-News*, 3 February 1998, 1. The phrase "up the river" connotes "to or in prison," but one is only sold *down* the river.

36. *Pittsburgh Post-Gazette*, 20 July 1995, A5; and *New York Times*, 25 July 1995, B1.

37. Ralph Ellison, "The Shadow and the Act," in idem, *The Collected Essays of Ralph Ellison*, ed. John F. Callahan (New York: Modern Library, 1995), 308.

Yeats, Group Claims, and Irishry

R. F. Foster

That strange word *Irishry* comes from "Under Ben Bulben," the poem traditionally placed last in the oeuvre of Irish poet and dramatist William Butler Yeats (1865–1939), since it ends proleptically with his own epitaph. The poem was dated 4 September 1938 by Yeats, four months before his death.

> Sing the peasantry, and then
> Hard-riding country gentlemen
> The holiness of monks, and after
> Porter-drinkers' randy laughter;
> Sing the lords and ladies gay
> That were beaten into the clay
> Through seven heroic centuries;
> Cast your mind on other days
> That we in coming days may be
> Still the indomitable Irishry.[1]

It comes as part of a classic late-Yeatsian admonition, to cast your mind on other days in order to imagine and ensure the future — while, perhaps, ignoring or evading the present. Furthermore, this is crystallized, again characteristically, in an archaic word: *Irishry*. One wonders who are (or were) the Irishry? This poem, written very late in Yeats's long and embattled life, gives a radically (and deliberately) limited answer. It is what he elsewhere called the "dream of the noble and the beggarman."[2] It is a definition of Irishness that excluded bourgeois Ireland (the culture of successful Catholic nationalist Ireland) and reinserted the eighteenth-century "planter" ascendancy, the Protestant elite whence Yeats himself derived. In the process, the deliberate appositions of the poem rather evade historical questions such as who had beaten the lords and ladies gay (the old Gaelic aristocracy) into the clay over seven centuries. But it does come as the climax of a long interrogation of his own relations to Irishness and, indeed, Irish nationalism — the "continual quarrel and continual apology," which he defined in his great essay of 1910, "J. M. Synge and the Ireland of His Time."[3]

To follow it requires a careful decoding of Irish *couches sociales* (social strata) and an equally careful "placing" of Yeats (as one antagonist said after the poet's death) in Irish life. It is also necessary to interrogate the changing opinions and political stances of Yeats in his own long and public lifetime. That is worth remembering when considering essays like Edward Said's "Yeats and Decolonisation,"[4] which tends to ignore questions of history and context and opts for seeing Yeats as the voice of the "Irish race" lifted against imperial domination. Certainly Yeats used literature as a form of assertion against the cultural domination of Englishness—particularly during the years when he lived largely in England and made Irishness culturally fashionable there. (The historic early British tours of the Abbey Theatre Company can be seen as an early instance of "empire strikes back" syndrome and, indeed, were so interpreted at the time.)[5] Yet it should equally be remembered that for long periods of his life, and after his death, Yeats was actually attacked by fellow Irish people for—in their exclusivist view—not being of the "Irish race" at all. It is also worth examining the versions promulgated by those who emphasize heavily what they see as Yeats's basic inability to speak for the nation, being—in Seamus Deane's phrase—infected by "the pathology of literary Unionism."[6] It is not that simple, and it never was.

Yeats's own radical nationalism, decisively embraced in his early youth, should be seen against his background. His Fenian period in the 1890s is, in the context of his career, a phase that is abandoned, then rediscovered during the revolution of 1916 to 1922, and then abandoned again. His poetry and prose both keep pace with and gloss these processes. Yet crude views of Yeats and his work in the context of Irish political resistance beg all sorts of questions and remind us how much work there is still to be done on the political, social, and even intellectual contexts of his life and work. For instance, Yeats and Catholicism is an almost untouched subject, although his attitude to the faith of the majority of his fellow countrymen is both absorbing in itself and central to his attitude toward Irishness. His recurrent imaging of the artist as priest, established around the turn of the twentieth century, has a particular resonance for an Irish Protestant determined to claim his place. In addition, the fervent Mariolatry of his unfinished autobiographical novel, *The Speckled Bird* (originally called *The Lilies of the Lord*),[7] reminds us not only what a person of the 1890s Yeats was but also how he, like another Irish poet Lady Isabella Augusta Gregory, felt necessarily excluded by their Protestantism from the conventional definition of the Irish family.

Indeed, another subject that has not been sufficiently tracked is Yeats's relation to radical nationalism—except, in part, by Conor Cruise O'Brien and Elizabeth Butler Cullingford.[8] It is closely related to the particular background of a déclassé Irish Protestant—from the echelons of clergymen and civil servants rather than grandees; estate stewards rather than landowners (although there was a little declining Yeats property, symbolically producing no rent by the 1880s and sold under the Land Commission: here, too, Yeats is an emblematic figure, if in rather an unexpected way). This describes Yeats's inheritance on his father's side. On his mother's side, the Pollexfen family were provincial bourgeoisie, millers, property developers, and town councillors—whom he would rewrite as merchants and mariners for autobiographical purposes, much as he rewrote his father's side as country gentry. It is a deliberately archaic presentation of a very tangible late-nineteenth-century social reality.[9]

This background of a declining elite at a time of social change often provides an acute vantage for a writer (as in late-nineteenth-century Russia); so it was for Yeats. It was further brought into focus by his father's decision to become a bohemian and transplant the family to the world of artists' studios in London in the 1880s and 1890s.[10] Penury was one result; but the other was an exposure to cosmopolitan and avant-garde life from an early stage and to ideas (like those of William Morris), which would remain more influential in Yeats's mind and art than is often realized. He would eventually seem proportionately less "Irish" to those who defined *Irishness* as a Catholic/Gaelic/ nationalist congruence. Yeats (and his family) was certainly nationalist— although even in that, they were going against the traditions of their background. From the mid-1880s, when he joined the old Fenian John O'Leary and his circle of Young Irelanders, until the turn of the century, Yeats's nationalism was—as current usage had it—"advanced" or even "extreme," partly, as he himself later wrote, to attract the political activist and patriot Maud Gonne, and partly to claim Ireland.[11] As the increasingly ascendant Catholic bourgeoisie and its spokespeople queried the credentials of people like him to qualify as Irish, he asserted them more and more strongly.

This is the theme of "To Ireland in the Coming Days," introduced quite late as the dedication poem of his *The Countess Kathleen, and Various Legends and Lyrics* (1894), after the bruising literary battles of the early 1890s. The poem is both a manifesto and an admonition: it makes the statement that you could be a Protestant occultist, rather than a Catholic Gael, and still be a true Irish nationalist. The message of the poem states, indeed, that occultism rather than Catholicism was a necessary precondition for Irishness.

> Nor may I less be counted one
> With Davis, Mangan, Ferguson
> Because to him who ponders well
> My rhymes more than their rhyming tell
> Of the dim wisdoms old and deep,
> That God gives unto man in sleep.
> For round about my table go
> The magical powers to and fro.
> In flood and fire and clay and wind
> They huddle from man's pondering mind,
> Yet he who treads in austere ways
> May surely meet their ancient gaze.
> Man ever journeys on with them
> After the red rose bordered hem
> . . . .
> I cast my heart into my rhymes
> That you in the dim coming times

May know how my heart went with them
After the red rose bordered hem.[12]

In this phase, up to about the turn of the century, the business of claiming Ireland involved two kinds of strategies: one negative, one positive. The negative mode involved the repudiation of the institutions of his caste, such as Trinity College, attacking Irish Protestantism and fervently advocating the mystical elements of Irish Catholicism. *The Speckled Bird*, again, bears witness to this, and so does his play *The Countess Cathleen* (1892), but it also testifies to Yeats's innocence, since it was promptly denounced by the Church and caused a great controversy because of its supposedly blasphemous content. This ungrateful reaction preoccupied him all his life. For some time after the debacle of 1899, he continued to preach the rejection of all English influences and to condemn the Irish eighteenth century, when Irish culture seemed trapped in a thin-blooded, Anglicized, colonial mode (ironic, given his later opinions and his later touting of Jonathan Swift and George Berkeley as the most essentially Irish figures of all).[13]

Yet there were positive strategies for claiming Ireland too, which provide one way of looking at Yeats's early work (and his later works as well). One was the study of folklore and fairy belief: a way of claiming the actual land of Ireland through asserting an authority over its legends, its traditions, its secret essence. This claim on Ireland could be crudely seen as another kind of landlordism. The agenda behind Yeats's versions of stories he collected is significant: another story is often being obliquely told. "Kidnappers," collected in *The Celtic Twilight* (1893), deals with a boy whose mother is spirited away by fairies. He tracks her down to Glasgow (which "in those days of sailing-ships seemed to the peasant mind almost over the edge of the known world") and finds her working in an underground cellar; "she was happy, she said, and had the best of good eating, and would he not eat? and therewith laid all kinds of food on the table; but he, knowing well that she was trying to cast on him the glamour by giving him faery food, that she might keep him with her, refused, and came home to his people in Sligo."[14] It is not hard to see in this a critique of emigration, family dispersal, and materialism, and an injunction to stay in one's native place.

Another intellectual strategy for asserting Irishness is also connected with the land—the idea of an occult brotherhood that would take its spiritual energy from specifically Celtic connections and the notion of Ireland as a Holy Land. For Yeats and his friends in the late 1890s, this took the form of a planned Celtic Order of Heroes, or Celtic Mystical Order.[15] This envisaged a fellowship that would provide a spiritual clerisy bound together by ritual, their training as adepts, and a complex system of rites and symbols. It attracted the political activist Maud Gonne, the leader of the Irish literary renaissance AE (George Russell), James and Margaret Cousins, Althea Gyles, Constance Markiewicz, and others—people from Irish Protestant backgrounds who had rejected the Unionist identifications of their parents and opted for art school, mysticism, and bohemianism. This conditioned them to assert Irishness through identification with Celticism rather than Catholicism. They constituted a marginal avant-garde, looking for a resolution to the political chaos and confrontations of Ireland after Irish nationalist leader Charles Stewart Parnell's shattering fall; they were also much influenced by international Celticism, in Brittany and Scotland as well as Ireland: Ernest Renan and Fiona Macleod showed the way forward as much as Standish James O'Grady and Yeats himself.

Yeats's third intellectual strategy for claiming Irishness succeeded the identifications of folklore and occultism and, in a way, subsumed them. This was his theatrical obsession from the turn of the century. A favorite quotation from Victor Hugo recurs: "in the theatre a mob becomes a people." The national theater would provide the bonding mechanism, the ritual, the magic, the priesthood of believers necessary for the forging of a new cultural identity — and he would be at the center of it.[16] He would also build into the theatrical enterprise, through his own plays, his version of ancient Irish legends, notably the Cuchulain cycle, which would articulate and promulgate the themes, characteristics, and uniqueness of a mythic Irish identity.[17] Often, in plays like *The King's Threshold* (1904), Yeats's work would also reflect the tensions in his own life and his own relationships with Irish conventions and expectations — and the opinions of the Irish majority, who so often repudiated him as elitist, suspect, decadent, and worse.

From early on, significantly, Yeats's ideas of the function of the theater were attacked by the new nationalism of Sinn Fein, under Arthur Griffith; and by journalists like David P. Moran, writing self-consciously in the name of the Catholic and nationalist majority, and decrying Yeats and his friends for being un-Irish and incapable of touching the national heart or soul.[18] From Yeats's side, in the first of his great polemics on the subject, "The Irish National Theatre and Three Kinds of Ignorance" (1903),[19] he made the point that extreme politics (that is, advanced nationalism) used to mean the politics of intellectual freedom; now, with the emergence of Griffith and Sinn Fein, it meant the inhibition of intellectual freedom, and the "deep digging in the pit of themselves," which was how artists approached reality. Even before this, his approach to the theater had set off warning bells even among sympathetic Catholic intellectuals — one of whom, Tom Kettle, decided that the implications of Yeats's art were worryingly un-Irish. Kettle wrote the following in 1903:

> Can it be that these petulant sayings, this fashion of pitting himself against "the mob," spring from the consciousness that the ideas which underlie and direct his art are essentially antagonistic to the ideas which underlie and direct the lives of the great majority of his countrymen? A philosophy, like an animal, can maintain itself only so long as it abides in harmony with his environment. Mr. Yeats will no doubt follow the path of his intellectual development whithersoever it leads him. But there is this danger: that his reading of life may diverge so widely from ours

that all his fine artistry will not save his work from automatic extinction — in Ireland at least.[20]

Kettle's "ours" is Catholic, but also conventionally nationalist.

Ironically, the theater project — once conceived as the forum for reconciliation of different sorts of Irishness — played an important part in distancing Yeats more and more from Irish majority opinion from 1899 to 1910. I choose the latter date because that is when he wrote his elegy for John Millington Synge, which was also perhaps his first autobiographical essay.[21] Synge's astonishing plays had focused the implicit conflict between what Yeats wanted the theater to do for Irish identity and how it was perceived by the majority of the Irish audience. That audience had largely stayed away from Yeats's plays, or greeted them with a dutiful respect while not really plumbing their implications. Synge's plays, however, possessed the theatrical magic and the impact of language, which made instant controversy — never more so than on the famous first night of *The Playboy of the Western World* (1907), when the audience rioted: not so much at the word *shift*, as Yeats would later claim, as at a portrayal of Irishness that did not fit with the conventions, or the self-image, of the newly confident nationalist bourgeoisie.

Yeats deliberately provoked public discussion on the theme, during which he took a more and more antagonistic line and with calculated offensiveness attacked the pieties of the majority in the name of artistic experiment.[22] Three years later, in 1910, recalling the events, he wrote that he stood watching the riots "knowing well that it meant the dissolution of a school of patriotism that had ruled me since my youth." And in his elegy to Synge, he queried the utility of all the revered early-nineteenth-century national images, inherited from the Young Ireland school of romantic nationalism, in which he had been tutored by John O'Leary and to which he had adhered in his younger days. Now, he said, the Irish had gained cultural confidence, and neither the pious stereotypes of Irish moral superiority nor ideal figures immobilized in a nationalist pantheon were needed any longer.

In a striking image (which he would later recycle), he wrote of the adherence to fixed ideas placing an obstruction in the stream of life, immobilizing thought and creativity into the worship of a stone image: "Even if what one defends be true, an attitude of defence, a continual apology, whatever the cause, makes the mind barren because it kills intellectual innocence.... A zealous Irishman especially if he lives much out of Ireland, spends his time in a never-ending argument about Oliver Cromwell, the Danes, the penal laws, the rebellion of 1798, the Famine, the Irish peasant, and ends by substituting a traditional casuistry for a country."

That essay marks the beginning of a period (1910–16) when Yeats defined his position against the conventional majority of Irish opinion. He began spending more time in England again, he stood out against Irish bourgeois opinion on issues like Hugh Lane's plans for a gallery of modern art in Dublin and the labor disputes of 1913. These conflicts produced some memorable philippics against the new Irish middle class as well as great public poems like "To a Wealthy Man" and "September 1913" that were presented as deliberate polemics and placed truculently on the op-ed page of the *Irish Times*, with accompanying leading articles planted by friends. The collection *Responsibilities: Poems and a Play* (1914) gathers these works together and establishes the Yeats of 1914 not only as a figure unafraid to scourge the ruling pieties of modern Irish life but also as someone acknowledging and even drawing back into a sense of ascendancy solitude.

Of the poems that express this, "September 1913" (originally called "Romance in Ireland") is particularly interesting. Its language, meter, and theme pay apparent homage to a standard ballad of the Young Irelanders, "The Green above the Red." Yeats's poem subverts its model, however, by claiming that real Irish nationalism, noble and self-sacrificing, belonged to eighteenth-century Irish Protestant rebels rather than contemporary Irish nationalists.

> Was it for this the wild geese spread
> The grey wing upon every tide;
> For this that all that blood was shed,
> For this Edward Fitzgerald died,
> And Robert Emmet and Wolfe Tone,
> All that delirium of the brave?
> Romantic Ireland's dead and gone,
> It's with O'Leary in the grave.[23]

A few weeks earlier he gave a deliberately offensive speech attacking the opponents of the art-gallery scheme, which directly anticipated the language of the poem's first stanza:

> There is a moment in the history of every nation when it is plastic, when it is like wax, when it is ready to hold for generations the shape that is given to it. Ireland is now plastic, and will be for a few years to come. The intellectual workers in Ireland see gathering against them all the bigotries—the bigotries of Dublin that have succeeded in keeping the "Golden Treasury" out of the schools, the bigotries of Belfast that have turned Nietzsche out of the public libraries. If Hugh Lane is defeated, hundreds of young men and women all over the country will be discouraged—will choose a poorer idea of what might be … if the intellectual movement is defeated Ireland will for many years become a little huckstering nation, groping for halfpence in a greasy till.[24]

Yeats was going to add "by the light of a holy candle" but struck it out. As the quotation indicates, he was also rediscovering Protestant family roots, and retiring into a kind of ascendancy mind-set, attacking "the barrenness of minds without culture" and declaring that the only bulwark against middle-class Irish philistinism was "a few educated men and the remnants of the old traditional culture among the poor." He even postulated that Ireland "may have to become irreligious, or unpolitical even, before she can change her habits." This was the dominant theme of his relations with Irish life in the period just before the outbreak of World War I in 1914.

These are also the years when constitutionally achieved Home Rule for Ireland seemed to be advancing in much the way that Yeats had advocated it. He did not align himself with advanced nationalists who saw it as an inade-quate installment; he appeared on Home Rule platforms and pressed the cause in interviews in America—although often stressing its function as rec-onciling the different kinds of Irishness (one of which he obviously repre-sented) and overcoming the bigotry, which he forcefully repeated in 1913 and 1914, which was part of Irish life. In one flight of inspired offensiveness, he remarked that Home Rule was necessary because it would educate Catholics mentally and Protestants emotionally (thus offending both).[25] Ireland, he told an American audience in 1914, was "no longer a sweetheart but a house to be set in order." With this, he distanced himself, yet again, from the language of traditional romantic nationalism and the tropes of the Gaelic *aisling* (vision poetry), in which Ireland appeared as a beautiful visionary woman, like the girl in Yeats's "The Song of Wandering Aengus" (1897).

Yeats's own kind of Irishness enabled him to live much of the year in London, moving from political dinner tables to the councils of the Royal Society of Literature, accepting a Civil List pension (and arranging one for Joyce) and refusing a knighthood. He was inevitably the object of much snip-ing from the Sinn Fein side of the political spectrum, as "Pensioner Yeats," and accused of every sin from imperialism to freemasonry. A new phase sets in after what was inaccurately called the Sinn Fein Rebellion of 1916, how-ever, which took Yeats by surprise; this led (thanks to a draconian British reaction) to a shift in Irish opinion in favor of advanced nationalism. Yeats's reactions may be charted in his letters. He was wrongheaded at first but rap-idly reassessed his opinion of those who had brought about the rising, and, very early on (no more than a week after the outbreak),[26] determined to turn this astonishing event into art. In the process, he aligned himself with the revo-lution, unlike most of his generation of visionary Celticists and Home Rule sympathizers who were sidelined by it.

The first of the poems in this process is "Easter 1916," written over the summer of 1916 but circulated privately and in secret. Yeats kept it out of print until 1920 due in part to diplomatic difficulties regarding his and Augusta Gregory's negotiations with the government over Hugh Lane's bequest of pictures claimed by both Dublin and London; but the delay also reflects the ambiguity of his own political stance as he cautiously moved toward the rebel side.

The poem is seen as his endorsement of their cause, recognizing that because of that doomed gesture of sacrifice, a "terrible beauty" had been born. Certainly he apotheosizes the rebel leaders, admitting he underesti-mated and trivialized them before the event. He was repositioning himself toward the "advanced nationalist" side of the Irish political spectrum—a volte-face from the direction in which he had been headed up to 1916. "Easter 1916" is really a poem about ambivalent feelings, however, and the central stanza returns to those images from "J. M. Synge and the Ireland of His Time," the stone and the stream. In that essay of 1910, he had prophetically written of nationalist "minds whose patriotism was great enough to carry them to the scaffold" but who "cried down natural impulse with the morbid persistence of minds unsettled by some fixed idea.... They no longer love, for only life is loved, and at last a generation is like a hysterical woman who will make unmeasured accusations and believe impossible things, because of some logical deduction from a solitary thought which has turned a portion of her mind to stone."[27] This central, gendered image, equating political zealotry and single-minded women, reveals that Yeats's mind was turning yet again to one woman in particular, who never acted as he wanted. Maud Gonne was behind this reflection of 1910; she is also invisibly present in the relevant section of "Easter 1916":

> Hearts with one purpose alone
> Through summer and winter seem
> Enchanted to a stone
> To trouble the living stream.
> The horse that comes from the road,
> The rider, the birds that range
> From cloud to tumbling cloud,
> Minute by minute they change;
> A shadow of cloud on the stream
> Changes minute by minute;
> A horse hoof slides on the brim,
> And a horse plashes within it;
> The long legged moor-hens dive,
> And hens to moor cocks call;
> Minute by minute they live;
> The stone's in the midst of all.
>
> Too long a sacrifice
> Can make a stone of the heart.
> O when may it suffice?[28]

Although the poem was finished at Coole, the first draft was written at Gonne's house in Normandy, as was the Synge essay. Both are texts that work on multiple levels. The poem, besides being a love poem written to Gonne, is—like the essay—an interrogation about the claims Irish history and Irish nationalism makes on the artist; the group versus the individual.

It also ushered in a period when Yeats rediscovered the Fenian note, the "Rose Tree" poems, and even a Fenian play, *The Dreaming of the Bones*

(1919). Both were withheld from publication at first but were produced with a flourish when confrontation between Britain and nationalist Ireland reached a decisive level. By the time the revolution was over and the treaty with Britain, which gave autonomy to twenty-six counties of Ireland, was signed, Yeats was rewriting his own history to put himself in the mainstream of the separatist current. He did this first in further installments of his autobiography, begun in 1920 or 1921; second, he did it in his famous speech accepting the Nobel Prize in Literature for 1923, which he used as an opportunity to state the thesis that would dominate Irish historiography of the period. According to Yeats, with Parnell's death in 1891 intellectual energy and political impetus turned into cultural revival, repudiating constitutional politics, and the transference mid-wifed a revolution in which he and his generation were the conductors of a radicalization that was both literary and political: they were the founding fathers of the new state, on a platonic level at least.[29] While concealing and eliding a good deal, this placed him in the center of the Irish experience, and aligned him with the new revolutionary class, rather than the old Home Rules (or the old Celticist mystics) now deposited on the scrap heap of history.

Yeats became a senator in the new state and, in many senses, a founding father in the real world. The tension between Yeats and the Irish majority continued, however. They flared up in the scandal over poems like "Leda and the Swan," in his brief support for the authoritarian and at least quasi-fascist Blue Shirt Party in the early 1930s, and in his swerve into new—and to many, shocking—literary directions in the later 1930s.

In the process, Yeats also rediscovered exactly those Irish traditions that he had repudiated as a young man, while trying to identify himself with the Catholic majority. From at least the mid-twenties, he was reevaluating the Irish eighteenth century, the Georgian ascendancy, the ruthless *sprezzatura*, the stylish nonchalance of "all who have held power in Ireland"—in many ways an invention, but a creative one.[30] Nietzsche had, in a sense, prepared the way for Yeats's version of Swift. The process may have begun crystallizing back in the key year of 1923, when he wrote "Meditations in Time of Civil War," which begins with a lyrical evocation of "Ancestral Houses":

> Surely among a rich man's flowering lawns,
> Amid the rustle of his planted hills
> Life overflows without ambitious pains;
> And rains down life until the basin spills.[31]

He goes on to query, however, whether violence and bitterness might not be essential to the achievement of a civilization and whether the current violence and bitterness of revolution and civil war are not, therefore, necessary in their way.

> O what if levelled lawns and gravelled ways
> Where slippered Contemplation finds his ease

And Childhood a delight for every sense,
But take our greatness with our violence?[32]

As usual, he was not afraid to ask difficult questions: the locution "what if" is central to "Easter 1916" as well. Nor was he afraid to offend. The "meditation" also centralizes his own house, or tower, in the west of Ireland, locating its origins in the mists of Ireland's violent and bitterly contested history, and projecting it into Ireland's future. Late in the sequence, he invokes an Irish identity for the postrevolutionary world:

We had fed the heart on fantasies,
The heart's grown brutal from the fare;
More substance in our enmities
Than in our love; O honey-bees,
Come build in the empty house of the stare.[33]

The last visionary stanzas, deliberately taking refuge in the scholar's and occultist's tower of the mind, are, however, hardly encouraging: "I See Phantoms of Hatred and of the Heart's Fullness and of the Coming Emptiness."[34] Behind it all, the old question of Irishness and group identification simmered. It still had not been resolved when Yeats died in 1939. Rapidly, the obituarists and newspaper columnists took up the question of his Irishness — and old enemies emerged to deny that he had ever been, in a "real" sense, Irish at all. There were series of articles on "placing W. B. Yeats" by cultural commissars like Stephen Quinn, Aodh de Blacam, Francis Shaw, and Timothy Corcoran. The oppositional tone is striking: note the "we" and "us" in this extract from de Blacam's piece in the *Irish Monthly* a few weeks after Yeats's death:

Yeats became more bitter than ever before, against what we hold most sacred. The indecency which marred so many of his past books now grew more horrid, and the latest book which he published, less than a year ago, was a repulsive play that we can excuse only by assuming that the mind which conceived it was unstrung. His poems, in the last dozen years, were morbid. He wrote of the blood of Calvary some lines so horrid that I could not quote them; one wonders how a publisher printed them... How ill this became the poet who had once charmed us with lines about the child that the Little People stole, the mice bobbing round the oatmeal chest in a country house, and the merry playing of the Fiddler of Dooney![35]

In other words, all the work since Yeats's early period of folkloric self-identification with Irish country lore disqualified him from Irishness. Almost simultaneously, a piece in the *Catholic Bulletin* made the point even more strongly:

During the last month the Anglo-Irish poet, William Butler Yeats, died. Immediately every newspaper on which we could lay hands, Irish and foreign, published enthusiastic accounts of this writer's work as a poet, playwright and critic. He was represented as the supreme man of letters writing in English in our time.

Now, we have no wish, when the man is newly dead, to deny him any credit to which he was entitled as an artist or a public man. We do not propose to recall in detail the many occasions on which conscientious Irish writers were obliged to condemn his work and to warn young Ireland against his influence. It is neither our wish nor our intention to usurp the place of Yeats's judge and to strike the balance of his account. Posterity will judge him in this world and he is already judged in the next. What we do insist upon is that a completely false idea of the man and of his achievements was given by those newspapers which published enthusiastic praises of his work and said nothing at all about his quarrel with the nation and his quarrel with Christianity.[36]

The "nation" is, therefore, identified with "Christianity," and "Christianity" with "Catholicism," neatly ruling Yeats out of the chosen group.

There were opposing views, but they came mainly from a dissident intelligentsia, of people like the writers Frank O'Connor and Sean O'Faolain. O'Connor specifically asserted that for all Yeats's Protestant background and Unionist family, not to mention his exotic affectations, his artistic personality was utterly Irish. O'Connor said of Yeats's writings that "generations of country blood in me responds and I am ashamed of writing as I seem to do in a foreign language."[37] Thus Yeats, the ascendancy Protestant, becomes—through his art—platonically more "Irish" than O'Connor himself (a town-bred Catholic Gael). Not everyone was so inclusively minded, or so imaginative. O'Connor and O'Faolain were themselves writers who were at odds with the imposed and exclusivist Irishness of the de Valera regime in the 1940s and 1950s; their books were banned, their private lives denounced by the clergy, and their professional lives blighted. They survived, however, as did Yeats. In fact, by 1948—nearly ten years after his death—his claims were made good when his remains were reinterred in Ireland in a ceremony that firmly emblematized him as a great national figure.

Of course, Yeats had the last word, having left behind for posthumous publication a "General Introduction to My Work," which could provide us with one conclusion:

No people hate as we do in whom the past is always alive. There are moments when hatred poisons my life and I accuse myself of effeminacy because I have not given it adequate expression...Then I remind myself that though mine is the first English marriage I know of in the direct family line, all my family names are English; that I owe my soul to Shakespeare, to Spenser, to Blake, perhaps to William Morris, and to the English language in which I think, speak and write; that everything I love has come to me through English. My hatred tortures me with love, my love with hate.[38]

Another option is that we could end as Yeats dictated, and as this essay began, with lines from "Under Ben Bulben":

Many times man lives and dies
Between his two eternities,
That of race and that of soul,
And ancient Ireland knew it all.[39]

If "race" (group claims) was, for Yeats, one of man's eternities, "soul" (self-consciously individualized creativity) was the other: the implicit conflict between them not only characterized his relationships with his fellow countrymen but profoundly affected his art as well as his life. Just as striking, perhaps, is the extent to which it still conditions, or even constructs, the study of his work by those who have come after him.

Notes

1. W. B. Yeats, *The Variorum Edition of the Poems of W. B. Yeats*, ed. Peter Allt and Russell K. Alspach (New York: Macmillan, 1968), 640.

2. W. B. Yeats, "The Muncipal Gallery Revisited," in idem, *The Variorum Edition* (note 1), 601–4; again, a very late poem.

3. Published by Cuala Press in 1910, and subsequently in W. B. Yeats, *The Cutting of an Agate* (New York: Macmillan, 1912), but most easily found in W. B. Yeats, *Essays and Introductions* (New York: Macmillan, 1961), 311–42. For a full commentary, see R. F. Foster, *W. B. Yeats: A Life*, vol. 1, *The Apprentice Mage: 1865–1914* (Oxford: Oxford Univ. Press, 1997), 417–21.

4. Edward W. Said, *Culture and Imperialism* (New York: Knopf, 1993), 220–38.

5. Foster, *W. B. Yeats* (note 3), 318–19.

6. See Seamus Deane, "Yeats and the Idea of Revolution," in idem, *Celtic Revivals: Essays in Modern Irish Literature, 1880–1980* (London: Faber & Faber, 1985). Declan Kiberd's essay "Inventing Irelands" is also relevant. Both essays are usefully reprinted in Jonathan Allison, ed., *Yeats's Political Identities: Selected Essays* (Ann Arbor: Univ. of Michigan Press, 1996), 133–46, 145–64, respectively; the collection contains much else relevant to the theme of this essay.

7. W. B. Yeats, *The Speckled Bird*, with variant versions ed. and annotated by William H. O'Donnell (Toronto: McClelland & Stewart, 1976).

8. Conor Cruise O'Brien's famous essay on Yeats's politics, "Passion and Cunning," has been reprinted many times—most recently in Allison, *Yeats's Political Identities* (note 6), which also has a useful extract from Elizabeth Butler Cullingford's *Yeats, Ireland and Fascism* (London: Macmillan, 1981).

9. Foster, *W. B. Yeats* (note 3), 528–31.

10. See William M. Murphy, *Prodigal Father: The Life of John Butler Yeats, 1839–1922* (Ithaca: Cornell Univ. Press, 1978), chaps. 3–7.

11. See W. B. Yeats, "The Stirring of the Bones," in idem, *Autobiographies* (London: Macmillan, 1955), 362–71.

12. Yeats, *The Variorum Edition* (note 1), 137–39; the lines quoted here are as they first appeared, not the final canonical version. For the circumstances of its publication, see Foster, *W. B. Yeats* (note 3), 119–24.

13. See Donald T. Torchiana, *W. B. Yeats and Georgian Ireland* (Evanston: Northwestern Univ. Press, 1966), chaps. 4 and 6.

14. W. B. Yeats, *The Celtic Twilight* (London: A. H. Bullen, 1902), 121–22.

15. The fullest description is in the appendix to *The Collected Letters of W. B. Yeats,* vol. 2, *1896–1900,* ed. Warwick Gould, John Kelly, and Deirdre Toomey (Oxford: Oxford Univ. Press, 1997), 663–69.

16. See James W. Flannery, *W. B. Yeats and the Idea of a Theatre: The Early Abbey Theatre in Theory and Practice* (Toronto: Macmillan, 1976; reprint, New Haven: Yale Univ. Press, 1989).

17. See Birgit Bramsbäck, *The Interpretation of the Cuchulain Legend in the Works of W. B. Yeats* (Uppsala: Lundequist, 1950).

18. On this old enmity, see Deirdre Toomey, "Moran's Collar: Yeats and Irish Ireland," *Yeats Annual* 12 (1996): 45–83.

19. See W. B. Yeats, *Uncollected Prose,* vol. 2, *Reviews, Articles, and Other Miscellaneous Prose, 1897–1939,* ed. John P. Frayne and Colton Johnson (London: Macmillan, 1975), 306–7.

20. Foster, *W. B. Yeats* (note 3), 298–99.

21. Foster, *W. B. Yeats* (note 3), 298–99.

22. See Foster, *W. B. Yeats* (note 3), 359–67, for a full discussion.

23. Yeats, *The Variorum Edition* (note 1), 289–90.

24. See Foster, *W. B. Yeats* (note 3), 494.

25. For this and other comments, see Foster, *W. B. Yeats* (note 3), 448, 513–14.

26. As established by the conversation with H. W. Nevinson on 1 May 1916, recorded in Ronald Schuchard, "An Attendant Lord: H. W. Nevinson's Friendship with W. B. Yeats," *Yeats Annual* 7 (1990): 90–130, 118.

27. Yeats, *Essays and Introductions* (note 3), 313–14.

28. Yeats, *The Variorum Edition* (note 1), 393.

29. See W. B. Yeats, "The Irish Dramatic Movement," in idem, *Autobiographies* (London: Macmillan, 1955), 559–72.

30. See Torchiana, *Georgian Ireland* (note 13).

31. Yeats, *The Variorum Edition* (note 1), 417.

32. Yeats, *The Variorum Edition* (note 1), 418.

33. Yeats, *The Variorum Edition* (note 1), 425.

34. Yeats, *The Variorum Edition* (note 1), 425.

35. See my essay "'When the Newspapers Have Forgotten Me': Yeats, Obituarists and Irishness," *Yeats Annual* 12 (1996): 172.

36. Cited in Foster, "Yeats, Obituarists and Irishness" (note 35), 169–70.

37. Published in *The Bell* 1, no. 5 (February 1941); as quoted in Foster, "Yeats, Obituarists and Irishness" (note 35), 176.

38. Edward Callan, *Yeats on Yeats: The Last Introductions and the "Dublin" Edition* (Dublin: Dolmen, 1981), 63.

39. Yeats, *The Variorum Edition* (note 1), 637.

Cultural Property and
Identity Politics in Britain

Robert J. C. Young

In the 1980s there occurred in Great Britain something known as the "crisis in English Studies." This was often associated with the advent of "theory," such as structuralism and poststructuralism, but the real crisis came with a challenge to the value of literature as such. Radical theorists such as Terry Eagleton and Peter Widdowson argued that literary critics should abandon literature and turn their hand to cultural studies instead.[1] This was not simply a Marxist argument that literature was not radical enough in political terms. In fact, Marxist literary critics had shown themselves quite content to analyze bourgeois authors, so long as the analysis itself constituted a Marxist critique. The reason for this new argument and for the development of the trauma of the "crisis in English Studies" was that research into the history of English literature as an academic subject in schools and universities had shown its complicity as an ideological form with the bourgeois state, that English literature had been explicitly set up in the *Newbolt Report on the Teaching of English in England* (1921)[2] and elsewhere as a device to resolve class conflict in Britain or to inculcate imperial culture and ideology in Ireland, India, and the Caribbean. The revelation of the class and nationalist ownership of the cultural property of English literature produced widespread disillusionment with the notion of literature itself. Literature almost became a dirty word, and certainly an enthusiasm for the literary became politically suspect. Since then, literature has been rehabilitated, largely as a result of its appropriation as a mode of self-expression and self-representation by women authors and those from ethnic minorities or former colonies overseas. Two decades later, everyone is happy: literature has become a space for the assertion and articulation of new forms of representation of different kinds of people and has thus become the cultural property of more than just members of the English upper middle classes. If literature formerly only reflected the class system by its structures of exclusion, it certainly now reflects the changed social structure of British postwar society.

The empire writes back, "We are here because you were there." This combative defensive slogan testifies to the dramatic transformation that has occurred in Britain since World War II. The British withdrew fairly rapidly from the countries that made up their empire after 1947, but no one anticipated that postcolonial Britain would itself be transformed in the next fifty years into a culture that incorporates diversity in such a radical new creative form. This reorientation has meant that English identity no longer comprises the singular scenario of a garlic-free world of pinstripe suits and clipped high-pitched staccato voices. It had never been just like that anyway, of course, but one of the more curious achievements of imperial culture was to impress on the world the properties of Englishness that encapsulated the identity only of its elite, ruling class. In the nineteenth century the class war was won at the level of representation as well as of political power. Of course, as Trotsky always stressed, it was the ruling upper classes with the power that were the imperialists. The unenfranchised working class had no choice. In the late twentieth century, however, the world began to perceive that the British as a whole come in a range of models, not only in class terms but also as a result of the increasing emphasis on the national and ethnic diversities contained within the not very United Kingdom of Great Britain and Northern Ireland.

As a result of this increasing emphasis on diversity, and as the "crisis in English Studies" indicated, English identity as such has been left almost in a vacuum. Everyone in Britain has been so busy deconstructing Englishness and English nationalism according to its identity in the past, that we have only recently begun to notice that it has been suffering somewhat of an identity crisis. No one is quite sure what properties constitute Englishness any more, aside from the continuing class snobbery of the abject remnants of the prewar middle and upper classes. This is a crisis not only for the English but also for everyone else in Britain like the Scots—and abroad in places like Australia—who defines his or her identity against them. There is, as it were, no same for the Other. One indication of this is that no one in Britain will admit to being English anymore. Whereas until the 1970s many people used to cover up any non-English ancestry, since the 1980s, people have suddenly rediscovered their forgotten Irish grandmother, Anglo-Indian grandfather, or Scottish roots. What used to be the most valuable attribute—being English—has lost its value in cultural terms, whereas what used to have a negative value—being Irish—has gained positive value. This is also true of that curious category "English literature," which is in the process of breaking up into its regional traditions and identities. In the same way, instead of the old imperialism of Standard English, today any self-respecting novelist has to write in the local vernacular, the stronger the better.

The assertion of literature as a regional cultural property is not, however, always straightforward. For example, Eagleton's book *Heathcliff and the Great Hunger: Studies in Irish Culture* (1995) was largely devoted to an analysis of Irish literary texts as the historical product of Irish culture.[3] The British Library cataloging description of the book points to continuing difficulties in asserting Irish literature as a national cultural property distinct from English.

Eagleton. Terry, 1943–
Heathcliff and the Great Hunger: Studies in Irish Culture
SUBJECT: English literature—Irish authors.

The questions that follow for an author are, therefore, How do you assert your own cultural property in literature if you write in English? How do you prevent your property from being appropriated to "English literature"? By writing in English, do you inevitably allocate your writing to the international literature property market, whose owners are the English and Americans? The role of English as an international language prompts interesting questions about cultural property. As the (paradoxical) lingua franca of the international community, English has great value as a cultural property in any non-English speaking country. At the same time, its cultural value is a negative one to the extent that its pull is so strong that writers of fiction increasingly write in English rather than in their own native language and therefore can only be read by a tiny proportion of their own population. It estranges a literature from its own culture—or rather, it estranges the novel from its own culture since poetry, for the most part, continues to be written in and for the vernacular. Fiction only becomes a valuable cultural property if it is written in one of the major languages of the world; however, by the same token, as a result it hardly remains the property of its own culture. The recent interest in postcolonial or commonwealth literatures—read fiction—in the West involves an interesting new form of cultural imperialism: as Indian literary critic Harish Trivedi has remarked, those arguing for the cultural value of postcolonial literatures tend to be from predominantly white settler colonies such as Australia and Canada. In any world anthology of postcolonial literatures in English, they then get all their literature in and occupy a massive space, whereas India, with eighteen indigenous languages, and with only 5 percent of its literature in English, is relegated to minor status. As far as the English-speaking world is concerned, this small percentage, as in Salman Rushdie's now-notorious *New Yorker* special issue on contemporary Indian fiction,[4] all of which was in English, becomes "Indian literature."

———

This covers cultural imperialism abroad; however, on the domestic front, things are less straightforward. Today British identity, which used to be so often just a synonym for Englishness, has given way before the resurgence of cultural nationalisms—particularly among the Scots and Welsh, who look to the success of Irish cultural nationalism for their political model. The arrival, for the most part, after World War II, of peoples from the Caribbean, South Asia, and Africa varied the mix. They transformed the situation decisively, not merely by the degree of cultural difference but also because their physical differences were not invisible. Their bodies were their cultural properties. Since the 1950s, British society, formerly divided up according to class interests, was challenged by new forms of minority politics. Of course, Britain always had a form—albeit a rather different form—of minority politics, in the sense that it had always been (and probably still is) ruled by a minority. The new forms of minority politics were different because they involved minorities who were not actually politically disenfranchised but rather disadvantaged solely because they were part of a minority.

Such politics, whether of ethnic minorities or the women's movement, involved conceptual as well as political strategies. They were similar in that both had to deal with a disadvantage resulting from physical markers of difference. Your identity was your property because you were determined by the properties of your body. Both groups had to contend with the prescription of biology as destiny and to counter the prejudiced assumption of social and cultural inferiority as an effect of biological difference. As a result, a parallel conceptual distinction was forged that disputed the cultural values that followed from the properties of biological difference: in the case of women, between the female (biology) and the feminine (culture); in the case of ethnic minorities, between race (biology) and ethnicity (culture). With a little help from Louis Althusser and Jacques Lacan, this was accompanied by an attack on essentialism. Any form of identification between the two now-distinct categories, biology and culture, was more or less denied—most famously in that awesome dictum that we must *never* confuse the phallus with the penis. In cultural criticism ever since, perhaps the worst sin of which you can accuse your opponent is falling into essentialism or biologism (or both). *Biologism* became the "b-word" with which you accused, and dismissed, your opponents. The separation of culture from biology allowed the active construction of positive identities in the place of the negative ones that had formerly been ascribed to the minority by the majority. In both cases the problem of what to do about the biological remained. Some feminists such as Judith Butler have moved to a view in which gender attributes are regarded not as expressive but performative, with nothing essential or biological determining them.[5]

Ethnicity was trickier. The initial form of the word, *ethnic*, originally simply constituted the adjectival form of the noun *race*. This term was, however, officially deconstructed at the United Nations Educational, Scientific and Cultural Organization (UNESCO) conference on race in 1950, which recommended that "the use of the term "race" be dropped, and the term 'ethnic group' be adopted instead."[6] The notion of an "ethnic minority" was invented in 1945, with *ethnicity* following in 1953 in order to provide a way of describing what the *Oxford English Dictionary*, in a significant hedge, calls "a group of people differentiated from the rest of the community by racial origins or cultural background, and usually claiming or enjoying official recognition of their group identity." We could infer from this that the ethnic minority has thus always been a political category based on the possession of certain properties. The category of race, insofar as it was connected to any biological basis, is now disavowed in favor of a cultural-political grouping. The notion of ethnicity allows the denial of any biological determinism and the claim from some that you can simply choose your ethnicity on the analogy of being able to choose your sexuality, or you can perform your ethnicity on the analogy of being able to turn gender into performance. What then do you do with the physical properties of difference? You cannot turn forms of ethnicity associated with the property of skin color into something entirely performative—although you can construct any performance you like from the signifier. The signifier may be floating, but you cannot choose to deny your ownership of it altogether if the majority, or even a minority of the majority, enforce its significance. This situation is nicely exposed in a passage in *The Lonely Londoners* (1956) by Sam Selvon:

> And Galahad would take his hand from under the blanket, as he lay there studying how the night before he was in the lavatory and two white fellars come in and say how these black bastards have [made] the lavatory dirty, and they didn't know he was there, and when he come out they say hello mate have a cigarette. And Galahad watch the colour of his hand, and talk to it, saying, "Colour, is you that causing all this, you know. Why the hell you can't be blue, or red or green, if you can't be white? You know is you that cause a lot of misery in the world. Is not me, you know, is you! I ain't do anything to infuriate the people and them, is you! Look at you, you so black and innocent, and this time so you causing misery all over the world!"
>
> So Galahad talking to the colour Black, as if is a person, telling it that is not *he* who causing botheration in the place, but Black, who is a worthless thing for making trouble all about....
>
> Galahad get so interested in this theory about Black that he went to tell Moses. "Is not we that the people don't like," he tell Moses, "is the colour Black."
>
> Moses tell Galahad, "take it easy, that is a sharp theory, why don't you write about it."[7]

Ethnicity and ethnic identity may be a cultural construction, so that you can contest and then construct your own identity. You cannot, however, refuse the materiality of the signifier, your skin-color property, if it has been given a social significance by others for you. In a racialized confrontation, you are owned by the color of your skin. The social meaning of its properties has already been written. Anyone who has ever suffered racism knows that. As Frantz Fanon wrote four years earlier in "The Fact of Blackness," in his *Peau noire, masques blancs* (1952; *Black Skin, White Masks*): "I am given no chance. I am overdetermined from without. I am the slave not of the 'idea' that others have of me but of my own appearance."[8] This explains why ethnicity still hovers uneasily on any complete denial of the biological. It also accounts for some of the differences in the models of cultural identity between, say, Scots and British African Caribbeans; namely, the Scots do not have the disadvantage—or advantage—of possessing the property that produces that flash of recognition from the English Other of a meaning that is already written. They have to assert it, to lay claim to it, through the invocation of cultural properties, of language, history, and place. The difference for anyone who is white in a white society is that you can turn the signifier on and off, as has been made clear from the variable force with which Scottish nationalism, and the variable forms of its ethnic identifications, has been asserted at different historical moments. Galahad, in *The Lonely Londoners,* had no such choice of identification with his black skin. Nor does anyone today with black skin, or indeed any skin that looks a shade away from "white."

Ethnicity, therefore, uneasily shadows race. The attempt to separate the biological from the cultural will always create an unsustainable dichotomy — even the scientific accounts were never just biological. The distinction between them can be reformulated by starting out with the fact that both share a set of common properties, cultural and biological. Whereas the thesis of race as the biological, ethnicity as the cultural, claims a complete separation between the two, if we think of race and ethnicity as possessing common forms of property, the similarities as well as the differences can become more clear. On the one hand, race gives greatest value to the property of the body, whose intrinsic properties then prompt the devaluation of all the other properties that a race may possess as comparatively peripheral. These other properties comprise a mere by-product of a particular physical and mental capacity, that is, a community with a shared history, geographical space, language, religion, culture, cultural aesthetic, cuisine, and so forth (no individual one of which is of course essential). Ethnicity, on the other hand, views ethnic identity in terms of a shared set of properties, of which history, language, religion, culture, and so on, are the determining properties and, therefore, the most valuable, while the properties of the communal body — skin color, physiognomy — although still essential, are comparatively peripheral and of no determining significance. The race, therefore, shares exactly the same properties with the ethnic group, but the cultural value of the different elements that define it differs radically.

There is one major conceptual difference, however, in ethnicity's claim apart from the relation to the biological, and that is a political one. Race as it was developed in the nineteenth century by racial theorists such as Joseph Arthur, comte de Gobineau, in his *Essai sur l'inégalité des races humaines* (1853–55), constituted a taxonomy of an absolute physical and cultural difference that would never change, resulting in a claim of a permanent hierarchy between the races.[9] Race, in other words, meant that the races were not only different but unequal and that difference meant inequality on a permanent basis. Today, with the transformation of the markers of difference into the category of ethnicity, the equation has been decisively rewritten: with ethnicity, you are allowed to be different, but this goes along with the recognition that, at a fundamental level, both in terms of intellectual and cultural capacity and in terms of political rights, you are essentially the same. This is why, incidentally, it makes no sense to reject universals for a postmodern particularity in the name of difference. In demanding general political rights, anyone is assuming universals. Identity involves both sameness and difference.[10]

Ethnicity, therefore, also amounts to a form of differential identity, and this constitutes the basis of identity politics. If ethnicity is a marker of difference, it is not fixed or essential; in other words, you can add properties or take them away. What the ethnic minority itself can do is attempt to reverse or shift the significance of the dominant culture's negative interpretation of the signifier in what V. N. Voloshinov called the struggle for the sign.[11] The minority can resist the dominant by becoming the agent of its own signification and cultural representation, which is what has been done with such success by Britain's ethnic minorities in the past three decades. This began with the antiracist movement and the politicization of the term *black* to describe all ethnic minorities who were subject to oppression. In recent years, that political solidarity among ethnic minorities, still observable in names such as the "Southall Black Sisters" who are, in fact, Asian, has broken down, with different groups seeking to establish individual, specific cultural identities.

Other forms of solidarity, however, have also developed in different ways through the politics of representation. The claim to self-representation, resistance through self-[re]presentation, has been articulated and achieved above all in the area of popular youth culture, particularly music. Indeed, black British, or perhaps more accurately, black Atlantic culture, so dominates the contemporary music scene that not only white but even Asian teenagers have started to emulate black street style and dress. This development undoes any multiculturalist assumption that each ethnic group will always pursue its own individual identity, its own form of self-expression. Rather, these forms of identification are common across different ethnic groups, who are more concerned with participating in contemporary youth subcultures and marking themselves with their forms of difference than with perpetuating discrete ethnic identities. This process forms the main subject of Hanif Kureishi's novel *The Buddha of Suburbia* (1990).[12] Such forms of identification do not stop at music; they can also be found in the popularity among the younger sections of different ethnic groups of Louis Farrakhan's Nation of Islam.

In 1987 Stuart Hall also remarked on this dynamic feature of contemporary black British culture. What he noticed was that those at the periphery of society seemed to be simultaneously at its center, those who had no economic or political property to hold the cultural property of greatest value:

> I've been puzzled by the fact that young black people in London today are marginalized, fragmented, unenfranchised, disadvantaged and dispersed. And yet, they look as if they own the territory. Somehow, they ... in spite of everything, are centred, in place: without much material support, it's true, but nevertheless, they occupy a new kind of space at the centre. And I've wondered again and again what it is about that long discovery-rediscovery of identity among blacks in this migrant situation, which allows them to lay a kind of claim to certain parts of the earth which aren't theirs, with quite that certainty. I do feel a sense of — dare I say — envy surrounding them. Envy is a very funny thing for the British to feel at this moment

in time—to want to be black! Yet I feel some of you surreptitiously moving toward that marginal identity.[13]

In contemporary British culture, marginal identity has become, Hall suggests, almost the typical or most widely felt form of identity. It is the property that everyone wants to have.

This characteristic feature of contemporary British culture is also true in a different way in the cultural and academic spheres. The Booker Prize has transformed the identity of contemporary British fiction by broadening the metropolitan mainstream to include many international writers in English, from Rushdie to Ben Okri to Arundhati Roy. These writers are balanced by those representing Britain's older ethnicities, such as Roddy Doyle. In the 1960s it was working-class culture that seized the void left at the center of a postimperial English identity, defining the "swinging London" of the Harold Wilson era. Oddly, perhaps, and against all expectations, in the course of the Thatcherite era, British ethnic minorities came to dominate the cultural self-representation of contemporary Britain, or rather England. Arguably, multi-cultural identity is more relevant to England than to Britain as a whole, in the sense that England, more than Wales or Scotland, tends to be represented as multicultural in this way (Ireland's multiculturalism, of course, is of an entirely different order, usually designated in negative terms as sectarianism).

At a cultural level, this is true above all perhaps of Rushdie's hybridized postcolonial London, but think also of the work of so many other writers—Kazuo Ishiguro, Timothy Mo, Sunetra Gupta, Joan Riley, Caryl Phillips, Merle Collins, and Diran Adebayo, to name but a few—together with films that seem to define—while transgressing—contemporary British hybridized culture such as *My Beautiful Laundrette* (1985) and *Sammy and Rosie Get Laid* (1987), both by Stephen Frears and Hanif Kureishi; or Gurinder Chadha's *Bhaji on the Beach* (1993); or Isaac Julien's *Looking for Langston* (1998) or his 1996 documentary on Fanon's *Black Skin, White Masks*. The work of such writers, filmmakers, and musicians is increasingly supported by those in the media, the arts councils, and the academy, who now see their duty as articulating the voices of the silenced, marginalized minorities of the present and the past. The same forces provide institutional funding from Channel 4 TV and the British Film Institute for black cinema and institution-alize such forms of cultural production in academic degree courses and in conferences held in and outside the United Kingdom, hosted by the British Council, a British government agency. All of this indicates that Britain's ethnic minorities have captured the cultural center ground, so much so that they have created what has become the dominant form of self-representation of English culture today. Ethnicity has been so successful in moving in on contemporary English culture that, as Stuart Hall observed, the margin has become the center.

Or has it? Despite Hall's claim that the margin has become the center, that is not how it often feels on the street. How can one account for this disparity?

Music provides the obvious answer: the music of youth cultures, as Dick Hebdige has shown, is always subcultural or countercultural. It is not the center itself but an act of resistance to the center.[14] Hall has mistaken the resistance to the center as the center. As black American culture makes clear, the cultural properties of what is cool and fashionable are not necessarily possessed by the center in terms of power and economic well-being. If the center lacks them, they can always be bought. Ethnicity gets commodified. The problem with any claim that minority artists and writers have become the center is that the status and, in many cases, the implicit aesthetic, of ethnic minority artists, writers, and academics is in some sense still guaranteed and authenticated by the continuing marginalization and social deprivation of Britain's ethnic minorities. The latter are no longer culturally marginalized, but economic disadvantage, particularly for African Caribbeans, is as great as ever. The emphasis on positive identities and on the politics of self-representation means that the signifier has started to float again. There has been a slippage between the representation and the real, between the image and the realities of poverty and social deprivation.

Moreover, as the Rushdie affair indicated, the problem with the representations of minorities by minority writers is that their cultural values are often implicitly directed at the white majority and constructed in terms which that majority will find sympathetic. Crudely, minority artists who endorse the dominant liberal view are celebrated. Those who do not, or whose work does not address the majority, or who do not work in the appropriate media, remain unheard and unregarded. The case of Rushdie's *Satanic Verses* brought out these issues in a very clear way. Here the British government found itself in the ultraliberal position of defending one of its former critics, because Rushdie's assertion of his right to liberal values (artistic freedom above morality) accorded with the government's position against that of so-called Islamic fundamentalism. What the outcry showed, however, is that Rushdie, like many ethnic minority artists, could not cash his claim to speak for the minority whom he had been presumed to represent. For once, the subaltern spoke and was heard. The minority refused to be treated as Rushdie's own cultural property, just as it refused to accept his recontextualization of the Qu'ran in a hybridized "composite" of translations, mediated, as Rushdie put it, "with a few touches of my own."[15] Rushdie had forged for himself the cultural identity of the antiracist spokesperson for Britain's ethnic minorities, promoting the liberal value of multicultural hybridization in his writing. But it was exactly these cultural values for which Rushdie was attacked by Muslims in Britain and elsewhere. With respect to any ethnic minority community, the issues remain: whose representations are represented and received, who authorizes them, and who controls them?

The gap between the representation and the represented not only operates at the level of cultural values. The celebration of the "new ethnicities" has sometimes participated in the tendency of identity politics in general to draw the political focus away from more mundane but material issues such as poverty, inequality, and disempowerment. In contemporary Britain, it is the poor who are the forgotten minority—the poor are now the unglamorous other who have been deprived of voice. Booker Prize winners notwithstanding, even fashionable ethnicity, wherever you go in Britain today, still lives in the poorest part of town.

Notes

1. Terry Eagleton, *Literary Theory: An Introduction* (Oxford: Blackwell, 1983); Peter Widdowson, ed., *Re-Reading English* (London: Methuen, 1982); and Robert J. C. Young, "The Politics of the Politics of Literary Theory," in idem, *Torn Halves: Political Conflict in Literary and Cultural Theory* (Manchester: Manchester Univ. Press, 1996), 84–112.

2. Henry John Newbolt, *The Newbolt Report on the Teaching of English in England* (London: His Majesty's Stationery Office, 1921).

3. Terry Eagleton, *Heathcliff and the Great Hunger: Studies in Irish Culture* (London: Verso, 1995).

4. Salman Rushdie, "Damme, This Is the Oriental Scene for You!," *New Yorker,* 23 and 30 June 1997, 50–61.

5. Judith Butler, *Gender Trouble: Feminism and the Subversion of Identity* (New York: Routledge, 1990).

6. UNESCO, *The Race Question in Modern Science: Race and Science* (New York: Columbia Univ. Press, 1961), 497.

7. Samuel Selvon, *The Lonely Londoners* (Harlow, Essex: Longman, 1985), 88–89.

8. Frantz Fanon, "The Fact of Blackness," in idem, *Black Skin, White Masks,* trans. Charles Lam Markmann (London: Pluto, 1986), 116; originally published as *Peau noire, masques blancs* (Paris: Éditions de Seuil, 1952).

9. Joseph Arthur, comte de Gobineau, *Essai sur l'inégalité des races humaines,* 4 vols. (Paris: Librairie de Firmin Didot frères, 1853–55).

10. Compare with Ernesto Laclau, "Universalism, Particularism and the Question of Identity," in John Rajchman, ed., *The Identity in Question* (New York: Routledge, 1995), 105.

11. V. N. Voloshinov, *Marxism and the Philosophy of Language,* trans. Ladislav Matejka and I. R. Titunik (New York: Seminar Press, 1973), 23.

12. Hanif Kureishi, *The Buddha of Suburbia* (London: Faber & Faber, 1990).

13. Stuart Hall, "Minimal Selves," in *Identity: The Real Me* (London: Institute of Contemporary Arts, 1987).

14. Dick Hebdige, *Subculture: The Meaning of Style* (London: Methuen, 1979).

15. Salman Rushdie, *The Satanic Verses* (London: Viking, 1988), 549.

Property, Shmoperty! Philip Roth, Postmodernism, and the Contradictions of Cultural Property

Ronald Bush

Cultural property rights are only as strong as the cultural identities that stand behind them and, ultimately, only as strong (or as weak) as the notion of cultural identity itself. Put another way, examining its proprietary attachments is an excellent way to get at the difficulties of a claim to cultural identity. Nor are these difficulties associated only with universalist objections to cultural authenticity (legal objections, say, to the way cultural property claims violate constitutive enlightenment notions such as individual rights). Poststructuralist theory, interrogating categories like authenticity and essence, also poses weighty challenges to endowing cultural groups with property rights.

Consider the implied premises of the most widely sympathetic struggle over cultural property now on the international stage—the Greek call for the return of the Elgin Marbles. To what Greek culture do the Parthenon sculptures belong—to the city-state of Pericles or the modern nation of Greece? If it is the latter, it must be that there is something authentic and essential in "Greek culture" that joins these two and separates them from the nineteenth- and twentieth-century culture of, for example, Great Britain, which once insisted that it was the true "heir" of Athenian democracy and civilization.[1] But if there is something authentically Periclean about modern Greece, does it inhere in every Greek descendant and is it uniformly represented in the expressions of Greek culture throughout the ages? If not, can some of these cultural expressions be exported? Which ones?

These questions get stickier when group claims on cultural property do not involve unique and material items like the Parthenon Marbles but immaterial or replicable things like folk motifs or folk music. Should there be strict controls on the transmission of traditional African music, whether it is explicitly sacred or simply retains a remnant of sacred significance? If the answer is yes, who has the right to exert those controls? Should, for example, the community impose them against the wishes of a contemporary indigenous musician who would sponsor their representation outside of their original context?

What about those cases where the representation of replicable material involves matters of the group's collective self-image, its reputation? For instance, in matters such as white America's First-Amendment license to impose pernicious stereotypes on the African American experience, does the

African American community have a right to exert control over such cases of its own "cultural property" because of the dangers it faces if it does not? When should a "culture" censor such representations for the sake of maintaining collective self-esteem, elevating its reputation among other competing groups, or discouraging potential persecution? Moreover, who is to arbitrate disputes in matters over what constitutes pernicious or distorting representation? What cultural body decides the limits of such censorship? What happens, to cite an actual instance, when African Americans quarrel about whether to censor Mark Twain's putatively sympathetic and memorably powerful use of the word *nigger* in *The Adventures of Huckleberry Finn?*

Most uncomfortably, what happens when such censorship applies not to figures outside a national or indigenous ethnic culture but to one of its own? Does no individual within a culture have the right to transfer or sell cultural property, even when he or she has produced it? In this last circumstance, the difficulties involved in deciding who and what constitute a culture become pronounced and painful, especially when cultural property is understood in connection with group reputation. On the one hand, did groups of African Americans, Muslims, Irish, or Jews have the right to censor authors such as Ralph Ellison, Salman Rushdie, James Joyce, or Philip Roth when they produced representations that offended many members of their communities? What is to say that such rebukes have more "authentic" cultural authority than the writing of the dissenters involved? On the other hand, as it seemed when Ellison, Rushdie, Joyce, and Roth all came under the heel of such pressure, might it be reasonable to regard matters such as "culture," "race," "identity," and "inalienable property" as in fact part of the problem rather than part of the solution?

Reasonable or not, this last suspicion has come to fuel the cultural critique we now associate with "modernism" and "postmodernism." Put another way, important modernist and postmodernist modes of self-consciousness have been generated by an understanding of the contradictions that notions of "cultural identity," "cultural authenticity," and "cultural property" have brought to the surface. In the fiction of James Joyce and Philip Roth, especially, and most vividly in Roth's recent *American Pastoral*, such issues form part of the literature's *donnée*. Nor is the attitude of this fiction toward cultural authenticity particularly sympathetic. To the contrary, in Roth's idiom the ridicule is all but palpable: "Cultural property?" you ask? Roth's answer all but screams: "Property? Shmoperty!"

The Artist and the Birth of a Nation: James Joyce as Prototype
The moral focus of both Joyce and Roth can be located in the way that they render what Roth once called the "country's private life,"[2] the way in which public idealizations and stereotypes shape the individual imagination. Of necessity, the two novelists start by probing with painful honesty their local milieu—their neighborhoods, their religious communities, the charisma exuded by their adolescent heroes. Almost inevitably, they precipitate them-

selves into life and death battles over what their communities consider unacceptable appropriation of this material, and they transform these battles into important subjects in their work.

In Joyce's case, which proved prototypical for the twentieth century, this struggle presented itself when he was sixteen and attending the premier performance of William Butler Yeats's play *The Countess Cathleen*. The play depicts some Irish peasants as ignorant and superstitious, and some of Joyce's most articulate contemporaries at school—the cream of the generation that would effect Ireland's separation from British colonialism—violently objected. They joined together to write a letter of protest to one of Dublin's newspapers, insisting that "we feel it our duty in the name and for the honour of Dublin Catholic students of the Royal University, to protest against an art, even a dispassionate art, which offers as a type of our people a loathsome brood of apostates."[3] Joyce refused to sign the letter and incurred the long-standing resentment of his cohort. For him, the incident acquired the status of an emblem of the situation of the modern writer and loomed large in his understanding of process that caused him to leave the emerging Catholic Ireland for good, even as he continued to claim the right to speak as an Irishman for the rest of his career.

To put it in terms more familiar to the 1990s, Joyce found himself in the position of a budding writer in anticolonial Africa and had encountered a now all-too-familiar pressure to synthesize a common past and legitimize the coherence of a future nation. The pressures of censorship in this situation are enormous. To revolutionaries, the primary mission of those unreliable creatures who style themselves artists is to solidify a national culture and its political identity. In a culturally discontinuous society, however (and what modern nation is not?), only ersatz or partisan national identities are uniform, and those writers who attempt to confect or idealize an image of national culture discover with surprise that their accounts accrue partisan support from certain political corners at home and appear unexpectedly exotic to certain readers abroad. Finally, however, these narratives are perceived as the propaganda they always were. Since the actual process of constituting group identity inevitably turns on conflict and struggle, novelists who make their living flogging anticolonial legitimation narratives are ultimately, to quote Anthony Appiah, seen to constitute only "a *comprador* intelligentsia…who mediate the trade in cultural commodities of world capitalism at the periphery. In the West, they are known through the Africa they offer; their compatriots know them…through an Africa they have invented for the world, for each other, and for Africa." After the revolution, Appiah adds acerbically, when the international market takes over, these writers universally share the experience of having sought "to naturalize…a nationalism that…failed."[4]

Joyce's youthful insight into this situation was profound, and much of his fictional technique was devoted, as we would now say, to deconstructing the bad faith of the politics of identity.[5] Another part of his reaction was more dramatic. Correctly gauging the likely public reaction to his questioning "the country's private life," and guessing that only card-carrying Irish nationalists would be allowed to thrive after the advent of Home Rule, he left Ireland and, with the exception of a handful of brief visits, never returned. When Ireland achieved its independence he kept his British passport, although he had been harassed by the British government during World War I, and he became, as he had earlier predicted he would, Ireland's first dissenter.[6] His battle to represent the fault lines of Irish identity was lifelong, but it was conducted at a distance. The distance did not, however, protect him from the vilification of his Irish contemporaries, any more than it protects him today from the continuing criticism of commentators like Terry Eagleton, who maintain their support for the means and goals of turn-of-the-twentieth-century Irish republicanism and continue to deprecate his position accordingly.[7]

Philip Roth: Demythologizing the World of the Respectable

Roth's battles in the American Jewish community began before the publication of his first book and have lasted over forty years. Roth, however, did not leave America but fought in place for the right to represent Jewish cultural material with the same kind of independence and skepticism with which Joyce had represented the Irish. Just after publishing the stories he was about to collect in the volume *Goodbye, Columbus* (1959), Roth was blasted by the elders of the American Jewish community. They argued, to invoke the words used by the playgoers horrified by *The Countess Cathleen*, that Roth's fiction, which depicted Jewish liars and adulterers, presented "a type of our people" as vicious reprobates. In letters Roth himself quoted in a famous essay entitled "Writing about Jews," Jewish elders charged that Roth's stories had "presented a distorted picture of the average Je[w]" and that he had done his best not only "to make people believe that all Jews are cheats, liars, connivers" but also to make "people—the general public—forget all the great Jews who have lived...all the Jews who live honest hard lives the world over."[8] The strongest accusation these letters leveled was that Roth had "len[t] fuel to anti-Semitism,"[9] a charge that Roth in his essay generalized as the crime of "*informing*.... I had informed on the Jews. I had told the Gentiles what apparently it would otherwise have been possible to keep secret from them: that the perils of human nature afflict the members of our minority."[10]

Roth, in other words, had turned traitor in a cultural battle whose dire possibilities the Holocaust had fifteen years previously realized. He had betrayed the tribe's secret shame, and he warranted a traitor's deserts. He recalled that a "rabbi and educator in New York City" wrote that "medieval Jews would have known what to do with him."[11] He had, by his representations of the Jewish community, reinforced anti-Semitic stereotypes, stereotypes whose perniciousness, the letter writers implied, would eventually fade away if non-Jews were prohibited from voicing them and if Jewish self-haters like Roth would become ashamed of rehearsing them.

These same charges were repeated in an even more outraged key ten years later, when Roth published what was, in the minds of the American Jewish community, his most scandalous and most shameful book, *Portnoy's Complaint* (1969). Roth was unrepentant, but the power of the accusations haunted and obsessed him. Ten years after that, in *The Ghost Writer* (1979), he endowed the charges with a combination of nightmarish intensity and burlesquelike overelaboration and inserted them into his fiction in the form of a letter written by one Judge Leopold Wapter, Newark's "most admired Jew" and a friend of the father of Nathan Zuckerman, Roth's fictional alter ego.[12] In the letter, Wapter asks the following questions, to which Nathan Zuckerman never replies, except by wondering to himself, "hadn't Joyce, hadn't Flaubert, hadn't Thomas Wolfe...all been condemned for disloyalty or treachery or immorality by those who saw themselves slandered in their works?"[13]

1. If you had been living in Nazi Germany in the thirties, would you have written such a story?
2. Do you believe Shakespeare's Shylock and Dickens's Fagin have been of no use to anti-Semites?
3. Do you practice Judaism? If so, how? If not, what credentials qualify you for writing about Jewish life for national magazines?
4. Would you claim that the characters in your story represent a fair sample of the kinds of people that make up a typical contemporary community of Jews?...
8. Can you explain why in your story, in which a rabbi appears, there is nowhere the grandeur of oratory with which Stephen S. Wise and Abba Hillel Silver and Zvi Masliansky have stirred and touched their audiences?
9. Aside from the financial gain to yourself, what benefit do you think publishing this story in a national magazine will have for (a) your family; (b) your community; (c) the Jewish religion; (d) the well-being of the Jewish people?
10. Can you honestly say there is anything in your story that would not warm the heart of a Julius Streicher or a Joseph Goebbels?[14]

In *The Ghost Writer,* Nathan Zuckerman reacts to such aspersions with paralytic rage, but in life Roth was not slow to defend himself, and his defenses were various and weighty. When we remember his replies, however, we first tend to remember their humanist convictions. First and foremost, Roth defended his freedom as an individual and an American Jew to use the experience of his own group and to represent what we have heard him call the "perils of human nature" in the shapes that he knew best — the social fabric of the postwar Jewish American community of Newark, the cadences (now also familiar in the stand-up routines of Lenny Bruce and the films of Woody Allen) of American Jewish humor, and the contours of Jewish folklore.

It is not necessary to rehearse this part of Roth's defense at length, however, because it seems that as long as one regards his quarrel simply as a struggle between propaganda and individual genius over the complexities of a universal human experience, his position is as vulnerable as his opponents to the sophistication of Roth's own fiction. In Roth's stories and novels, claims to such universal humanity are repeatedly unmasked as deceptions that majority groups construct to naturalize the contingency of their social values or that minority groups entertain to gain advantage in the game of cultural politics. Roth even goes so far as to insert such positions in the mouths of his fictional alter egos so that he can interrogate them in a Joycean way — by placing a recognizable image of his own weakness for them at the center of stories whose ironies then call them into question.

Given his own fundamental assumptions as a novelist, then, Roth has little to stand on when he invokes universal experience or universal genius to justify his representations of Jewish America. And were these assertions the only weapons in his arsenal, there would be little to choose between his defenses and his detractors' charge that he is only a "fool" of the gentile community, a naif playing into anti-Semitic hands. It is worth recalling, therefore (as I first recalled while rereading his essays), that Roth did not exclusively or even primarily rest his claim to Jewish materials on his grasp of human verities. Instead, the more interesting part of his critical defense is as Joycean as his fiction. Thus he avers in an essay entitled "Imagining Jews" that "the task for the Jewish novelist has *not* been to go forth [a phrase that Joyce put in the mouth of his ironized self-representation of "An Artist as a Young Man"] to forge in the smithy of his soul the *un*created conscience of his race, but to find inspiration in a [cultural] conscience [Roth calls it a prototype] that has been created and undone a hundred times over in this century alone.... [It is his task] to imagine what *he* [as a Jew] is and is not, must and must not do."[15] In Roth's account, the nub of this obligation is first to recognize the "myriad" of conflicting "prototypes" that as humans we hold about one another individually and in groups, and especially as Jews. For Jews in the twentieth century have no choice but to recognize that "strongly held ideas as to what a Jew in fact is" have been held by figures as different (this is Roth's list) as Theodor Herzl, Chaim Weizmann, Vladimir Jabotinsky, Adolf Hitler, Joseph Goebbels, Jean-Paul Sartre, Meir Kahane, and Leonid Brezhnev, all of whom put themselves on record about it in a major way.[16] Jewish fiction and Jewish identity must be realized, Roth argues, not simply by *imagining* Jews but by "imagining Jews *being* imagined" — that is, by creating Jewish identity out of the shards of previous creations — and in that wilderness of mirrors conduct what he calls a "baffled, claustrophobic struggle" for clarity.[17]

These remarks, in their self-consciousness about the multilayered, constructed, and antiessentialist quality of group identity, answer, it seems, to the skepticism in Anthony Appiah's remarks. On the one hand, Appiah insisted that the only stories that colonized groups want to hear about themselves are tales of unified identity. The tales, useless for their intended purposes, succeed in circulating as political commodities generously compensated by politicians on the make. On the other hand, Appiah argues, more rigorous postcolonial writing adopts the techniques of postmodern irony and questions rather than reinforces notions of cultural authenticity. Thus Appiah concludes that postcolonial writing, which first presents itself as a more traditional alternative to modernist narrative, is ultimately transformed by similar stylistic imperatives.

(What he might have said but did not is that the first occasions of such experimental styles even in European fiction were themselves engaged with the contradictions of postcolonial identity—in places such as Joyce's Ireland.[18])

The word *commodity* was just used, but one might just as easily use the more pertinent word, *property*. The notion of "cultural property" has been proposed as a legal instrument with which minority or indigenous groups can fend off external exploitation at the same time as they empower themselves to license and control internally or externally produced group representations. (As Marlon Ross argues in his essay in this volume, such formulas have even been enshrined in the precedents of American law to bolster and solidify the "reputation" of the white and black races during the period following Reconstruction.) So conceived along lines concordant with older racist law, such "property," like the identity of the groups that claim it, is authentic and inalienable.

In the modern world, however, neither property nor identity can work in that way. In almost any imaginable contemporary context, property and commodity are synonymous. The same may be said about those kinds of group identities that are formed, consolidated, or reinforced by means of their proprietary attachments. No less than the idea of universal human experience, the ideal of authentic property or identity in the modern world is a Pandora's box loaded with perils that the last twenty years of twentieth-century nationalist insurgence have made all too apparent.

Nevertheless, in the cultural property movement the ideal of inalienable property continues to insinuate a compelling nostalgia—one that is romanticized and compounded by its association with obvious historical injustices, such as the case of the Elgin Marbles. It is this nostalgia, along with its ineluctable affiliation with the way we think about group identity, that is at the center of Roth's recurrent concerns, emerging in its most intense form in his powerful book of 1997, *American Pastoral,* the story of a Jewish American high-school athlete-cum-demigod named Seymour Levov. Levov, nicknamed "the Swede" because of his fair hair and regular features, in the first flush of business success buys a colonial stone house in a town founded during the American Revolution and becomes a near-perfect representative of a Jewish one-hundred-percent American. His achievement and happiness are subsequently—and, it seems, inevitably—destroyed, however, by a teenage daughter who turns domestic terrorist during the Vietnam War, and whose rebellion and implacable hostility unsettle all that the Swede has thought and done. Levov's fall, we are finally compelled to realize, arises precisely out of the paradoxes of ownership and cultural identity. Hence Roth's title, where "pastoral" refers to the perfect attainment of Americanness by a third-generation immigrant. The book's most provocative epiphany occurs three-quarters through it, when Roth has the Swede wisecracking to his old-fashioned Jewish mother, and maintaining that he has bought his colonial house because "I want to own the things that money can't buy."[19]

As the ruin of Roth's protagonist shows us, however, nothing that money can't buy *can* be owned, and anything that can be owned must be bought and paid for — in cash or destroyed illusions. In Roth's analysis, when we ignore this truth and pretend otherwise, as we do when we try to supply metaphysical wraiths like "America" or "Jewishness" with the false solidity of inalienable property, we find that they cannot but betray our faith and upset our trust. As *American Pastoral* suggests, it is absurd to talk about the reality of group identity when even the idea of personal identity is, in the human world of unconscious motivation, untenable. So in the novel, an older and wiser Nathan Zuckerman discovers the "picture we have of one another. Layers and layers of misunderstanding. The picture we have of *ourselves*. Useless. Presumptuous. Completely cocked-up. Only we go ahead and we *live* by these pictures. That's what she is, that's what he is, this is what I am. This is what happened, this is *why* it happened."[20] "The worst lesson that life can teach [is, he says,] that it makes no sense."[21]

Nor is the ability of the artist or intellectual to clarify matters of personal or group identity any less hopeless. In the novelist's case,

> you fight your superficiality, your shallowness, so as to try to come at people without unreal expectations, without an overload of bias or hope or arrogance, as untanklike as you can be, sans cannon and machine guns and steel plating half a foot thick; you come at them unmenacingly on your own ten toes instead of tearing up the turf with your caterpillar treads, take them on with an open mind, as equals, man to man, as we used to say, and yet you never fail to get them wrong. You might as well have the *brain* of a tank. You get them wrong before you meet them, while you're anticipating meeting them; you get them wrong while you're with them; and then you go home to tell somebody else about the meeting and you get them all wrong again. Since the same generally goes for them with you, the whole thing is really a dazzling illusion empty of all perception, an astonishing farce of misperception. And yet what are we to do about this terribly significant business of *other people,* which gets bled of the significance we think it has and takes on instead a significance that is ludicrous, so ill-equipped are we all to envision one another's interior workings and invisible aims? . . . The fact remains that getting people right is not what living is all about anyway. It's getting them wrong that is living, getting them wrong and wrong and wrong and then, on careful reconsideration, getting them wrong again. That's how we know we're alive: we're wrong.[22]

The reason the novelist (along with the rest of us) gets people wrong is that what makes people real to themselves and to us is a myth that Roth in his prose associates with the "boundary of the individual's identity and experience" — a "barrier of personal inhibition, ethical conviction and plain old monumental fear" that often corresponds with both "the problematical nature of moral authority and of social restraint and regulation."[23] As this "boundary" or "barrier" of identity exerts a dubious and life-threatening "claim" on a libidinal life that is not bounded, continuous, decorous, or ethical, it is the job of the novelist to counter it by the techniques of "irony, pathos, ridicule,

[and] humor."[24] The transgressive messiness of actual (as opposed to mythical) humanity requires the novelist to be equally transgressive—to show life as more outrageous than we expected and to expose the conventions of society and its fictions. The outrageousness of postmodern fiction, finally, exists to subvert the myths of *identity* and (as Roth's boyhood idol Henny Youngman did) to "demythologiz[e] the world of the respectable."[25]

In Roth's world, it is when we feel we are *not* wrong—when we feel we can read our own and others' identities—that we are lost. It is when we succumb to the myth of group identity and embrace what Roth calls the "American" or "Jewish" "pastoral" (thereby subjecting ourselves to the manifold false claims that misguided individual members of a group make "to being the legitimate moral conscience of the community"[26]) that we are propelled, like Swede Levov, into the tragic farce that is Roth's signature as a novelist. It is this subjection, no less than the bomb that his daughter throws, that transports the Swede "out of the longed-for American pastoral and into...the fury, the violence, and the desperation of the counterpastoral—into the indigenous American berserk."[27]

Cultural property? In Roth's understanding, cultural property taken straight is one of the most dangerous poisons there is, to be ranked right up there with the other mythologies of "the country's private life" such as conservative or utopian politics. Furthermore, although Roth is rightly famous for his fury against the former, it is the latter that has most recently drawn his wrath. In *I Married a Communist* (1998), he remembers "those rapturous revolutionary days when everyone craving for change programmatically, naively—madly, unforgivably—underestimates how mankind mangles its noblest ideas and turns them into tragic farce. Heave-ho! Heave-ho! As though human wiliness, weakness, stupidity, and corruption didn't stand a chance against the collective, against the might of the people pulling together to renew their lives and abolish injustice."[28]

Nonproprietary Identities and Jewish Doubleness

Despite Roth's fundamental aversion to the idea of ethnic identity, how else can one think of him but as a Jewish writer? After all, in his essay "Writing about Jews," Roth tells us he cannot *not* write about Jews. They are what he knows, and without them the flavor of his fiction would disappear, just as "most of those jokes beginning 'Two Jews were walking down the street' lose a little of their punch, if one of the Jews, or both, is disguised as an Englishman or a Republican."[29] Commenting on this remark, Hermione Lee notes that Roth's world shares a great deal with the sensibility of Sigmund Freud's *Jokes and Their Relation to the Unconscious*, where Freud insists that "the Jew functions in his deepest imagination...as his own other, his own inferior, and he must consequently laugh at himself.... This [Freud concludes] is the famous Jewish humour." She adds, however, that the flavor of Roth's humor does not so much mirror such humor as struggle with it. It is true that Roth's characters are, in fact, all, as Alexander Portnoy realizes, living the only lives they have "in the middle of a Jewish joke." But, as Portnoy also knows, *"it ain't no joke!"* Lee concludes that *"Portnoy's Complaint* is more than the ultimate Jewish joke; it is a joke *against* Jewish humour. Roth's protest against the rabbi's or Jewish mother's self-limiting idea of Jewishness is the same as Portnoy's complaint at being trapped inside a Jewish joke."[30]

The sensibility of Roth's fiction, in other words, does not correspond to some authentic "Jewishness" but rather grows out of contesting the prevailing idea that there is an authentic Jewishness. Through this contest it arrives at what it holds to be a more sophisticated notion of identity. This other kind of identity is for Roth necessarily local, for him Jewish, for that is the kind he has at hand. It has a *negative* inflection, however; one that grows out of a fallen knowledge of all those previous imaginings of Jews. Like Appiah's sense of postcolonial narrative, it affiliates itself with the necessary ironies and discontinuities of the postmodern novel — as in books like *The Counterlife* (1987) and *Operation Shylock* (1993), where identity is fractured into multiple lives, multiple relations with history and community, all with no easy resolution. Not surprisingly, it retains a striking family resemblance to those ironic traditions of Jewish American humor in which everything can be changed by changing the inflection of a word. These traditions fuse ethnic representations of Jews undercutting their historical oppressors with a more generalized dramatization of the way language and literature can unsettle the "right" and the "real." Take, for example, the classic Jewish story of "a little Jewish tailor" on the day of Joseph Stalin's assumption of power:

Standing on Lenin's tomb in Red Square, Stalin was acknowledging the acclamation of the masses. Suddenly he raised his hands to silence the crowd.

"Comrades," he cried. "A most historic event! A telegram of congratulations from Leon Trotsky!"

The crowd could hardly believe its ears. It waited in hushed anticipation.

"Joseph Stalin," read Stalin. "The Kremlin. Moscow. You were right and I was wrong. You are the true heir of Lenin. I must apologize. Trotsky."

A roar erupted from the crowd.

But in the front row a little Jewish tailor gestured frantically to Stalin.

"Psst!" he cried. "Comrade Stalin."

Stalin leaned over to hear what he had to say.

"Such a message! But you read it without the right feeling."

Stalin once again raised his hands to still the excited crowd. "Comrades!" he announced. "Here is a simple worker, a Communist, who says I did not read Trotsky's message with the right feeling. I ask that worker to come up on the podium himself to read Trotsky's telegram."

The tailor jumped up on the podium and took the telegram into his hands. He read:

"Joseph Stalin. The Kremlin. Moscow."

Then he cleared his throat and sang out: "You were *right* and I was *wrong? You are the true heir of Lenin? I* should *apologize?"*[31]

In the story the simple insertion of a question mark changes the entire force of the telegram, suggesting how problematic words and the things they create can be, and how the apparent solidities of history and identity can be undermined by language in an instant. If there is a Jewish identity to be brought out here, it is at one with this power of ironic negation.

The source of identity conceived in this alternative way, and one of Roth's talismanic terms, is *doubleness*. Thus the enormous cost of the perfection of Swede Levov's "American pastoral" is, his ethnic heritage effaced, to acknowledge "no striving, no ambivalence, no doubleness—just the style, the natural physical refinement of a star."[32] Without "doubleness," however, there can be only catastrophe. Roth's account of both the Jewish and American condition requires us to remember contingency and conflict, and his insistence strongly recalls W. E. B Du Bois's famous account of American Negro life as a "double-consciousness," a "history of strife" in which "one ever feels his twoness—an American, a Negro; two souls, two thoughts, two unreconciled strivings; two warring ideals in one dark body, whose dogged strength alone keeps it from being torn asunder."[33] In Roth this historical condition is universalized. To be double is to be human. To pretend otherwise is to court ruin.

Thus transformed, the notion of ethnic "identity" (now circumscribed by scare quotes) positions itself in opposition not to the alternative identities of other cultural communities but to the kind of false "pastoral" that Roth links with the ownership of cultural property through Swede Levov's colonial house. Recall Roth's comment about the loss involved in altering jokes "beginning 'Two Jews were walking down the street.'" The jokes, he says, lose "a little of their punch" if one of the Jews, or both, is disguised as an Englishman or a Republican. They lose their punch not because Englishmen or Republicans have positive alternative identities of their own, however, but because they are both instances of a false and willed denial of doubleness. "Englishman" here connotes the false "English pastoral" of, say, Shakespearean idolatry, which is a different kind of joke entirely. And to tell a Republican joke for Roth requires a language so obscene it could probably not be repeated in an academic screed, forcing me simply to invoke Roth's wildly funny but ferocious book about Tricky Dick Nixon, *Our Gang* (1971).

How much credence should we give to Roth's postmodern skepticism about cultural identity and its proprietary attachments? How does his brief against the Jewish establishment hold up against the assertions made by ethnic and indigenous communities with long and painful histories of being demonized and exploited by the hurtful representations of outsiders? As the passionate and persuasive argument of many of the essays in this volume documents, the jury is still out on these matters, but Roth's utterances about them seem too compelling to ignore.

Notes

1. See Timothy Webb, "Appropriating the Stones: The 'Elgin Marbles' and English National Taste" in this volume.

2. Philip Roth, *Reading Myself and Others* (New York: Farrar, Straus & Giroux, 1975), 122. Subsequent references will be abbreviated as *RMO*.

3. Quoted in Richard Ellmann, *James Joyce* (New York: Oxford Univ. Press, 1959), 69.

4. Kwame Anthony Appiah, "Is the Post- in Postmodernism the Post- in Postcolonial?" *Critical Inquiry* 17, no. 2 (1991): 336–57, esp. 348–49.

5. See, for example, Vincent J. Cheng, *Joyce, Race, and Empire* (Cambridge: Cambridge Univ. Press, 1995).

6. See Herbert Gorman, *James Joyce* (New York: Farrar & Rinehart, 1939; revised 1948, Rinehart), 412.

7. See Terry Eagleton, *Heathcliff and the Great Hunger: Studies in Irish Culture* (London: Verso, 1995), 269 ff.

8. Roth, *RMO* (note 2), 160.

9. Roth, *RMO* (note 2), 160.

10. Roth, *RMO* (note 2), 161.

11. Roth, *RMO* (note 2), 160.

12. Philip Roth, *The Ghost Writer* (New York: Farrar, Straus & Giroux, 1979); reprinted as the first part of *Zuckerman Bound* (New York: Farrar, Straus, & Giroux, 1985), 96. Subsequent references will be abbreviated as *GW*.

13. Roth, *GW* (note 12), 110.

14. Roth, *GW* (note 12), 102–4.

15. Roth, *RMO* (note 2), 245–46.

16. Roth, *RMO* (note 2), 245–46.

17. Roth, *RMO* (note 2), 245.

18. On this subject, see Ronald Bush, "Monstrosity and Representation in the Postcolonial Diaspora: *The Satanic Verses*, *Ulysses*, and *Frankenstein*," in Elazar Barkan and Marie-Denise Shelton, eds., *Borders, Exiles, Diasporas* (Stanford: Stanford Univ. Press, 1998), 234–56.

19. Philip Roth, *American Pastoral* (Boston: Houghton Mifflin, 1997), 307. Subsequent references will be abbreviated as *AP*.

20. Roth, *AP* (note 19), 64.

21. Roth, *AP* (note 19), 81.

22. Roth, *AP* (note 19), 35.

23. Roth, *AP* (note 19), 64.

24. Roth, *AP* (note 19), 85.

25. Roth, *AP* (note 19), 81.

26. Roth, *AP* (note 19), 84–85.

27. Roth, *AP* (note 19), 86.

28. Philip Roth, *I Married a Communist* (Boston: Houghton Mifflin, 1998), 74–75.

29. Roth, *RMO* (note 2), 158.

30. See Hermione Lee, *Philip Roth* (London: Methuen, 1982), 38, which gives the citations from Freud and *Portnoy's Complaint*.

31. As told in Rabbi Joseph Telushkin, *Jewish Humor: What the Best Jewish Jokes Say about the Jews* (New York: W. Morrow, 1992), 121–22.

32. Telushkin, *Jewish Humor* (note 31), 20.

33. W. E. B. Du Bois, *The Souls of Black Folk: Essays and Sketches* (Chicago: A. C. McClurg, 1903; reprinted New York: Signet Classic Edition, 1969), 45. Roth's sophistication about identity politics in fact owes much to the experience of African Americans, principally the experience of Ralph Ellison. Ellison negotiated the same quagmire of authenticity and recrimination earlier in the century, and Roth learned a great deal from it. In *Reading Myself and Others* (note 2), 166–67, he notes that

> a book like Ralph Ellison's *Invisible Man* [New York: Random House, 1952] for instance, seems to me to have helped many whites who are not anti-Negro, but who do hold Negro stereotypes, to surrender their simpleminded notions about Negro life.... [Yet] Just as there are Jews who feel that my books do nothing for the Jewish cause, so there are Negroes, I am told, who feel that Mr. Ellison's work has done little for the Negro cause and probably has harmed it.

Alan Cooper, in *Philip Roth and the Jews* (Albany: State Univ. of New York Press, 1996), 5, reminds us that Roth, in *The Facts* (New York: Farrar, Straus & Giroux, 1988), presents a scene in which he is menaced by a mob at Yeshiva University and is extricated by Ellison. Cooper calls the event ironic, implying that it says something about Roth that Roth himself does not know. I suspect that the irony is deliberate, however; here Roth is underlining how he was helped by Ellison's sophistication in earlier and comparable situations.

Biographical Notes on the Contributors

Jonathan Arac is Orlando Harriman Professor of English and Comparative Literature at Columbia University, where he also serves as chair of the department. His publications include the monographs *Critical Genealogies* (1987) and *Huckleberry Finn as Idol and Target* (1997) and the edited volumes *Postmodernism and Politics* (1986) and *After Foucault* (1988). Currently he is researching the problem of identity in the intellectual history of the United States, with special attention to the work of Ralph Ellison.

Elazar Barkan is professor of history and cultural studies at Claremont Graduate University, where he also serves as chair of cultural studies. A cultural historian who writes about cultural politics and human rights, he is the author of *The Retreat of Scientific Racism* (1992) and *The Guilt of Nations* (2000) and the coeditor of *Prehistories of the Future* (with Ronald Bush, 1995) and *Borders, Exiles, Diasporas* (with Marie-Denise Shelton, 1998).

Ronald Bush is Drue Heinz Professor of American Literature and a fellow of Saint John's College at Oxford University. An expert on Anglo-American modernism, his writings include *The Genesis of Ezra Pound's "Cantos"* (1976) and *T. S. Eliot: A Study in Character and Style* (1983). He also coedited *Prehistories of the Future* (with Elazar Barkan, 1995). He is currently working on a critical biography of James Joyce.

Clemency Coggins is professor of archaeology and of art history at Boston University and an associate with the Peabody Museum of Archaeology and Ethnology at Harvard University. The editor of *Artifacts from the Cenote of Sacrifice, Chichén Itzá, Yucatán* (1992), she specializes in Maya and Mesoamerican archaeology, the uses of cultural property, and the international trade in antiquities.

R. F. Foster is Carroll Professor of Irish History and a fellow of Hertford College at Oxford University. He has published widely on Irish history, society, and politics in the modern period, as well as on Victorian high politics and culture. *The Irish Story* (2001) and the prize-winning first volume of *W. B. Yeats: A Life* (1997) are his most recent books. He is now completing the second volume of this authorized biography.

Patty Gerstenblith is professor of law at DePaul University College of Law in Chicago. A specialist in law and cultural heritage, she has been editor-in-chief of the *International Journal of Cultural Property* since 1995 and has served on the United States Cultural Property Advisory Committee since 2000. Her latest publication is "The Public Interest in Restitution of Cultural Objects," which appeared in the *Connecticut Journal of International Law* (2001).

Richard L. Jantz is professor of physical anthropology at the University of Tennessee, Knoxville, where he also serves as the director of the Forensic Anthropology Center. His research interests include quantitative variation in recent humans, skeletal variation in Americans (recent and ancient), the peopling of the New World, and forensic anthropology. He is the coeditor of *Skeletal Biology in the Great Plains* (with Douglas W. Owsley, 1994).

Hélène La Rue is university lecturer and a fellow of Saint Cross College at Oxford University. She has been curator of the musical collections of the Pitt Rivers Museum since 1981 and curator of the Bate Collection of Musical Instruments since 1995. Her teaching and research range across the fields of ethnomusicology; the music of Europe, China, and Japan; and the history and development of musical instruments.

Claire L. Lyons is collections curator at the Getty Research Institute, where she oversees acquisitions, exhibitions, and programs related to archaeology and ancient art. She has written extensively on the history of archaeology, antiquities collecting, and cultural property issues. Among her publications are a monograph on the archaic cemeteries of Morgantina, Italy, and the edited volumes *Naked Truths* (with Ann Koloski-Ostrow, 2000) and *The Archaeology of Colonialism* (with John K. Papadopoulos, 2002).

Douglas W. Owsley is curator and division head of physical anthropology at the National Museum of Natural History, Smithsonian Institution. His research in the areas of osteology, bone and dental pathology, and forensic anthropology has led to the publication of over 155 articles and essays. He is the coeditor of *Bioarchaeology of the North Central United States* (with Jerome Rose, 1997), the coeditor of *Skeletal Biology in the Great Plains* (with Richard L. Jantz, 1994), and a member of the editorial board of the *Journal of Forensic Sciences*.

Darrell Addison Posey, at the time of his death in May 2001, was director of the Programme for Traditional Resource Rights of the Oxford Centre for Environment, Ethics and Society at Mansfield College and an associate fellow of Linacre College at Oxford University. An anthropologist and ethnobiologist well known for his interdisciplinary research on Amazonia and his advocacy of indigenous rights, he received the United Nations Environment Programme's Global 500 Award for Environmental Achievement in 1993. He published numerous scientific articles and books, most recently *Cultural and Spiritual Values of Biodiversity* (2000) and *Kayapó Ethnoecology and Culture* (2002).

Marlon B. Ross is professor of English and Afro-American Studies at the University of Virginia. He is the author of *The Contours of Masculine Desire: Romanticism and the Rise of Women's Poetry* (1989) as well as an array of published essays on eighteenth- and nineteenth-century British literature, African American studies, and gender and queer theory. He is completing a book on the cultural formation of African American manhood in twentieth-century American politics and society.

Ngahuia Te Awekotuku is visiting professor at the Maori and Psychology Research Unit of the University of Waikato, where she is principal investigator for a three-year research project on the origins, technology, narratives, and practice of *Ta Moko*. A Maori cultural activist for over three decades, she has published the collection of short stories *Tahuri* (1989), a volume of articles and speeches *Mana Wahine Maori* (1991), and a monograph, *He Tikanga Whakaaro: Research Ethics in the Maori Community* (1991). Her research interests focus on Maori and Pacific art and on sexuality, ritual, and transgression.

Timothy Webb is Winterstoke Professor of English at the University of Bristol. Among his publications are *The Violet in the Crucible* (1976), *English Romantic Hellenism, 1700–1824* (1982), and editions of the poetry of Percy Bysshe Shelley and W. B. Yeats. He is coeditor of *Shelley's "Devils" Notebook* (with P. M. S. Dawson, 1993) and *The Faust Draft Notebook* (with Nora Crook, 1997). Currently he is working on *Bristol: Romantic City, The Book of Stones,* and an edition of Leigh Hunt's *Autobiography*.

Robert J. C. Young is professor of English and critical theory and a fellow of Wadham College at Oxford University. A specialist in postcolonial theory, he is the author of the monographs *White Mythologies* (1990), *Colonial Desire* (1995), *Torn Halves* (1996), and *Postcolonialism: An Historical Introduction* (2001). Since 1998, he has served as the general editor of *Interventions: International Journal of Postcolonial Studies*.

Illustration Credits

Unless otherwise noted, illustrations are from the collections of the authors and are reproduced with their permission. The following sources have also granted permission to reproduce images in this book:

55   Photo: Courtesy Towneley Hall Art Gallery and Museum, Burnley, Lancashire/Bridgeman Art Library, ref. no. THA2288

102   From Museu Barbier-Mueller Art Precolombí, Barcelona, *Ritual Arts of the New World: Pre-Columbian America* (Milan: Skira, 2000), 10. Photo: Henri Stierlin, Geneva, Switzerland

104   David Alfaro Siqueiros, *Ethnography* (1939), enamel on composition board, 48 ⅛ x 32 ⅜ in. (122.2 x 82.2 cm). The Museum of Modern Art, New York. Gift of Abby Aldrich Rockefeller. Photograph © 2001 The Museum of Modern Art, New York

119   Photos: Courtesy Ira Block, New York

244   By permission of the British Library. From "A Collection of Drawings by A. Buchan, S. Parkinson, and J. F. Miller Made in the Countries Visited by Capt[ain] Cook in His First Voyage; also of Prints Published in Hawkesworth's *Voyages* of Biron, Wallis and Cook, as well as in Cook's Second and Third Voyages, Vol[ume] First," British Library, Add. MS 23920, fol. 54(a). Photo: © The British Library, London

249, fig. 2   From David Wood, ed., *Torture Garden: A Photographic Archive of the New Flesh* (London: Creation Books, 1996), 62. Photo: © Jeremy Chaplin; reprinted with the permission of Ron Athey and Jeremy Chaplin

252   Courtesy Rikirangi Moeau

263   Copyright © 2001 by the New York Times Co. Reprinted by permission

281   © W. Tjark Reiss Estate. Photo: Courtesy Department of Special Collections, Charles E. Young Research Library, University of California, Los Angeles

283   Photo: Courtesy Department of Special Collections, Charles E. Young Research Library, University of California, Los Angeles

287   © W. Tjark Reiss Estate. Photo: Courtesy Department of Special Collections, Charles E. Young Research Library, University of California, Los Angeles

288, fig. 19   Winold Reiss, *Roland Hayes (1887–1976), Singer,* National Portrait Gallery, Smithsonian Institution, Gift of Lawrence A. Fleischman and Howard Garfinkle with a matching grant from the National Endowment for the Arts. © W. Tjark Reiss Estate. Photo: Courtesy National Portrait Gallery,

Smithsonian Institution, Washington, D.C., NPG.72.81

288, fig. 20   The Getty Research Institute wishes to thank The Crisis Publishing Co., Inc., the publisher of the magazine of the National Association for the Advancement of Colored People, for authorizing use of this work

291   Courtesy Marianetta Porter. Photos: *Persona #1,* Marianetta Porter; *Persona #2, Persona #3:* Tim Thayer, Detroit

Index

Issues & Debates
A Series of the Getty Research Institute Publications Program

In Print
Art in History / History in Art: Studies in Seventeenth-Century Dutch Culture
Edited by David Freedberg and Jan de Vries
ISBN 0-89236-201-4 (hardcover), ISBN 0-89236-200-6 (paper)

American Icons: Transatlantic Perspectives on Eighteenth- and Nineteenth-Century American Art
Edited by Thomas W. Gaehtgens and Heinz Ickstadt
ISBN 0-89236-246-4 (hardcover), ISBN 0-89236-247-2 (paper)

Otto Wagner: Reflections on the Raiment of Modernity
Edited by Harry Francis Mallgrave
ISBN 0-89236-258-8 (hardcover), ISBN 0-89236-257-X (paper)

Censorship and Silencing: Practices of Cultural Regulation
Edited by Robert C. Post
ISBN 0-89236-484-X (paper)

Dosso's Fate: Painting and Court Culture in Renaissance Italy
Edited by Luisa Ciammitti, Steven F. Ostrow, and Salvatore Settis
ISBN 0-89236-505-6 (paper)

Nietzsche and "An Architecture of Our Minds"
Edited by Alexandre Kostka and Irving Wohlfarth
ISBN 0-89236-485-8 (paper)

Disturbing Remains: Memory, History, and Crisis in the Twentieth Century
Edited by Michael S. Roth and Charles G. Salas
ISBN 0-89236-538-2 (paper)

Looking for Los Angeles: Architecture, Film, Photography, and the Urban Landscape
Edited by Charles G. Salas and Michael S. Roth
ISBN 0-89236-616-8 (paper)

The Archaeology of Colonialism
Edited by Claire L. Lyons and John K. Papadopoulos
ISBN 0-89236-635-4 (paper)

In Preparation
Representing the Passions: Histories, Bodies, Visions
Edited by Richard Meyer
ISBN 0-89236-676-1

Situating El Lissitzky: Vitebsk, Berlin, Moscow
Edited by Nancy Perloff and Brian Reed
ISBN 0-89236-677-X

Designed by Bruce Mau Design Inc.,
Bruce Mau with Chris Rowat and Daiva Villa
Coordinated by Anita Keys
Type composed by Archetype in Sabon and News Gothic
Printed and bound by Transcontinental, Litho Acme, Montreal,
on Cougar Opaque

Issues & Debates
Series designed by Bruce Mau Design Inc., Toronto, Canada